The Microsoft AI Human Resources Handbook

Optimizing the Employee Experience with the Microsoft Tech Stack

Ana Inés Urrutia de Souza

Apress®

The Microsoft AI Human Resources Handbook: Optimizing the Employee Experience with the Microsoft Tech Stack

Ana Inés Urrutia de Souza
Zurich, Zürich, Switzerland

ISBN-13 (pbk): 979-8-8688-1780-9　　　　　　　ISBN-13 (electronic): 979-8-8688-1781-6
https://doi.org/10.1007/979-8-8688-1781-6

Managing Director, Apress Media LLC: Welmoed Spahr
Acquisitions Editor: Ryan Byrnes
Editorial Project Manager: Gryffin Winkler

Cover designed by eStudioCalamar

Cover image designed by Lisa from Pexels (pexels.com)

Distributed to the book trade worldwide by Springer Science+Business Media New York, 1 New York Plaza, New York, NY 10004. Phone 1-800-SPRINGER, fax (201) 348-4505, e-mail orders-ny@springer-sbm.com, or visit www.springeronline.com. Apress Media, LLC is a Delaware LLC and the sole member (owner) is Springer Science + Business Media Finance Inc (SSBM Finance Inc). SSBM Finance Inc is a **Delaware** corporation.

For information on translations, please e-mail booktranslations@springernature.com; for reprint, paperback, or audio rights, please e-mail bookpermissions@springernature.com.

Apress titles may be purchased in bulk for academic, corporate, or promotional use. eBook versions and licenses are also available for most titles. For more information, reference our Print and eBook Bulk Sales web page at http://www.apress.com/bulk-sales.

Any source code or other supplementary material referenced by the author in this book is available to readers on GitHub. For more detailed information, please visit https://www.apress.com/gp/services/source-code.

If disposing of this product, please recycle the paper

For the ones who supported me –
by blood,
by choice,
or by belief.

Table of Contents

About the Author

 **Ana Inés Urrutia de Souza** is a Microsoft Most Valuable Professional (MVP) since 2020, an HR tech strategist, and a member of the Harvard Advisory Council. With a background in psychology and over a decade of experience in human resources technology, she brings a thoughtful, people-centered perspective to digital transformation in the workplace.

Ana helps organizations across the globe rethink and modernize their HR operations using Microsoft Dynamics 365, Power Platform, Microsoft 365, and other integrated tools. Her work spans from strategic design to hands-on implementation, always focused on practical outcomes that serve both employees and business goals.

Since 2020, Ana has been an active voice in the Microsoft ecosystem and a consistent contributor to the global HR tech dialogue. She maintains a blog where she writes regularly on topics such as digital HR, process automation, employee experience, data strategy, and platform governance – making complex concepts accessible to professionals at all levels.

Ana is also a dedicated community builder. She organizes events across Europe, co-hosts the D365 Community Call, and frequently speaks at international conferences. Beyond her technical and advisory roles, she supports peers and teams in defining strategic direction, crafting brand narratives, and creating cohesive visual identities for their initiatives.

Her work is defined by a strong commitment to clarity, relevance, and collaboration – helping teams work smarter, not just faster, and building systems that feel intuitive, purposeful, and aligned with real human needs.

About the Technical Reviewer

 **Adrià Ariste Santacreu** is a software developer, technical architect, and Microsoft Business Applications MVP with over 15 years of experience specializing in Microsoft Dynamics 365 Finance and Operations. Adrià is an expert in integration design, implementation, Application Lifecycle Management (ALM), X++, and automation, having worked with the Dynamics ERP since Axapta 3.0.

Passionate about innovation and continuous learning, Adrià regularly shares his expertise as a speaker at Microsoft events around the globe, empowering professionals and organizations to effectively leverage technology.

Acknowledgments

To the friends who offered food, floors, distractions, and perspective – you know who you are.

To Juan, Bert, and Peter – thank you for believing in me when it mattered most.

To the editor who made this possible, and to the companies that gave me the space to build what later became chapters.

Thanks to Adriá for reading drafts with a sharp eye and honest feedback – exactly what I and the book needed.

And to the Microsoft community – thank you for the space to share, the challenges that sharpened my thinking, and the support that made this work better.

Introduction

The field of Human Resources has changed dramatically in the last decade – not just in how it operates but in how it's perceived. HR is no longer just about policies and personnel files. It's about designing systems that support people, data, and decisions at scale. And that requires the right technology.

This book is a practical guide for anyone working at the intersection of HR and technology. Whether you're an HR professional navigating digital transformation, an IT consultant supporting a People team, or a business leader rethinking your HR systems – this book is for you.

At the center of this transformation is Microsoft's HR tech ecosystem. You may already be using parts of it – Dynamics 365, Microsoft 365, Power Platform, LinkedIn, Teams, or Viva – but the real value comes from understanding how they work together. That's what this book aims to unpack.

We start by grounding you in **Dynamics 365 Human Resources**, covering how to implement it, configure security, migrate data, and prepare for go-live. The focus is on giving you a step-by-step understanding of the product – not just its features but how to actually use them to meet real-world needs.

From there, we expand into the broader Microsoft landscape, with chapters on

- **Power Platform** – for reporting, automation, and custom workflows tailored to HR processes

- **Microsoft Teams and Viva Learning** – for improving internal communication, engagement, and continuous learning

- **LinkedIn** – not just as a social platform but as a powerful tool for sourcing, branding, and strategic workforce planning

- **Security and Governance** – covering compliance, access management, and data integrity across the stack

- **Discovery and Implementation Frameworks** – with templates, workshop tips, and delivery advice from the field

In addition to practical guidance, you'll also find **templates, checklists, and action prompts** to help you apply what you're learning right away. This book is built for doers – whether you're designing a process, presenting to a stakeholder, or configuring a solution. You'll be able to move from insight to execution without needing to start from scratch.

This isn't a sales pitch or a theoretical overview. It's written from experience – with the same tools, questions, and client conversations many of you are navigating today.

For **HR professionals**, you'll find support in

- Making sense of the Microsoft HR stack – without needing to be a tech expert

- Mapping technology to real HR processes, like onboarding, performance, or internal mobility

- Learning just enough about Power Platform to automate the painful bits

- Using collaboration and learning tools to improve how teams work and grow

For **IT professionals**, this book helps you

- Understand the unique needs of HR – and where they differ from other business areas

- Implement, integrate, and secure Microsoft HR tools

- Support user adoption and change management across HR teams

- Extend functionality using Power Platform and Microsoft Graph

Each chapter is written to stand on its own – so you can jump straight to what's most useful for your current project. The structure moves from core system setup to broader ecosystem opportunities, and then into implementation best practices.

If you're looking for a way to bring your HR tech vision to life – without getting lost in buzzwords or oversimplified solutions – this book is meant to be a hands-on companion. Whether you're designing your first digital process or scaling your existing systems, the goal is simple: make Microsoft tools work *for* people, not the other way around.

PART I

Introduction to Microsoft HR Solutions

CHAPTER 1

The HR Tech Revolution

The evolution of human resources is a testament to the transformative power of technology. Historically, HR was primarily a transactional function, focused on administrative tasks such as payroll, benefits, and record-keeping. These functions were often paper-based and labor-intensive, limiting HR's strategic impact on the organization.

The advent of computers in the mid-20th century marked the beginning of HR's digital transformation. Early HR technology systems automated routine tasks, freeing up HR professionals to focus on more strategic initiatives. However, these systems were often siloed and lacked the capabilities to provide actionable insights.

Today, the HR Tech Revolution is in full swing. HR departments have embraced a wide array of technologies, including cloud-based HR information systems (HRIS), applicant tracking systems (ATS), performance management software, and learning management systems (LMS). These tools have significantly improved efficiency, accuracy, and accessibility of HR data. Top-tier strategy consulting firms contend that human resources are at a critical juncture. They assert that technology is revolutionizing HR function, shifting it toward a data-centric approach where informed decisions are the cornerstone of success.

Moreover, the integration of artificial intelligence (AI) and machine learning is revolutionizing HR processes. AI-powered chatbots are enhancing employee self-service, while predictive analytics enables HR to anticipate workforce needs and optimize talent management strategies. Recent studies from leading industry analysts highlight that HR technology is no longer solely focused on operational efficiency. Instead, there is a growing emphasis on crafting immersive and tailored employee experiences throughout the entire organizational life cycle.

Looking ahead, the future of HR tech holds immense potential. Emerging technologies such as augmented reality (AR) and virtual reality (VR) are poised to revolutionize recruitment, training, and employee development. Additionally, the burgeoning field of predictive analytics will equip HR professionals with deeper insights into workforce trends, enabling them to optimize talent strategies and make data-driven decisions.

In conclusion, the HR Tech Revolution has propelled HR from a transactional function to a strategic business partner. By embracing technology and leveraging data, HR departments can drive organizational success, foster employee engagement, and build high-performing teams. The journey is far from over, and as technology continues to evolve, HR professionals who can adapt and innovate will be at the forefront of shaping the future of work.

The Evolving HR Landscape and the Role of Technology

The human resource's function is undergoing a profound transformation, shifting from a primarily administrative role to a strategic business partner. This evolution is driven by a confluence of factors, including demographic shifts, the rise of the knowledge worker, and the increasing globalization of business. As the International Labour Organization (ILO) emphasizes, the world of work is undergoing rapid change, necessitating a forward-thinking approach to labor and social policies. At the heart of this transformation is technology, which is reshaping the way HR operates and delivers value.

Traditionally, HR departments were primarily focused on transactional tasks such as payroll, benefits administration, and record-keeping. These functions were often time-consuming and labor-intensive, limiting HR's ability to contribute strategically to the organization. However, the advent of technology has significantly altered this landscape. HR information systems (HRIS) have emerged as essential tools for managing employee data, streamlining processes, and generating valuable insights. These systems have enabled HR to move beyond transactional activities and focus on more strategic initiatives.

Moreover, the increasing complexity of the modern workplace has necessitated a more holistic approach to talent management. The rise of the knowledge worker, characterized by individuals with high levels of education and expertise, has placed a premium on attracting, developing, and retaining top talent. HR departments are tasked with creating a culture that fosters innovation, engagement, and employee well-being. To achieve this, HR professionals must leverage technology to support talent acquisition, development, and retention strategies.

Globalization has further expanded the scope of HR's responsibilities. Managing a geographically dispersed workforce requires HR to adapt to different cultural, legal, and regulatory environments. Technology plays a crucial role in facilitating cross-border collaboration, communication, and compliance. Additionally, HR must ensure that talent acquisition strategies are aligned with the global business strategy.

In summary, the HR function is experiencing a period of rapid evolution, driven by a combination of demographic, economic, and technological factors. By embracing technology and leveraging its potential, HR departments can become more strategic, efficient, and effective in supporting organizational goals.

These trends are reshaping the world of work, as emphasized by the International Labour Organization (ILO). At the heart of this transformation is technology, which is reshaping the way HR operates and delivers value.

Demographic Shifts: A New Era of Workforce Composition

The composition of the workforce is undergoing a profound transformation, driven by factors such as aging populations, increasing birth rates in certain regions, and changing educational attainment levels. This demographic shift is reshaping the talent landscape and presenting new challenges and opportunities for HR.

A key aspect of this demographic shift is the increasing diversity of the workforce. Organizations are becoming more inclusive, with employees from different cultures, ethnicities, genders, and generations working together. This diversity brings a wealth of perspectives and ideas, but it also requires HR to develop strategies for managing a diverse workforce effectively.

Generational differences are another important dimension of demographic change. Baby boomers, Generation X, Millennials, and Generation Z each have unique values, expectations, and preferences. HR must adapt its policies and practices to meet the needs of different generations, while also fostering collaboration and understanding between them.

Furthermore, the educational attainment levels of the workforce are evolving. The proportion of individuals with higher education degrees is increasing, leading to a more skilled and knowledgeable workforce. However, this also creates challenges in terms of talent acquisition and retention, as organizations compete for top talent with advanced qualifications.

In conclusion, demographic shifts are reshaping the workforce and creating new opportunities and challenges for HR. By understanding these trends and developing strategies to manage a diverse and evolving workforce, organizations can gain a competitive advantage.

The Rise of the Knowledge Worker

The emergence of the knowledge worker has fundamentally transformed the nature of work. Characterized by their reliance on intellectual capital rather than physical labor, knowledge workers are the driving force behind innovation and economic growth. This shift has profound implications for organizations and HR functions alike.

As knowledge becomes the primary asset, the role of employees has evolved. They are no longer mere cogs in a machine but strategic contributors to an organization's success. This necessitates a focus on talent development and retention, as organizations compete fiercely to attract and retain individuals with specialized skills and expertise.

Moreover, the rise of the knowledge worker has led to a shift in organizational culture. Traditional hierarchical structures are giving way to more flat and collaborative environments. Employees are empowered to take ownership of their work and contribute to decision-making processes. HR must foster a culture of innovation, learning, and growth to support the needs of knowledge workers.

In conclusion, the knowledge worker has become a cornerstone of modern organizations. To thrive in this new era, HR must adopt a strategic approach to talent management, focusing on employee development, engagement, and well-being.

Globalization: A New Frontier for HR

Globalization has reshaped the business landscape, transforming how organizations operate and compete. This interconnected world presents both challenges and opportunities for HR functions. Managing a global workforce requires a strategic approach to talent acquisition, development, and management.

One of the key challenges is building a globally competent workforce. HR must identify and develop talent with the necessary intercultural skills, language proficiency, and global mindset. Additionally, ensuring equitable employment practices across different regions is crucial for maintaining a positive employer brand.

Technology plays a pivotal role in managing a global workforce. Collaboration tools, HR information systems, and talent management platforms enable seamless communication and operations across borders. However, HR must also navigate complex legal and regulatory environments in different countries.

Furthermore, globalization has increased competition for talent. Attracting top talent from a global pool requires a strong employer value proposition and effective talent acquisition strategies. Additionally, HR must focus on employee engagement and retention to prevent talent attrition.

In conclusion, globalization has transformed the HR function, demanding a strategic and agile approach. By embracing technology and developing a global mindset, HR can effectively manage a diverse workforce and contribute to organizational success.

Technology As a Catalyst for HR Transformation

Technology has emerged as a powerful catalyst for revolutionizing HR processes. By automating routine tasks, providing data-driven insights, and enhancing employee experiences, technology is transforming the way HR functions operate. This section explores specific examples of how technology is being leveraged to improve HR efficiency, effectiveness, and strategic impact.

Artificial intelligence (AI) is rapidly reshaping the human resources landscape. This chapter explores how AI is being leveraged to optimize various HR processes beyond recruitment. From talent acquisition to employee development, AI is driving efficiency, improving decision-making, and enhancing the overall employee experience. By understanding the potential of AI, HR professionals can unlock new opportunities and gain a competitive advantage.

AI-Powered Recruitment

AI has revolutionized the way organizations identify and attract talent. AI-powered chatbots have become indispensable tools in the recruitment process. These virtual assistants can handle a wide range of tasks, from answering frequently asked questions to scheduling interviews. For instance, a leading tech company has implemented an AI chatbot that can provide candidates with real-time information about open positions, company culture, and benefits, freeing up HR professionals to focus on building relationships with top talent.

Furthermore, AI-driven applicant tracking systems (ATS) have streamlined the resume screening process. By analyzing candidate data, these systems can identify the most qualified applicants, reducing time-to-fill and improving the quality of hires. A global financial services firm has successfully deployed an AI-powered ATS that can accurately predict job performance based on candidate profiles, leading to a significant increase in hiring success rates.

Social Media Recruitment

Social media platforms have become essential channels for talent acquisition. Companies across various industries are leveraging platforms like LinkedIn, Twitter, and Instagram to connect with potential candidates. A retail giant, for example, has successfully used Instagram to target young, creative talent through visually appealing content and influencer partnerships.

Moreover, social media analytics provide valuable insights into candidate behavior and preferences. By monitoring social media conversations, HR teams can identify emerging talent pools and tailor their recruitment strategies accordingly. A technology company has effectively used social listening to understand the pain points of software engineers and develop targeted recruitment campaigns.

In conclusion, AI and social media have transformed the recruitment landscape, enabling organizations to identify and attract top talent more efficiently and effectively. By harnessing the power of these technologies, HR departments can enhance candidate experience, reduce time-to-fill, and build high-performing teams.

Onboarding: Enhancing the New Hire Experience

Onboarding is a critical stage in the employee life cycle that sets the tone for an individual's tenure within an organization. Traditional onboarding processes can be time-consuming and inefficient. However, technology has emerged as a powerful tool to streamline and enhance this crucial phase.

Online Onboarding Platforms

Online onboarding platforms have become indispensable in creating a seamless and engaging new hire experience. These platforms centralize information, automate tasks, and provide a consistent onboarding journey for all employees. By digitizing paperwork, assigning tasks, and delivering interactive content, organizations can accelerate the time-to-productivity for new hires. For example, a multinational technology company has implemented an online onboarding platform that includes interactive modules, virtual meet-and-greets, and access to company resources, resulting in increased employee satisfaction and reduced time-to-onboarding.

Gamification During Onboarding

Gamification has emerged as a compelling approach to enhance employee engagement during the onboarding process. By incorporating game-like elements, organizations can transform onboarding into an interactive and enjoyable experience. For instance, a financial services firm has developed a gamified onboarding program that includes quizzes, challenges, and rewards for completing tasks. This approach has boosted employee engagement and knowledge retention.

In conclusion, technology has revolutionized the onboarding process, enabling organizations to create more efficient, engaging, and impactful experiences for new hires. By combining online platforms with gamification elements, HR departments can accelerate time-to-productivity, improve employee satisfaction, and foster a strong sense of belonging.

Learning and Development: Empowering Employees Through Technology

Learning and development (L&D) have become strategic imperatives for organizations seeking to foster a high-performance culture. Technology has emerged as a powerful tool to enhance the effectiveness of L&D initiatives.

E-Learning and Online Courses

E-learning platforms and online courses offer a flexible and accessible approach to employee development. These digital learning solutions provide employees with the opportunity to learn at their own pace and convenience. For example, a healthcare organization has implemented an e-learning platform that offers a comprehensive library of courses on patient care, compliance, and leadership development. This platform has enabled employees to access training materials from anywhere, anytime, enhancing knowledge retention and skill development.

Immersive Learning with VR and AR

Virtual reality (VR) and augmented reality (AR) are transforming the learning experience by creating immersive and interactive training environments. VR can be used to simulate real-world scenarios, allowing employees to practice complex tasks in a safe and controlled environment. For instance, a manufacturing company has developed a VR training module for new employees to learn equipment operation without risking physical injury.

AR, on the other hand, overlays digital information onto the real world, providing employees with context-specific guidance and support. For example, a field service technician can use AR glasses to access repair manuals and troubleshooting steps while working on equipment in the field.

By combining e-learning, VR, and AR, organizations can create a comprehensive and engaging learning ecosystem that supports employee growth and development.

Performance Management: Data-Driven Development

Performance management has undergone a significant transformation, shifting from annual appraisals to continuous feedback and development-oriented processes. Technology has played a crucial role in this evolution.

Performance management software has become indispensable in streamlining the performance evaluation process. These tools facilitate goal setting, performance tracking, and feedback delivery. By automating administrative tasks, HR professionals can dedicate more time to coaching and developing employees. For example, a professional services firm implemented performance management software that enables employees to set objectives, track progress, and receive regular feedback from managers and peers. This has fostered a culture of continuous improvement and enhanced employee engagement.

Additionally, performance management software can provide valuable data-driven insights into employee performance trends. By analyzing performance metrics, organizations can identify areas for improvement, allocate resources effectively, and make informed talent decisions. For instance, a retail company utilized performance data to identify high-potential employees and tailor development plans accordingly.

In conclusion, performance management software has transformed the way organizations manage employee performance. By automating processes, providing data-driven insights, and fostering continuous feedback, these tools contribute to a more effective and employee-centric performance management system.

Employee Engagement: The Pulse of the Organization

Employee engagement is a critical driver of organizational success. To foster a high-performance culture, HR departments must prioritize understanding and enhancing employee engagement. Technology has emerged as a powerful tool for measuring, analyzing, and improving employee experience.

Leveraging Data for Engagement

Employee engagement surveys and analytics tools provide invaluable insights into employee sentiment, job satisfaction, and overall well-being. By collecting and analyzing employee feedback, HR professionals can identify trends, pinpoint areas of strength and weakness, and measure the impact of engagement initiatives. For example, a technology company implemented pulse surveys to gather real-time feedback on employee morale, enabling them to address issues promptly and prevent employee churn.

Moreover, advanced analytics can help HR departments identify correlations between employee engagement and key performance indicators (KPIs). By understanding these relationships, organizations can prioritize engagement initiatives that drive business outcomes. A healthcare provider utilized employee engagement data to correlate job satisfaction with patient outcomes, demonstrating the direct impact of employee engagement on organizational performance.

Actionable Insights for Improvement

The data collected through employee engagement surveys and analytics must be translated into actionable insights. HR professionals can use this information to develop targeted initiatives that address employee needs and concerns. For example, if survey results indicate a lack of career development opportunities, HR can implement mentorship programs, leadership development initiatives, or tuition reimbursement benefits.

Additionally, employee engagement data can be used to measure the effectiveness of HR programs and initiatives. By tracking changes in employee engagement over time, organizations can assess the impact of their efforts and make necessary adjustments.

In conclusion, employee engagement is a critical factor in organizational success. By leveraging technology to gather data, analyze trends, and implement targeted initiatives, HR departments can create a more engaged and productive workforce.

Summary

The HR function has undergone a profound transformation, evolving from a transactional to a strategic role. Technology has been the catalyst for this evolution, enabling HR to optimize processes, enhance employee experiences, and drive business outcomes. By leveraging AI, automation, and data analytics, HR departments can create a more efficient, effective, and employee-centric organization.

From talent acquisition to employee engagement, technology has reshaped the entire employee life cycle. By embracing these advancements, HR can build high-performing teams, foster a positive work culture, and contribute significantly to organizational success. As the world of work continues to evolve, HR professionals who can harness the power of technology will be at the forefront of driving organizational performance and shaping the future of work.

Introduction to Microsoft's HR Tech Stack and Its Benefits for HR and IT

The HR technology landscape has undergone a dramatic transformation in recent years. Organizations are increasingly seeking integrated solutions that streamline processes, improve decision-making, and enhance the employee experience. This shift has paved the way for the emergence of comprehensive HR tech stacks.

Microsoft has positioned itself as a leading provider of HR technology solutions. Its suite of applications offers a holistic approach to managing the employee life cycle, from recruitment to retirement. By combining traditional HR functionalities with emerging technologies like artificial intelligence (AI), Microsoft empowers organizations to drive innovation and achieve strategic business objectives.

The integration of AI into HR processes is no longer a futuristic concept but a present-day reality. By harnessing the power of AI, organizations can unlock new possibilities for improving efficiency, enhancing decision-making, and delivering exceptional employee experiences.

In the following sections, we will delve deeper into the core components of Microsoft's HR tech stack and explore the benefits it offers to both HR and IT departments.

HR Transformation and Technology

The HR function is undergoing a significant transformation, shifting from a primarily administrative role to a strategic business partner. This evolution is driven by factors such as demographic shifts, the rise of the knowledge worker, and globalization. Technology, particularly AI, is playing a crucial role in enabling HR departments to streamline processes, improve decision-making, and enhance employee experiences.

Summary

Chapter 1 explored the profound transformation of the HR function from an administrative support role to a strategic driver of business success. This shift has been powered by rapid technological advancements – ranging from early digital tools to the present-day integration of artificial intelligence, automation, and data analytics. The chapter highlighted how HR technology enhances operational efficiency, supports strategic talent management, and fosters a more personalized and engaging employee experience.

Key global forces such as demographic shifts, the rise of knowledge workers, and globalization are reshaping workforce expectations and organizational structures. In parallel, emerging technologies like AI, AR/VR, and predictive analytics are redefining recruitment, onboarding, learning, and performance management.

As HR continues to evolve, technology remains its most critical enabler. By embracing innovative tools and platforms, HR professionals are better equipped to attract and retain talent, support organizational agility, and shape the future of work.

CHAPTER 2

Understanding HR Solution Architecture

Core Components of the Microsoft HR Tech Stack and Their Interrelationships

Microsoft has emerged as a leading provider of comprehensive HR technology solutions that address the evolving needs of modern organizations. The company's HR tech stack is designed to empower HR departments and IT teams to create a more efficient, data-driven, and employee-centric workplace. By integrating a range of tools and platforms, Microsoft offers a holistic approach to talent management, employee experience, and operational excellence.

This section delves into the core components of Microsoft's HR tech stack, highlighting the role of AI and other advanced technologies in transforming HR processes. Through a deep dive into these solutions, readers will gain insights into how Microsoft can help organizations build a smarter workforce and achieve their business objectives.

Microsoft Dynamics 365 for Human Resources: A Comprehensive HR Foundation

Microsoft Dynamics 365 for Human Resources serves as the cornerstone of a robust HR technology strategy. This cloud-based solution offers a comprehensive suite of tools designed to streamline HR processes, enhance decision-making, and elevate the overall employee experience. By unifying core HR functionalities within a single platform, organizations can achieve greater efficiency, accuracy, and strategic focus.

© Ana Inés Urrutia de Souza 2025
A. I. Urrutia de Souza, *The Microsoft AI Human Resources Handbook,*
https://doi.org/10.1007/979-8-8688-1781-6_2

Core HR Functionalities: Empowering HR Professionals

At the heart of Dynamics 365 for Human Resources lies a comprehensive set of core HR functionalities that address the fundamental needs of organizations. These include performance management, benefits administration, compensation planning, learning and development, time and attendance, expense management, and leave and absence management.

- **Performance management** capabilities enable organizations to align employee goals with business objectives, provide regular feedback, and conduct performance reviews. By centralizing performance data, HR professionals can identify top performers, assess training needs, and inform compensation decisions.

- **Benefits administration** simplifies the enrolment, eligibility, and management of employee benefits. Through self-service options and automated processes, Dynamics 365 for Human Resources streamlines benefits administration, reduces administrative burden, and enhances employee satisfaction.

- **Compensation management** empowers organizations to develop and implement competitive compensation strategies. By centralizing compensation data, HR professionals can analyze salary structures, conduct equity analyses, and ensure compliance with labor regulations.

- **Learning and development** functionality supports employee growth and development by tracking training completion, managing certifications, and delivering personalized learning experiences. By providing employees with access to relevant learning content, organizations can enhance skills and knowledge.

- **Time and attendance** management simplifies time tracking, overtime calculations, and absence management. Through integration with payroll systems, Dynamics 365 for Human Resources ensures accurate and efficient time and attendance processing.

- **Expense management** automates expense report submission, approval, and reimbursement processes. By streamlining expense management, organizations can reduce errors, improve compliance, and enhance employee satisfaction.

- **Leave and absence management** simplifies leave requests, approvals, and accruals. By providing employees with self-service options and managers with visibility into team absences, Dynamics 365 for Human Resources optimizes workforce planning and scheduling.

By consolidating these core HR functions into a unified platform, Dynamics 365 for Human Resources provides organizations with a solid foundation for managing their human capital.

Dynamics 365 for Human Resources offers a robust suite of tools to streamline the talent acquisition process. By integrating candidate management, job postings, and onboarding, organizations can enhance their ability to attract, engage, and hire top talent.

Talent Acquisition with Microsoft Dynamics 365 for Human Resources

Candidate Management

The talent acquisition module within Dynamics 365 for Human Resources provides a centralized platform for managing candidate information. Key features include:

- **Candidate profiles:** Comprehensive profiles capturing candidate details, work experience, skills, and preferences

- **Resume parsing:** Automated extraction of candidate information from resumes, saving time and improving data accuracy

- **Applicant tracking:** Efficiently managing the candidate journey through the recruitment process, including status updates, communications, and feedback

- **AI-powered candidate matching:** Leveraging AI algorithms to identify candidates whose skills and experience closely align with job requirements

Job Postings and Sourcing

Dynamics 365 for Human Resources empowers organizations to create compelling job postings and distribute them across multiple channels. Key features include:

- **Job description creation:** Building detailed and engaging job descriptions that accurately reflect role requirements and company culture

- **Job board integration:** Posting jobs on various job boards and career websites to increase visibility

- **Social media recruiting:** Leveraging social platforms to attract passive candidates and build employer branding

- **Sourcing tools:** Accessing talent pools and databases to identify potential candidates

Onboarding New Hires

A seamless onboarding experience is crucial for employee satisfaction and retention. Dynamics 365 for Human Resources offers tools to streamline the onboarding process, including:

- **New hire setup:** Creating and managing new employee records, including personal information, job details, and benefits enrolment

- **Task management:** Assigning onboarding tasks to new hires and tracking completion

- **Document management:** Storing and sharing essential onboarding documents

- **Welcome kits:** Creating personalized welcome kits to introduce new hires to the company culture and resources

By leveraging Dynamics 365 for Human Resources, organizations can optimize the talent acquisition process, enhance candidate experience, and improve time-to-hire.

Employee Self-Service: Empowering Your Workforce

Employee self-service (ESS) is a cornerstone of modern HR. It empowers employees to manage their HR-related information and processes independently, freeing up HR teams to focus on strategic initiatives. Dynamics 365 for Human Resources offers a robust ESS platform that enhances employee engagement and satisfaction.

Core ESS Functionalities

Dynamics 365 for Human Resources provides employees with a self-service portal to access and manage various HR-related tasks, including:

- **Personal information:** Updating contact details, emergency contacts, and personal information

- **Benefits enrolment:** Selecting and managing benefit plans, dependents, and changes

- **Time and attendance:** Submitting time-off requests, viewing time-off balances, and tracking time worked

- **Expense management:** Submitting expense reports, tracking approvals, and viewing reimbursement status

- **Learning and development:** Accessing training materials, enrolling in courses, and tracking certifications

- **Performance management:** Viewing performance goals, providing self-assessments, and accessing performance feedback

By providing employees with easy access to HR information and processes, ESS fosters a sense of ownership and autonomy. It also reduces the administrative burden on HR teams, allowing them to focus on strategic initiatives and employee development.

Manager Self-Service: Empowering Effective Leadership

Manager Self-Service (MSS) is a critical component of Dynamics 365 for Human Resources, providing managers with the tools they need to effectively manage their teams. By streamlining administrative tasks and providing insights into team performance, MSS empowers managers to focus on developing their employees and driving business results.

Core MSS Functionalities

Dynamics 365 for Human Resources offers a range of functionalities to support managers in their roles:

- **Team management:** Overseeing team structure, reporting relationships, and organizational changes

- **Performance management:** Setting goals, conducting performance reviews, and providing feedback to employees

- **Time and attendance:** Approving time-off requests, managing overtime, and monitoring team attendance

- **Expense management:** Approving expense reports submitted by team members

- **Talent management:** Identifying development needs, creating succession plans, and managing employee performance

- **Leave and absence management:** Approving leave requests and managing team absences

By empowering managers with the right tools and information, Dynamics 365 for Human Resources helps organizations build a strong leadership pipeline and drives employee engagement.

Microsoft Viva: The Evolution of Employee Experience

Microsoft Viva is a comprehensive employee experience platform designed to enhance employee engagement, productivity, and well-being. It sits at the strategic layer of the HR architecture, providing a holistic view of employee experiences.

The concept of employee experience (EX) has gained significant prominence in recent years, driven by several factors:

- **The Great Resignation:** The COVID-19 pandemic highlighted the importance of employee well-being and work-life balance, leading to a surge in resignations. Organizations realized that investing in employee experience is crucial for attracting and retaining top talent.

- **Remote Work:** The shift to remote work during the pandemic necessitated new tools and strategies for maintaining employee engagement and productivity.

- **Focus on Culture:** Companies recognized the importance of fostering a positive and inclusive company culture to drive employee satisfaction and performance.

Microsoft Viva: A Response to Evolving Needs

Microsoft Viva was launched in response to these evolving trends. It aims to address the challenges and opportunities presented by the changing nature of work. By providing a centralized platform for employee engagement, learning, communication, and insights, Viva empowers organizations to create a more connected, productive, and fulfilling workplace.

Key Features and Benefits:

- **Enhanced Communication:** Viva Amplify enables organizations to communicate effectively with employees across various channels, ensuring everyone is aligned and informed.

- **Community Building:** Viva Connections facilitates employee connections and fosters a sense of belonging, promoting collaboration and knowledge sharing.

- **Personalized Insights:** Viva Insights provides employees with data-driven recommendations to improve their productivity, focus, and well-being.

- **Learning and Development:** Viva Learning delivers personalized learning experiences, supporting employee growth and development.

- **Recognition and Feedback:** Viva Engage enables employees to recognize and appreciate their colleagues, fostering a positive work culture.

The Future of Employee Experience

As the world of work continues to evolve, employee experience will remain a top priority for organizations. Microsoft Viva is well-positioned to help companies navigate these challenges and create a thriving workplace culture. By leveraging technology to enhance employee engagement, productivity, and well-being, Viva can contribute to organizational success and employee satisfaction.

Viva Amplify: A Strategic Communication Platform

Viva Amplify is a powerful communication tool designed to enhance employee engagement and alignment within organizations. It serves as a centralized platform for distributing company-wide messages, announcements, and updates, ensuring that all employees receive consistent and timely information.

Goals:

- **Improve communication efficiency:** By providing a single platform for distributing messages, Viva Amplify streamlines communication processes and reduces the risk of information silos.

- **Enhance employee engagement:** By delivering relevant and timely information, Viva Amplify can foster a sense of connection and belonging among employees.

- **Drive alignment:** By ensuring that all employees are informed about company goals, initiatives, and updates, Viva Amplify helps to drive alignment and cohesion within the organization.

Target Audience:

Viva Amplify is primarily targeted at HR professionals, communications teams, and company leaders. It is also a valuable tool for employees who want to stay informed about company news and updates.

Role in the Organization:

Viva Amplify plays a strategic role in the organization by providing a foundation for effective communication. It helps to

- **Build a strong company culture:** By fostering open and transparent communication, Viva Amplify can help to create a positive and inclusive company culture.

- **Improve employee satisfaction:** By keeping employees informed and engaged, Viva Amplify can contribute to higher levels of employee satisfaction and retention.

- **Drive business outcomes:** Effective communication is essential for achieving business goals. By ensuring that employees are aligned and informed, Viva Amplify can help to drive performance and productivity.

Architectural Position:

Viva Amplify sits at the strategic layer of the HR architecture. This means that it is a high-level tool that supports the overall goals and objectives of the organization. By providing a platform for effective communication, Viva Amplify helps to create a strong foundation for other HR initiatives.

Viva Connections: A Strategic Community Building Platform

Viva Connections is a powerful tool designed to foster employee connections and build a strong sense of community within organizations. It provides a centralized platform for employees to connect with each other, share information, and participate in community activities.

Goals:

- **Enhance employee engagement:** By creating opportunities for employees to connect with each other and participate in community activities, Viva Connections can help to improve employee engagement and satisfaction.

- **Foster a sense of belonging:** Viva Connections can help employees to feel like they are part of a larger community, which can boost morale and productivity.

- **Improve knowledge sharing:** By providing a platform for employees to share information and best practices, Viva Connections can help to improve knowledge sharing and collaboration.

Target Audience:

Viva Connections is primarily targeted at employees, but it can also be a valuable tool for managers and HR professionals who want to foster a strong company culture.

Role in the Organization:

Viva Connections plays a strategic role in the organization by providing a platform for community building and employee engagement. It helps to

- **Improve employee retention:** By creating a positive and supportive work environment, Viva Connections can help to improve employee retention.

- **Enhance collaboration:** Viva Connections can facilitate collaboration between teams and individuals, leading to better outcomes.

- **Strengthen company culture:** By fostering a sense of community and belonging, Viva Connections can help to strengthen the company culture.

Architectural Position:

Viva Connections sits at the strategic layer of the HR architecture. This means that it is a high-level tool that supports the overall goals and objectives of the organization. By providing a platform for community building and employee engagement, Viva Connections helps to create a strong foundation for other HR initiatives.

Viva Insights: A Strategic Productivity and Well-Being Platform

Viva Insights is a powerful tool designed to help organizations improve employee productivity and well-being. It provides employees with personalized insights and recommendations based on their work patterns and habits.

Goals:

- **Improve employee productivity:** By providing employees with data-driven insights into their work habits, Viva Insights can help them to identify areas where they can improve their productivity and efficiency.

- **Enhance employee well-being:** Viva Insights can help employees to identify signs of burnout and stress and provide them with recommendations for improving their work–life balance.

- **Optimize organizational processes:** By analyzing employee data at the organizational level, Viva Insights can help organizations to identify bottlenecks and inefficiencies in their workflows.

Target Audience:

Viva Insights is primarily targeted at employees, but it can also be a valuable tool for managers and HR professionals who want to improve employee productivity and well-being.

Role in the Organization:

Viva Insights plays a strategic role in the organization by providing data-driven insights into employee productivity and well-being. It helps to

- **Improve employee retention:** By helping employees to manage their workload and reduce stress, Viva Insights can help to improve employee retention.

- **Enhance organizational performance:** By optimizing workflows and improving employee productivity, Viva Insights can help to enhance organizational performance.

- **Foster a culture of well-being:** Viva Insights can help to create a culture where employee well-being is a priority.

Architectural Position:

Viva Insights sits at the operational layer of the HR architecture. This means that it is a tool that provides data and insights to support decision-making at the individual and organizational level. By providing employees with personalized recommendations, Viva Insights can help to drive positive change and improve overall organizational performance.

Viva Engage: A Strategic Employee Engagement Platform

Viva Engage is a powerful tool designed to foster employee engagement and recognition within organizations. It provides a platform for employees to connect with each other, share ideas, and celebrate achievements.

Goals:

- **Enhance employee engagement:** By creating opportunities for employees to connect with each other and participate in community activities, Viva Engage can help to improve employee engagement and satisfaction.

- **Foster a positive company culture:** Viva Engage can help to create a positive and supportive company culture by encouraging employees to recognize and appreciate each other's contributions.

- **Improve employee retention:** By creating a sense of belonging and community, Viva Engage can help to improve employee retention.

Target Audience:

Viva Engage is primarily targeted at employees, but it can also be a valuable tool for managers and HR professionals who want to foster a strong company culture.

Role in the Organization:

Viva Engage plays a strategic role in the organization by providing a platform for employee engagement and recognition. It helps to

- **Improve employee morale:** By creating a positive and supportive work environment, Viva Engage can help to improve employee morale.

- **Enhance collaboration:** Viva Engage can facilitate collaboration between teams and individuals, leading to better outcomes.

- **Strengthen company culture:** By fostering a sense of community and belonging, Viva Engage can help to strengthen the company culture.

Architectural Position:

Viva Engage sits at the strategic layer of the HR architecture. This means that it is a high-level tool that supports the overall goals and objectives of the organization. By providing a platform for employee engagement and recognition, Viva Engage helps to create a strong foundation for other HR initiatives.

Viva Learning: A Strategic Learning and Development Platform

Viva Learning is a powerful tool designed to support employee learning and development. It provides a centralized platform for accessing training resources, tracking progress, and measuring learning outcomes.

Goals:

- **Improve employee skills:** By providing employees with access to relevant and up-to-date training resources, Viva Learning can help them to develop the skills they need to succeed in their roles.

- **Enhance employee performance:** By supporting employee learning and development, Viva Learning can help to improve employee performance and productivity.

- **Drive organizational growth:** By investing in employee development, organizations can create a skilled and engaged workforce that is capable of driving growth and innovation.

Target Audience:

Viva Learning is primarily targeted at employees, but it can also be a valuable tool for managers and HR professionals who want to support employee development.

Role in the Organization:

Viva Learning plays a strategic role in the organization by providing a platform for employee learning and development. It helps to

- **Improve employee retention:** By investing in employee development, organizations can create a more engaging and rewarding work environment, which can help to improve employee retention.

- **Enhance organizational agility:** By ensuring that employees have the skills they need to adapt to changing business needs, Viva Learning can help organizations to remain agile and competitive.

- **Foster a culture of learning:** Viva Learning can help to create a culture where learning and development are valued and encouraged.

Architectural Position:

Viva Learning sits at the strategic layer of the HR architecture. This means that it is a high-level tool that supports the overall goals and objectives of the organization. By providing a platform for employee learning and development, Viva Learning helps to create a strong foundation for other HR initiatives.

Viva Glint: A Strategic Employee Engagement Platform

Viva Glint is a powerful tool designed to measure and improve employee engagement within organizations. It provides a platform for conducting employee engagement surveys and analyzing the results.

Goals:

- **Measure employee engagement:** Viva Glint provides a comprehensive framework for measuring employee engagement and satisfaction.

- **Identify areas for improvement:** By analyzing survey results, organizations can identify areas where they need to improve employee experience.

- **Track progress:** Viva Glint enables organizations to track changes in employee engagement over time and measure the impact of their initiatives.

Target Audience:

Viva Glint is primarily targeted at HR professionals and managers who want to improve employee engagement.

Role in the Organization:

Viva Glint plays a strategic role in the organization by providing data-driven insights into employee engagement. It helps to

- **Improve employee retention:** By identifying and addressing issues that are affecting employee engagement, Viva Glint can help to improve employee retention.

- **Enhance organizational performance:** High levels of employee engagement are correlated with better business outcomes. By improving employee engagement, Viva Glint can help to enhance organizational performance.

- **Foster a positive company culture:** By understanding the factors that are driving employee engagement, organizations can create a more positive and supportive company culture.

Architectural Position:

Viva Glint sits at the strategic layer of the HR architecture. This means that it is a high-level tool that supports the overall goals and objectives of the organization. By providing data-driven insights into employee engagement, Viva Glint helps to create a strong foundation for other HR initiatives.

Viva Pulse: A Strategic Employee Feedback Platform

Viva Pulse is a powerful tool designed to gather and analyze employee feedback within organizations. It provides a platform for conducting short, targeted surveys and analyzing the results.

Goals:

- **Gather employee feedback:** Viva Pulse provides a simple and efficient way for organizations to gather feedback from employees on a variety of topics.

- **Identify areas for improvement:** By analyzing survey results, organizations can identify areas where they need to improve employee experience.

- **Track changes:** Viva Pulse enables organizations to track changes in employee sentiment over time and measure the impact of their initiatives.

Target Audience:

Viva Pulse is primarily targeted at HR professionals and managers who want to gather employee feedback and improve employee experience.

Role in the Organization:

Viva Pulse plays a strategic role in the organization by providing a platform for gathering employee feedback. It helps to

- **Improve employee engagement:** By understanding the factors that are affecting employee engagement, organizations can take steps to improve it.

- **Enhance organizational performance:** High levels of employee engagement are correlated with better business outcomes. By gathering employee feedback and addressing their concerns, Viva Pulse can help to enhance organizational performance.

- **Foster a culture of transparency:** Viva Pulse can help to create a culture where employees feel comfortable sharing their feedback and ideas.

Architectural Position:

Viva Pulse sits at the strategic layer of the HR architecture. This means that it is a high-level tool that supports the overall goals and objectives of the organization. By providing a platform for gathering employee feedback, Viva Pulse helps to create a strong foundation for other HR initiatives.

Summary of Microsoft Viva Solutions

Microsoft Viva is a comprehensive suite of employee experience platforms designed to enhance employee engagement, productivity, and well-being. It includes the following key components:

- **Viva Amplify:** A communication platform for distributing company-wide messages and updates.

- **Viva Connections:** A community-building platform for fostering employee connections and collaboration.

- **Viva Insights:** A productivity and well-being platform that provides personalized insights to employees.

- **Viva Engage:** An employee engagement platform for recognizing and appreciating employee contributions.

- **Viva Learning:** A learning and development platform for providing access to training resources and supporting employee growth.

- **Viva Glint:** An employee engagement survey platform for measuring and improving employee satisfaction.

- **Viva Pulse:** A feedback platform for gathering employee input and insights.

These solutions work together to create a holistic employee experience platform that supports employee engagement, productivity, and well-being. By leveraging Viva, organizations can improve employee satisfaction, enhance organizational performance, and create a positive and supportive company culture.

The Power Platform: A Low-Code Revolution

The Power Platform is a suite of low-code development tools from Microsoft that empowers organizations to create custom business applications without extensive coding knowledge. It emerged as a response to the growing demand for organizations to build applications quickly and efficiently, bridging the gap between business needs and IT resources.

For business specialists, the Power Platform is a game-changer. It allows them to take control of their own application development, creating tailored solutions that address specific business challenges and drive efficiency. This empowers them to become more strategic and innovative.

The Power Platform also benefits IT departments by reducing their workload. By delegating application development to business specialists, IT teams can focus on more strategic initiatives and complex projects. Additionally, the Power Platform provides a centralized platform for managing and governing custom applications, ensuring consistency and compliance.

Citizen developers, individuals with limited coding experience but a deep understanding of their business domain, can leverage the Power Platform to build solutions that address their unique needs. This democratization of application development empowers organizations to innovate and respond to changing market conditions more effectively.

Core Components of the Power Platform: Power Apps

Power Apps, a cornerstone of the Power Platform, offers two primary development approaches: model-driven and canvas apps. These versatile tools empower organizations to create a wide range of custom applications tailored to their specific needs, including HR solutions.

Model-Driven Apps: A Structured Foundation

Model-driven apps are built on a preexisting data model, often leveraging existing data sources like Microsoft Dynamics 365 or Dataverse. This structured approach makes them ideal for creating complex business applications with predefined entities, relationships, and workflows.

HR Use Cases for Model-Driven Apps:

- **Employee onboarding:** Create a comprehensive onboarding app that automates tasks, provides access to essential resources, and tracks progress.

- **Performance management:** Develop a performance management app to set goals, track progress, and conduct performance reviews.

- **Time and attendance:** Build a time tracking app to manage employee hours, calculate overtime, and handle leave requests.

- **Expense management:** Create an expense management app to streamline expense reporting, approvals, and reimbursement processes.

- **Benefits administration:** Develop a benefits enrolment and management app to simplify the process for employees.

Canvas Apps: A Flexible Canvas for Customization

Canvas apps offer a more flexible and customizable approach, allowing developers to create visually appealing and interactive interfaces without extensive coding. They are ideal for building apps with unique requirements or highly customized user experiences.

HR use cases for Canvas Apps:

- **Employee self-service:** Create a visually appealing and user-friendly self-service portal for employees to manage their personal information, benefits, and time-off requests.

- **Recruitment:** Build a recruitment app with a visually appealing interface to attract and engage top talent.

- **Training and development:** Create interactive training modules using canvas apps to enhance employee learning experiences.

- **Employee surveys:** Develop custom surveys to gather employee feedback and measure satisfaction.

- **Custom reporting:** Create custom reports and dashboards to visualize HR data and gain insights into your workforce.

Building on Existing HRIS Solutions

Both model-driven and canvas apps can be used to extend and enhance existing HRIS solutions. By integrating with platforms like Microsoft Dynamics 365 for Human Resources, Power Apps can provide additional functionality, automate processes, and improve user experience. For example, a canvas app could be built on top of Dynamics 365 to provide a more visually appealing and user-friendly interface for employee self-service.

Core Components of the Power Platform: Power Automate

Power Automate is a powerful workflow automation tool that enables organizations to streamline processes, automate tasks, and integrate applications. It offers a wide range of capabilities, from simple automation workflows to complex robotic process automation (RPA) solutions.

Key Features of Power Automate:

- **Workflow automation:** Create automated workflows to streamline processes across various applications and services.

- **Robotic process automation (RPA):** Automate repetitive tasks on your desktop using RPA bots.

- **Connectors:** Connect to a wide range of applications and services, including Microsoft 365, Dynamics 365, Salesforce, and many others.

- **Triggers and actions:** Trigger workflows based on events or conditions and perform actions to automate tasks.

- **Logic and decision-making:** Use conditional statements and branching logic to create complex workflows.

- **Data manipulation:** Transform and manipulate data using various functions and expressions.

HR Use Cases for Power Automate

Power Automate can be used to automate a wide range of HR processes, including:

- **Onboarding automation:** Automate tasks such as sending welcome emails, assigning tasks, and providing access to company resources.

- **Leave request automation:** Automatically approve or reject leave requests based on predefined rules.

- **Expense report automation:** Automate the process of submitting, reviewing, and approving expense reports.

- **Performance review automation:** Automate the process of sending performance review reminders and collecting feedback.

- **Recruitment automation:** Automate tasks such as posting job openings, screening resumes, and scheduling interviews.

- **Data synchronization:** Automate the synchronization of data between HR systems and other applications.

Integrating Power Automate with HRIS Solutions

Power Automate can be integrated with existing HRIS solutions to create a more streamlined and efficient HR workflow. For example, you can use Power Automate to

- **Trigger workflows based on HRIS events:** Automate tasks when employees join, leave, or change roles.

- **Sync data between HRIS and other systems:** Keep data in sync between your HR system and other applications, such as payroll or time and attendance systems.

- **Enhance employee self-service:** Create automated workflows to support employee self-service tasks, such as requesting time off or updating personal information.

By leveraging Power Automate, organizations can significantly reduce manual effort, improve efficiency, and enhance the overall employee experience.

Core Components of the Power Platform: Power BI

Power BI is a powerful business intelligence tool that enables organizations to visualize data, create interactive reports and dashboards, and gain valuable insights. It offers a comprehensive set of features for data analysis, reporting, and sharing.

Key Features of Power BI:

- **Data ingestion:** Connect to a wide range of data sources, including databases, spreadsheets, cloud services, and on-premises systems.

- **Data modeling:** Create data models to define relationships between data entities and establish data hierarchies.

- **Data visualization:** Create interactive visualizations such as charts, graphs, maps, and tables.

- **Dashboards:** Design custom dashboards to combine multiple visualizations into a single view.

- **Reporting:** Create reports to present data in a structured and informative format.

- **Sharing and collaboration:** Share reports and dashboards with colleagues and stakeholders.

- **Natural language queries:** Ask questions in natural language to get answers from your data.

HR Use Cases for Power BI

Power BI can be used to analyze HR data and gain valuable insights into your workforce. Some common HR use cases include:

- **Employee turnover analysis:** Analyze employee turnover rates, identify trends, and understand the reasons behind attrition.

- **Performance analysis:** Track employee performance metrics, identify top performers, and identify areas for improvement.

- **Compensation analysis:** Analyze compensation data to ensure fair and equitable pay practices.

- **Diversity and inclusion analysis:** Analyze workforce demographics to assess diversity and identify areas for improvement.

- **Talent acquisition analysis:** Track recruitment metrics, measure time-to-hire, and identify effective sourcing channels.

- **Learning and development analysis:** Track employee training completion rates, measure the impact of training programs, and identify skill gaps.

Integrating Power BI with HRIS Solutions

Power BI can be integrated with your HRIS solution to provide a centralized platform for HR analytics. By connecting to your HR data, you can create custom reports and dashboards that provide valuable insights into your workforce.

Key benefits of integrating Power BI with your HRIS:

- **Improved data accessibility:** Easily access and analyze HR data from a single platform.

- **Enhanced decision-making:** Gain valuable insights into your workforce to make data-driven decisions.

- **Improved employee experience:** Use Power BI to create interactive dashboards that provide employees with insights into their performance and development.

- **Enhanced compliance:** Use Power BI to track compliance with labor laws and regulations.

By leveraging Power BI, organizations can gain a deeper understanding of their workforce, identify areas for improvement, and make data-driven decisions to improve HR outcomes.

Core Components of the Power Platform: Power Pages

Power Pages is a low-code platform that enables organizations to create custom websites and portals without extensive coding knowledge. It offers a wide range of templates, components, and customization options to help you build engaging and informative websites.

Key Features of Power Pages:

- **Templates:** Choose from a variety of pre-built templates to get started quickly.

- **Components:** Customize your website with a wide range of components, including buttons, forms, images, and more.

- **Integration:** Integrate your website with other Power Platform components, such as Power Apps and Power Automate.

- **Customization:** Tailor your website to your specific needs using CSS and JavaScript.

- **Mobile optimization:** Create websites that are optimized for mobile devices.

HR Use Cases for Power Pages

Power Pages can be used to create a variety of HR-related websites, including:

- **Employee self-service portals:** Provide employees with a convenient way to access HR information and services.

- **Career websites:** Attract top talent with a visually appealing and informative career website.

- **Intranet portals:** Create a central hub for internal communication and collaboration.

- **Learning management systems:** Deliver training and development content through a custom website.

- **Vendor portals:** Manage relationships with vendors and suppliers through a dedicated portal.

Integrating Power Pages with HRIS Solutions

Power Pages can be integrated with your HRIS solution to create a more seamless and unified employee experience. For example, you can use Power Pages to create a custom employee self-service portal that integrates with your HRIS to provide employees with access to their personal information, benefits, and time-off requests.

Key benefits of integrating Power Pages with your HRIS:

- **Improved employee experience:** Provide employees with a convenient and user-friendly way to access HR information and services.

- **Enhanced communication:** Create a central hub for internal communication and collaboration.

- **Streamlined processes:** Automate HR processes and reduce manual effort.

- **Improved branding:** Create a visually appealing and consistent website that reflects your company's brand.

By leveraging Power Pages, organizations can create custom websites that meet their specific HR needs and improve the overall employee experience.

Core Components of the Power Platform: Copilot Studio

Copilot Studio is a powerful tool that enables organizations to create intelligent virtual agents (chatbots) and automate workflows using a conversational interface. It offers a wide range of features for building and managing agents and bots.

Key Features of Copilot Studio:

- **Agent creation:** Create custom agents with natural language capabilities.

- **Bot development:** Build automated workflows and processes using a conversational interface.

- **Integration:** Integrate your agents and bots with other Power Platform components and third-party applications.

- **Training:** Train your agents and bots to understand and respond to user queries.

- **Analytics:** Track agent and bot performance to identify areas for improvement.

HR Use Cases for Copilot Studio

Copilot Studio can be used to create a variety of HR-related agents and bots, including:

- **HR chatbots:** Provide automated HR support to employees, answering common questions and resolving issues.

- **Recruitment chatbots:** Screen candidates and schedule interviews.

- **Onboarding assistants:** Guide new employees through the onboarding process.

- **Learning assistants:** Provide personalized learning recommendations and support.

- **Performance review assistants:** Help employees and managers prepare for and conduct performance reviews.

Integrating Copilot Studio with HRIS Solutions

Copilot Studio can be integrated with your HRIS solution to provide automated HR support and improve employee experience. For example, you can create a chatbot that can answer common HR questions, such as how to request time off or access benefits information.

Key benefits of integrating Copilot Studio with your HRIS:

- **Improved employee experience:** Provide employees with 24/7 access to HR support.

- **Increased efficiency:** Automate routine HR tasks and reduce manual effort.

- **Enhanced customer service:** Provide a better customer experience for employees and external stakeholders.

By leveraging Copilot Studio, organizations can create intelligent virtual agents that can automate HR processes, improve employee experience, and enhance organizational efficiency.

Combining Power Platform Components for HR solutions

The Power Platform offers a flexible and customizable suite of tools that can be combined to create powerful HR solutions. Here are five scenarios where Power Platform components can be used together to address specific HR challenges:

1. **Comprehensive HR onboarding solution:**

   - **Power Apps:** Create a visually appealing and user-friendly onboarding app that guides new employees through the process.

   - **Power Automate:** Automate tasks such as sending welcome emails, assigning tasks, and providing access to company resources.

   - **Power BI:** Track onboarding progress and measure the effectiveness of the onboarding process.

2. **Enhanced employee self-service portal:**

   - **Power Apps:** Build a custom employee self-service portal with a user-friendly interface.

   - **Power Automate:** Integrate with your HRIS to automate tasks such as updating personal information, requesting time off, and enrolling in benefits.

   - **Power BI:** Provide employees with personalized dashboards that show their benefits information, time-off balances, and performance metrics.

3. **AI-Powered recruitment solution:**

   - **Power Apps:** Create a recruitment app with features such as job postings, candidate applications, and scheduling interviews.

   - **Power Automate:** Automate tasks such as sending job offers and scheduling interviews.

   - **Power Virtual Agents:** Create a chatbot to answer candidate questions and provide initial screening.

   - **Power BI:** Analyze recruitment data to identify effective sourcing channels and improve time-to-hire.

4. **Integrated performance management system:**

   - **Power Apps:** Build a performance management app with features such as goal setting, performance reviews, and feedback.

   - **Power Automate:** Automate tasks such as sending performance review reminders and collecting feedback.

   - **Power BI:** Analyze performance data to identify top performers, identify areas for improvement, and inform compensation decisions.

5. **Personalized learning and development platform:**

   - **Power Apps:** Create a personalized learning platform with features such as course catalogues, enrolment, and progress tracking.

   - **Power Automate:** Automate tasks such as sending course reminders and tracking completion.

   - **Power BI:** Analyze learning data to identify skill gaps, measure the effectiveness of training programs, and provide personalized recommendations.

By combining these Power Platform components, organizations can create powerful and flexible HR solutions that address their specific needs and improve employee experience.

Power Platform Architecture and Integration with HRIS and ERP Solutions

The Power Platform sits at the application layer of the enterprise architecture, providing a flexible and scalable platform for building custom applications. Its seamless integration with various data sources, cloud services, and on-premises systems enables organizations to create end-to-end solutions.

The Power Platform and HRIS systems can be integrated to extend and enhance HR functionality. By connecting to HR data, Power Platform components can automate processes, provide additional features, and improve user experience. For example, Power Automate can automate onboarding tasks, Power Apps can create custom employee self-service portals, and Power BI can analyze HR data to gain insights into the workforce.

Similarly, the Power Platform can integrate with ERP systems to create a more unified and streamlined business solution. By connecting to ERP data, Power Platform components can automate cross-functional processes, provide additional functionality, and improve data visibility.

Integrating Power Platform with HRIS and ERP systems offers several benefits, including:

- **Improved efficiency:** Streamline processes and reduce manual effort.

- **Enhanced data visibility:** Gain a more comprehensive view of your business by integrating data from HR and ERP systems.

- **Increased productivity:** Empower employees with tools and automation to improve their productivity.

- **Better decision-making:** Make data-driven decisions based on insights from HR and ERP data.

- **Improved employee experience:** Provide employees with a more seamless and integrated experience.

By leveraging the Power Platform, organizations can create a more integrated and efficient business solution that spans HR and ERP systems. This can help to improve productivity, reduce costs, and enhance overall business performance.

Summary

This chapter provided an in-depth exploration of Microsoft's HR solution architecture, emphasizing the interconnectivity and strategic layering of tools like **Microsoft Dynamics 365 for Human Resources**, **Microsoft Viva**, and the **Power Platform**. Dynamics 365 serves as a comprehensive foundation for core HR operations and talent management, while Viva enhances employee experience through communication, engagement, learning, and feedback modules. The Power Platform supports agility and customization, enabling organizations to build tailored HR applications, automate workflows, and drive data-driven insights. Together, these technologies form a scalable, integrated ecosystem that empowers HR and IT to collaborate more effectively, improve employee satisfaction, and align HR functions with organizational goals.

PART II

Deep Dive into Core HR Solutions

CHAPTER 3

Dynamics 365 Human Resources

Capabilities of Dynamics 365 Human Resources

Dynamics 365 Human Resources (D365 HR) is an extensive solution that supports the entire employee life cycle from hiring to retirement. It provides HR professionals and organizations with tools for talent acquisition, onboarding, core HR management, performance tracking, compensation, and offboarding – all within a unified platform. D365 HR helps companies handle HR tasks more smoothly, meet compliance requirements, and create a better experience for employees. This section explores the key functional areas of D365 HR, aligning them with stages of the employee journey and illustrating how the system can be utilized in various industry scenarios.

Talent Acquisition and Recruitment

At the start of the employee journey, Dynamics 365 Human Resources offers functionality to manage talent acquisition. The process begins when HR teams or line managers submit a recruitment request, which triggers the end-to-end workflow of filling an open position. This includes posting job openings, sourcing candidates, and tracking applications through each stage. Recruiters and hiring managers collaborate within the system: recruiters manage candidate data and communication directly in D365 HR, while hiring managers can raise position requests, review applicants, and participate in interviews and selection. The system maintains a centralized repository of candidate profiles and application history, with the flexibility to link a single candidate to multiple job applications as needed.

Dynamics 365 Human Resources natively supports integration with external recruiting platforms such as LinkedIn. Many organizations use a dedicated Applicant Tracking System (ATS) or LinkedIn Talent Solutions for sourcing candidates; D365 HR can integrate with these tools to smoothly transition candidates into the HR system once a hiring decision is made. For example, a common process is to enter a recruiting request for a new position in Dynamics 365 Human Resources, this initial request triggers the end-to-end workflow. From there, recruiters can source candidates via LinkedIn or another ATS, and then import or transition the selected candidate into D365 HR as a new employee record once hired. This ensures that all critical hire data is captured in the HR system without duplicate entry. By supporting both built-in recruiting projects and external integrations, D365 HR provides flexibility in talent acquisition strategies.

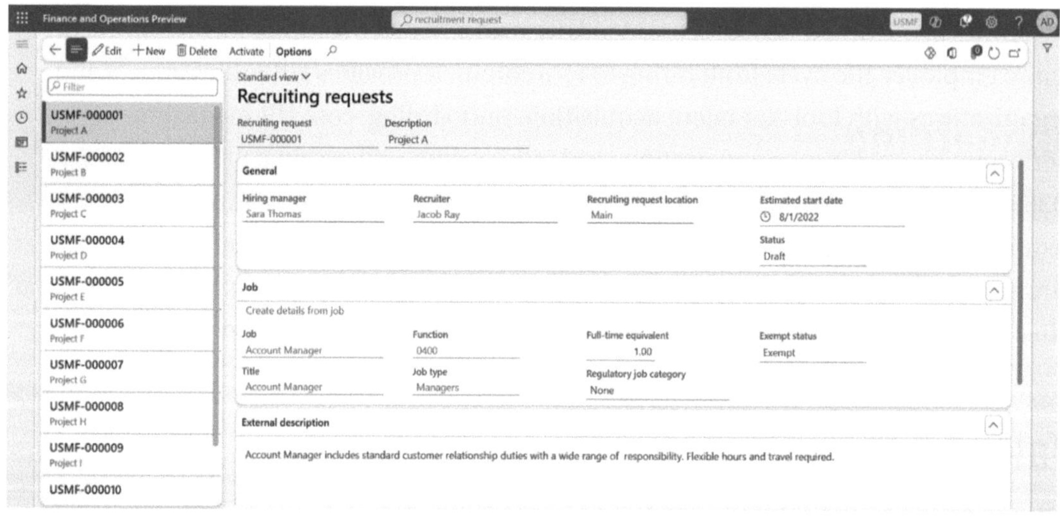

Figure 3-1. *Example of a recruitment project in Dynamics 365 HR, showing an open position with candidates and application stages*

Moreover, integration can now be extended using the Recruiting add-on, a model-driven Power Platform app, which deepens the connection between recruitment efforts and D365 HR. The add-on, available in public preview, is built on Power Apps, Power Automate, Dataverse, and Power Pages, and embeds Copilot to assist with different recruitment activities. When a hiring manager creates a recruiting request, a recruiting project is created and the information is sent through Power Automate to Recruitment add-on, and once a candidate is selected, the data flows back into D365 HR, completing the round trip.

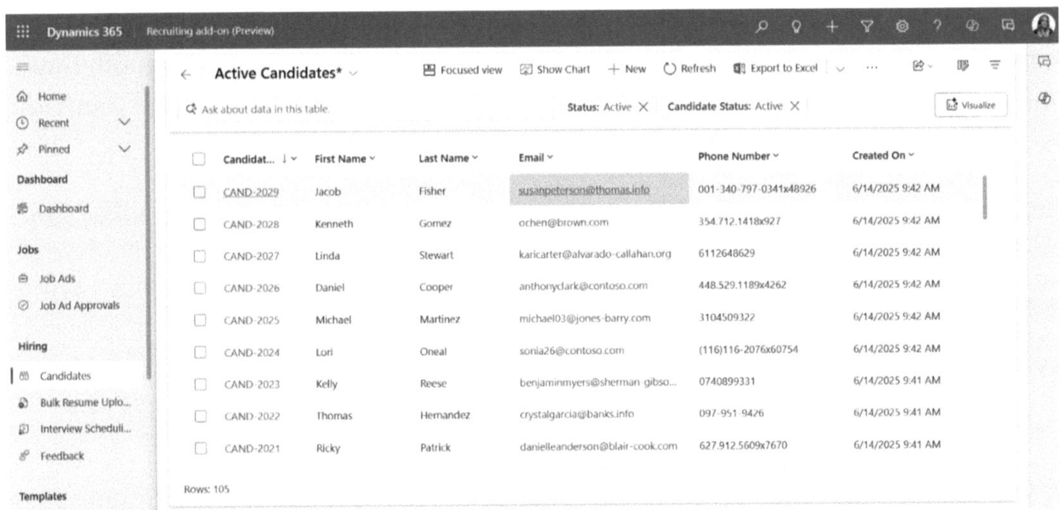

Figure 3-2. *Recruiting add-on app showing candidates and application stages for an open position*

Onboarding New Employees

Successful onboarding is critical for new hire engagement, and D365 HR includes robust tools to manage and automate the onboarding process. The cornerstone of onboarding in Dynamics 365 HR is the Task Management workspace, which enables HR to define onboarding checklists and assign tasks to various stakeholders. As soon as a hire is confirmed and the employee record is created, an onboarding checklist can be triggered for that new employee. The checklist might include tasks for the new hire (such as completing HR forms or mandatory training) as well as tasks for others, like IT setting up equipment or a manager scheduling introductory meetings. All these tasks are consolidated so that HR and managers can track progress and ensure nothing is missed in bringing the new employee onboard.

Dynamics 365 HR's task management is designed to be flexible and scalable. HR teams can create a library of reusable task templates to standardize onboarding across roles or locations. Tasks can be grouped and even assigned to a task group (for example, an "IT setup team" of several members) so that anyone in that group can pick up the task and complete it. Each onboarding checklist ties into a calendar that respects working days and holidays, helping to set realistic due dates for each task. Moreover, tasks can be scheduled relative to the employee's start date – including in advance (using negative offset days) so that certain preparatory steps (like creating accounts or preparing a workspace) are completed before the first day. This ensures a smooth Day One experience for the new hire. HR administrators can monitor the checklist status and receive alerts for any delayed tasks, allowing proactive follow-up.

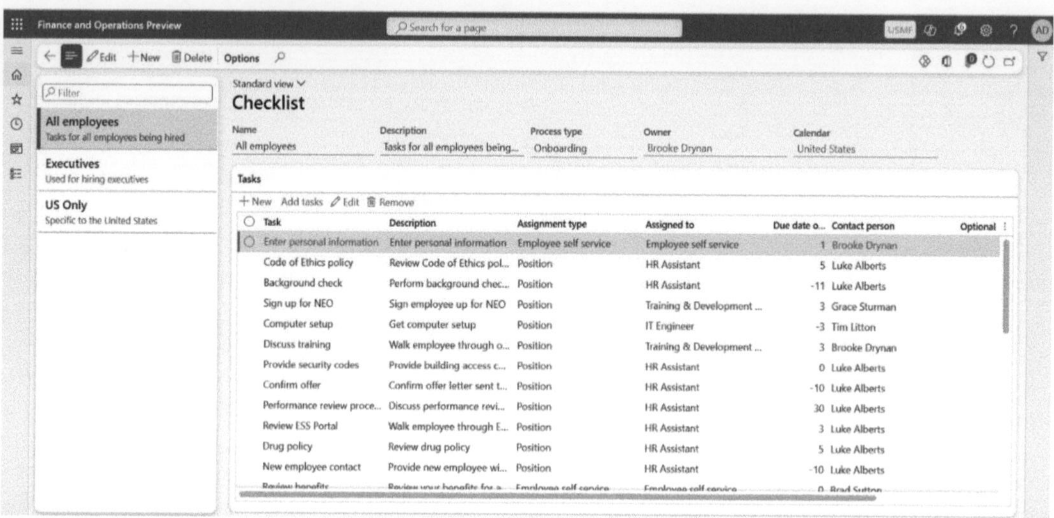

Figure 3-3. *Onboarding checklist in Dynamics 365 HR Task Management module*

Beyond administrative tasks, D365 HR supports a positive onboarding employee experience. New hires can log into the Employee Self-Service portal (ESS) or Self-Service – depending on the preferences set in parameters for workspace name – to see their onboarding tasks, upload personal information, and familiarize themselves with company resources. Some organizations configure a "new employee welcome" page to guide newcomers through their first week. For example, the onboarding checklist might include a task prompting the new employee to complete a compliance training module. While the employee can view and acknowledge the task through the self-service interface, the actual training content is typically delivered via an external Learning Management System (LMS) or through integrated tools like Microsoft Viva Learning. At the same time, a designated buddy or mentor could have tasks reminding them to meet with the newcomer for a tour or coffee chat. By assigning responsibilities across HR, IT, managers, employee and buddies, Dynamics 365 HR helps create a structured yet welcoming onboarding process.

Core HR Management (Employee Records and Organization)

Once an employee is onboarded, Dynamics 365 Human Resources serves as the central system of record for all employee information and organizational data. HR professionals can maintain detailed employee profiles that include personal details, job assignments, contact information, skills, certifications, performance history, and more. Having rich employee profiles in one place enables better connections and insight, for instance, a profile might show an employee's career history and skills, which managers can review when considering project assignments or succession plans. The system also supports document management for HR, allowing storage of important employee documents (such as contracts, identification, or performance documents) in a secure manner.

Organizational structures are configurable in D365 HR to mirror the company's actual structure. HR can set up legal entities (companies), departments, jobs (generic roles or titles), and positions (specific instances of jobs that are filled by employees). This configuration underpins many HR processes. For example, each position is associated with a manager, which by default defines the reporting hierarchy used for performance reviews. D365 HR uses this position hierarchy for workflows (such as automatically routing a leave request to an employee's manager). HR specialists or enterprise architects can configure multiple hierarchy types, aside from the managerial hierarchy, there can be project or matrix hierarchies for other reporting relationships. These hierarchies are useful in scenarios like global companies with complex reporting lines, or where functional managers and project managers are in different roles.

Critically, D365 HR also supports compliance and record-keeping needs in core HR. The system can track required certifications or work authorizations and prompt HR when renewals are due. It provides standard fields and modules for regulatory data (for example, in some jurisdictions, tracking an employee's work eligibility, or emergency contacts is important). Role-based security ensures that sensitive personal data (like government IDs, medical information, or compensation) is only accessible to authorized HR users, protecting employee privacy. The HR Analytics capabilities (delivered via built-in integration with Power BI) enable organizations to monitor headcount, turnover rates, and other key HR metrics over time. This helps HR leaders analyze workforce trends and make data-driven decisions about talent management.

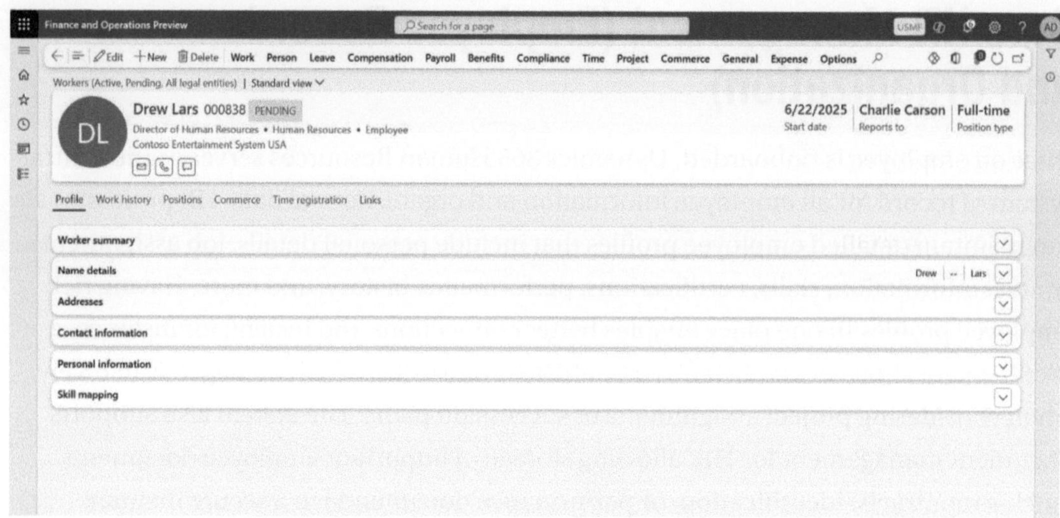

Figure 3-4. *Employee record page in Dynamics 365 HR*

Leave and Absence Management

Managing employee time off is another core capability of Dynamics 365 Human Resources. The Leave and Absence workspace in D365 HR provides a centralized and flexible framework for defining leave and time-off plans. HR can configure various types of leave (such as vacation, sick leave, parental leave, or any custom leave types) and define rules for accrual and carry-over. Using these types, HR creates leave plans that specify how employees accrue time off (for example, a vacation plan might grant a certain number of hours per month) and what the maximum balances are. Employees are enrolled in the appropriate plans, and the system can automatically calculate accruals and update balances. This automation ensures that leave benefits are consistently applied and that both employees and managers have an accurate view of available time off.

Employee self-service (ESS) is a key part of leave management: workers can easily view their leave balances and submit time-off requests through the self-service portal or even directly within Microsoft Teams. For instance, an employee could open the HR app in Teams or the ESS, check how many vacation days they have remaining, and then fill out a leave request form for upcoming dates. The interface is intuitive, showing their current balances and any company holidays or blackout dates that might affect the request. Once submitted, D365 HR uses workflow rules to route the leave request for approval. Typically, the request goes to the employee's manager, who can approve or reject it, and the system will update the calendar and balances accordingly. The approval process can be done in Dynamics HR system, or through integrated Teams notifications, making it convenient for managers to respond promptly.

D365 HR also supports more complex absence management scenarios. In some industries – for example, manufacturing or field service – the direct line manager may not be the one who handles daily leave approval. To accommodate this, the system allows configuration of an Absence Manager role with an alternate approval hierarchy. An absence manager can be a supervisor responsible for approving time off for a group of employees across different departments or locations. For example, on a production shop floor, a shift supervisor might act as the absence manager for all production workers on that shift, even though those workers formally report to managers in another department. Dynamics 365 HR lets HR define a custom hierarchy (e.g., a "Leave approvers" hierarchy) and assign positions to it so that leave requests route to the designated absence manager instead of the default manager. This flexibility is valuable for organizations with non-traditional management structures or where operational needs dictate a different approval workflow. All leave approvals, whether by direct managers or absence managers, are captured in the system to maintain a complete audit trail.

From an analytical perspective, the Leave and Absence module provides reporting on time-off usage. HR and business managers can analyze absence trends – for instance, identifying departments with higher sick leave usage or visualizing overall workforce availability across the year. Such insights help in workforce planning and in designing wellness initiatives, if needed. In summary, D365 HR's leave management capabilities ensure that employees have a clear and easy way to take the time off they've earned, while the organization maintains oversight and control over scheduling and compliance with leave policies.

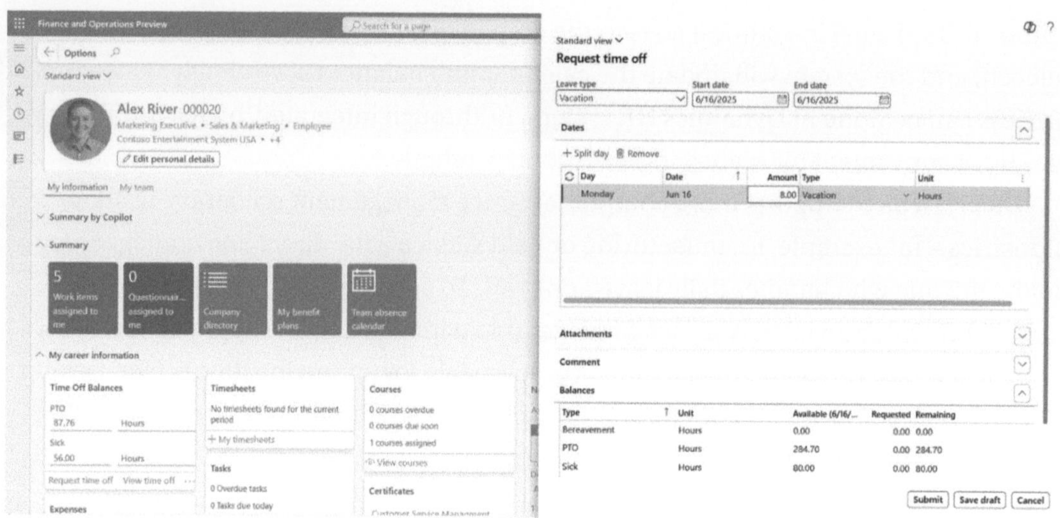

Figure 3-5. *Screenshot: Employee self-service leave request form in Dynamics 365 HR, showing available leave balance and fields to request time off*

Compensation and Benefits Management

Competitive and well-managed compensation and benefits programs are crucial for employee satisfaction and retention. Dynamics 365 Human Resources includes modules to administer both compensation (salaries, bonuses, etc.) and benefits (health insurance, retirement plans, etc.), tying them into the employee life cycle.

On the compensation side, HR can set up fixed compensation plans to handle salaries or hourly wages, and variable compensation plans for bonuses, incentives, or stock awards. The system supports defining compensation structures such as pay grades or bands with associated ranges. Each employee's compensation can be recorded in their profile, including history of pay changes. During annual salary reviews or merit increase cycles, D365 HR can assist by providing worksheets or processes where managers propose pay changes that HR can approve and apply across the organization. All compensation changes are tracked, ensuring transparency and historical record-keeping. For example, if an employee gets a promotion, the HR specialist can update their position assignment and associated compensation in D365 HR, triggering any workflow for approval, if required. The new salary will then be effective from the designated date and visible to payroll or finance systems through integration.

In terms of benefits management, D365 HR allows organizations to configure benefit plans (like medical, dental, vision insurance, or company pension plans) and manage employee enrollment. HR can define each benefit plan's options, costs (employee contribution vs. employer contribution), and eligibility rules. Employees can then enroll in benefits through the self-service portal, especially during an open enrollment period or when they have a qualifying life event (such as marriage or birth of a child). The system can process life events, meaning if an employee's marital status changes or they have a new dependent, HR can record that life event and open a special enrollment window for them to adjust their benefits. This ensures compliance with policies and regulations that govern benefits changes.

D365 HR's benefit management capabilities are designed to handle complex scenarios and provide flexibility. For example, different groups of employees might be eligible for different plans, or a company operating in multiple countries may have distinct benefit offerings per country. The system supports these variations by allowing configurations per legal entity or employment category. Additionally, benefits administration in D365 HR can integrate with payroll providers so that deductions and contributions are accurately reflected in paychecks. Although Dynamics 365 HR itself does not process payroll, it can export compensation and benefit deduction data to payroll systems (such as Ceridian Dayforce or other third-party payroll solutions) to ensure seamless payroll processing.

Overall, the compensation and benefits features in Dynamics 365 Human Resources help HR teams maintain structured and fair reward systems. By automating calculations (like prorating salary for mid-period changes or computing benefit costs) and keeping all information in one system, D365 HR reduces manual effort and errors. Employees, in turn, benefit from clarity – through self-service they can view their current compensation details, total rewards statements, and enrolled benefits. This transparency and ease of access contribute to higher employee trust and engagement.

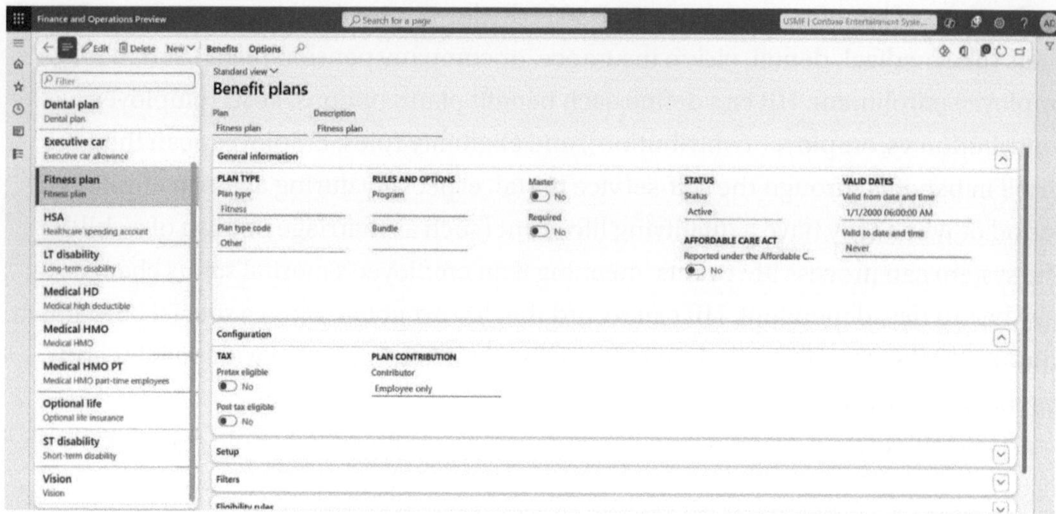

Figure 3-6. *(Screenshot: Example of a benefit enrollment screen in Dynamics 365 HR, showing available benefit plans and selection options for an employee during open enrollment)*

Performance Management and Employee Development

An ongoing part of the employee journey is performance management and professional development. Dynamics 365 Human Resources provides integrated tools to set goals, track performance reviews, and manage employee skills and training, thereby supporting a continuous development cycle.

The performance management module in D365 HR covers the process of setting employee objectives (goals), collecting feedback, and conducting performance evaluations. HR can configure performance review templates that define the criteria and format for appraisals – for example, establishing sections for competencies, goals, and manager feedback. Employees and managers can collaboratively set performance goals in the system, aligning individual objectives with broader organizational targets. These goals are tracked in D365 HR over the review period, and both employees and supervisors can update progress notes or results. During the review cycle, the system offers a dedicated Performance journal where employees can record achievements, milestones, or feedback they've received throughout the year. This journal functions like a personal log of performance-related events (such as successful project completion or customer kudos), which the employee can choose to share with their manager. Managers similarly can keep notes on their team members' performance in manager journals. When it's time for the formal review, having this documented history makes the evaluation process more evidence-based and comprehensive.

A typical performance review in D365 HR might involve the employee completing a self-assessment form, the manager entering their evaluation, and possibly a calibration step by a second-level manager or HR. The system supports capturing ratings (e.g., a numeric score or qualitative rating for each goal or competency) and feedback comments. All this happens within the HR system's Performance review pages, ensuring that the data is stored centrally and can be analyzed later. For example, HR could generate reports on average competency ratings across the company or track completion status of performance reviews for compliance. Managers also use the system to document performance feedback and coaching conversations throughout the year, not just at formal review time. This encourages a culture of continuous feedback.

In conjunction with performance tracking, Dynamics 365 Human Resources emphasizes employee development and learning. The system can manage a catalog of skills and competencies that are relevant to the organization. HR or managers can record each employee's skills, proficiencies, certifications earned, and any required qualifications for their role. There is functionality to map these competencies to job roles – for instance, a "Project Manager" job might require leadership, budgeting, and a certification in project management. D365 HR can then track which employees meet or exceed those qualifications and which might have gaps. This ties into development plans: if an employee aspires to a role or needs growth in certain areas, their manager or an L&D specialist can create a development plan in the system. Development plans might include enrolling in training courses, pursuing a certification, or gaining specific on-the-job experiences. The employee development module and performance features work hand-in-hand; goals in the performance module can include development goals (like "Complete advanced Excel training by Q4") and those can be tracked just like business goals.

The solution also supports administering training and courses. Organizations can set up internal training events or link to external learning systems. D365 HR can keep a record of courses offered, and employees can be registered for courses through the system. After completion, their profile gets updated with the new skills or certifications. While Dynamics 365 Human Resources does not offer native integration with LinkedIn Learning, organizations can leverage Microsoft Viva Learning and Power Platform tools to connect learning experiences across the Microsoft ecosystem. This ensures that an employee's learning progress is visible when considering their performance and career progression.

Crucially, D365 HR takes advantage of the broader Dynamics 365 ecosystem to enhance performance and development. For example, integration with Dynamics 365 Customer Voice (one of Microsoft's survey tools) allows HR to gather 360-degree feedback or employee engagement survey results and link them to performance insights. An organization might use Dynamics 365 Customer Voice to conduct an annual employee satisfaction survey or to collect peer feedback for a manager's review. Those insights, once captured, can be analyzed alongside performance data to provide a more holistic view of an employee's growth and areas for improvement. Additionally, emerging capabilities with AI and analytics in HR systems are enabling more proactive talent development, such as identifying skill gaps across the workforce and recommending training courses or mentoring to close those gaps. While these AI-driven features are evolving, Microsoft's vision is that D365 HR can use machine learning to suggest personalized development opportunities or even predict attrition risk by analyzing engagement and performance trends.

From goal setting to annual reviews, and from skill tracking to continuous learning, Dynamics 365 Human Resources supports a full spectrum of performance and talent development activities. This helps organizations foster a high-performance culture where employees receive regular feedback and opportunities to grow.

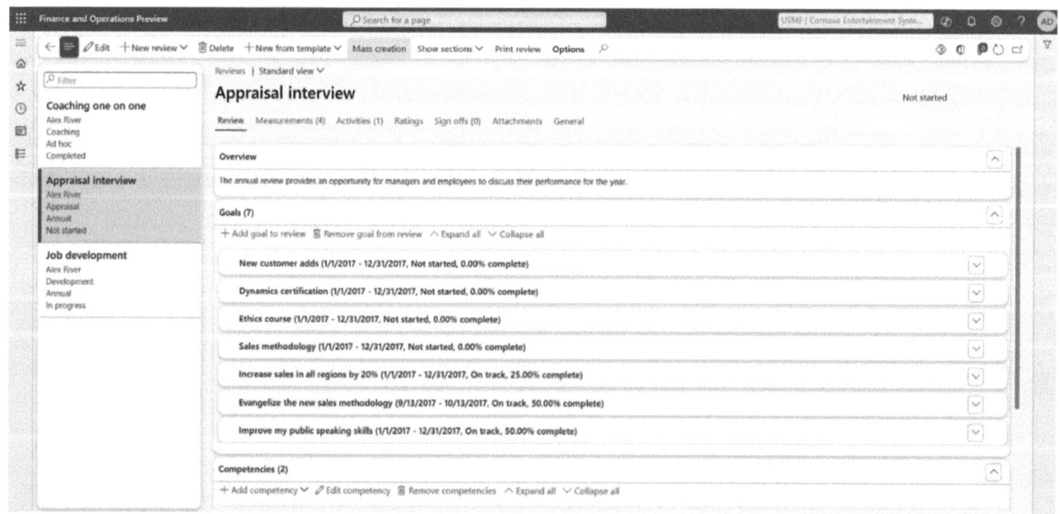

Figure 3-7. *(Screenshot: Performance review form in Dynamics 365 HR, illustrating an employee's goals, manager's ratings, and feedback comments)*

Employee and Manager Self-Service

One of the strengths of Dynamics 365 Human Resources is the emphasis on self-service, empowering employees and managers with direct access to HR information and processes. Instead of relying on HR personnel for every update or request, employees can use the Employee Self-Service (ESS) portal to handle many tasks on their own, and managers can use the Manager Self-Service (MSS) view to oversee their teams. This not only improves efficiency but also engages the workforce by giving them ownership of their data and requests.

In the ESS portal, an employee can perform a variety of actions: update personal information (such as contact details, address, or emergency contacts), view their compensation details, request time off, enroll in benefits during open enrollment, and track their performance goals and reviews. The interface is user-friendly, often presented as a dashboard or a set of tiles for each major area (e.g., "My Information," "Time off," "Performance," "Benefits"). For instance, if an employee moves to a new address, they can log into ESS and submit that address change which, once approved by HR, updates their record globally. Similarly, employees can use the self-service to view their remaining vacation balance and submit a leave request in a matter of clicks. The convenience of ESS is further enhanced by integration with tools like Microsoft Teams; employees can interact with a bot or app in Teams to check time-off balances reflecting a modern approach to employee experience.

Manager Self-Service provides people managers with an overview of their team and tools to take action on HR tasks related to their direct reports. Through MSS, a manager can see an org chart of their team, review team members' profiles (limited to relevant information such as roles, tenure, objectives), and approve or deny requests (like leave requests, travel expense approvals if integrated, or performance submissions). Managers can also initiate actions such as requesting a new position or starting a transfer process for an employee from their team view. The system facilitates team performance tracking – a manager can quickly glance at goal completion status across their team or check which of their employees have pending performance reviews to complete. In essence, MSS acts as a one-stop shop for managers to handle HR-related responsibilities efficiently, without needing to navigate through complex administrative menus or involve HR for routine approvals.

Self-service capabilities are especially valuable in large organizations and in decentralized environments. For example, in a consulting firm, consultants on the go can update their emergency contact or banking information themselves through ESS, ensuring HR records are up-to-date without back-and-forth emails. In a retail chain, store managers using MSS can see part-time staff schedules and approve shift swap requests (if integrated with scheduling systems) in real time. D365 HR's self-service is also accessible via mobile devices, which is critical for industries like construction or field services where workers may not have desktop access but can use a phone or tablet to access HR self-service.

From an HRIS (HR Information Systems) specialist perspective, enabling and configuring self-service involves deciding what data fields employees and managers can see and edit. D365 HR provides security roles and personalization options so that, for example, employees might be allowed to edit their contact info but not their job details, or managers can view their team's compensation ranges but not edit them. This configurability ensures that self-service rolls out in a controlled, secure manner. The result is a more agile HR function: routine updates and requests are handled directly by those involved, and HR staff can focus on strategic activities rather than clerical ones. Microsoft reports that this kind of employee empowerment leads to higher satisfaction, as people feel they have immediate access to the information they need and a direct channel to handle HR matters.

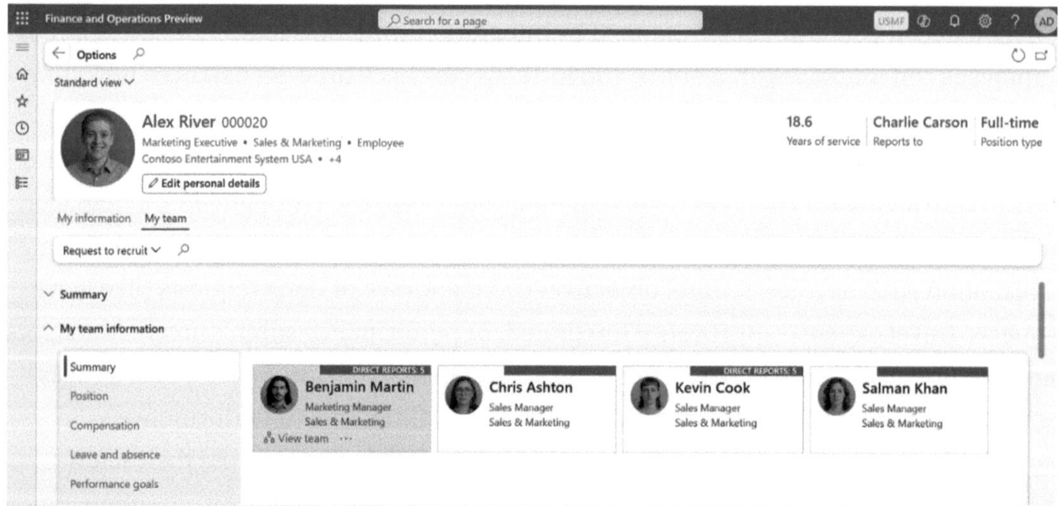

Figure 3-8. *(Screenshot: Manager Self-Service dashboard in Dynamics 365 HR, showing a team overview with each member's key info and pending approval requests)*

Offboarding and Transitions

The employee journey eventually comes to a transition point, whether it's an internal transfer/promotion or an exit from the organization. Dynamics 365 Human Resources supports these transitions with processes for offboarding departing employees and managing internal changes, ensuring consistency and compliance up to the last day of employment.

For internal transfers or promotions (often referred to as employee transitions), D365 HR can facilitate changes in an employee's position, department, or location. HR can use the system to initiate a transfer action, which updates the employee's record (new manager, new role, compensation change if applicable, etc.) effective on a specified date. Such changes can trigger transitional checklists similar to onboarding. For example, if an employee is moving to a new department, a transition checklist might include tasks like "Collect old equipment and issue new equipment," "Update system access rights," or "Introduce employee to the new team." Dynamics 365 HR's Task Management, as mentioned earlier, is used not only for onboarding but also for these transitions and offboarding processes. This ensures all stakeholders complete necessary steps when someone changes roles – from the old department and the new department alike.

Offboarding, the process that occurs when an employee is leaving the organization, is handled with equal importance in D365 HR. An offboarding checklist can be created to manage the exit process, whether it's a resignation, retirement, or involuntary leave. The checklist typically includes tasks like arranging exit interviews, revoking system access, returning company property (laptop, ID cards), providing benefits information (such as pension plan offboarding), and ensuring final payroll and paperwork are processed. When HR marks an employee for termination in the system with a last working day, they can attach the appropriate offboarding checklist which will assign tasks to the relevant parties – IT, payroll, the employee's manager, facilities (for access card retrieval), and so on. For instance, the IT department might automatically receive a task to disable the user's accounts on their last day, and Facilities might get a notice to prepare exit paperwork or remove the person from the security roster. The employee themselves might get a task via self-service to complete an exit survey or schedule an interview with HR.

Consistency in offboarding is critical for compliance and knowledge transfer. D365 HR helps by providing a structured approach so that each departure is handled professionally and no steps are missed. This is especially important in regulated industries or in roles with sensitive information. Additionally, the system maintains a record of the offboarding tasks completed for each employee, which is useful if any issues arise later (for example, proving that company assets were returned or that the employee received required notifications upon exit).

From an analytics standpoint, the offboarding data ties into broader HR metrics. HR can analyze reasons for leaving recorded during offboarding interviews (if tracked in the system) and feed that into retention strategies. Moreover, offboarding marks the end of one employee life cycle, and trends like turnover rates can be monitored. Dynamics 365 Human Resources can be configured to work with other tools to even predict or flag potential attrition risks before offboarding happens, by analyzing engagement and performance indicators. While offboarding itself is reactive, the data collected can proactively improve future talent acquisition and retention plans.

In summary, D365 HR treats offboarding and internal transitions as structured processes, much like onboarding. By doing so, it ensures that the employee's journey – whether ending or evolving – is handled with diligence and that the organization maintains continuity. It also means that every stage of the hire-to-retire life cycle is managed within the same system, giving HR a complete view of each employee's history from start to finish.

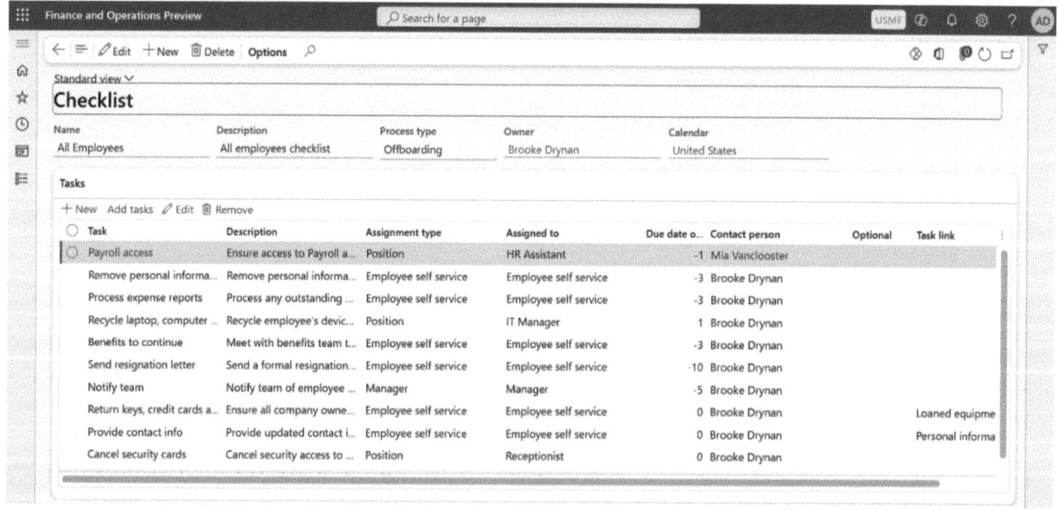

Figure 3-9. *(Screenshot: Offboarding checklist in Dynamics 365 HR, showing tasks such as exit interview scheduling, equipment return, and system access removal for a departing employee)*

Configuration and Customization Options for HR Professionals

While Dynamics 365 Human Resources provides rich out-of-the-box functionality, every organization has unique requirements. HR professionals, HRIS specialists, and consultants can configure and extend D365 HR to fit specific business needs without extensive development effort. This section discusses how to tailor the system – from initial setup of HR modules to advanced customizations – and provides examples such as industry-specific adjustments. The goal of configuration and customization is to leverage the standard capabilities of D365 HR while aligning them with an organization's processes, terminology, and structure, ensuring a best fit HR solution.

Core System Setup and Organizational Configuration

Implementing Dynamics 365 HR begins with configuring the foundational HR structures. This involves defining the organizational elements like legal entities (companies), business units, departments, jobs, and positions. HR or system administrators use the configuration interface to input these elements so that the software mirrors the company's hierarchy and roles. For example, HR can create all the job titles (jobs) relevant to the business – such as "Software Engineer," "HR Manager," "Production Supervisor" – and then create position records for each headcount slot under those jobs (like "Software Engineer I in IT Department, reports to IT Manager"). By organizing the workforce into this structure, later processes (approvals, reporting, analytics) can utilize the relationships. Consultants often guide HR teams through this setup during implementation to ensure alignment with how the organization operates. A manufacturing company might set up a department for each plant location and position hierarchies that reflect both the operational reporting and a separate safety supervision line. Dynamics 365 HR supports multiple hierarchy types, so one can configure a matrix structure if, for instance, employees report administratively to one manager but on projects to another – this is especially useful in consulting or project-based industries.

Another key part of initial configuration is setting global HR parameters and policies in the system. D365 HR allows HR administrators to define rules such as the default probation period for new hires, the review period frequency (annual, semi-annual), or standardized date settings for benefit enrolment periods. HR parameters also cover things like number sequence codes for employee IDs, settings for privacy (who can view certain personal data), and integration keys if connecting to other systems. For example, if integrating D365 HR with a finance system, part of the configuration would involve mapping the financial dimensions (like department or cost center) with HR departments so that costs of an employee can flow correctly to Finance. These configurations ensure that once the system goes live, everyday transactions (hiring an employee, posting a job, approving leave) follow the company's rules and feed into the right channels.

Security configuration is another foundational element. The system comes with predefined security roles (such as HR manager, HR assistant, manager, employee) which have role-based access controls. HRIS specialists will review and adjust these roles to match the organization's governance. For instance, an HR Manager role might be given access to view and edit all employee records, whereas a manager role (for line managers) can only see their team's records and has no access to confidential fields like salaries of peers. D365 HR's security model is quite granular – you can adjust permissions on forms, reports, and even specific fields. A practical example: a company might create a special role for "Compensation Analyst" who can edit salary data but cannot view certain personal info, combining elements of HR and Finance roles. Configuring these roles properly is crucial for compliance (e.g., ensuring GDPR-sensitive data is restricted) and for allowing the self-service features to work appropriately (employees only see their own data, managers only their team's data, etc.).

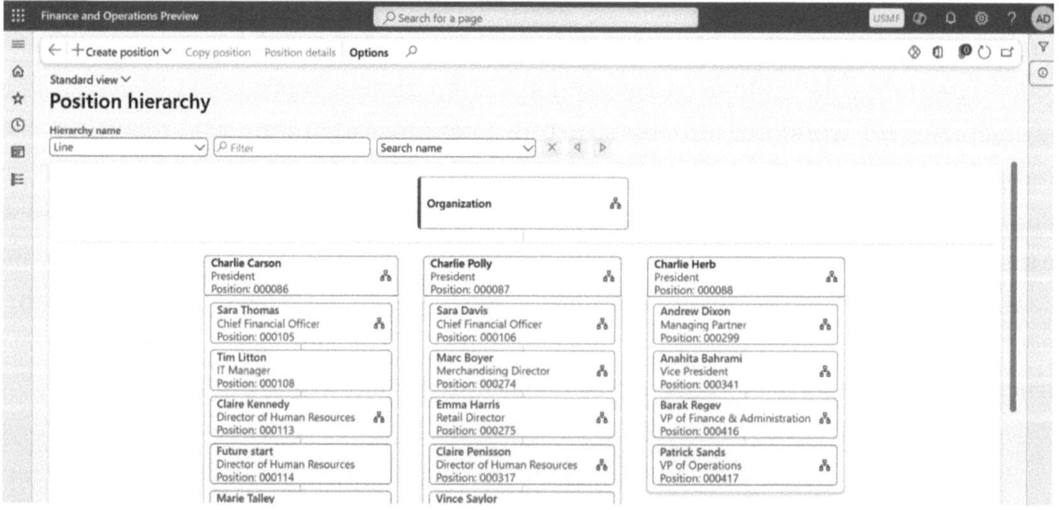

Figure 3-10. *(Screenshot: Dynamics 365 HR – Example of organizational hierarchy setup, showing departments, jobs, and positions configured for a sample company)*

Tailoring Talent Acquisition and Onboarding Processes

Dynamics 365 Human Resources can be adapted to match an organization's specific recruiting and onboarding workflows. In talent acquisition, while the system's Recruitment projects feature provides a basic structure, HR teams often have unique stages or data they want to capture about candidates. Through configuration, HR can define custom stages for recruitment (for example, adding stages like "Technical Interview" or "Culture Fit Interview" if those are part of the hiring process). It's also possible to add custom fields to the applicant or application records if additional information needs to be tracked – such as an "Interview Score" or "Referral Source." D365 HR supports creating custom fields without coding, directly through the interface by system administrators. This means if the default candidate form doesn't include a field for "University Ranking" and the HR team deems it important for their hiring analysis; a custom field can be added and will then be available on the form and in reports.

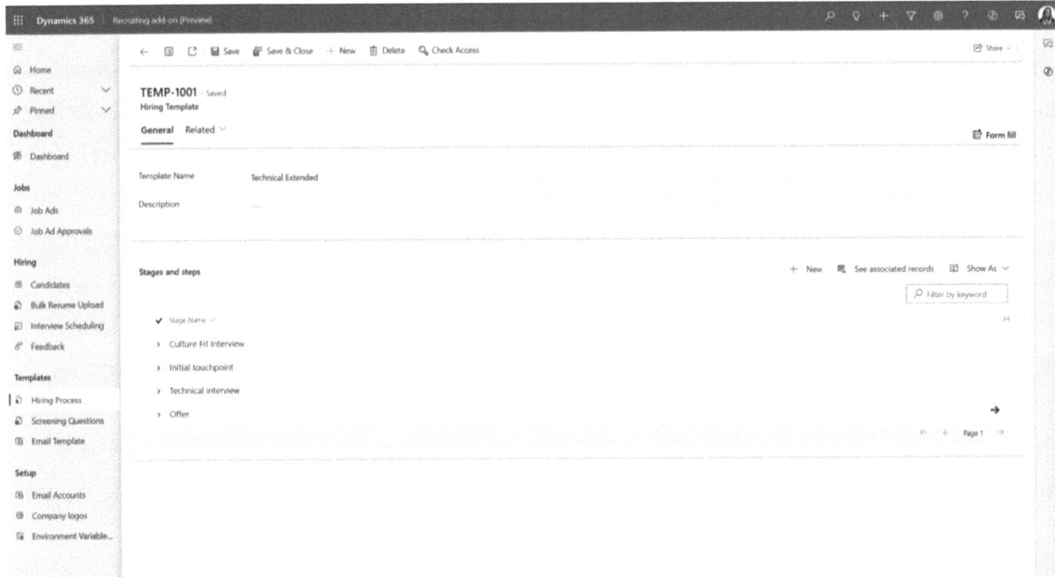

Figure 3-11. *(Screenshot: Dynamics 365 HR Recruiting add-on. Example of customized stages in an interview process)*

For onboarding, companies often have their own sets of tasks and rituals to welcome a new hire. Dynamics 365 HR's task management is highly configurable: HR can create multiple onboarding checklist templates tailored to different roles or regions. For example, the onboarding steps for a new factory worker might differ from those for a new software developer. A factory worker's onboarding might include specific safety training and equipment issuance tasks, whereas a developer's checklist might involve software setup and team meet-and-greets. The system allows HR to maintain these distinct templates and choose the appropriate checklist when hiring an employee (or even automate the selection based on role). Additionally, each task in the checklist can be configured with details such as the description, the assignee (by default or by role), and relative due date. If an organization uses external systems or tools for onboarding (such as a separate Learning Management System for training), D365 HR tasks can include links or instructions to use those systems, ensuring nothing falls through the cracks.

Another aspect of tailoring the hiring process is configuring workflow approvals if needed. While hiring an employee in D365 HR is typically an HR action, some companies require managerial approval or budget approval for new positions or hires. D365 HR can relate to Power Automate or use its internal workflow engine (in the merged Finance & Operations infrastructure) to route an approval request. For instance, when a recruiter finishes entering a new hire's details, an automatic workflow could send a notification to the finance controller to approve the position's budget allocation before finalizing the hire. These kinds of custom workflow steps can be set up during implementation to enforce internal controls.

A practical industry example: In public sector or education institutions, hiring often mandates additional steps like background checks or board approvals. D365 HR can be configured to include a "Background Check" stage in recruitment and not allow the hiring process to complete until a background check clearance field is marked as passed. HR specialists could configure a simple rule or use Power Automate to integrate with a background check provider – once the result comes back, the system updates the candidate's status, and only then can the recruiter move them to "hire" stage. By configuring these kinds of process specifics, Dynamics 365 HR is transformed from a generic system into a tailored solution that mirrors the organization's exact hiring policies and ensures compliance with all necessary steps.

Customizing the Employee Experience and Self-Service

Every organization may want to present information slightly differently to its employees and managers or capture additional data pertinent to their workforce. Dynamics 365 Human Resources provides several avenues for customization of the user experience, especially in the self-service pages.

One common customization is the use of custom fields to extend data capture. As mentioned, administrators can add custom fields on many forms in D365 HR. For example, an HR team in a healthcare company might add a custom field on the employee record for "Medical License Number" to track professional licenses of doctors and nurses. Once added, this field can be exposed on the employee's profile both for HR's view and optionally on the self-service profile so the employee can update it if it changes. The system ensures that these custom fields are also available in Dataverse and for reporting, meaning any unique data points captured become part of the organization's HR database for analytics and integration.

The layout and content of self-service can also be tailored. While deep changes to UI require development, there are configuration options such as choosing which tiles appear on the self-service homepage and what links or actions are provided. HR might decide to enable a tile for "Submit Idea" if they have integrated a suggestion program or hide a tile for "Benefits" if benefits enrollment is handled in a different system. Additionally, D365 HR can incorporate Power Apps or custom pages into the self-service menu. For instance, if an organization has a specialized employee survey or a rewards nomination form built in Power Apps, it can be embedded into the HR self-service interface so that employees see it in the same portal. This kind of extension is valuable for providing a one-stop shop for all employee needs.

Another key area of customization is notifications and workflows that underpin the self-service actions. By default, D365 HR will send out notifications for things like approved leave requests or when a manager completes a performance review. HRIS specialists can customize the content and timing of these communications. They might include company-specific instructions in the template of the "Onboarding welcome email" that the system sends to new hires, for example. Using Power Automate, organizations can also build additional automation: imagine when a new hire is marked "Hired" in D365 HR, an automated email could be sent to the IT department outside of the task management system, or a Teams message could notify the team channel that a new colleague is joining next week – these are custom automations that extend the standard capabilities.

From an enterprise architect's perspective, ensuring the user experience is aligned with corporate IT standards might involve branding and integration. While Dynamics 365 applications have a standard look, companies can usually apply their logo and adjust some color schemes. More importantly, integration with single sign-on (Microsoft Entra ID) means employees use the same credentials and possibly a company portal to access D365 HR self-service, making it a smooth part of the digital workplace. If the organization uses a broader employee portal or intranet (like SharePoint or Viva Connections), links to D365 HR pages or even embedded D365 HR web parts can be provided so that from the intranet an employee could, say, see their remaining vacation balance live. Such integrations are often configured during implementation to drive higher adoption of self-service by meeting employees where they already spend time.

In summary, Dynamics 365 HR's flexible architecture (built on the Microsoft Power Platform and Dataverse in many respects) allows a high degree of customization to the employee and manager experience. HR teams can introduce custom fields, adjust page layouts, create tailored communication, and even embed HR functions into other platforms. All these adjustments are done while maintaining the core integrity of the system – ensuring that updates from Microsoft won't break the customizations and that supportability remains high. The result is a personalized HR system that still benefits from cloud updates and innovations.

Workflow Automation and Approvals

Many HR processes require approvals or multistep workflows and configuring these is a critical part of tailoring Dynamics 365 HR to organizational policies. Out of the box, certain processes like leave requests, expense approvals (if integrated), and performance reviews have built-in workflow logic (for example, a leave request routes to the employee's manager automatically). However, HR professionals often need to fine-tune these or add new workflow approvals for other actions, such as job changes, compensation adjustments, or new position creation.

Dynamics 365 Human Resources (especially when deployed on the unified Finance and Operations infrastructure) leverages a robust workflow engine that allows point-and-click configuration of approval routes. For instance, if a company policy dictates that any salary increases above 10% must be approved by the HR Director, an approval workflow can be set such that when a manager submits a compensation change for an employee, the system checks the percentage increase. If it exceeds the threshold, it adds an extra approval step to the HR Director; otherwise, it might only require the immediate manager's approval. Similarly, for recruiting, an organization might require that any new position (new headcount) be approved by Finance before recruiting begins. In D365 HR, one can configure a workflow on the position request process: the hiring manager's request flows to the Finance Manager, then to HR for final approval. All approvals are tracked, and the requester can see the status (pending, approved, etc.) in the system.

Another tool in the arsenal is Microsoft Power Automate, which can be used alongside D365 HR to create more complex or cross-application workflows. Power Automate (part of the Power Platform) can listen to events in D365 HR via the Dataverse integration – for example, "a new employee record is created" or "an employee's address is changed" – and then perform actions or approvals as defined. A use case for this could be onboarding: upon a new hire record being created, a Power Automate flow could automatically create a user account in Microsoft Entra ID, add them to relevant distribution lists, and send a welcome email with instructions, complementing the tasks assigned within D365 HR. While D365 HR's internal workflow handles the HR-side tasks, Power Automate can handle communications and integrations with other systems. HRIS specialists configure these flows with a low-code approach, ensuring that the HR process connects smoothly with IT, facilities, or any other departments' processes.

Importantly, D365 HR's workflows can accommodate alternate hierarchies and roles as discussed earlier. Configuring the absence approval to follow an alternate hierarchy (such as an "Absence manager") is done by defining that hierarchy and setting the leave workflow to use it. This is a configuration step that allows the system to route approvals not strictly according to the line reporting. As another example, consider expense approvals: perhaps line managers approve expenses up to a certain amount, but anything beyond needs a director's approval. If expense management is integrated with D365 HR self-service (via Dynamics 365 Finance or a third-party), the same principle of hierarchy and conditional approval steps can be applied.

One area where workflow configuration intersects with industry needs is in compliance-related approvals. In healthcare, a hiring decision might need approval from a credentialing committee if the role is a clinician. In finance industries, a termination (offboarding) might need approval from a legal or compliance officer if the person has access to sensitive financial data. D365 HR's flexible workflow setup means these additional approval layers can be incorporated. HR and consultants will map out the required approvals for each process during the design phase and implement them so that the system automatically enforces these rules. This reduces reliance on manual email approvals and ensures auditable records of who approved what and when.

Role-Based Access and Security Customization

Security and proper access control are paramount in an HR system, as it contains highly sensitive personal and organizational data. Dynamics 365 Human Resources comes with a set of predefined security roles and privileges, but configuring these to match the company's governance model is an important step. HR administrators, often with the help of enterprise architects or IT security teams, will customize role-based access control in D365 HR.

Each role in D365 HR (like "Human Resources Administrator," "HR Assistant," "Manager," "Employee," "Compensation Manager," etc.) has specific permissions. During implementation, these are reviewed. For example, the default "Manager" role allows viewing of certain details for the manager's direct reports – such as contact info, leave balances, and performance goals – but not their pay or personal sensitive data. If an organization wants managers to also see their team's training completion records, the security role can be extended to grant that access. Conversely, some organizations might want to lock down data further; perhaps only a very limited set of HR personnel should be able to see employees' social security numbers or national IDs. In D365 HR, one can create a custom role (e.g., "HR Payroll Specialist") that has access to identification numbers for tax paperwork, while a regular "HR Generalist" role might not include that access. The system's security configuration interface allows administrators to tweak these settings without coding – by selecting duties and privileges included in each role.

A scenario requiring security customization is when external consultants or contractors are given limited access to the system. Suppose a company outsources some recruiting activities to an external recruiter: D365 HR could be configured with a role that allows that recruiter to enter candidate records and update application statuses, but not to access any other HR data like employee records or compensation information. This principle of least privilege is followed by creating a tailor-made security role, perhaps called "External Recruiter," and assigning it to those external user accounts. The role might only permit access to the recruitment project forms and nothing else. This way, Dynamics 365 HR acts as a controlled collaboration platform with third parties as well, without compromising data security.

Another example is the Absence manager role discussed earlier. This is not just a concept for approvals; in D365 HR, it can be a security role that grants designated users the ability to manage leave for certain employees outside their direct team. Configuring this involves setting up the role and linking it to the absence hierarchy so that those users can see and approve the requests for those employees. It's a combination of security and functional configuration.

Overall, customizing security in D365 HR ensures that the principle of *segregation of duties* is upheld. Enterprise architects will ensure that no single role has conflicting permissions (for instance, the person who can approve compensation changes should perhaps not be the same person who can initiate and pay them, to prevent fraud – unless checks are in place). Dynamics 365 provides auditing capabilities as well, logging changes to records and, if enabled, tracking who viewed certain information. HRIS admins can configure retention policies for audit logs as required by compliance.

In summary, while end users of D365 Human Resources see a seamless application tailored to their needs, behind the scenes, a careful configuration of roles and permissions governs what each user can do. This customization step is often invisible to the general user but is crucial for a successful and secure HR system deployment.

Integrations and Extensibility (LinkedIn, Teams, Power Platform, etc.)

No HR system exists in isolation, and Dynamics 365 Human Resources is designed to integrate and extend within the larger Microsoft ecosystem and with third-party solutions. HRIS specialists and enterprise architects will typically configure several integrations to ensure data flows smoothly between D365 HR and other applications like payroll providers, job boards, time tracking systems, or ERP modules.

A primary integration point for many organizations is payroll. D365 HR contains the core employee data, compensation, benefits deductions, and time-off records, but often an external payroll system is responsible for calculating pay and handling tax withholdings. Microsoft provided an out-of-the-box integration to Ceridian Dayforce in the past, and even though direct support ended in 2023, the capability demonstrated how data can be exchanged between D365 HR and payroll systems. Today, integration can be achieved through middleware or APIs. HR consultants configure D365 HR to export required data (new hires, terminations, pay changes, hours of leave taken) on a regular schedule to the payroll system. This could be done via Data Entities and Power

Automate or using an iPaaS (integration platform as a service) connector. Conversely, once payroll is processed, any relevant results (like year-to-date tax info or leave balance adjustments) can be imported back into D365 HR. The result is a cohesive HR-payroll process where employees see one version of their information, and administrators don't have to manually reenter data across systems.

Integration with LinkedIn is another valuable configuration, especially for talent acquisition. Microsoft owns LinkedIn, and Dynamics 365 has provided connectors to LinkedIn Talent Solutions. By configuring this, HR can post jobs from D365 or at least receive applicant data directly from LinkedIn. For example, when a candidate applies via LinkedIn, their profile details can flow into D365 HR's recruitment project as an application record. Likewise, hiring managers could view LinkedIn profiles of candidates side-by-side with internal data. While the dedicated Attract app was retired, core D365 HR can still utilize LinkedIn Recruiter system connectivity to optimize sourcing. Setting this up might involve API keys and mapping fields, tasks typically handled by a technical consultant during system integration.

The integration with Microsoft Teams is increasingly a highlight of D365 HR. HR professionals can configure a Teams integration such that employees and managers interact with HR processes without leaving Teams. For instance, a Teams agent (powered by Copilot Studio) can be deployed to answer common HR questions like "How much vacation do I have left?" or "What is the company holiday schedule?" D365 HR provides an app for Teams where employees can request time off directly in Teams and get a response in the chat interface. To enable this, administrators follow the setup to connect D365 HR with the organization's Teams environment and publish the HR app to users. This kind of integration drives up usage of the HR system by meeting users in a platform they use daily and is a relatively straightforward configuration since Microsoft supplies the template app.

Another facet of extensibility is using the Power Platform (Power Apps, Power BI, Power Automate) to build on D365 HR. We already discussed Power Automate for workflows; similarly, Power BI can be used to create custom HR analytics dashboards beyond the standard reports. Microsoft often provides a starter Power BI content pack for Human Resources, which consultants can deploy and then customize to include specific metrics the organization cares about (e.g., diversity ratios, training hours, or predictive analytics for turnover). This might involve pulling data from D365 HR (via Dataverse or analytical data export) and combining it with other data sources like survey results or industry benchmarks. The resulting dashboards can be embedded back into D365 HR's interface for HR managers to view under an "Analytics" section, or into Teams/SharePoint for broader management consumption.

Finally, many organizations will leverage ISV (Independent Software Vendor) solutions and partner apps that extend D365 HR. Microsoft's Dynamics ecosystem includes numerous third-party add-ons – for example, advanced recruiting systems, benefits administration platforms, or time-clock systems – which have pre-built connectors to Dynamics 365. Configuring these typically involves installing the solution (often via Microsoft AppSource) and then setting up connection parameters. For instance, a specialized attendance tracking system might feed employee clock-in/clock-out data into D365 HR's leave and absence module to deduct hours from leave balances or to feed into payroll. The ability to centralize data by integrating various applications with D365 HR ensures that HR managers and business leaders can rely on Dynamics 365 as the single source of truth for people data.

In summary, a significant portion of an HR consultant's work in a D365 HR implementation is making sure the system talks to others. By using provided APIs, connectors, and the Power Platform, Dynamics 365 Human Resources can be woven into the organization's application landscape. This extensibility means D365 HR not only automates HR processes internally but also connects with broader business processes – from finance to project management – creating a unified, agile enterprise system.

Industry-Specific Configurations and Examples

While the core HR processes are common across industries, different sectors often have unique requirements or emphases. Dynamics 365 Human Resources, through its flexible configuration, can be adapted to meet these industry-specific needs. Here we highlight a few examples of how D365 HR might be tailored for industries:

Manufacturing: In a manufacturing environment, managing shift workers and ensuring compliance with labor regulations (like OSHA safety training in the United States) are top priorities. D365 HR can be configured with certification tracking – for instance, ensuring that forklift operators have a valid certification recorded in their employee profile and sending alerts when renewals are due (important for safety compliance). The leave management configuration can use the absence manager hierarchy so that a plant floor supervisor (absence manager) approves time off for production staff, as discussed earlier. Also, integration with Dynamics 365 Supply Chain or Commerce can allow sharing of worker availability for shift scheduling. A manufacturing company might also configure the compensation module to handle shift differentials (additional pay for night shifts), which can be done by setting up multiple compensation plans or pay rate adjustments that apply based on the position or schedule.

Professional Services/Project-based organizations: In consulting firms or IT services, the skills and project assignments are critical. D365 HR's competency management is configured with a rich library of skills and proficiency levels tailored to the services offered (e.g., specific programming languages, project management methodologies, client industry knowledge). HR can use the system's skill mapping to projects by integrating with Dynamics 365 Project Operations – meaning that when a new project is being resourced, the project operations module can query the HR module for people with the required skills and availability. To facilitate this, HR might configure additional fields like "Available from date" for each consultant or use the workforce scheduling integration in the Microsoft ecosystem. Performance reviews in this industry might occur after each project, so the performance module could be used in a more frequent, project-end review cycle rather than an annual cycle – something HR can set as a policy and reflect by triggering performance review processes multiple times a year.

Retail: Retail companies have large frontline workforces with high turnover and a need for quick onboarding. In D365 HR, the onboarding templates for retail roles (like store associate or cashier) are configured to be very streamlined – focusing on essentials that need to be done before the employee starts on the shop floor, such as completing a brief orientation and registering in the point-of-sale system. Integration with Dynamics 365 Commerce (for store operations) means HR can share data like employee positions and skills (e.g., who is trained on the cash register vs. stocking) with the store scheduling system. Retail also often has complex benefits eligibility (e.g., variable hour employees qualifying for benefits only after a period). HR can configure D365 HR's benefit plans with eligibility rules that automatically include or exclude employees based on their job type or hours worked, thereby handling this complexity. Additionally, the self-service in a retail context might be configured with simpler mobile access, knowing many retail staff will use their phones – so HR might emphasize the Teams mobile app integration for leave requests, as not all employees will log into a desktop portal.

Healthcare: Healthcare providers require tracking of licenses, continuing education, and often have scheduling systems for clinical rotations. D365 HR's course management can be leveraged to schedule and track mandatory trainings (like HIPAA compliance training, or medical education credits). HR can configure life events in benefits specifically to accommodate frequent status changes (for example, many healthcare workers may change from full time to part time or vice versa, affecting benefits). Another unique aspect is managing multiple positions – a nurse might work in two departments part-time. Dynamics 365 HR can support multiple position assignments per worker; configuring this properly allows each assignment to have its own compensation and leave eligibility. The security model might be adjusted as well so that departmental managers only see the portion of a shared employee relevant to their department. These fine-grained configurations ensure that even complex employment scenarios common in healthcare are well managed.

Across all industries, HR consultants use the configuration tools of D365 HR to tune the system. The underlying theme is that the application is versatile: by adjusting parameters, definitions, and workflows, it can handle union rules in one scenario, commission-based pay in another (like in sales organizations), or academic tenure tracking in an education context. Microsoft often releases new features in wave updates that target specific industry needs, and those can be enabled via the Feature Management workspace in D365 HR. For example, if a new feature for benefits management is released (perhaps supporting new retirement plan rules), an HRIS admin can turn it on for their environment and configure its settings to use it.

Summary

In conclusion, Dynamics 365 Human Resources provides a robust foundation that HR professionals can configure and customize extensively. By aligning the system with the employee journey – from recruiting the right talent, onboarding them effectively, nurturing their development and performance, managing their rewards and time off, and finally handling their transition or exit – organizations ensure they are leveraging technology to enhance every step of that journey. The combination of rich built-in capabilities and flexible customization options makes D365 HR suitable for a wide range of industries and scenarios, all while maintaining a single, integrated source of truth for the workforce. With careful planning and configuration, it becomes not just an HR database, but a strategic tool for talent and organizational management.

CHAPTER 4

Dynamics 365 Human Resources Implementation Guide

Implementing Dynamics 365 Human Resources (D365 HR) requires careful planning across environment setup, security, data migration, integrations, and more. This guide provides a comprehensive, step-by-step overview for administrators and project teams.

Environment Provisioning and Setup

Provisioning a D365 HR environment is done through the Power Platform Admin Center using the unified Finance and Operations infrastructure. Each D365 HR environment is essentially a Finance & Operations app running within a Power Platform environment with an associated Dataverse instance. This unified approach means you can have multiple Dynamics 365 apps (HR, Sales, etc.) and Power Platform components in one environment with a common Dataverse database, simplifying administration.

Step 1: Requesting the Environment

The actual deployment is self-service: from the Power Platform admin center's Environments section, create a new environment, add a Dataverse database, and select *Enable Dynamics 365 apps* with the Human Resources application template. This will provision the necessary HR solution and linked Finance & Operations infrastructure behind the scenes.

© Ana Inés Urrutia de Souza 2025
A. I. Urrutia de Souza, *The Microsoft AI Human Resources Handbook*,
https://doi.org/10.1007/979-8-8688-1781-6_4

Each environment you provision will come with a dedicated Dataverse instance and the linked HR app services. Make sure you have the appropriate license and available storage capacity in the tenant (at least 1 GB for database and file each) before provisioning. Choose a region for the environment that aligns with your organization's data residency and compliance requirements (D365 HR supports a broad range of geographies and languages).

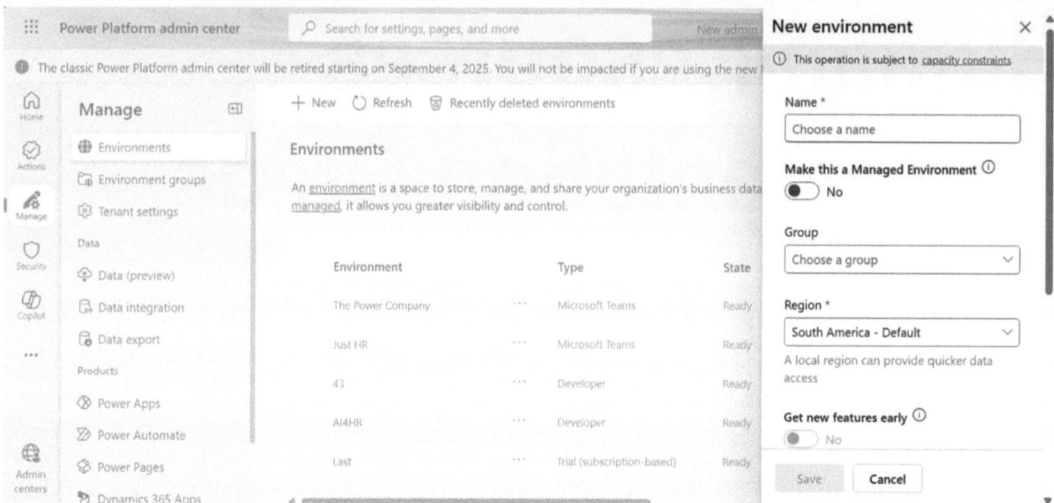

Figure 4-1. *Provisioning a Dynamics 365 Human Resources environment via Power Platform Admin Center*

Step 2: Choosing the Right Environment Type

When creating the environment, select the appropriate type: Sandbox or Production. A base D365 HR subscription typically includes one Production and one Sandbox environment. Use Sandbox environments for development, configuration, and testing. They contain all HR functionality but allow safe experimentation. Production environments are for live use with real data and users. You cannot deploy a *Production* environment until you have completed Microsoft's go-live readiness process, which ensures your project is prepared for production use.

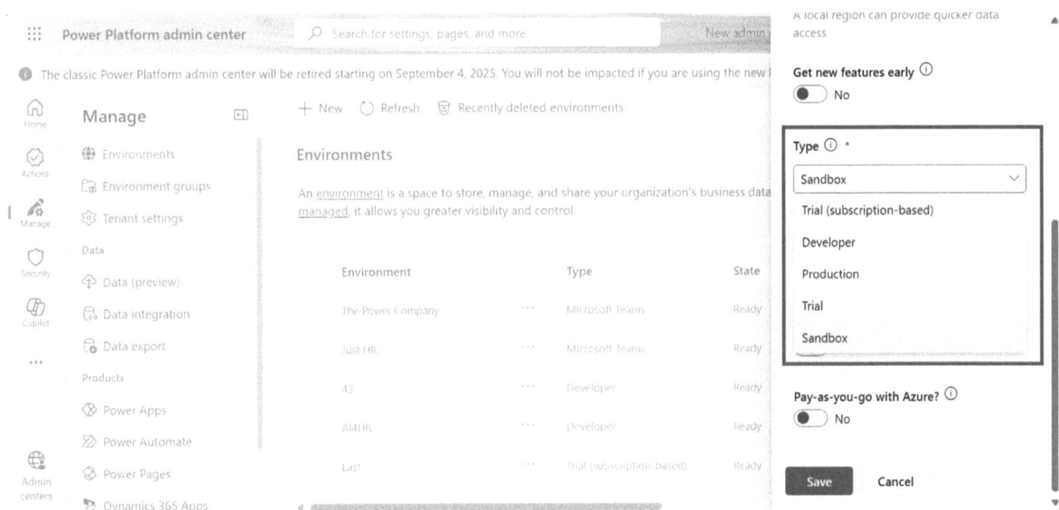

Figure 4-2. *Environment types in Power Platform admin center*

It's not recommended to use a Dataverse-only environment (one without the HR app deployed) for D365 HR. A "Dataverse-only" environment would lack the Finance and Operations HR back-end, so it cannot run the HR module. Always ensure you deploy the full HR app into the environment. Also consider the region and language needs: the environment's region should match your organization's location or compliance requirements (for example, EU data centers for European employee data), and language packs can be enabled to support localized user experiences.

Step 3: Linking to Microsoft Entra ID

Every D365 HR environment is bound to a Microsoft Entra ID tenant for identity and access management. User accounts and security roles in D365 HR are managed through Microsoft Entra ID – you must grant users access by adding their Microsoft Entra ID accounts to the HR environment and assigning appropriate roles. Upon provisioning, the account that created the environment (often a service account or global admin) is the administrator by default. You will need to add other users (such as HR staff, managers, employees) via the Users form in D365 HR and associate them with their Microsoft Entra ID User IDs.

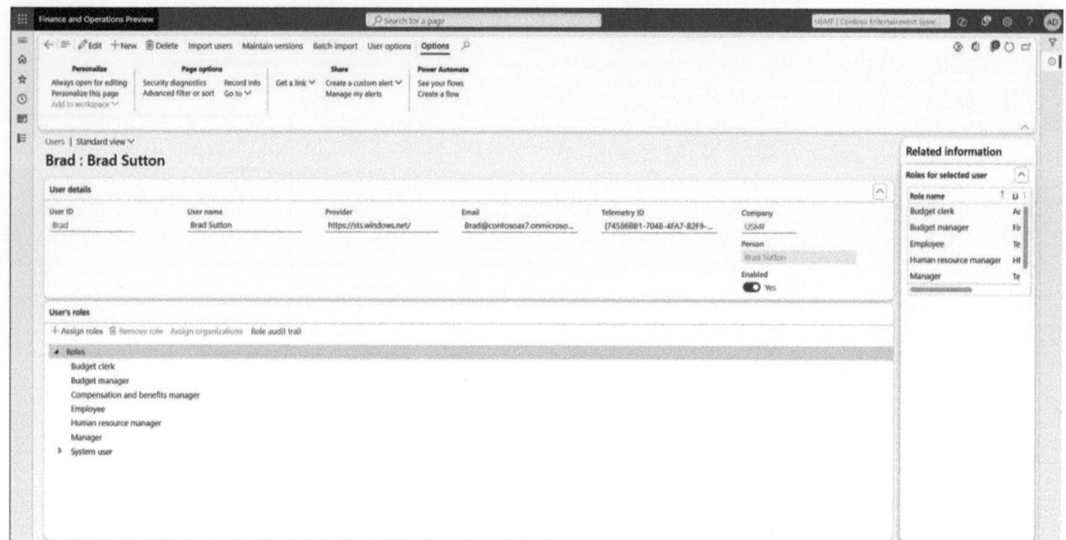

Figure 4-3. *User creation form in Dynamics 365 Human Resources*

Ensure that the HR environment's Microsoft Entra ID tenant is the one where all your employees reside. If your organization uses multiple directories, the environment will only recognize identities from the tenant it's linked to (usually the tenant where the licenses are provisioned). All authentication is handled by Microsoft Entra ID – D365 HR simply uses those identities and enforces role-based access within the application. In practice, this means no separate username/password management in HR; just assign existing Microsoft Entra ID users to the system.

Tip   It's good practice to create a Microsoft Entra ID security group for HR users and assign licenses and environment access to that group. This way, adding or removing someone from HR is as simple as updating group membership, which can also be automated.

Security Configuration and Custom Roles

Once the environment is up, establishing a secure access model is critical. Dynamics 365 Human Resources uses the same role-based security model as other Finance and Operations apps. In this model, access is granted to roles, not directly to users. Each security role aggregates a set of permissions (to menus, fields, actions) via underlying *privileges* and *duties*. Users are assigned one or more roles based on their job responsibilities, which in turn gives them the necessary privileges to perform their tasks. A user with no role has no access at all by default.

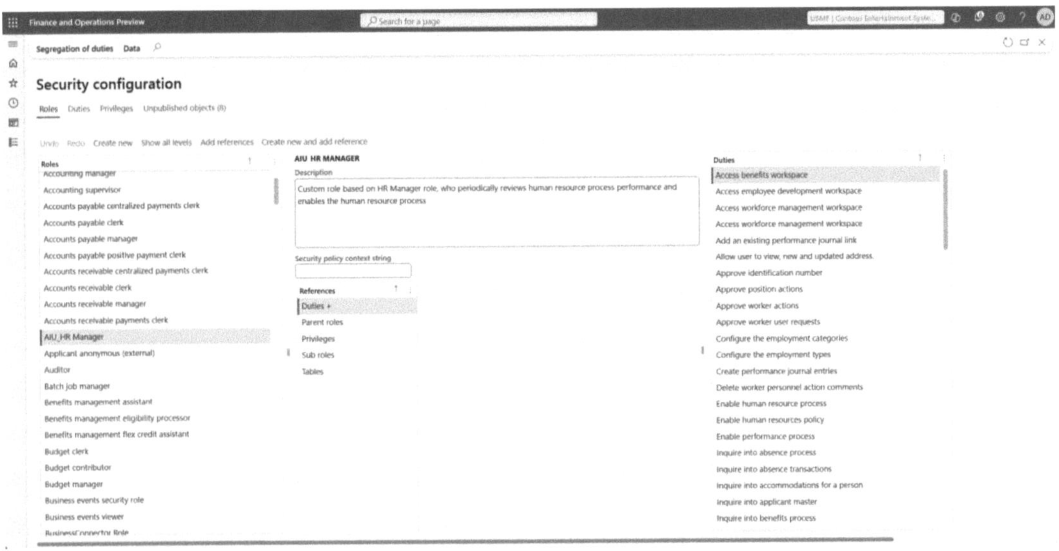

Figure 4-4. *Custom role created in Dynamics 365 Human Resources*

Step 1: Understanding the Role Hierarchy

Security in D365 HR is hierarchical and aligned with business functions. At the lowest level, permissions grant access to individual objects (specific forms, reports, or fields). Permissions group into privileges, which correspond to a certain action or task (for example, a privilege might allow "maintain worker personal details" or "approve leave requests"). Duties are higher-level groupings of privileges that represent parts of a business process (e.g., a duty to "manage employee information" might encompass privileges for maintaining addresses, positions, etc.). Finally, a role is composed of duties and privileges needed for a job role in the organization.

D365 Human Resources comes with several default security roles tailored to common HR personas:

- HR Manager: Broad privileges across the HR module. Users in this role can typically manage employee records, employment details, compensation, leave, and perform most HR configurations. An HR Manager can do almost all HR tasks (except system admin functions).

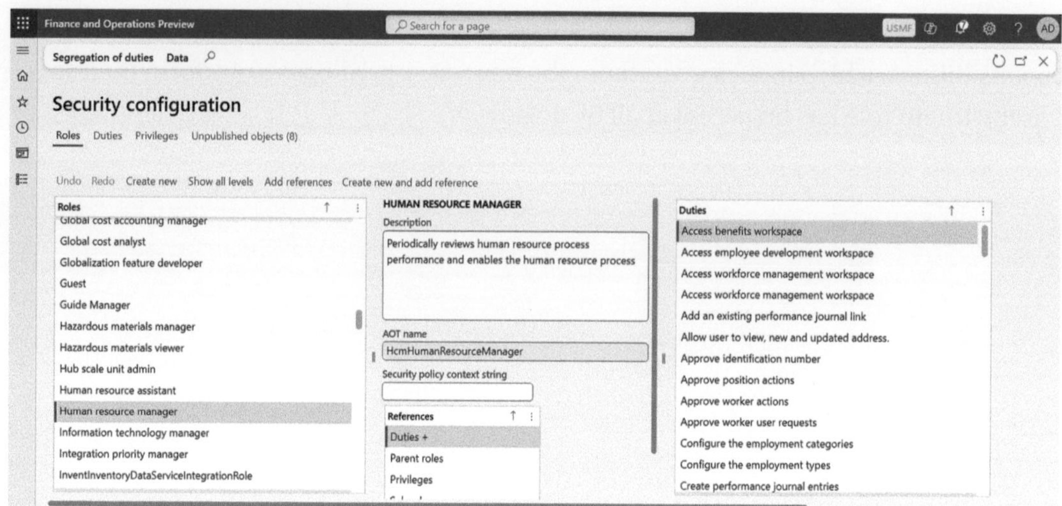

Figure 4-5. *Human Resources Manager role and duties*

- HR Assistant: A more limited HR staff role. HR Assistants can view and edit many HR records as well, but organizations might restrict certain sensitive areas. For example, an HR Assistant might help with maintaining addresses or onboarding info, but perhaps not have access to confidential performance reviews or executive compensation by default. (These specifics can be adjusted as needed.)

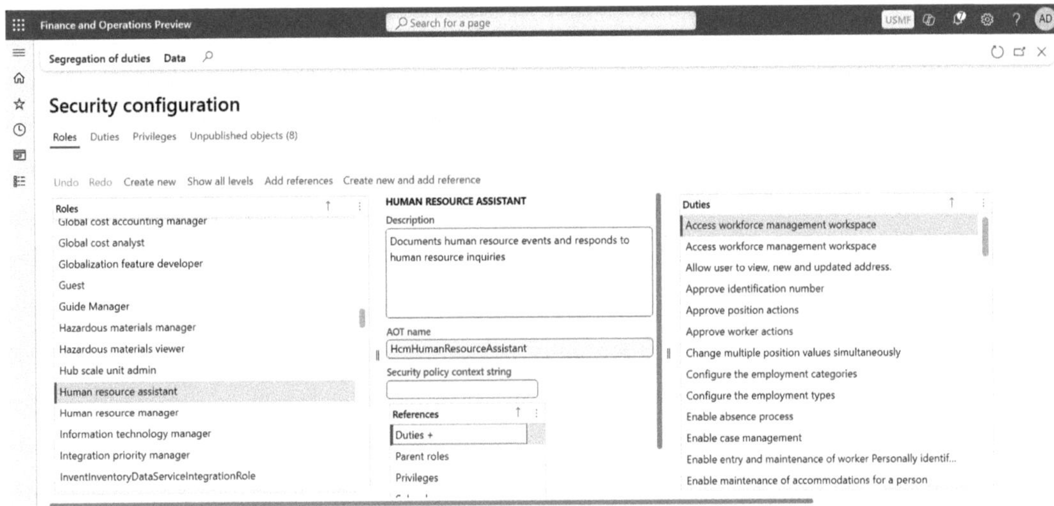

Figure 4-6. *Human Resources Assistant role and duties*

- Employee (Self Service): A very restricted role allowing an employee to view and update their own information. This role enables access to Employee Self Service workspace, where a worker can see their profile, benefits, time-off balance, submit leave requests, etc. They cannot see other employees' data.

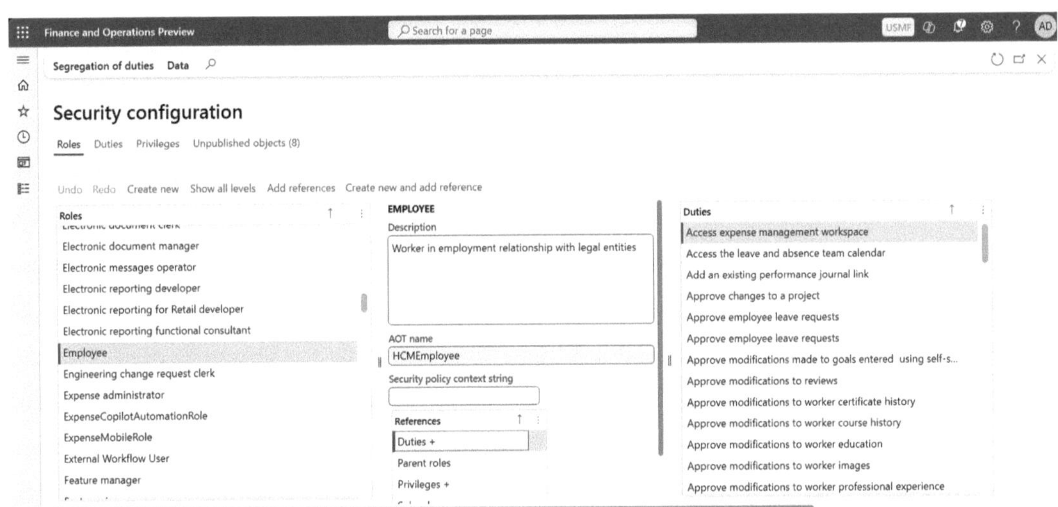

Figure 4-7. *Employee role and duties*

- Manager (Self Service): This role is for line managers to view information about their direct reports. Managers with this role can approve leave or changes for their team and view their team's profiles and performance entries but not edit core HR records. They also have the Employee self-service capabilities for their own info.

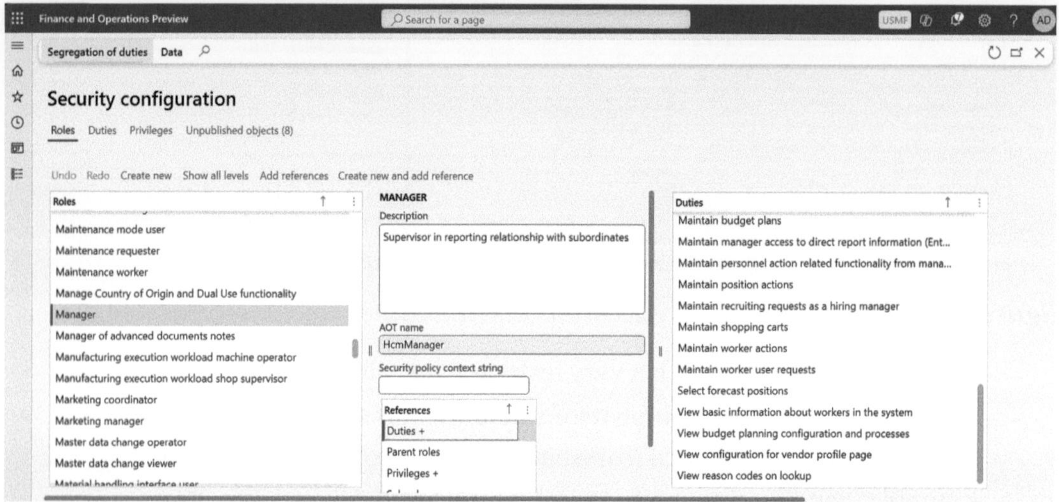

Figure 4-8. *Manager role and duties*

- System Administrator: Full access to all areas of the system (not just HR). This role is typically only for IT or system admins and has every privilege, including configuration, user management, and integration settings.

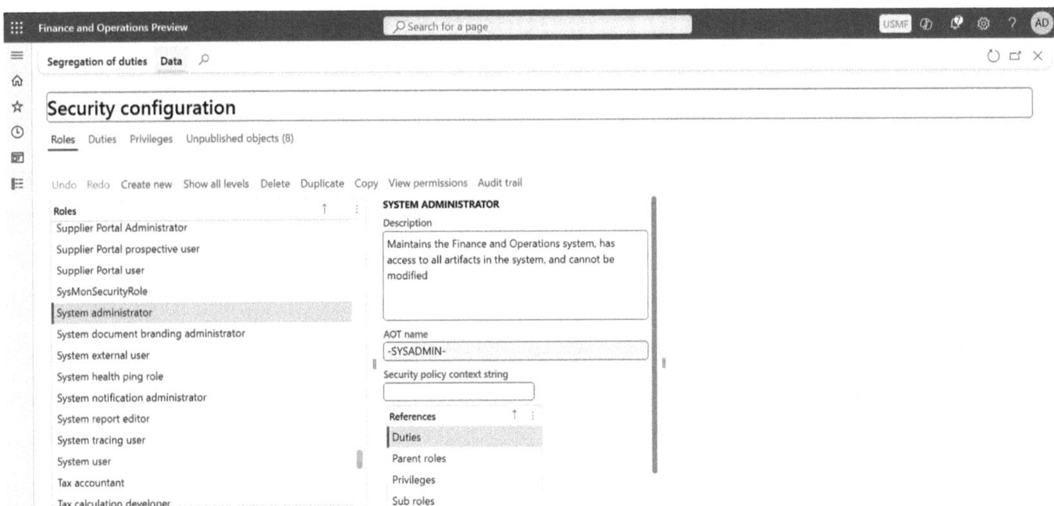

Figure 4-9. *System administrator role and duties*

Each role *bundles specific duties and privileges* relevant to that job. For example, the Manager role likely includes duties for approving employee leave and viewing team data, but not the duty to edit organization-wide HR parameters. The HR Manager role includes duties like maintaining worker records, managing positions and jobs, processing compensation, etc. Meanwhile, the Employee role's duties are limited to "maintain own info" and "view own info." By structuring roles this way, D365 HR ensures people only see or do what their role permits – effectively a whitelisting approach where nothing is accessible unless a role explicitly grants it.

Note   In D365 F&O security, it's possible to set up automatic role assignment rules based on data. For instance, you could configure that all workers who are managers (i.e., have reports in the system) get the Manager Self Service role assigned, or all employees get the Employee Self Service role by default. This can reduce admin effort in security maintenance. Consider using this feature so new hires and new managers are automatically given the proper self-service roles as their data is entered, ensuring they have access from day one.

Step 2: Custom Roles and Fine-Tuning Access

While the out-of-the-box roles cover common scenarios, most implementations will require some custom security roles or tweaks. You might create customs for specific positions (e.g. Payroll Specialist, HR Benefits Administrator) or modify existing ones to remove or add privileges. Using the Security configuration interface, you can copy an existing role as a starting point, then add/remove duties or privileges. Always follow the principle of least privilege: give users the minimum access they need to perform their job.

A common customization example is handling sensitive personal data. Fields like employee salary, identification numbers, or performance notes can be restricted. You can create a custom duty that excludes access to, say, the Compensation screens, and assign HR Assistants a role without that duty if you want to "whitelist" salary access only to HR Managers. Conversely, you might have a role that is read-only for audit purposes or a role just for running reports.

Whitelisting in this context means explicitly granting access to data and functions only to certain roles. By default, if a role doesn't include a privilege, the user can't do that action or see that data. For example, only the System Administrator role might have access to system setup areas (through a "Maintain system parameters" privilege). Only HR Managers might have the privilege to edit performance reviews, while HR Assistants have the privilege to read but not change them. Review each role's duties and adjust permissions so that compliance requirements are met – especially regarding who can view personally identifiable information (PII) or make critical changes.

Finally, ensure to test the roles thoroughly. Use a test user for each role and verify what that user can see/do in the system. It's important to catch any excessive permissions (if a role can see data, it shouldn't) or missing permissions (preventing the user from completing a process). D365 security diagnostics or a "User role evaluator" tool can help simulate access. Remember that security changes might require users to sign out and back in to take effect.

Data Migration Strategy

Migrating HR data from legacy systems (such as SAP HCM, Oracle PeopleSoft, Workday, Ceridian Dayforce, or even Excel spreadsheets) into D365 Human Resources is a major part of implementation. A structured data migration strategy will ensure a smooth transition with minimal disruption. D365 HR shares its data management framework with Finance & Operations apps, meaning we can leverage standard Data Entities and import tools to load data in bulk.

Step 1: Planning the Scope

Start by defining which data will be migrated from the old system. Not all historical data may need to come over; focus on what's required for day-one operations and compliance. Key data categories typically include:

- Core employee records: Personal information (name, contact info, birth date), employment start dates, identities (employee ID, etc.).

- Organizational data: Jobs, positions, department structures, business units, and legal entities that employees belong to.

- Compensation and benefits: Current salary or wage, pay grade, benefit enrollments or eligibility.

- Leave and absence balances: Remaining vacation days, sick leave balances, any carry-over from previous periods.

- Performance and talent records: Performance reviews, goals, certificates or training records (if available and needed).

- Historical payroll info: You might optionally import some payroll-related info such as last pay date, year-to-date totals, or bank account details if integrating with payroll. However, detailed payroll history is often kept in the old system, or a data warehouse rather than fully migrated.

Be clear on time scope as well: will you bring in just active employees and the last year of data? Five years of history? Often, core HR data (like employment history) is kept, but payroll transaction history might be left out to simplify the project. Work with HR and compliance officers to identify any data retention requirements.

Importantly, determine if the new D365 HR environment will share data with an existing D365 Finance & Operations environment or if it's stand-alone. If your company already uses D365 Finance (F&O) for ERP, you may have an existing set of global data: for example, your legal entities, financial dimensions, and even some worker records might already exist in F&O and will carry into HR. In such cases, the HR implementation can leverage that data (no need to recreate legal entities or duplicate employee records – in fact, the system will unify them). If the HR implementation is completely new (no prior D365 F&O), then you'll need to load all foundational data from scratch.

Step 2: Using Data Entities and the Data Management Framework

Dynamics 365 provides a Data Management Framework (DMF) which uses Data Entities as the means to import and export data. Each data entity represents a logical set of data (usually corresponding to a major HR concept). Examples of relevant entities in D365 HR include:

- HcmWorkerEntity – The main employee (worker) record, including personal details

- HcmEmploymentEntity – Employment details for the worker (position assignment, employment dates, employment type)

- HcmJobEntity – Job definitions (title, descriptions, compensation level, etc.)

- HcmPositionEntity – Position instances (a specific role in a department, linked to a Job and a department/legal entity)

- HcmPositionHierarchyEntity – Organizational hierarchy relationships if maintaining org chart

- HcmCompFixedPlanEntity – Fixed compensation plans or salary records

- HcmBenefitEnrollmentEntity – Benefit enrollment records (if applicable)

- HcmLeaveRequestEntity – Leave and absence transactions or balances

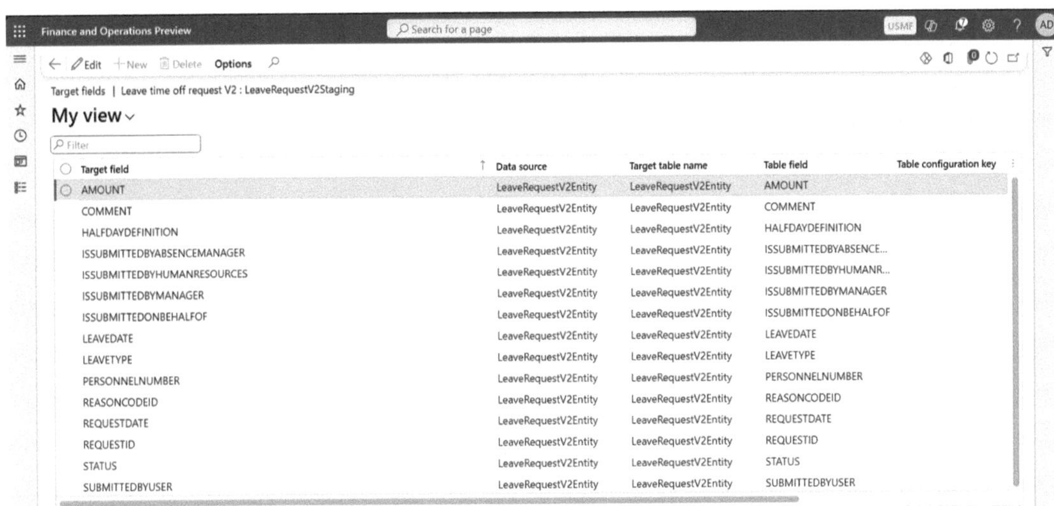

Figure 4-10. *Leave request entity target fields*

Microsoft provides many of these entities out-of-the-box, and they can be accessed in the HR Data management workspace. Whenever possible, use the standard entities rather than custom builds, as they already encapsulate the required validations and table mappings. You can export templates for these entities (Excel or CSV format) to fill with data or connect through integration tools.

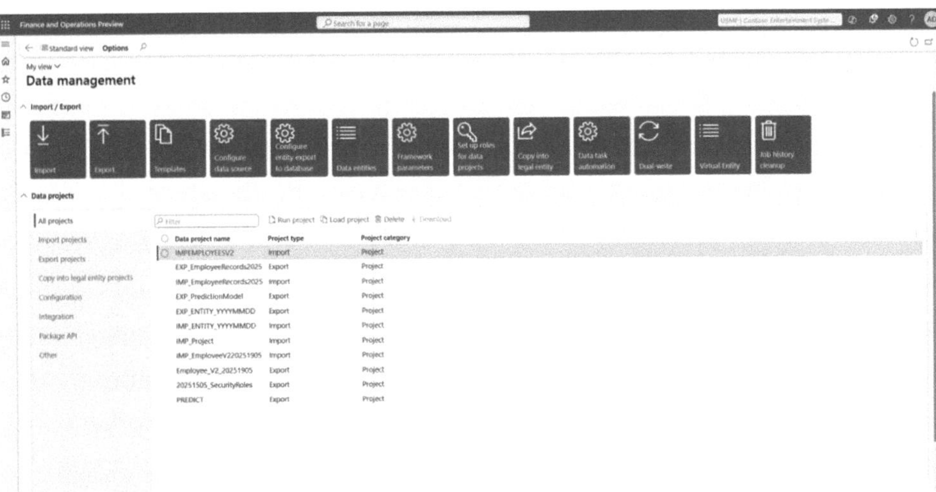

Figure 4-11. *Data Management workspace showing various import and export data projects in Dynamics 365 Human Resources. This is where admins organize and manage data migration efforts by HR entity type*

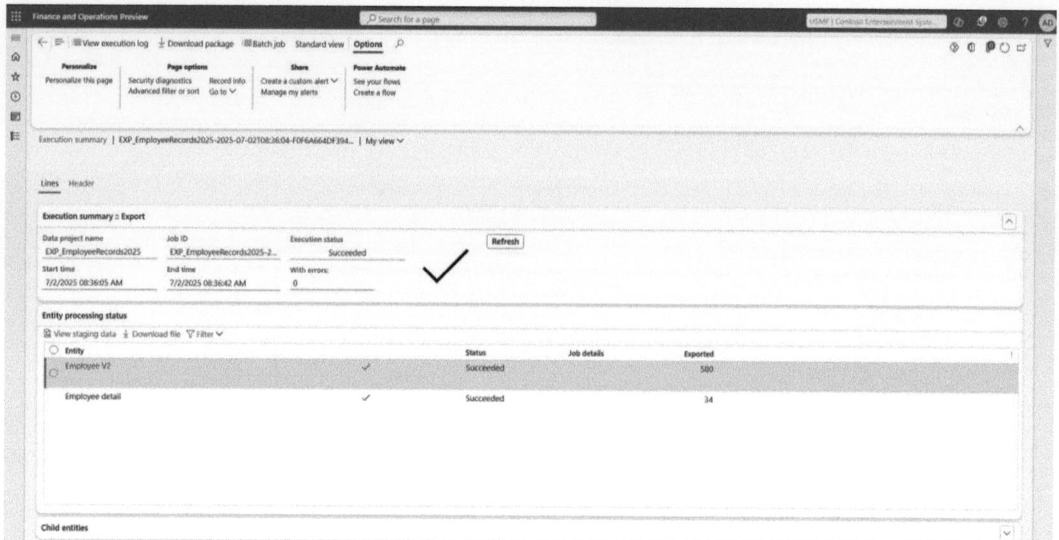

Figure 4-12. *Detail view of a data export project configured for employee records. Selected entities like "Employee V2" and "Employee Detail" are exported in Excel format for data transformation or archival*

Data Entities handle a lot of complexity, but you must still be mindful of data dependencies when planning the import sequence. For example:

- Legal entities (the company/organization units) should be created before importing employees, because each worker is attached to a legal entity.

- Departments and jobs should be loaded before positions, and positions before worker assignments, because a Position record references a job and department, and a Worker's employment references a position.

- Workers (basic person records) can be created before their detailed employment assignments, or together in one package if the entity supports it. Often, it's easier to import the person first (HcmWorker), then employment (which links person to position).

- Compensation plans and benefits setup should exist before you load current compensation or benefit enrolments for workers.

- Leave and absence plans should be configured before loading leave balances.

Respecting these dependencies is crucial – if you attempt to import data out of order, you'll encounter errors (for instance, importing a worker with a position that doesn't exist yet will fail). The Data Management Framework allows grouping entities in a data project and even sequencing them. It's wise to break the migration into logical waves (e.g., Foundation data, then Employee core data, then related transactional data).

Also note, if your D365 HR environment is merged with an existing F&O environment, some data may already be present. For example, if Finance was using the HR module in the past, you might find that some workers or global address book records exist. In that case, migration might involve mapping or cleansing that existing data rather than importing afresh. Always do an analysis of the current state of the environment.

Step 3: Preparing and Validating the Data

Data preparation often happens outside the system, using tools like Excel, Power Query, or scripting to extract from the legacy system and transform to the D365 format. Key preparation steps include:

- Data cleansing: Fix obvious errors or inconsistencies in legacy data. Ensure names, dates, and key fields are correct and not missing. Remove duplicate records (for example, make sure you don't have the same employee twice).

Field	Raw/Legacy Data Example	Cleansed/System-Ready Example	Notes
First Name	jon	Jon	Capitalization corrected
Hire Date	31/02/2020	**Removed/flagged for review**	Invalid date corrected or flagged
Employee ID	12345, 12345	12345	Duplicate removed
Email Address	maria@@company..com	maria@company.com	Obvious formatting error fixed

Figure 4-13. *Data cleansing example*

- Mapping values: Align legacy codes to D365 values. For instance, legacy job codes or department IDs might need to be mapped to new ones in D365. If the legacy system had country codes that differ from ISO codes used in D365, translate them. Common mappings involve things like gender codes, marital status, leave type codes, etc. – these must match the option set values in D365 HR.

Field	Legacy Value	Mapped D365 Value	Notes
Gender Code	M	Male	Mapped to option set values in D365
Department ID	DEPT001	HR-01	Aligned to D365 department structure
Marital Status	S	Single	'S' translated to readable, standardized value in D365
Leave Type	ANL	Annual Leave	Legacy codes expanded to full values used in D365 HR
Country Code	UK	GB	Mapped to ISO standard used in D365

Figure 4-14. *Mapping values example*

- Lookup references: Verify that all referenced data exists in the target. If an employee's record says their location is "New York Office," make sure "New York Office" exists as a location in D365 or decide how to handle it (maybe as a department or address). Ensure every position's job exists, every worker's position exists, every worker's manager (if specified) is also being loaded.

Entity	Reference Field	Legacy Value	Action or Transformed Value	Notes
Employee	Location	NYC Office	New York HQ	Ensured this location exists or renamed accordingly in D365
Position	Job ID	JB_321	JOB-HR-001	Validated that job exists in D365 before import
Worker	Manager ID	000999 (non-existent)	**Flagged for remediation**	Manager must also exist as an employee in the data set
Worker	Position ID	POS_XYZ (missing)	**Flagged or added**	Referential integrity must be maintained

Figure 4-15. *Lookup references example*

- Field lengths and formats: D365 fields have specific length and format requirements. For example, worker ID might be 15 characters max; phone numbers might need country codes separated, etc. Adjust your data to meet these requirements to avoid import truncation or errors.

Field	Legacy Format	D365-Compliant Format	Notes
Worker ID	00000012345678901	000000123456789	Truncated to 15-character limit
Phone Number	(123)456-7890	+1 123 456 7890	Reformatted with country code and spacing
Zip Code	123	00123	Padded to meet 5-digit requirement
Date	12.31.2021	2021-12-31	Converted to ISO standard (yyyy-mm-dd)

Figure 4-16. *Field lengths and formats example*

- Test small samples: Before importing thousands of records, do a trial run with a handful of representative records for each entity. This will flush out issue with mapping and format in a manageable way. Use the Data ManageMent workspace to import these and check for errors in the Execution log. After each import, validate the data in the application. Run queries or open forms in D365 HR to ensure records look correct. For example, after importing employees and their positions, go to an employee's record and confirm their job title and department shows up properly via the position assignment. Check that leave balances match what was in the old system. If possible, have the HR users do a spot-check or even a full UAT (User Acceptance Testing) on migrated data – this helps catch anything that looks off early.

Step 4: Execution Sequence and Golden Environment

When it's time to perform the full migration, plan a logical sequence of data loads respecting dependencies. One common approach is

1. Foundation data first: legal entities, business units, departments, jobs, compensation plans, leave plans – the static setup info.

2. Positions and org hierarchy: load positions after jobs/ departments, then if needed, the position hierarchy (so managers are assigned).

3. Workers and employment: import core worker personal data, then their employment details (which attach them to positions, companies, etc.). This might include hiring date, employment type, and manager's link.

4. Compensation and benefits: once workers exist, load their current fixed compensation (salary or hourly rate records), and any benefit enrolments or pension details.

5. Leave balances and performance records: load any time-off balance for each worker and import performance goals or reviews if those are being brought over.

6. Additional records: such as skills, certificates, attachments, etc., as needed.

Phase	Data Type	Examples	Dependencies / Notes
Foundation	Legal Entities	Company A, Subsidiary B	Must be loaded first
Foundation	Business Units	Sales Division, Support Services	Foundation for departments
Foundation	Departments	Finance, IT, HR	Required for position links
Foundation	Jobs	HR Specialist, IT Manager	Used by positions and employment
Foundation	Compensation Plans	Hourly Rate Plan, Annual Salary Plan	Required before compensation records
Foundation	Leave Plans	Annual Leave 25 Days, Sick Leave Unlimited	Required before leave balances
Org Hierarchy	Positions	POS001: HR Specialist in HR Dept	Requires jobs/departments to exist
Org Hierarchy	Position Hierarchy	POS001 reports to POS000	Enables manager assignment
Worker & Employment	Personal Info	Name, DOB, National ID, Email	Workers must exist for other links
Worker & Employment	Employment	Hire Date, Full-time/Part-time, Entity	Linked to legal entity, job, position
Worker & Employment	Position Assignment	Worker John Doe → POS001	Depends on positions being loaded
Worker & Employment	Manager Assignment	John Doe's Manager: Jane Smith → POS000	Relies on valid position hierarchy
Comp & Benefits	Compensation	70,000 EUR/year, Monthly	Workers must be in system
Comp & Benefits	Benefits Enrollment	Gold Medical, Standard Pension	Workers and benefit plans must exist
Leave & Performance	Leave Balances	10.5 days remaining	Leave plans and workers must be loaded
Leave & Performance	Performance Reviews	2023: Exceeds Expectations	Optional, based on system use
Leave & Performance	Goals	Leadership training by Q4	Optional, links to worker goals
Enrichments (Optional)	Skills	Project Management, B2 German	Enhances worker profiles
Enrichments (Optional)	Certificates	PMP, SAP Training	Optional metadata for skills tracking
Enrichments (Optional)	Attachments	Resume PDF, Contract, Work Permit	Linked to worker record

Figure 4-17. *Execution Sequence example*

It's generally recommended to migrate module by module or entity group by group, validating each set, rather than a "big bang" where everything is imported in one go. This way, you can catch errors in one area (e.g., position load fails) and fix it before it cascades to dependent data (like worker import).

Many projects designate a "Golden Environment" for migration and configuration. This is a dedicated environment (often a UAT or Sandbox) where all data loads and configurations are done first to reach a perfect, validated state. The golden environment serves as the master copy of the system setup. You can perform multiple trial migrations here until data is clean and complete. At go-live, you then replicate the golden environment data into Production (either by fresh import or by a database copy, if allowed). This approach ensures that by the time you load Production, you have already ironed out issues. Microsoft recommends doing a mock cutover in a sandbox environment using the final migration packages. This practice helps you refine the steps and document a detailed cutover checklist of all data packages to import and in what order. Having a checklist is especially important if you don't have a separate gold environment to freeze configurations – it acts as your guide during the real cutover.

Also, remember that data ownership lies with the client's team. HR data is sensitive and should be handled securely. Typically, the client's HR or IT data owners should be responsible for extracting and validating the data. Consultants can assist with mapping and importing, but it's best practice (and often a compliance requirement) that the client reviews and signs off the final data. Consultants should not arbitrarily change or "clean" data without client approval – any anomalies should be flagged for the client to decide how to address. This ensures accountability and accuracy of HR records.

Entity Load Sequence for Initial Implementation

This section outlines the required entity load sequence for an initial implementation of Dynamics 365 Human Resources. The structure presented follows a wave-based approach, grouping entities by dependencies and functional area. Master data is the primary focus, as it provides the foundational elements necessary for HR operations. Transactional data should only be included if the data is recent – preferably no older than two years – to avoid overloading the system with historical information that is unlikely to provide value in daily operations. Use the information below as a reference; some entities may apply for your scenario, and others might be missing. Use the Data entities section within Data Management to search for additional items.

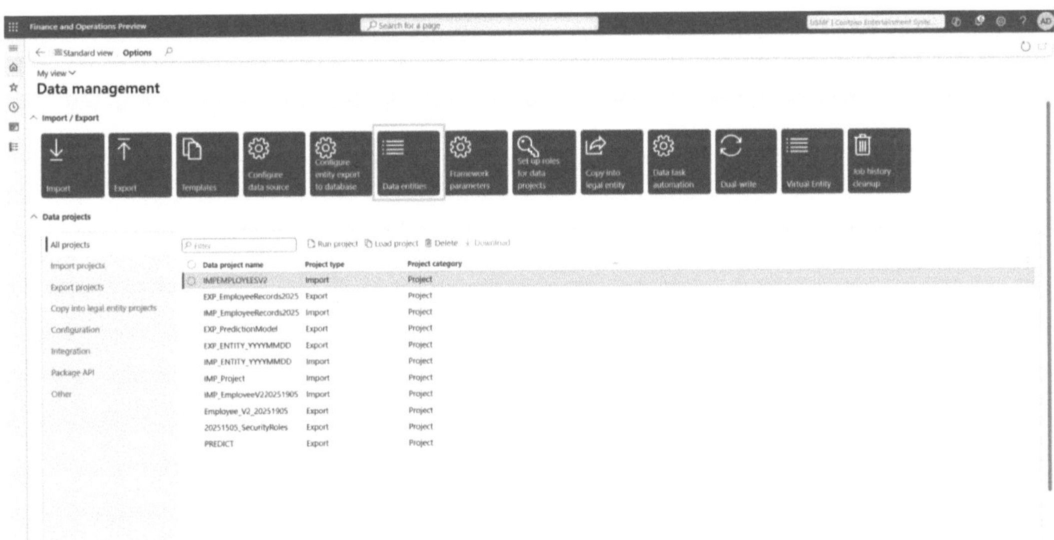

Figure 4-18. *Data entities section within Data Management*

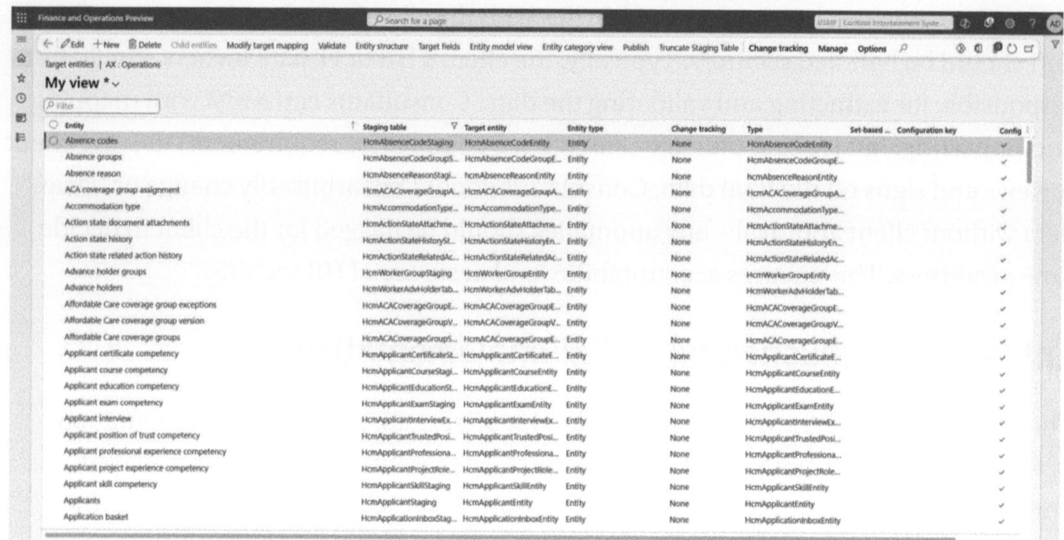

Figure 4-19. *Data entities details within Data Management*

Wave 0 – System Switches and Parameters

- HcmSharedParametersStaging – Cross-company HR settings

- HcmParametersStaging – Legal-entity-specific configuration

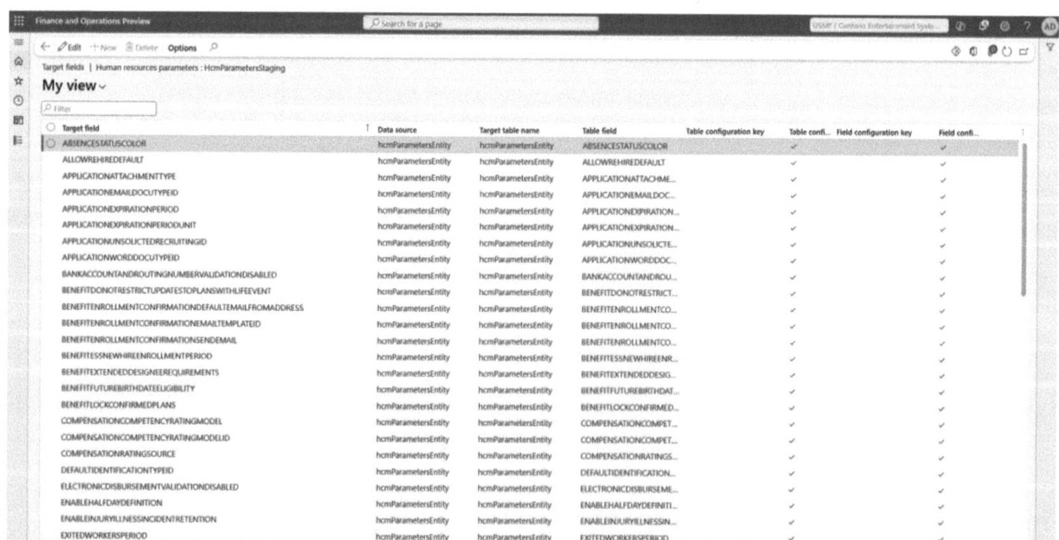

Figure 4-20. *Human Resources Parameters entity target fields*

Wave 1 – Foundational Lookups (No Foreign Keys)

- HcmLanguageCodeStaging
- HcmAccommodationTypeStaging
- HcmIdentificationTypeStaging
- HcmReasonCodeStaging
- HcmEthnicOriginStaging
- HcmVeteranStatusStaging
- HcmMediaTypeStaging
- HcmSkillTypeStaging ➤ HcmSkillStaging/HcmSkillDualWriteStaging
- HcmCertificateTypeStaging (+ Attachments)
- HcmEducationDegreeStaging
- HcmEducationDisciplineCategoryStaging
- HcmEducationDisciplineStaging
- HcmMeasurementStaging
- HcmRatingModelStaging
- HcmRatingLevelStaging

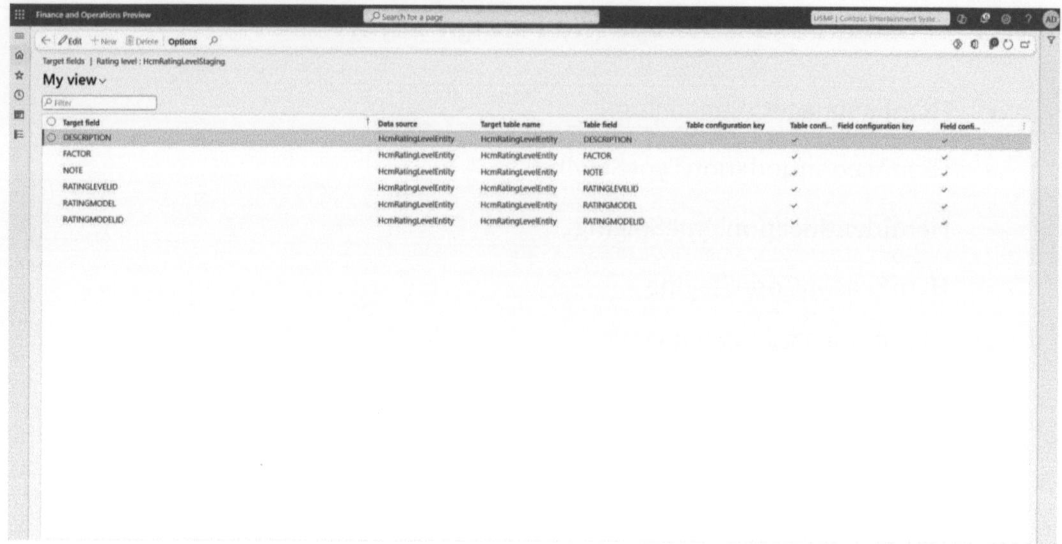

Figure 4-21. *Rating level entity target fields*

Wave 2 – Regulatory and Organizational Structure

- HcmRegulatoryEstablishmentStaging

- HcmRegulatoryEstablishmentDetailStaging

- HcmLaborUnionStaging

- HcmLaborUnionAgreementStaging

- HcmUnionAgreementDurationStaging

- HcmWorkCalendarHolidayStaging ➤
  HcmWorkCalendarHolidayLineStaging

- HcmOnboardingLibraryTaskGroupStaging ➤
  HcmOnboardingLibraryTaskStaging

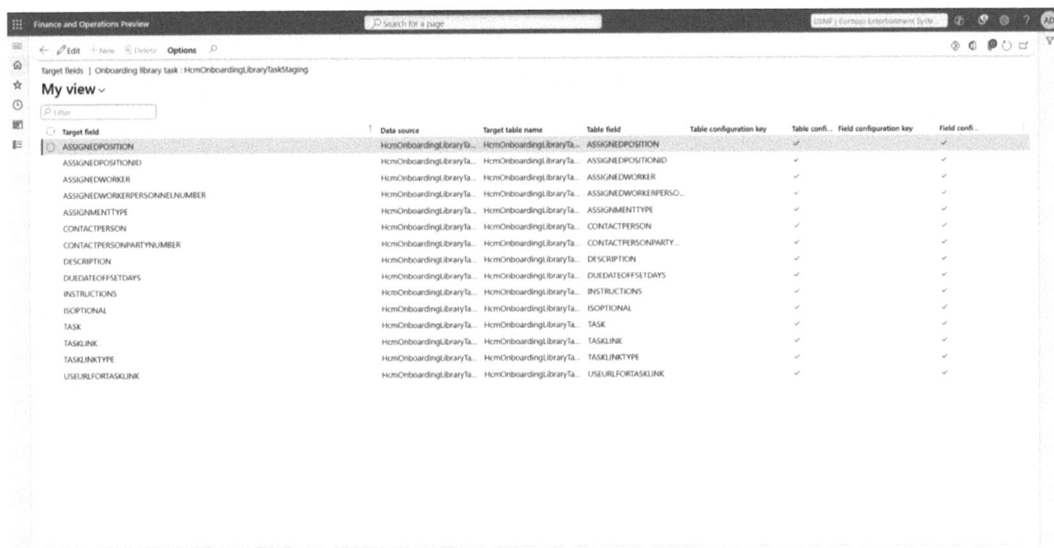

Figure 4-22. *Onboarding library task entity target fields*

Wave 3 – Jobs, Job Templates and Responsibilities

- HcmJobFamilyStaging

- HcmJobTypeStaging

- HcmJobBaseStaging ➤ HcmJobStaging/HcmJobDualWriteStaging

- HcmJobPreferredSkillStaging

- HcmJobPreferredCertificateStaging

- HcmJobPreferredEducationDisciplineStaging

- HcmJobPreferredExamStaging

- HcmJobPreferredScreeningStaging

- HcmJobResponsibilityStaging

- HcmJobTaskAssignmentStaging

- HcmJobTaskStaging

- HcmJobTemplateStaging and related templates

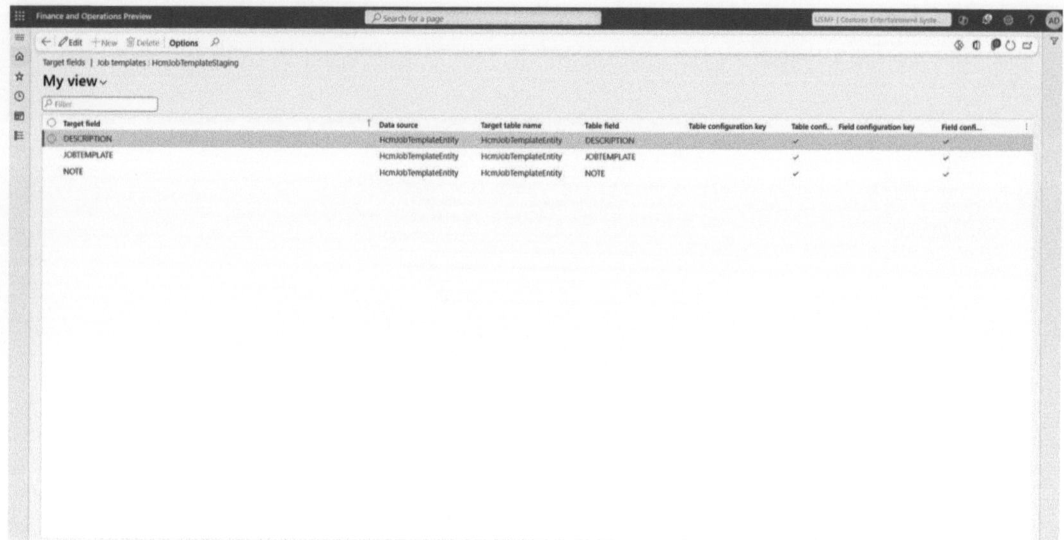

Figure 4-23. *Job templates entity target fields*

Wave 4 – Positions and Hierarchies

- HcmPositionTypeStaging

- HcmPositionBaseStaging ➤ HcmPositionStaging/ HcmPositionV2Staging

- HcmPositionDefaultDimensionStaging/DualWrite/ CrossCompanyExport

- HcmPositionDurationStaging

- HcmPositionForecastStaging / V2

- HcmPositionUnionAgreementStaging

- HcmPositionHierarchyTypeStaging ➤ HcmPositionHierarchyStaging

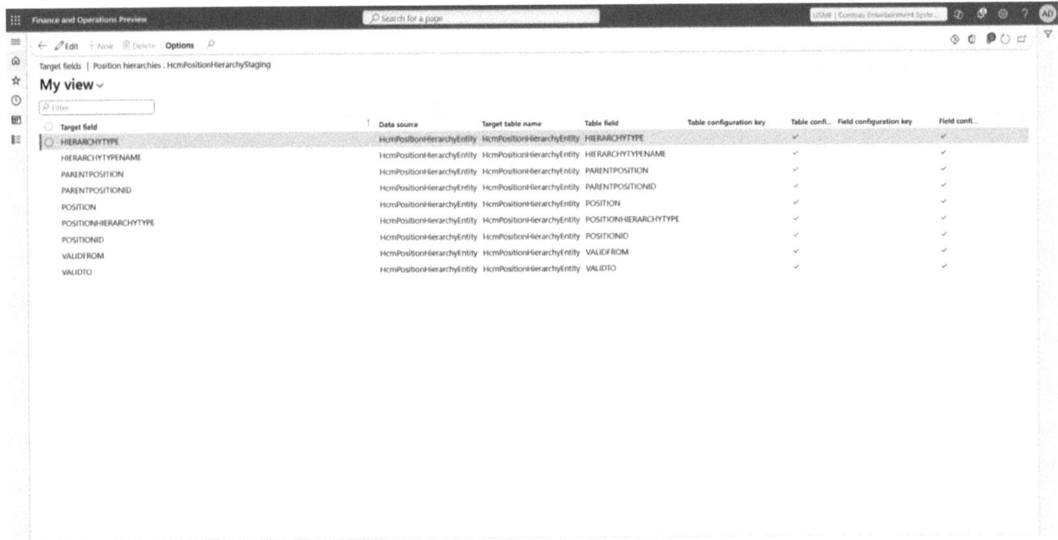

Figure 4-24. *Position hierarchy entity target fields*

Wave 5 – Compensation Framework

- HcmPayRateConversionStaging

- HcmCompensationRegionStaging

- HcmCompensationLevelStaging

- HcmCompensationReferencePointStaging ➤
  HcmCompensationReferencePointSetupLineStaging

- HcmCompensationGridStaging

- HcmCompensationStructureStaging/DualWrite variants

- HcmCompensationEligibilityLevelStaging

- HcmCompensationEligibilityRuleStaging

- HcmCompVarPlanTableStaging/V2

- HcmCompensationMeritIncreaseTargetStaging

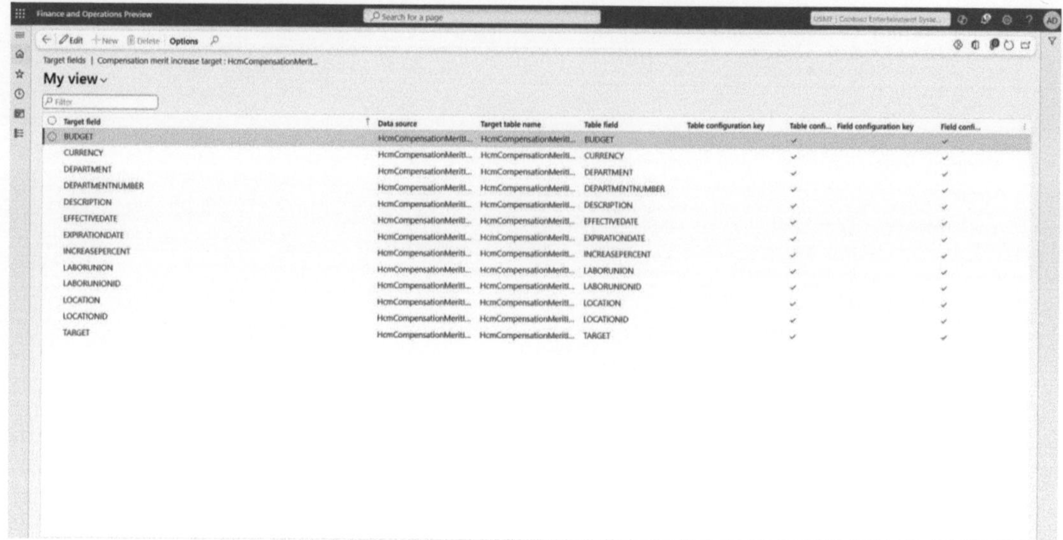

Figure 4-25. *Compensation merit increase target entity target fields*

Wave 6 – Benefit Framework

- HcmBenefitTypeStaging ➤ HcmBenefitOptionStaging

- HcmBenefitPlanStaging ➤ HcmBenefitStaging

- HcmBenefitEligibilityPolicyStaging ➤ Rule Types ➤ Rules ➤ Benefits ➤ Workers

- HcmBenefitExpirationGroupStaging

- HcmBenefitExpirationStatusStaging

- HcmACACoverageGroupStaging and related ACA entities

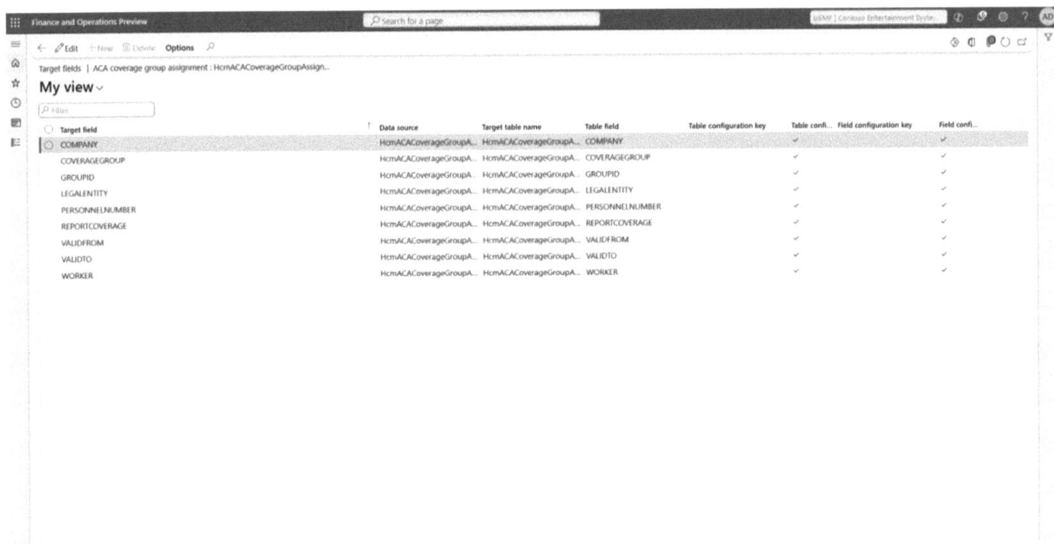

Figure 4-26. *ACA coverage group assignment entity target fields*

Wave 7 – Learning, Performance, and Recruiting Scaffolding

- HcmCourseTypeStaging and related certificate, skill, education profiles

- HcmCourseGroupStaging, HcmCourseHotelStaging, HcmCourseRoomStaging

- HcmCourseTableStaging, HcmCourseV2Staging

- HcmGoalHeadingStaging ➤ HcmGoalTemplateStaging ➤ HcmGoalSettingsGoalsEntityStaging

- HcmDiscussionTemplateStaging ➤ HcmDiscussionSettingsDiscussionTemplatesStaging

- HcmRecruitingMediaStaging ➤ HcmRecruitingProjectStaging ➤ HcmRecruitingRequestStaging

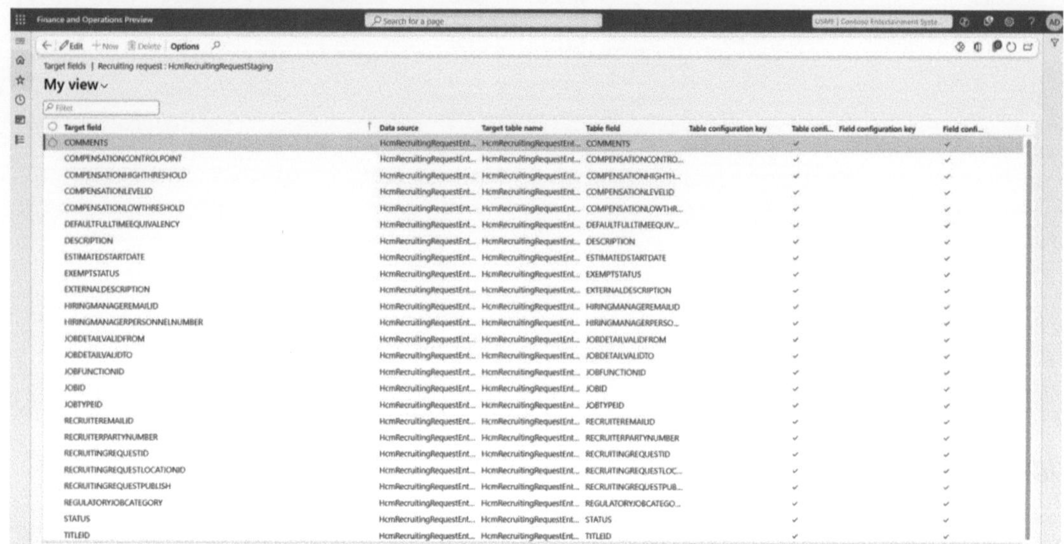

Figure 4-27. *Recruiting request entity target fields*

Wave 8 – People: Persons, Workers, and Employments

- HcmPersonDetailsStaging

- HcmPersonAddressStaging

- HcmPersonIdentificationNumberStaging

- HcmWorkerStaging/HcmWorkerBaseStaging

- HcmEmploymentStaging/HcmEmploymentV2Staging

- HcmPersonEducationStaging,

- HcmPersonSkillStaging, HcmWorkerCourseStaging, etc.

- HcmWorkerPrimaryPositionStaging

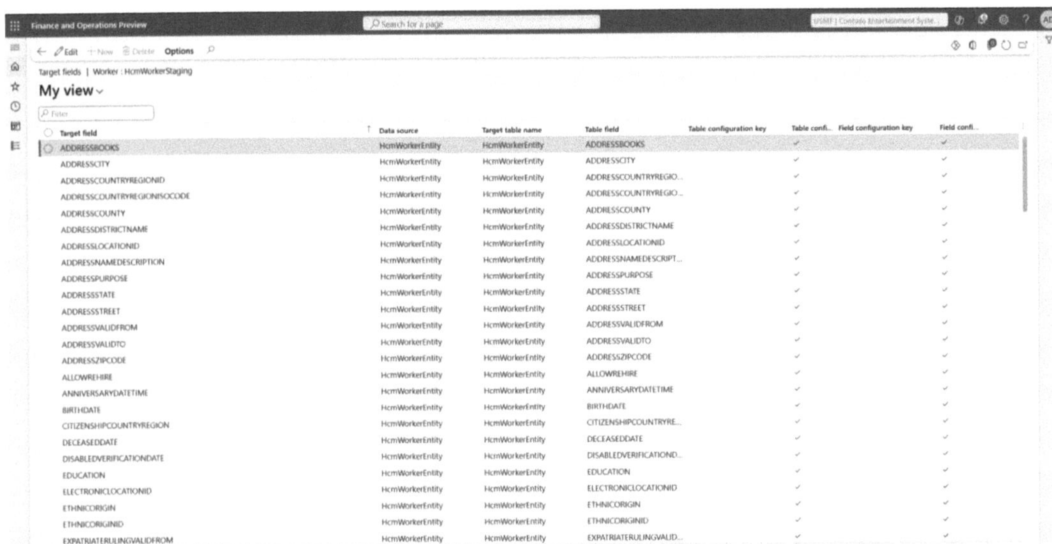

Figure 4-28. *Worker entity target fields*

Wave 9 – Individual Compensation and Benefits

- HcmCompFixedEmplStaging/
  HcmWorkerActionCompEmplHistoryStaging

- HcmVariableCompensationEnrollmentStaging and overrides

- HcmWorkerEnrolledBenefitStaging

- HcmCoveredDependentRelationshipStaging

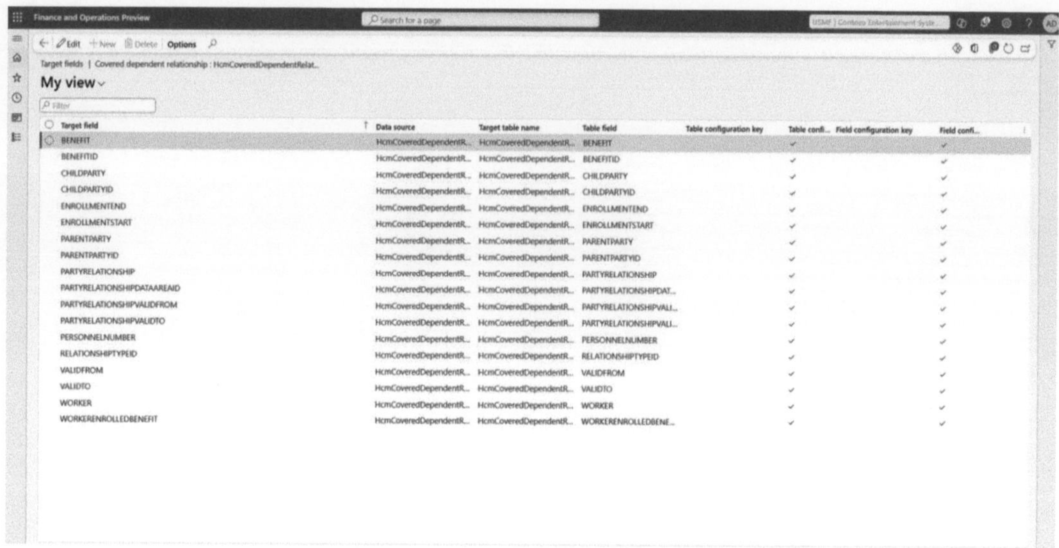

Figure 4-29. *Covered dependent relationship entity target fields*

Wave 10 – Talent, Learning, and Performance Transactions

- HcmDiscussionStaging,

- HcmDiscussionGoalStaging

- HcmDiscussionPerfJournalEntryStaging

- HCMCourseParticipantStaging

- HcmWorkerTaskAssignmentStaging, HcmWorkerTaskStaging

- HcmWorkerActionHistoryStaging,
  HcmOnboardingWorkerChecklistHeaderStaging, etc.

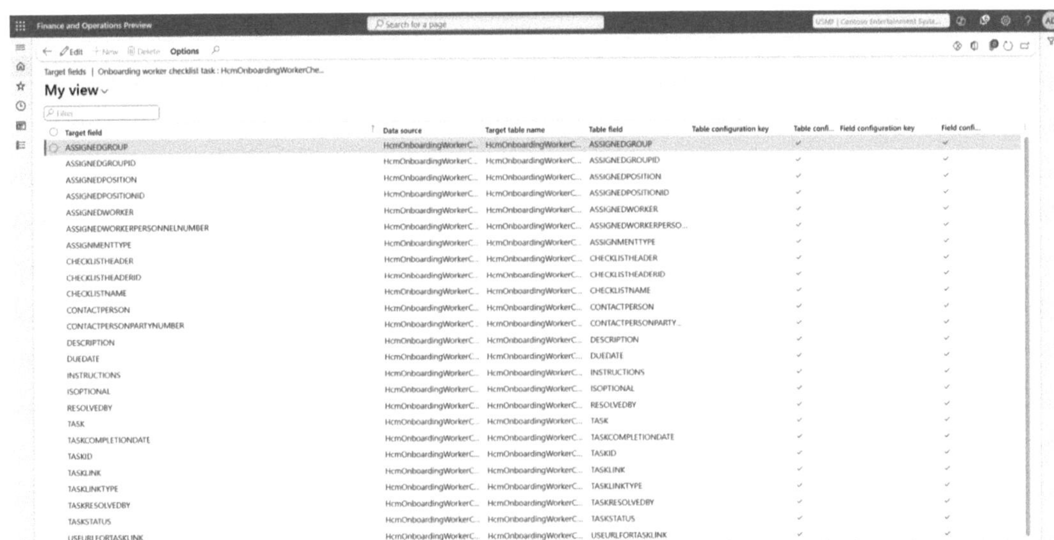

Figure 4-30. *Onboarding worker checklist task entity target fields*

Integration with Payroll Systems

Most organizations implementing D365 Human Resources will need to integrate it with an external payroll system (or multiple, if operating in different countries). D365 HR does not process pay slips or taxes itself (unless you also use D365 Finance payroll for certain regions), so a seamless flow of data to the payroll provider is crucial. The integration strategy can vary from simple file exports to API-based, near-real-time sync. Microsoft provides a Payroll Integration API in D365 HR to facilitate common scenarios.

Step 1: Define Payroll Data Requirements and Cut-Off

Begin by identifying what data needs to flow to payroll and when. Typical data that the payroll system requires from HR includes:

- Employee master data: Personal details (name, address, SSN or Tax ID) and employment info (hire date, employment type, department, etc.) for new hires or changes.

- Salary and pay rate: The base pay rate (annual salary or hourly wage), and any changes to it, since payroll will calculate earnings from this.

- Variable pay and allowances: Bonuses, commissions, overtime hours, or any recurring allowances/deductions (like a car allowance or union dues) that need to be passed for that pay period.

- Time/leave data: If the HR system tracks hours worked or approved overtime, this may need to go to payroll (unless a separate Time & Attendance system handles it). Similarly, if an employee took unpaid leave or used certain leave that affects pay, payroll should know the balances or the hours to deduct.

- Benefits and deductions: Employee benefit selections that have payroll contributions (e.g., health insurance premium, retirement contributions) and any changes in those deductions.

- Banking and pay method: The employee's bank account details or payment method (for direct deposit) – these might be maintained in HR or directly in payroll, depending on processes.

Decide on the cut-off dates and frequency of integration. For example, if payroll runs on the 25th of each month, you might set a cut-off that any changes after the 20th go into next month's cycle. Clarify with the payroll team: when is the latest HR can send data for the current payroll? This will drive your integration schedule (e.g., daily sync, or a batch file after each pay period end). It's often wise to run parallel payroll cycles during the first month of go-live: continue running the old system or a shadow calculation in parallel to the new one to verify there are no discrepancies.

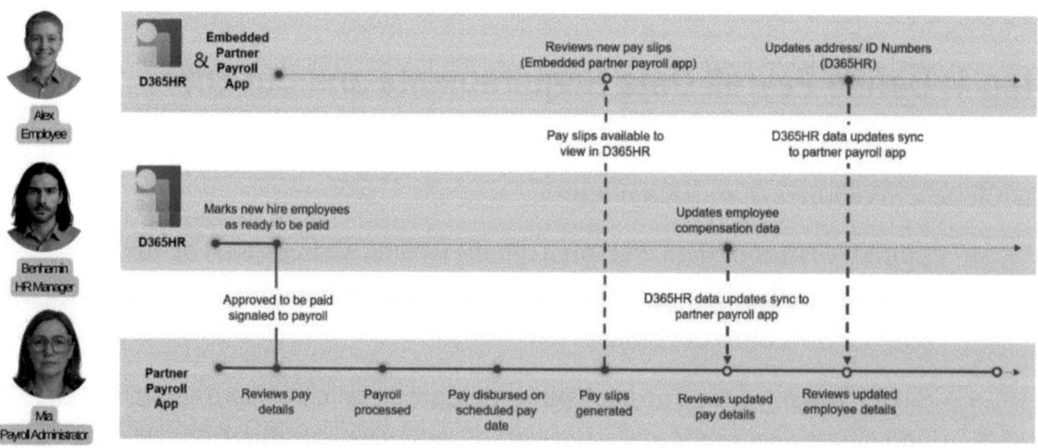

Figure 4-31. *Payroll integration API*

Step 2: Utilizing the Payroll Integration API

Dynamics 365 HR includes a simplified Payroll integration capability introduced in recent releases. Essentially, the HR system can mark an employee record as "ready for payroll" and expose all relevant data via dedicated Dataverse entities or OData feeds to be pulled by the payroll system. When you hire or update an employee in D365 HR (profile, salary, deductions, etc.), the integrated payroll system can pull this information through the API for processing payroll. The integration covers updates too – any changes in HR (like a salary increase or address change) will be available for the payroll system to fetch before the next run.

To enable this, D365 HR provides:

- A feature to mark an employee as "Ready to pay." This is usually a checkbox or status on the employee record. Only employees marked ready will be picked up by the integration, allowing HR to control when a new hire should start being paid.

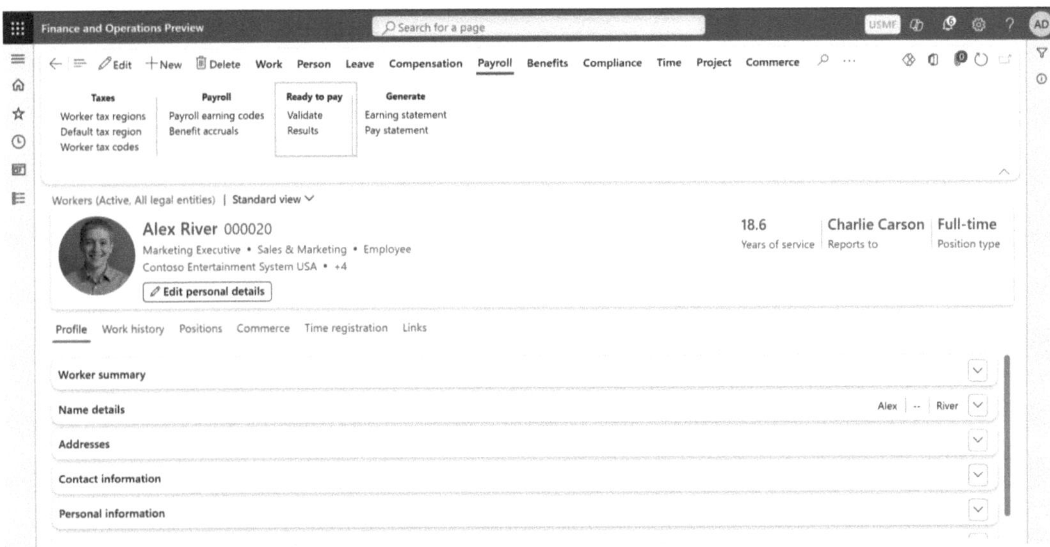

Figure 4-32. *Ready to pay features within worker record*

- A set of payroll integration data entities (often prefixed with Payroll or under the mshr_ virtual tables) that expose necessary data. These include things like Payroll Employee Entity (personal and job info), Payroll Position, Payroll Job, Payroll Fixed Compensation, etc. Essentially, these are views of HR data tailored for payroll consumption.

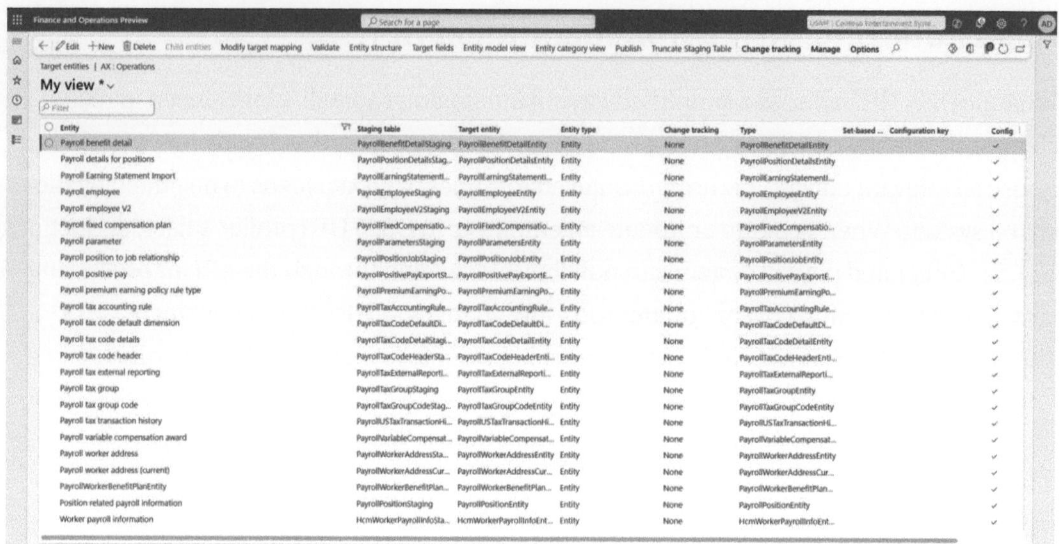

Figure 4-33. *Payroll entities*

- OData APIs to query and retrieve these entities. The payroll system (or integration middleware) can use the Dataverse Web API to query employees marked ready to pay and get their info in JSON or XML format. The API respects changes: for example, using change tracking or filtering by last modified date to only pull incremental changes.

In practice, you might configure a Power Automate flow to run on a schedule (e.g., nightly) that calls the D365 HR payroll OData endpoint, retrieves all new/changed records, and then passes them to the payroll system's input. The integration can be one-way (HR -> payroll) for things like employee data and deductions. In some cases, there is also a return integration (payroll -> HR) for posting results such as pay slip info or year-to-date balances, but that's optional and often not implemented initially.

Be sure to also set up the Payroll integration parameters in D365 HR. Under HR > Setup > Human Resources Parameters > Payroll integration, configure things like the identification type to use (e.g., whether to use the employee's personnel number or another ID as the key for payroll), and enable the use of a special payroll address if needed. These parameters ensure the data flows with the correct identifiers and addresses expected by payroll.

Step 3: Testing and Local Compliance

Payroll integrations must be tested thoroughly with realistic data. Perform end-to-end tests for a sample set of employees:

- New Hire flow: Create a new employee in D365 HR, mark as ready for pay, and verify that the payroll system received all necessary info to set up that employee.

- Pay Change: Modify a salary in HR, and confirm the change is reflected for that employee in the payroll input.

- Termination: If an employee is terminated in HR, ensure the payroll system knows to stop paying after the termination date (this might be part of the data feed or a separate flag).

- Leave Without Pay or absences: If an employee took unpaid leave and you track that in HR, ensure that either the hours or a flag is communicated to payroll so that salary can be prorated accordingly.

- Deductions and benefits: If HR manages benefits, test that an update in HR (e.g., employees increase their pension contribution) flows to payroll for the next pay cycle.

Pay special attention to local compliance requirements in each country's payroll. For instance, in Switzerland, you might need to send specific codes for different allowance types or ensure the data matches Swiss decimal format and pension scheme IDs. In Germany, tax class and social insurance numbers must be accurately transferred. The payroll provider often has a defined template or API schema for input – align the D365 HR integration to that. You may need to do some data transformation (for example, converting D365's country/region codes to the payroll's expected country codes, or combining certain fields to match a legacy format).

Also clarify the format of data exchange. If not using the API, will you generate a CSV file or an XML to send to payroll? D365 HR's Data Management can export to Excel or CSV, if needed, on a periodic schedule. Some organizations use an SFTP file drop for payroll data. If using the API approach, ensure the connectivity (perhaps use a Microsoft Entra ID application for authentication to Dataverse API, or the payroll vendor's integration tool supports OAuth to Dataverse).

Finally, establish clear cut-off and reconciliation processes. For example, after you send the data for a pay period, any further HR changes effective in that period should be held off or clearly communicated to payroll. Post-payroll, you might import payroll results back into D365 HR, such as actual paid amounts or tax info, if desired (though not mandatory). At minimum, consider importing final pay slip documents or summaries into D365 HR or an employee portal so that employees and HR can reference pay stubs in the HR system (alternatively, many companies just let the payroll system handle pay slip distribution).

Microsoft's payroll integration API is designed to minimize manual intervention and ensure consistent data between HR and payroll. By using it, one can reduce duplicate data entry and related errors. As with other integrations, monitor it closely during the first few payroll cycles and have a fallback plan (e.g., the ability to manually input something into payroll last-minute if an integration issue arises) to avoid impacting employees' pay.

For more details on the payroll integration API and setup, refer to Microsoft's documentation on the [Payroll integration API introduction].

Integration with Identity and Access Management

Beyond payroll, another critical integration is between D365 Human Resources and your organization's identity and security ecosystem. Since HR is the system of record for employees, there are opportunities to streamline user account provisioning and ensure security policies stay in sync with HR data. Microsoft Entra ID (formerly Microsoft Entra ID) integration features can enable some of this.

Step 1: Synchronize User Accounts from Microsoft Entra ID

Dynamics 365 HR relies on Microsoft Entra ID for user authentication, so there's already a basic integration: any user accessing HR must exist in Microsoft Entra ID and be granted access to the HR environment. However, many organizations want to go further and automate the provisioning of those Microsoft Entra ID user accounts when a new employee is hired (or disable when they leave). Traditionally, admins had to manually create a Microsoft Entra ID account for a new hire or use scripts/imports – which is duplication of effort since the hire's information is entered in D365 HR as well.

New integration capabilities (planned for late 2024/2025) address this by allowing HR-driven identity provisioning. The idea is to enter the employee data once in D365

HR (as part of hiring/onboarding), and the integration will automatically create the corresponding user account in Entra ID (Microsoft Entra ID) with that information. For example, when an HR Manager adds a new hire into D365 HR (with details like name, job title, department, personal email, etc.), the system can trigger the creation of a Microsoft Entra ID account (with username, organizational information, etc.) for that person. Likewise, if the employee's name or title is updated in HR, it could flow to Microsoft Entra ID; and if an employee is terminated in HR, the integration could automatically disable or flag their Microsoft Entra ID account.

This Entra ID integration eliminates the need for separate CSV uploads or custom scripts to sync employee info between HR and IT systems. It reduces administrative overhead and the risk of errors from data retyping. According to Microsoft's release plans, the integration ensures that employee profiles are always up-to-date across HR and Microsoft Entra ID, improving security and consistency. In technical terms, this might be achieved via the Microsoft Entra ID provisioning service using D365 HR as a source, or via Power Automate flows connecting to the HR API and Microsoft Entra ID Graph/API.

Status: As of the 2024 Wave 2 release plan, the Entra ID integration for HR was in preview with general availability expected around April 2025. This means it may require enabling a preview feature or additional configuration. Keep an eye on Microsoft's documentation for the setup steps once it's officially released. Early adopters have noted the benefit of not having to double-enter data, and it's a highly requested feature (no longer maintaining separate spreadsheets to feed IT accounts).

Step 2: Map Roles and HR Data to Security Policies

HR data often contains valuable information about a person's role in the organization – their job title, department, manager, location, etc. Your identity and security systems can leverage this information to enforce policies. For instance:

- Dynamic Groups in Microsoft Entra ID: You can create dynamic group membership rules in Entra ID based on user attributes (which can include department, job title, etc.). If D365 HR is populating those attributes on the Microsoft Entra ID user (either manually or via the new integration), you could have a group for "All Managers" that automatically includes anyone whose job title in Microsoft Entra

ID equals "Manager" or who has direct reports in HR. That group might be used to grant access to a Management SharePoint site or a specific application. Similarly, a dynamic group for each department could drive license assignments or app access specific to that department.

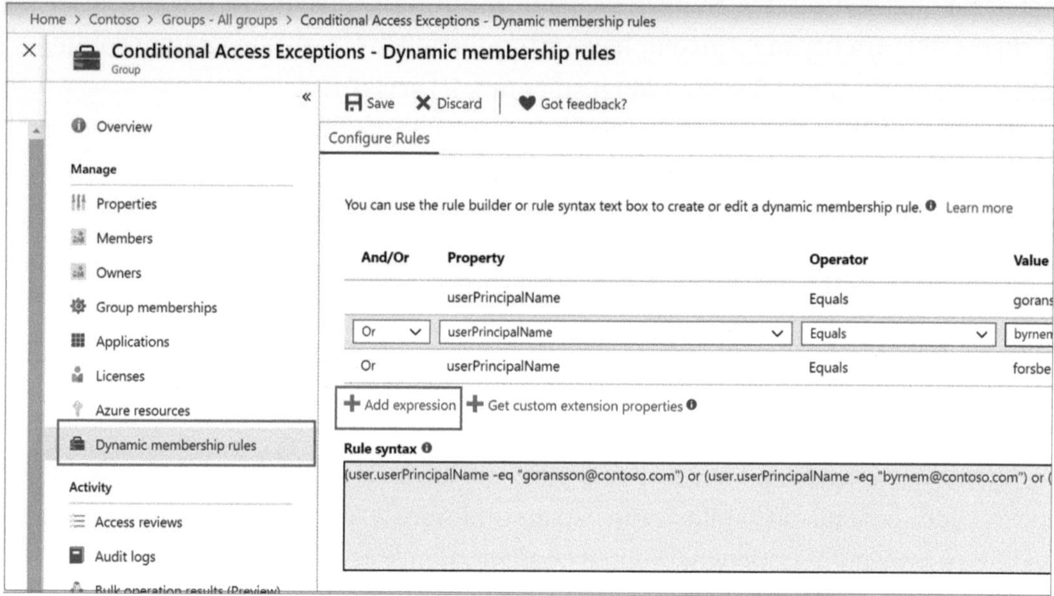

Figure 4-34. *Dynamic membership rules*

- Conditional Access Policies: Microsoft Entra ID Conditional Access can restrict or allow certain resources based on attributes. For example, if HR marks an employee as a contingent or external contractor (perhaps via an "employment type" field), you might map that to a Microsoft Entra ID attribute and enforce that contractors can only access certain apps or must pass extra MFA. Ensuring HR's data flows into Microsoft Entra ID attributes is key for such policies.

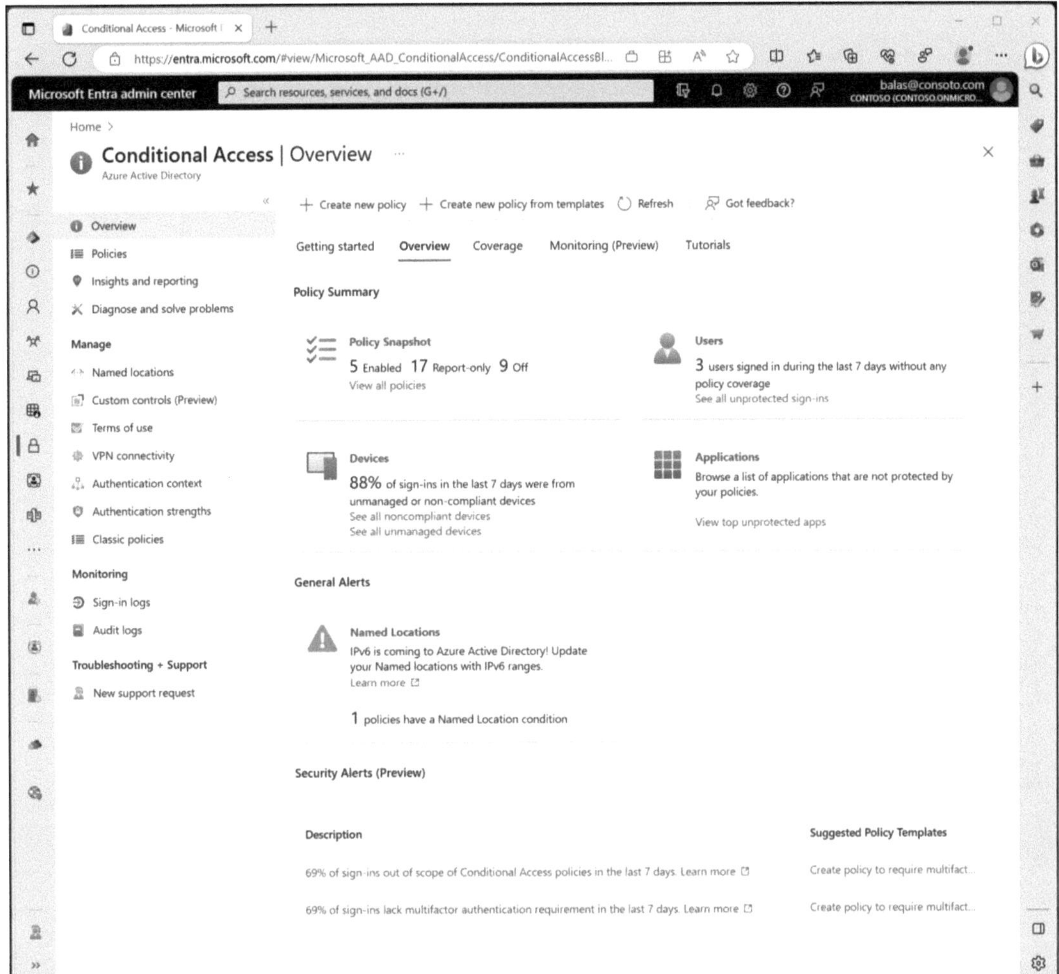

Figure 4-35. *Conditional Access Policies*

- License provisioning: Some organizations also automate license assignments based on roles or department. If HR marks someone as in Sales, an automation could license them for Dynamics 365 Sales or for a particular training portal. Tools like Microsoft Identity Governance (Entitlement Management) can use rules that tie into user properties (sourced from HR) to assign access packages.

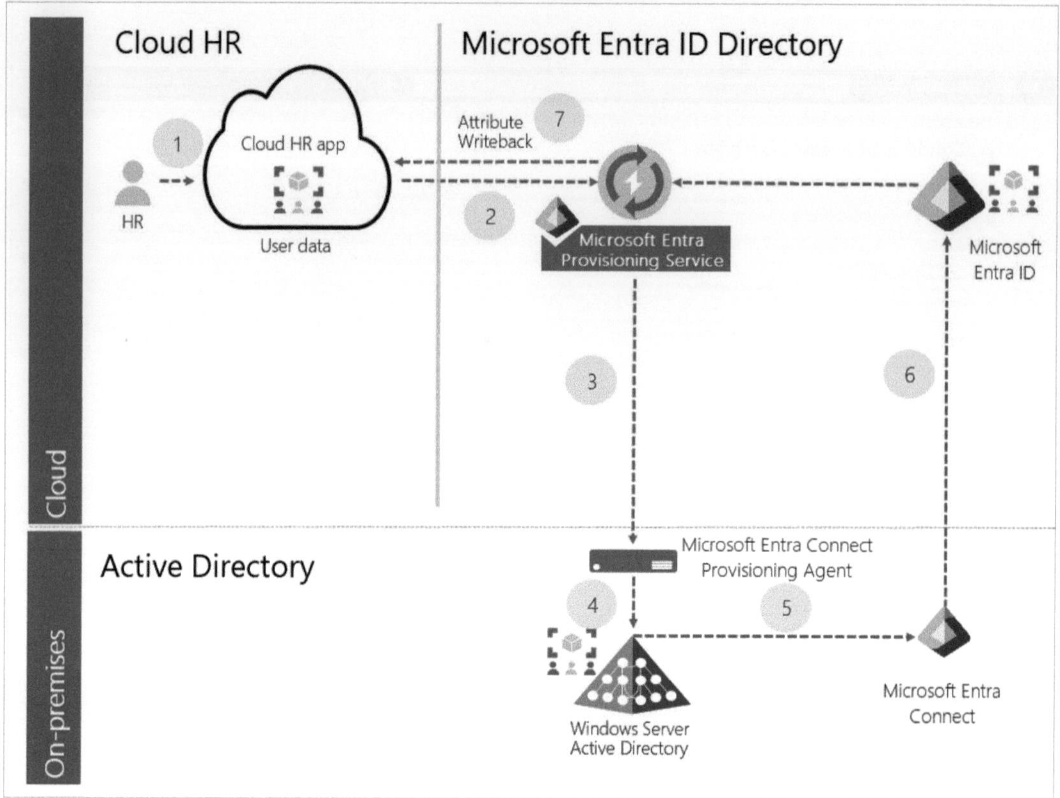

Figure 4-36. *License provisioning*

In D365 HR itself (and the underlying F&O security), you can set up automatic role assignment rules for the HR application roles as mentioned earlier. For example, "if a person is an employee of company X, assign them the Employee self-service role" or "if a person's position is of type Manager, assign the Manager role." This uses HR data to keep application roles in sync without manual labor. Configure these in the System administration > Security > Automatic role assignments area.

Lastly, ensure HR and IT coordinate on a joiner–mover–leaver process. When HR enters a new hire, not only is their Microsoft Entra ID account created but also think about notification to IT for equipment and building access, etc. Conversely, when HR processes a termination, IT should be immediately alerted (via workflow or integration) to disable accounts, collect equipment, and so on. Dynamics 365 HR can integrate with IT service management systems or identity governance solutions to kick off these workflows. For instance, Power Automate could detect a termination record and send a message to an IT ticketing system or trigger an access review.

Step 3: Identity Governance and Compliance

For organizations with advanced security or regulatory needs, integrating D365 HR with Microsoft Entra ID Governance features can add an extra layer of control:

- Access Reviews: You can configure periodic access reviews in Entra ID for critical HR security groups or roles. For example, every quarter has HR leadership review who is in the "HR Manager" role group, with data from HR about their current job. Because HR is the source of truth for who holds what position, you can cross-verify that only the right people retain high-privilege roles. If someone's role changed in HR (e.g., an HR Manager moved to a different role), an access review can catch that and remove their old access.

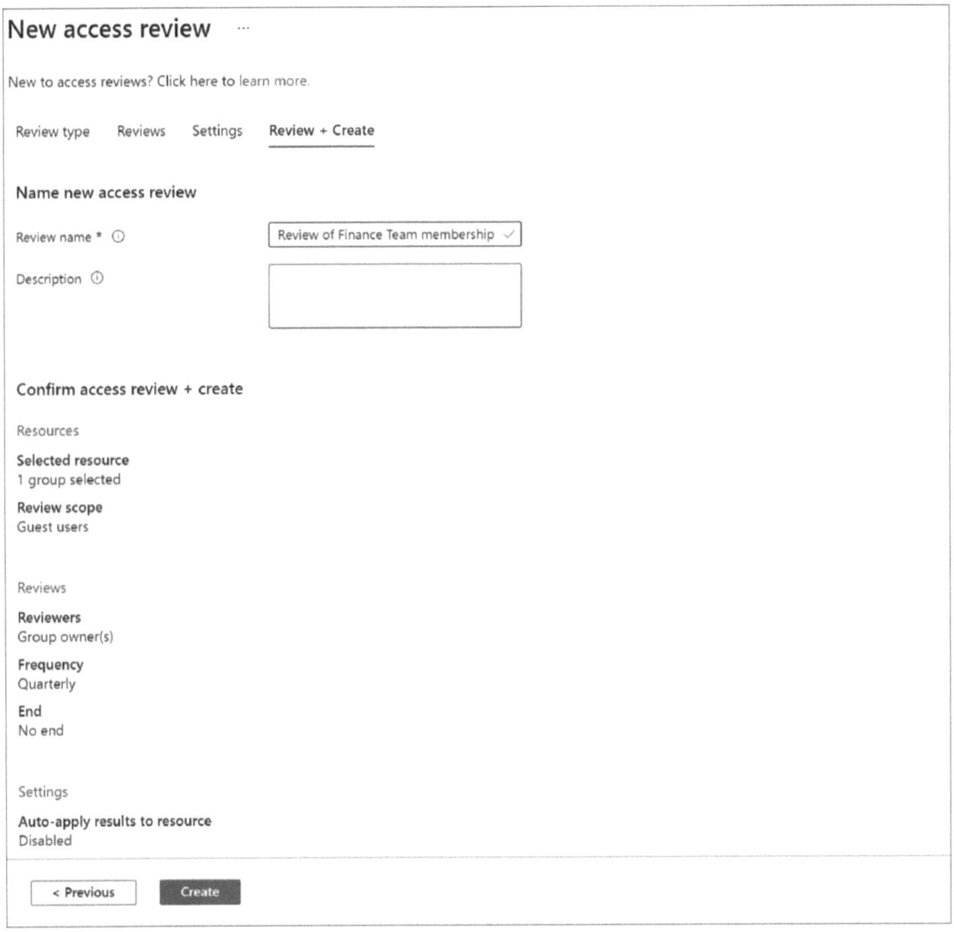

Figure 4-37. *Access review*

- Segregation of Duties (SoD): HR systems sometimes need to enforce that certain roles should not be combined (to prevent fraud or errors). While D365 has role definitions, you might use an identity governance tool to report if a single user somehow got assigned two roles that should be mutually exclusive. Maintaining such rules requires coordination between HR, IT, and possibly the finance security team.

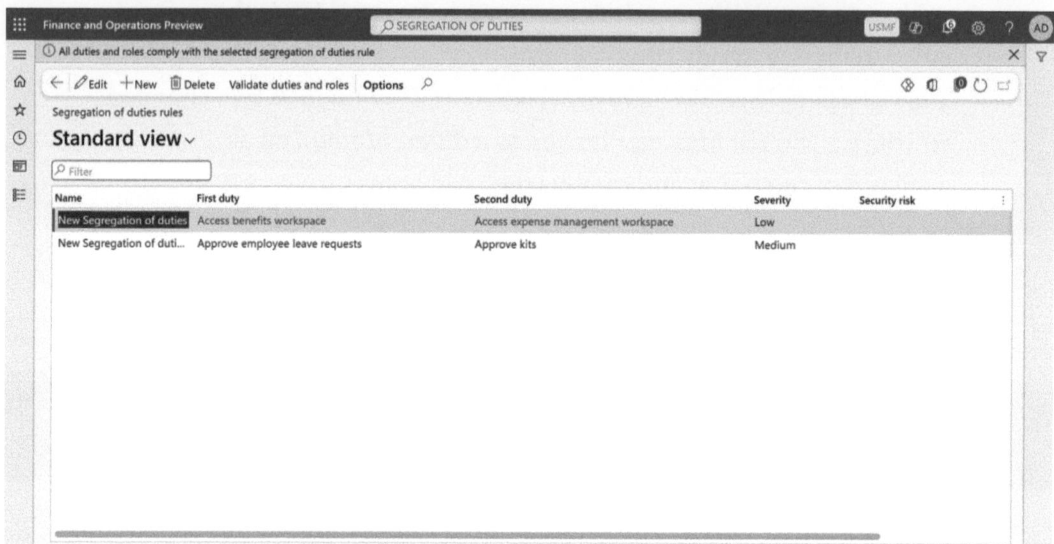

Figure 4-38. *Segregation of duties*

- Audit and Compliance Reporting: Ensure that auditing is enabled in the Power Platform admin center for the Dataverse environment used by D365 Human Resources, so that user activity is logged for traceability and compliance. These logs can be retained indefinitely in Dataverse and viewed through the Power Platform admin center. While audit logs themselves are not directly streamed to Azure Monitor or SIEM, related telemetry and activity data can be exported using diagnostic settings for advanced analysis. If your organization uses Microsoft Purview or other compliance tools, integrate D365 HR's Dataverse environment to classify and protect personal HR records.

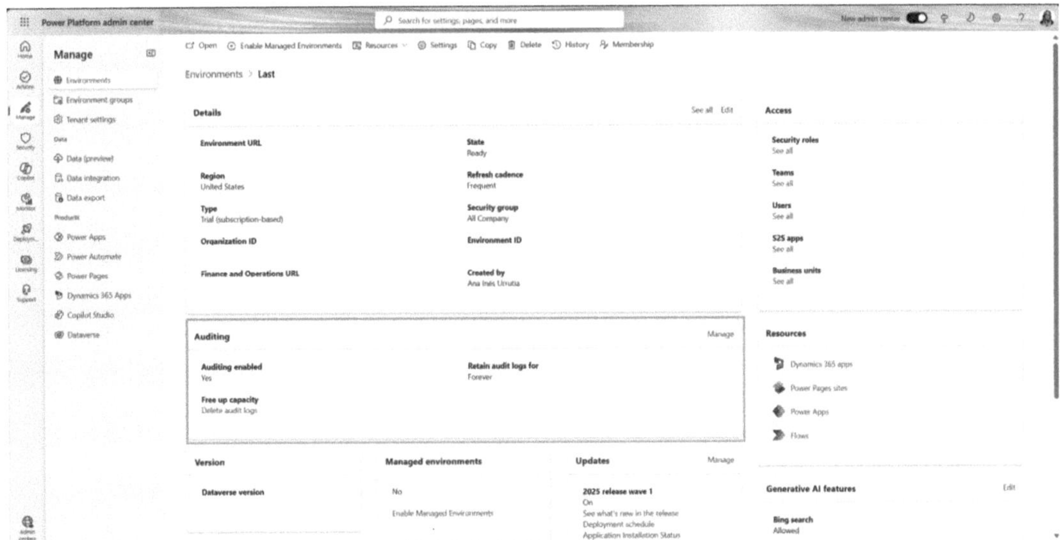

Figure 4-39. *Audit in Power Platform admin center*

In summary, the integration of HR with your identity management ensures a smooth flow from an HR event (hire, move, terminate) to the IT actions (account create/update/delete and access adjustments). Microsoft's 2025 wave features (like the Entra ID integration) underscore this focus on eliminating duplicate data entry and strengthening security by keeping HR and MICROSOFT ENTRA ID in lockstep.

Final Preparation and Go-Live

As implementation nears completion, thorough preparation for go-live is essential. This phase is about ensuring everything is in place, tested, and accepted by stakeholders before you flip the switch to make D365 HR the system of record. Below is a Pre-Go-Live Checklist of critical items, followed by some go-live tips:

Pre-Go-Live Checklist

- Security roles assigned and tested: Double-check that every user who needs access to the system has been added as a user in the environment and has the correct security roles. Test user access for different roles (e.g., an employee can submit a leave request, a manager can approve a report's leave, HR can update an employee record, etc.). Verify that no user has more access than necessary – for example, a regular manager should not see organization-wide HR settings. Adjust role assignments or security configurations if any discrepancies are found.

- Data migration validated: Ensure all intended data is loaded and verified in the system. This includes a final reconciliation of counts and key figures – for example, number of active workers in D365 HR vs. legacy system, random sampling of employee records to ensure personal info is correct, spot-checking that every department and job made it over, and that leave balances match. Any critical errors or missing data should be resolved before go-live. It's much easier to fix data with the system in implementation mode than after users are actively using it. If possible, have business users sign off that the data (especially HR master data) is accurate and complete.

- Workflows and automations tested: D365 HR often uses workflows for approvals (for example, an approval workflow for a position change or a leave request). Make sure all such workflows are configured with the correct approvers and conditions and run end-to-end tests for each one. For instance, submit a test leave request as an employee and confirm it routes to the right manager for approval and sends notifications as expected. If there are any Microsoft Power Automate flows or custom scripts (for integrations or alerts), test them with real-world scenarios and confirm they trigger and execute properly. Also test any business processes like hiring or termination: go through the steps an HR user would do to hire a new employee and verify all sub-processes (like user provisioning, paperwork generation, notifications) work in concert.

- Integrations connected and monitored: By this stage, all integrations (to payroll, to identity systems, to other third-party apps) should be in place. Do a final test of each integration in a sandbox or using sample data: for example, trigger a payroll export and ensure the payroll system received it; create a new test user and see if the MICROSOFT ENTRA ID integration picks it up, etc. It's also important to set up monitoring/alerts for integrations – for example, if a nightly payroll sync fails or encounters errors, there should be an alert (email or dashboard) so the team can address it quickly. Ensure that error handling processes are defined (what happens if an integration fails on go-live day? Who is on call to fix it and what is the fallback?)

- Compliance and access policies in place: Review that the system's configuration meets any compliance or legal requirements. For example, if there's sensitive personal data, ensure proper security roles guard it (and possibly enable the D365 feature to mask or secure fields if needed). If operating in EU or other regions with strict data protection, verify that the audit logs are enabled and data retention policies are set (perhaps personal data deletion or retention is configured as per GDPR needs). Check that notifications (like privacy consent forms or notifications to employees) are set up if those are required by law. Additionally, ensure all legal entities that you operate in have been set up in the system and any localization features (like specific fields or reports for certain countries) are enabled and tested. For instance, if you're using D365 HR in Switzerland, test that you can record a Swiss AHV number in the worker's identity info; in France, test the CPF number or birth city fields, etc., as relevant.

- User training and documentation completed: While not a system configuration per se, it's crucial that end-users (HR staff, managers, employees) have been trained on the new system before go-live. Confirm that training sessions were held, materials or quick guides distributed, and that users know how to perform their day-to-day tasks in D365 HR. Also ensure the support team is ready to handle questions – they should have an admin guide or at least know how to troubleshoot common issues (like "user can't see X, likely missing role Y" etc.).

- Go-live support plan: Line up the support structure for the go-live period. Typically, a hyper-care team (mix of implementation consultants and key power users) should be available during the first week(s) of go-live to quickly respond to any problems. Have a clear communication channel for users to report issues (a dedicated Teams channel or war-room, for example).

Category	Checklist Item	Status
Security roles assigned and tested	Verify all users are added to the environment with correct security roles	
Security roles assigned and tested	Test access for different roles (employee, manager, HR)	
Security roles assigned and tested	Ensure no user has more access than necessary	
Data migration validated	Reconcile data counts (e.g., number of active workers)	
Data migration validated	Sample employee records to validate personal information	
Data migration validated	Spot-check departments, jobs, leave balances	
Data migration validated	Resolve any critical data issues before go-live	
Workflows and automations tested	Test workflows for correct approvers and end-to-end functionality	
Workflows and automations tested	Validate leave request approval and notification flow	
Workflows and automations tested	Run tests for Power Automate flows and custom scripts	
Workflows and automations tested	Simulate business processes like hiring/termination	
Workflows and automations tested	Ensure provisioning, notifications, and forms are triggered	
Integrations connected and monitored	Test all integrations with sandbox or sample data	
Integrations connected and monitored	Validate integration with Microsoft Entra ID	
Integrations connected and monitored	Set up monitoring/alerts for integration failures	
Integrations connected and monitored	Define error handling and fallback for go-live	
Compliance and access policies in place	Validate security roles for sensitive data access	
Compliance and access policies in place	Enable audit logs and configure data retention policies	
Compliance and access policies in place	Ensure legal entity and localization configurations are complete	
Compliance and access policies in place	Verify GDPR or local compliance requirements are met	
Compliance and access policies in place	Test localization fields for country-specific requirements	
Compliance and access policies in place	Set up consent and privacy notifications, if required	
User training and documentation completed	Confirm training sessions held and guides distributed	
User training and documentation completed	Verify support team readiness with documentation	
Go-live support plan	Establish go-live hyper-care team	
Go-live support plan	Set up user support and communication channels	

Figure 4-40. *Pre-go-live checklist*

Go-Live Tips

- Plan a blackout window for cutover: Coordinate with HR and IT leadership on a cutover date and time. During cutover, freeze changes in the legacy HR system. For example, you might pick a weekend or payroll period end. Communicate to all users that from, say, Friday 5 PM, the old system is read-only, and no further HR updates should be made except emergency changes, until Monday 8 AM when D365 HR is live. This window is used to perform the final data migration (loading any delta changes since the last mock run, e.g., any new hires or terminations in the last week) and final validations. It also gives IT a buffer to resolve any issues. Announce clearly when the new system will be available to employees and how they will access it (URL, credentials, etc.).

- Execute a final mock cutover/test run: If possible, do one full dress rehearsal of the go-live process in a non-production environment shortly before the actual go-live. This includes running through the final data migration with the latest data, toggling any feature flags or settings to production mode, and simulating Day 1 in the life of the system. Microsoft recommends using a sandbox environment to do a mock cutover using your cutover checklist. This will highlight any last-minute tasks you might have missed (for example, needing to update number sequence counters or a workflow activation). Incorporate those findings into your plan.

- Keep parallel systems for a short period (if feasible): For critical functions like payroll or time tracking, some organizations run them in parallel for the first cycle. For instance, continue using the old payroll system to calculate the month's salaries as a backup, even while the new system is being fed by HR – then compare results. This safety net can catch discrepancies without impacting employees. Similarly, if you had an external leave management system and you're moving that into D365 HR, you might allow a parallel run or at least keep the old system data intact for a month until you trust everything in D365 HR (just don't let employees double-enter requests). This may not always be possible, but for high impact processes, it's worth the consideration.

- Enable auditing and monitoring: Upon go-live, turn on user activity logs and any auditing features in D365 HR (if not already on). This helps track changes and can be invaluable if issues arise ("Why did Jane's address disappear? Oh, there's an audit log that it was edited by X user on day 2 of go-live"). Also monitor system performance closely – check the environment's Health metrics in the admin center, ensure integration run times are normal, etc. Early detection of performance bottlenecks or errors allows you to react before they escalate.

- Communication is key: During cutover and go-live, keep communication channels open. Send an email or Teams announcement to all employees about the new system, including how to access support. Encourage feedback and have a quick method to disseminate fixes or workarounds if a common issue is discovered. For example, if many users report they can't login due to missing licenses, quickly communicate the resolution ("We identified an issue with license assignment, please hold on, fixing now"). A positive and transparent communication plan will help user adoption and patience.

- Post go-live review: After the first week or two, convene the project team to review how go-live went. Document any issues that occurred and how they were resolved, as well as any remaining tasks (perhaps there are still some data that need to be cleaned up or a report to be tweaked). This will serve as a lesson learned and ensure nothing falls through the cracks once the project formally closes and transitions to support mode.

By covering all these bases, the go-live will be much smoother, and the HR team can confidently transition to using Dynamics 365 HR as their primary system.

AI and Copilot for Administrators

Microsoft is increasingly infusing AI capabilities across the Dynamics 365 platform. In D365 Human Resources, many of the initial Copilot features have been end-user oriented. However, administrators and implementation teams can also leverage AI-driven tools to simplify their work and improve outcomes. Here are some ways AI and Copilot can assist in a D365 HR implementation and beyond:

Step 1: AI in Data Preparation and Migration

Cleansing and transforming data for import can be tedious. Tools like Power Query in dataflows and Excel now have AI-assisted transformations. During migration, if you have unstructured legacy data (like resumes or contract documents), AI Builder in the Power

Platform can help. AI Builder's form-processing or text-recognition models could extract structured data from scanned documents. For instance, if you have legacy performance review PDFs that you want to import key data from, an AI model could pull out employee name, review rating, etc., which you then feed into D365 HR. Another example is using AI Builder to classify or categorize training certificates or skills from old records to match the new skill taxonomy in D365.

In summary, AI can accelerate data prep by handling the heavy lifting of parsing and cleaning, which reduces manual errors and effort, but it still requires human oversight.

Step 2: Natural Language Automation and Support

Implementing integrations or custom processes often involves building Power Automate flows or writing scripts. Copilot features in Power Automate allow you to describe what you want in natural language and get a suggested flow. For example, "Notify HR via Teams when a new employee is hired in D365 HR and create a new hire checklist task list" – Copilot can draft a flow with triggers and actions which you can then adjust. This lowers the bar for creating automation around D365 HR.

Additionally, consider using Copilot in Dynamics 365 Human Resources features that Microsoft has delivered and those that are in development phase. These might include AI suggestions in the admin interface – such as recommending security roles for a new user based on their job (using learning from the org), or identifying anomalies in data (e.g., "These 5 employees have unusually high benefit deductions compared to peers, check if data is correct").

On the support side, if you integrate D365 HR with a chatbot or Agent for employees, AI can help deflect basic HR inquiries ("How do I update my address?") which reduces the load on HR admins. While this is end-user facing, it benefits admins by decreasing repetitive questions.

Step 3: AI-Powered Recruiting and Talent Management

One of the most exciting AI enhancements is in the new Recruiting add-on for D365 Human Resources (currently in preview as of 2025). This add-on introduces a modern applicant tracking system (ATS) built on Power Platform, with AI features to streamline hiring. Key AI-driven capabilities include:

- Outlook-integrated interview scheduling: The system can automatically find available time slots by checking the Outlook calendars of interviewers and candidates, propose meeting times, and send out invites. This is enhanced by AI to optimize scheduling, reducing back-and-forth emails.

- Teams integration for interviews: Interviews can be conducted via Microsoft Teams with the recruiting app capturing feedback. It simplifies the process for hiring managers and panel members to join interviews and input their notes.

- AI-enhanced resume processing: You can bulk-upload resumes or have candidates email their resumes, and the AI will parse them to create candidate profiles in the system. This saves recruiters from manual data entry. The AI can also suggest interview questions or highlight key experience from the resume.

- Automated candidate communication: The add-on can send personalized emails to candidates – for example, to schedule interviews or provide updates – using templates that can be dynamically filled. Copilot can help draft engaging emails or job descriptions based on a few prompts.

- Intelligent candidate matching (planned): We expect AI to assist in ranking or matching candidates to job requirements in the future, perhaps by analyzing resumes vs. job descriptions, or using LinkedIn integration to find best fits.

Even outside of the recruiting module, AI can aid talent management. For example, if using LinkedIn Talent Insights integration or other AI services, you might get recommendations on career paths for employees, or AI-generated learning plans based on an employee's role and performance gaps. Microsoft's Copilot vision includes assisting managers in writing performance reviews or helping employees with career development questions by referencing HR data and broader knowledge.

As an HR administrator, your role will be to enable and govern these AI features: deciding which ones to turn on, training users on them, and monitoring their suggestions for appropriateness. Always ensure that AI-generated content is reviewed by an HR professional (e.g., a Copilot drafting a job description should be checked for bias or accuracy). Microsoft typically allows configuration of AI compliance settings, such as filtering out sensitive info.

In conclusion, while AI and Copilot tools are optional and still emerging in the HR space, they offer tangible benefits. They can reduce manual work (like parsing documents or scheduling), provide insights that would be hard to obtain otherwise, and accelerate configuration through natural language commands. Embracing these tools can speed up your implementation and deliver ongoing improvements in HR operations.

Summary

Implementing Dynamics 365 Human Resources is a multifaceted project that, when done correctly, sets HR up for strategic success. To recap the key areas:

- Robust Environment Provisioning: Plan your environments early (Production, Sandbox, etc.) and deploy via the unified Power Platform admin center. Ensure the environment is linked to the correct Microsoft Entra ID tenant and meets regional compliance needs. Proper setup here provides a stable foundation for the rest of the project.

- Strong Security and Role Governance: Leverage D365's role-based security model to control access. Use default roles as a starting point and customize as needed to fit your organization's policies. Ensure sensitive data is only visible to whitelisted roles. Consider setting up automatic role assignments and keep security testing in scope to prevent any privilege gaps or overruns.

- Thorough Data Migration with Standard Entities: Use the Data Management Framework and out-of-box entities to import legacy HR data in a controlled sequence. Clean and map data meticulously to avoid issues. A golden environment approach and multiple trial runs are recommended. Remember that accurate HR data is the bedrock of user trust in the new system.

- Durable Integrations (Payroll, Identity, etc.): Integrate D365 HR with downstream systems like payroll using the provided API for a seamless flow of employee and pay information. Align on cut-off dates and verify compliance requirements for each integration. Similarly, connect HR with Microsoft Entra ID/Entra ID to automate user account life cycle and reduce duplicate data entry. Solid integrations ensure HR data doesn't live in a silo but actively drives enterprise processes.

- Go-Live Readiness and Change Management: Before go-live, use a comprehensive checklist to ensure everything is ready – security, data, workflows, integrations, user access, and support plans. Conduct user training and UAT to gain buy-in. A well-managed cutover (with a fallback plan) will minimize disruption. Post go-live, monitor the system closely and be responsive to user feedback during the stabilization period.

- Continuous Improvement with AI and Automation: After the basics are in place, take advantage of Microsoft's AI capabilities and Copilot to further enhance the HR solution. Whether it's accelerating administrative tasks, improving data quality, or empowering recruiters with AI-driven tools, these innovations can help HR teams work smarter. Keep an eye on new releases – D365 HR is evolving quickly, with features like AI-assisted recruiting and Entra ID integration poised to add significant value as they mature.

By focusing on these areas, an organization can successfully implement Dynamics 365 Human Resources as a core platform for HR management. The end result is not just a one-time software rollout but a foundation for ongoing HR transformation – one that enables the HR department to operate efficiently, securely, and with the flexibility to adapt as the company grows or regulations change. With the right preparation and the powerful tools at hand (from automation to AI), HR can shift more time from administrative tasks to strategic people initiatives, fulfilling the true promise of a modern HR system.

CHAPTER 5

Power Platform for HR: Modernizing Workflows, Reports, and Dashboards

Introduction

HR departments today face intense pressure to move faster, personalize employee services, and adapt to constant change. Yet many HR teams are still bogged down by legacy systems, siloed spreadsheets, and manual processes that slow them down. Studies show that HR staff spend as much as 57–73% of their time on repetitive administrative tasks, leaving little time for strategic work. HR managers lose over 14 hours per week on tasks that *could* be automated. These inefficiencies not only strain HR capacity (more than half of HR departments report being understaffed) but also impact employee satisfaction and business agility.

Microsoft's Power Platform offers an alternative: a low-code suite that HR and IT teams can use together to build apps, automate workflows, and create data insights *without* replacing the core HRIS (such as Dynamics 365 Human Resources). With relatively little technical effort, HR professionals can streamline processes across the employee life cycle – from onboarding to offboarding – using tools they control. The payoff isn't just efficiency: in a Microsoft survey of thousands of workers, 89% of employees with access to automation and AI tools felt more fulfilled, because they could spend time on work that really matters. In other words, automating the drudgery frees HR to focus on people and strategy.

A. I. Urrutia de Souza, *The Microsoft AI Human Resources Handbook*,
https://doi.org/10.1007/979-8-8688-1781-6_5

This chapter explores how each component of the Power Platform can transform HR operations and employee experience. We'll cover all five tools – Power Automate, Power Apps, Power Pages, Power BI, and Copilot Studio (formerly Power Virtual Agents) – with detailed implementation guides, realistic examples, and best practices. You'll see how to build workflows, reports, and automated dashboards to streamline HR processes in practical ways, using real-world scenarios and metrics (e.g., time saved, efficiency gains). We'll also introduce Microsoft's emerging Project "Sophia" (AI-powered Business Agents) as a glimpse into next-generation HR workflows. Throughout, the tone is accessible yet expert-led, aimed at both HR leaders and IT professionals working together on digital transformation. Let's dive into the Power Platform toolkit and how it empowers HR to deliver more value with less effort.

Power Automate: Workflow Automation for HR Operations

Power Automate allows HR teams to design automated workflows ("flows") that connect systems, send timely notifications, and eliminate tedious manual tasks. It acts as a tireless HR assistant, running processes in the background so nothing falls through the cracks. Many routine HR processes that once required emails and data entry can be streamlined with Power Automate. For example, HR departments use it to automate processes such as:

- New Hire Onboarding: Trigger onboarding tasks across IT, Facilities, HR, and managers when a new hire record is created. For instance, as soon as HR enters a new employee into the HRIS, a flow can automatically send a welcome email, create an IT account request, notify Facilities to prepare a workspace, and assign the hiring manager an onboarding checklist. *(This ensures a consistent Day 1 experience.)*

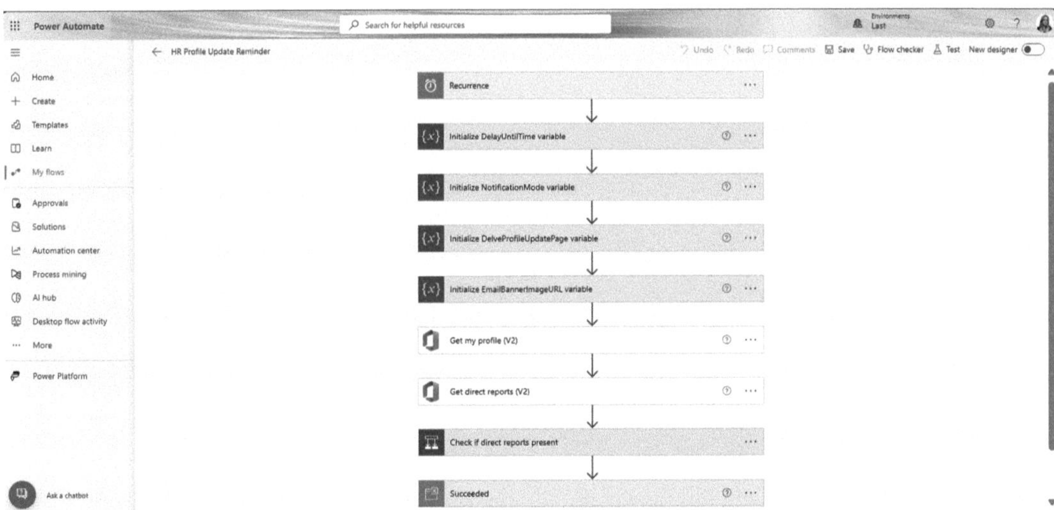

Figure 5-1. *HR Profile update reminder: an example of a Power Automate template to use*

- Leave Approvals: Route leave requests through multistep approvals and send reminders if approvals are delayed. Instead of HR manually chasing managers for vacation request approvals, a flow can handle the routing and nudging. Managers get an approval card in Teams or email; if they don't respond in, say, 3 days, the flow can escalate to their boss. This speeds up response times and keeps employees informed.

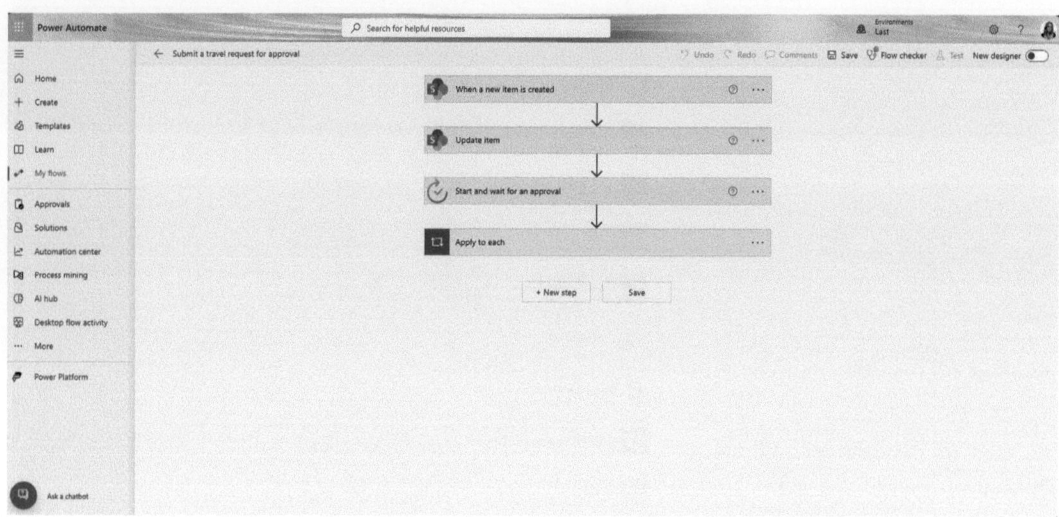

Figure 5-2. *Part 1: Submit a travel request for approval workflow.*

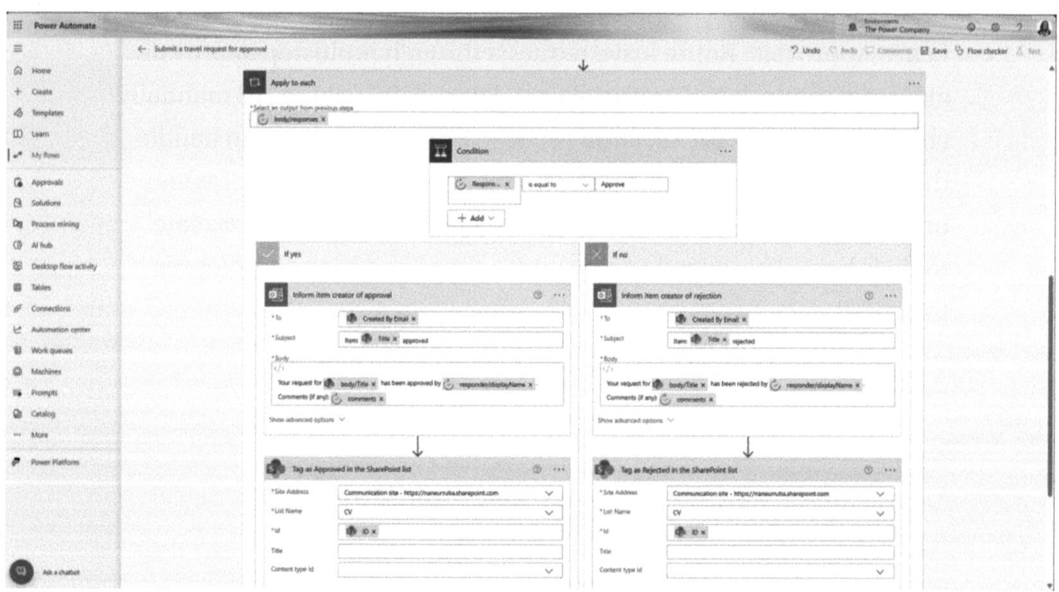

Figure 5-3. *Part 2: Submit a travel request for approval workflow.*

- Policy Acknowledgments: Distribute updated HR policies to all employees and track their acknowledgment. Power Automate can post the new policy on Power Pages or SharePoint, email employees a link, and collect digital read-receipts. HR can see who hasn't acknowledged and send automatic follow-up reminders, ensuring compliance.

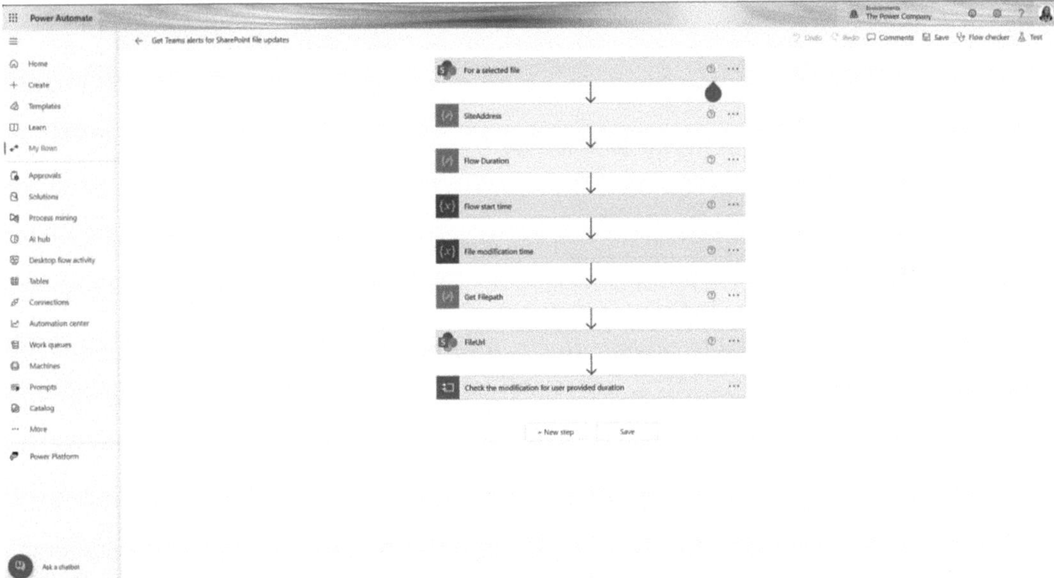

Figure 5-4. *Document acknowledgment notification workflow*

When a file is updated – signature, changes, or similar – a notification is sent to the designed contact, another example of a template in Power Automate ready to use.

- Performance Review Alerts: Automatically send evaluation reminders at 30-, 60-, and 90-day intervals (or any schedule). For example, after a new hire's start date, trigger check-in survey links to the manager at the 30/60/90-day marks, or remind employees and supervisors about annual review deadlines. This replaces spreadsheet trackers with a "set it and forget it" flow.

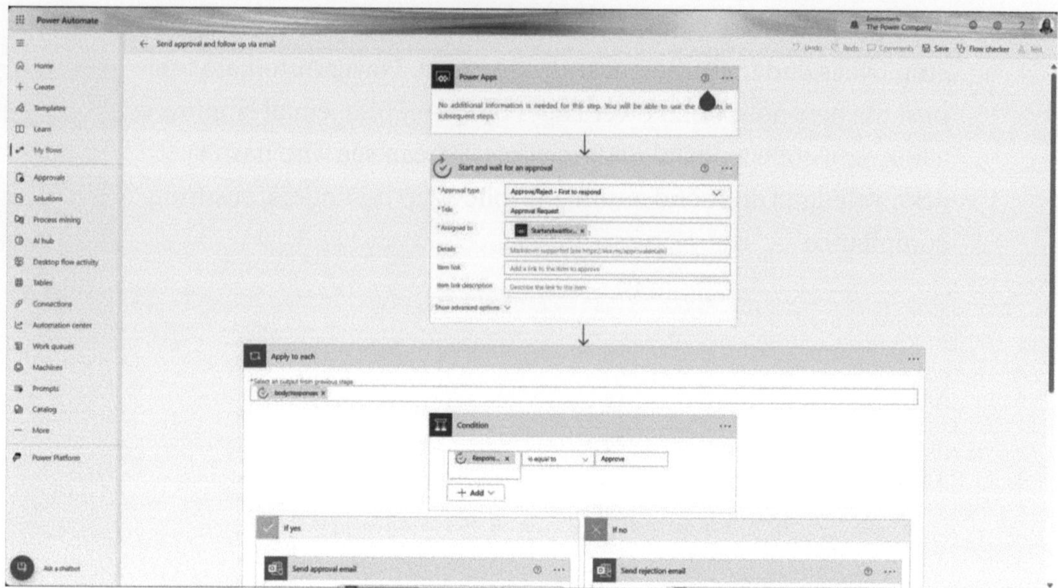

Figure 5-5. *Power Automate review alerts. Assuming the performance reviews are stored in Power Apps.*

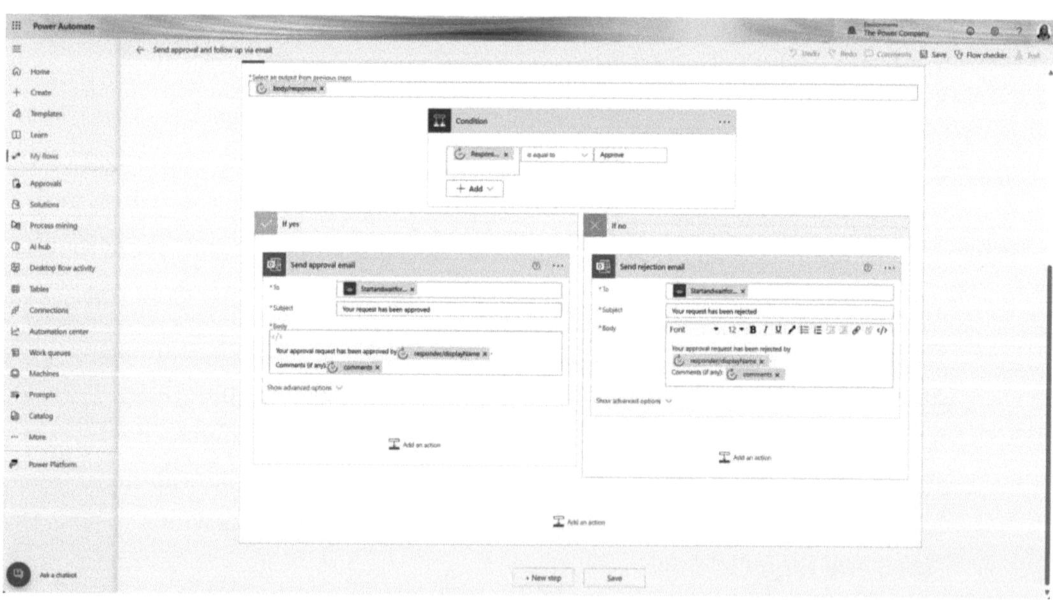

Figure 5-6. *After approval or not, the review is submitted Power Automate will act based on the condition.*

Strategically, designing HR workflows with Power Automate involves some forethought:

- Build logic around dependencies: Identify business rules and prerequisites. *Example:* only trigger certain IT setup tasks if the new hire is an internal transfer (who may already have equipment), or skip background check steps if the person is re-hired within 6 months. Implementing these conditional branches ensures the flow handles exceptions and doesn't create noise.

- Define escalation paths: Decide what happens if an approval or task sits too long. For instance, if a manager hasn't approved a leave request in 5 days, the flow could auto-notify *their* manager or ping a backup approver. This prevents processes from stalling silently.

- Use environment variables and templates: So that the same flow can be reused across departments, business units, or regions with minimal changes. For example, you might parameterize an "Onboarding Flow" to handle slightly different emails or task lists per country, without maintaining separate flows. Reuse is key to managing automation at scale.

Implementation Steps: If you're an HR or IT leader looking to implement Power Automate for HR workflows, here's a step-by-step guide:

1. Identify High-Impact Processes: Start by listing HR processes that are repetitive, paper-based, or prone to delays. Good candidates are onboarding, offboarding, leave approvals, expense approvals, policy sign-offs, etc. Engage HR team members to pinpoint pain points (e.g., "we spend too much time sending reminders for X"). Prioritize one process to automate first – ideally one with clear benefits (time saved, fewer errors).

2. Map the Current Workflow: Document the steps, people involved, and systems used in the manual process. For example, map out how a leave request currently flows from employee to manager to HR, including all emails. This becomes the blueprint for your automated flow. At this stage, involve both HR process owners and an IT Power Platform specialist to ensure you capture the details and any technical considerations (like where data is stored).

3. Build in Power Automate (Iteratively): Using the flow designer, start building the automated version. Power Automate offers many pre-built templates for common HR scenarios – leverage them as a starting point. For instance, there's a template for onboarding that creates tasks in Planner and sends emails. You can customize these templates to fit your needs. Build the flow step by step: triggers (what kicks it off, e.g., "new item in SharePoint list" or a scheduled recurrence), actions (e.g., "create Teams message," "update record in HR database"), and conditions (for branching logic). If you're new to Power Automate, the HR and IT team might do this jointly: HR provides the logic and rules, IT helps with technical connectors and best practices.

4. Test with Sample Data: Before rolling out, run the flow with test cases. For example, create a dummy new hire in a test environment and ensure all the automated tasks fire correctly – the welcome email goes out, the accounts are created, etc. Check that permissions are correct (e.g., the flow can write to a SharePoint list, or read from the HR system) and that error handling is in place (what if an email address is missing?). It's wise to conduct a small pilot: maybe use the flow for the next 2–3 real new hires but still monitor manually, to catch any issues.

5. Deploy and Educate Users: Once validated, publish the flow to the production environment. Make sure any managers or employees involved know about the new automated process. For instance, if managers will start receiving Teams approval cards instead of emails from HR, give them a heads-up and quick instructions. From a governance perspective, document the flow (what it does, who owns it) in an HR operations manual or IT knowledge base.

6. Monitor and Refine: Power Automate provides run history and analytics. After deployment, keep an eye on the flow runs – are there failures or delays? Perhaps add alerting (e.g., an email to HR IT if a flow fails or if it takes unusually long). Gather feedback from end users: *Did the onboarding flow cover all tasks?*

Are the notifications timed well? Use that input to adjust timing, add missing steps, or improve wording in communications. Automation is not "set and forget" – continuous improvement will help you squeeze maximum efficiency and employee satisfaction from each flow.

One huge advantage of Power Automate for HR is the integration of AI assistance (Copilot) for building flows. HR users can now *describe* the workflow they need in plain English, and Power Automate will draft a flow for them. For example, you might simply tell Copilot: *"Create a flow that sends an onboarding checklist via Teams to a new hire, one day before their start date, and also assign a task to IT to set up their laptop."* The AI will generate a draft workflow with those steps laid out, which you can then tweak as needed. This drastically lowers the barrier for non-technical HR staff to create their own automations. Early users report that Copilot can produce a decent first version of a flow in seconds – something that might take an hour to configure manually. While you'll still want an expert to review the flow (for accuracy and edge cases), it speeds up the development cycle and empowers HR to ideate solutions quickly.

Fictional Scenario – Automate in Action: *NOVAX Manufacturing,* a mid-sized company with 500 employees, used to onboard new hires through a flurry of emails. HR sent forms to the new hire, IT and Facilities got separate emails for equipment and desk setup, and managers often forgot to schedule initial trainings. It took two weeks on average for a new employee to be fully set up. After implementing a Power Automate flow for onboarding, NOVAX cut the onboarding completion time to one week (a 50% faster ramp-up). The flow orchestrated everything: new hires now automatically get a welcome email with all forms on Day 1, managers receive a Teams reminder to schedule training within the first week, and IT tickets for equipment are created instantly. HR reports they save about 5 hours of admin work per hire, and new hires are productive sooner. This kind of improvement is echoed elsewhere – companies using HR automation have seen onboarding time reduced by up to 80% in some cases, though 50% is a more typical achievable goal. The key is that *no one has to "remember" the process – the workflow just runs.*

Exercise (Automating an HR Process): Identify one HR process in your organization that is currently manual and time-consuming – for example, tracking employee trainings or handling travel expense approvals. Sketch out the steps on paper or a whiteboard. Then, using Power Automate, create a new flow that automates that process. *For instance, if you chose travel expense approvals:* build a flow that triggers when an employee submits an expense form (perhaps from Microsoft Forms or a SharePoint list), automatically routes it to the appropriate manager for approval, and notifies Finance once approved. Include at least one conditional branch (e.g., if the amount is over $1,000, add an extra Finance approval step). Test your flow with a sample submission. In a workshop setting, have each team demo their flow and discuss how it could save time or reduce errors. This exercise will give you hands-on experience in turning a manual HR task into an automated workflow using Power Automate.

Power Apps: Self-Service HR Apps and Tools

Power Apps enables HR to build custom applications and digital forms with minimal coding. Think of Power Apps as a toolkit to create employee-facing apps that solve specific HR needs – often replacing Excel files, emails, or even paper forms with a more user-friendly app. These apps can run on web or mobile, and can be as simple or sophisticated as needed. The beauty for HR is the *speed*: instead of waiting months for IT to develop a bespoke tool, HR professionals (with some training or IT support) can spin up a working app in weeks or even days. This puts more self-service capabilities directly into employees' and managers' hands, reducing the back-and-forth with HR for routine tasks.

Some real examples of HR apps built with Power Apps include:

- Training Nomination Portal: An app where employees and managers can browse upcoming training sessions, nominate attendees, and view past attendance history. For instance, NOVAX's HR team created a training catalog app – employees open the app to see what courses are available, click to nominate themselves or a team member, and the app logs the nomination for HR to review. Managers can see who on their team has completed what training. This replaced a clunky process of emailing an HR inbox to sign up for training.

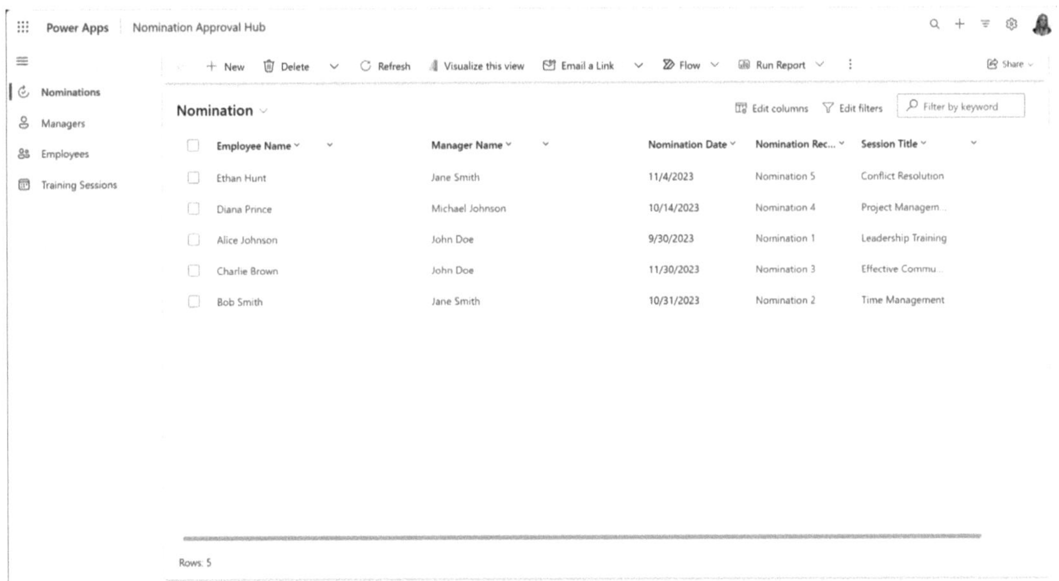

Figure 5-7. *Training nomination approval model-driven app*

- HR Document Center: A secure app for employees to upload or download HR documents (such as contracts, certifications, policy acknowledgments). Instead of sending sensitive documents via email, employees use the app to upload files directly to a secure SharePoint or Dataverse location, where HR can review and store them. Likewise, HR can publish documents (e.g., total rewards statements or updated policies) for individual employees to retrieve. This kind of app improves data security and gives employees 24/7 access to their HR files.

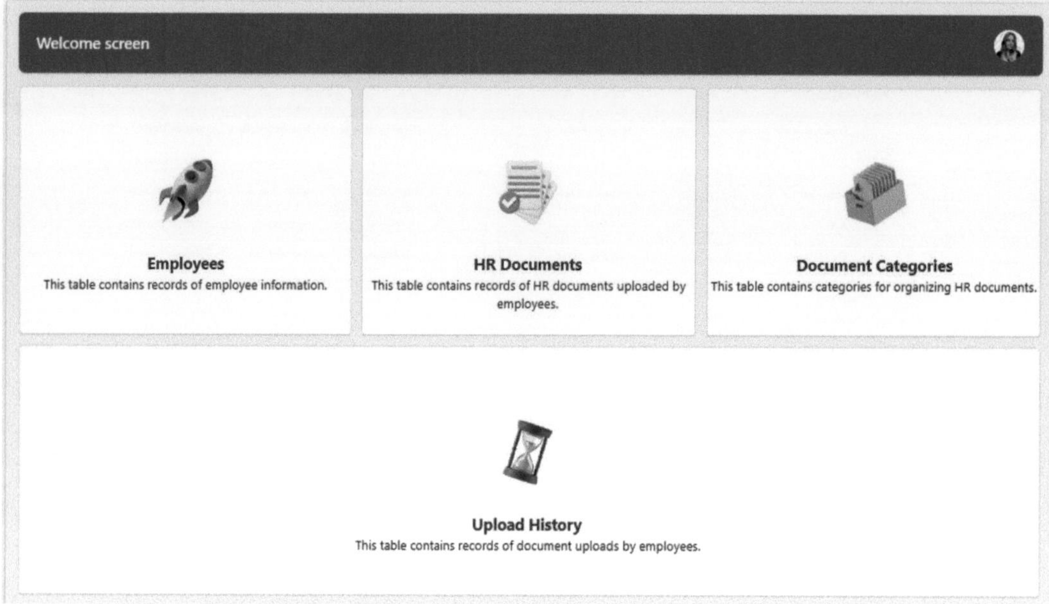

Figure 5-8. *HR document center Canvas app*

- Position Request App: Designed for HR business partners or managers to request creation of a new position or role. The app might include a form to fill in role details, justification, and budget information, and it kicks off an approval workflow (often integrated with Power Automate) for finance and HR approval. By standardizing position requests in an app, the organization can ensure all necessary info is captured and approvals are tracked – no more inconsistent emails when a manager wants to open a new role.

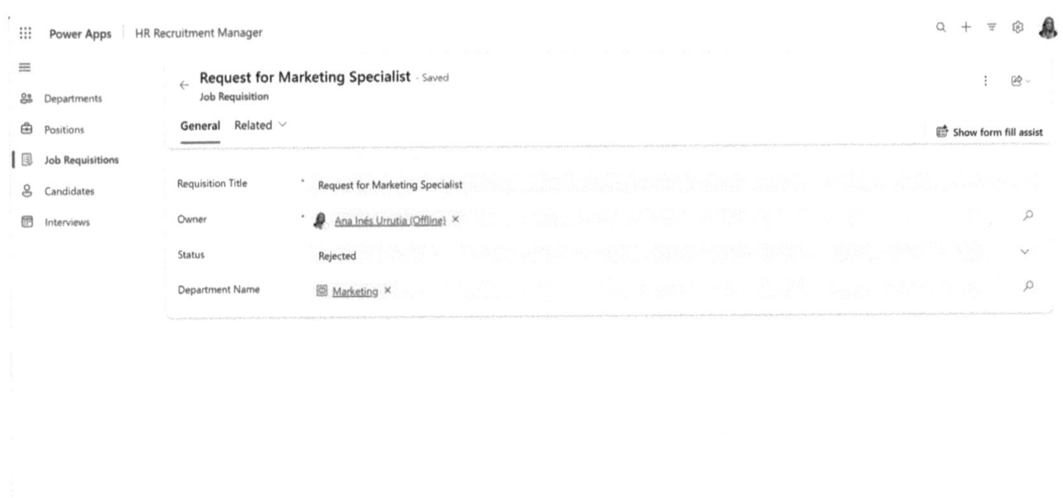

Figure 5-9. *Job requisitions screen in model-driven app*

- Return-to-Work Form: A mobile-friendly app used, for example, in scenarios like a pandemic or medical leave. Employees can fill out a health attestation or provide required info before returning on-site, including uploading test results or certificates and checking acknowledgment boxes (consent, etc.). Power Apps can leverage device features, so an employee could take a photo of a doctor's note with their phone and upload it directly. HR then monitors submissions through the app. This dramatically simplifies collecting and organizing such information compared to manual methods.

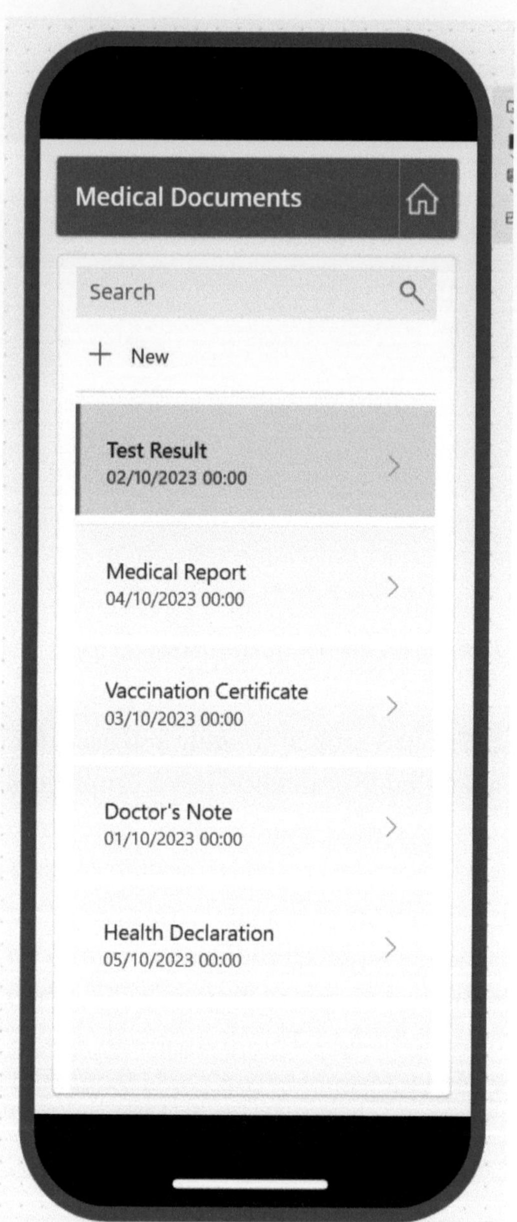

Figure 5-10. *Medical document screen from return-from-work canvas app mobile version*

These examples show the versatility of Power Apps for HR. When building an HR app, you typically have two approaches in Power Apps:

- Canvas Apps – These start with a blank canvas and give you pixel-perfect control over the UI. You drag-and-drop text fields, buttons, galleries, etc. onto screens and design exactly how you want it to look. Canvas apps are great for highly tailored apps (e.g., a branded employee portal) or mobile scenarios where you need to optimize for touch and small screens. HR can make the app visually engaging and intuitive, with freedom in layout. The Training Nomination and Document Center examples above could be canvas apps because they likely need a custom look and feel.

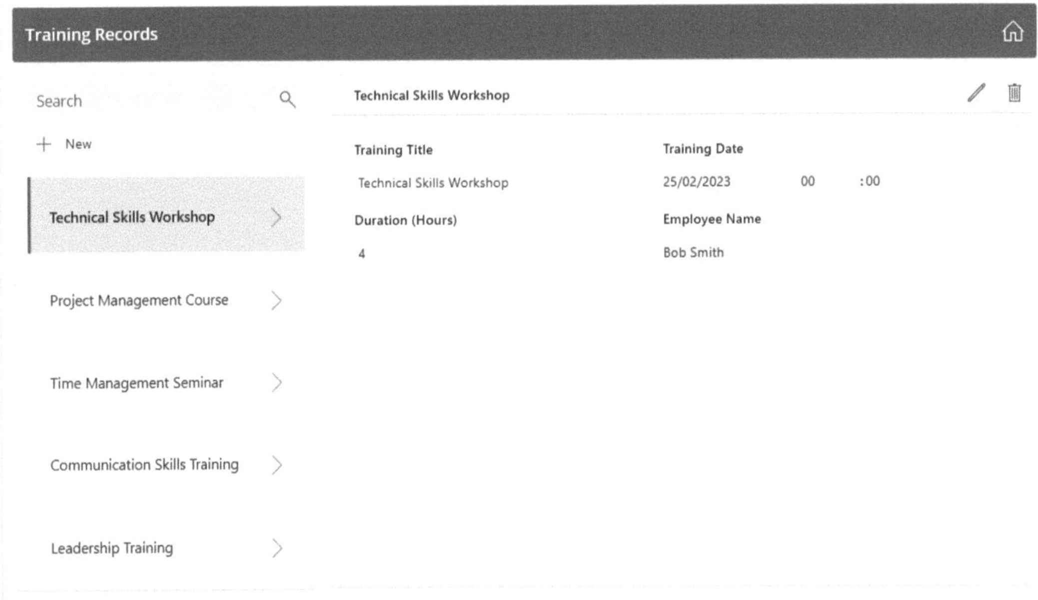

Figure 5-11. *Training record canvas app*

- **Model-Driven Apps** – These are data-centric applications built on Microsoft Dataverse, the underlying **low-code platform** for Power Platform. Dataverse provides not only data storage but also integrated capabilities for security, workflows, business rules, and automation. In model-driven apps, you define data tables, relationships, and forms, and the app is generated around this data model with a standardized, responsive UI. These apps are well-suited for complex, relational business processes – for example, an internal HR app to manage positions and job requisitions might use Dataverse tables for Departments, Positions, and Candidates, automatically generating views and forms for data entry and review. The user interface aligns with Dynamics 365 standards, making it ideal for structured HR scenarios where data consistency and integration with Dataverse security roles and workflows are important.

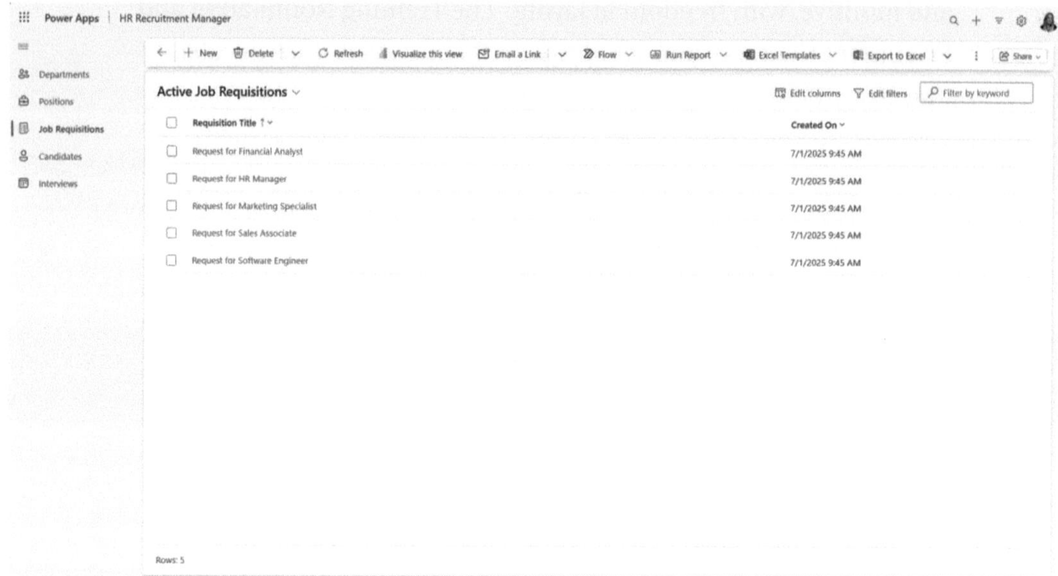

Figure 5-12. *HR Recruitment Manager model-driven app*

In practice, HR teams choose the approach based on the problem. If user experience and simplicity for employees are top priority, they lean toward Canvas Apps. If the app is more for HR power-users managing structured data (and you want to leverage Dataverse with possibly minimal design work), model-driven might fit.

Implementation Steps: How can HR leaders and IT implement Power Apps solutions for HR needs? Here's a guide:

1. Identify the Use Case and Audience: Start with a specific problem or opportunity. Are you trying to empower *employees* (self-service) or *HR staff* (internal tool)? Is the goal to replace a paper form, consolidate an Excel tracker, or provide a new service? For

example, say you want to reduce the emails to HR for updating personal info – that points to an employee self-service app for profile updates. Knowing *who* will use the app (and how) guides all design decisions.

2. Plan the Data Source: Apps need to store or retrieve data. Decide where the data will live. Options include Dataverse (preferred for complex apps or if you already use D365 HR, since employee data might sync there), SharePoint lists (good for simpler needs or if you're already using SharePoint for HR documents), or even Excel or other connectors. For instance, an "HR FAQ app" might pull questions and answers from a SharePoint list maintained by HR. An "Employee Directory app" could use Dataverse or the Office 365 users connector. IT can help set up the right data source and connectors and ensure HR has the right access.

3. Choose Canvas vs. Model-Driven: Based on the use case. If you need a custom user interface or it's mostly a form for employees, Canvas is likely best. If it's an internal tool managing records (and you don't mind a standard UI), model-driven can save time. Sometimes you might even use Power Pages (covered in the next section) if the target users are external or if you need a full website experience. But for most internal apps, Canvas or Model-Driven will do. For example, if building a *Performance Review app* for managers to enter ratings, a Canvas app could provide a tailored experience; a model-driven approach could work if integrated with D365 data models.

4. Build the App (Iteratively): Use Power Apps Studio to start building. Microsoft offers templates and sample apps; you can open these to learn or jumpstart development. Begin with basic screens: for example, for a Document Center app, start with a login/home screen, an upload form, and a gallery listing uploaded documents. Focus on functionality first (make sure the app can perform the needed tasks), then refine the design (make it intuitive and on-brand). HR subject matter experts should work closely with the app maker to ensure it meets real user needs. It's

common to do a quick demo to a few end users for feedback while still in development.

5. Ensure Security and Compliance: Before rolling out, think about data security. If the app shows personal or sensitive data, implement proper access controls. With Power Apps connected to Dataverse or SharePoint, you can leverage security roles or item-level permissions. For instance, an employee shouldn't see another's HR documents – so the Document Center app must filter data to the current user. Test that the security works (IT can attempt to use the app as a test user to verify they only see what they should). Also consider if any data (like health info on a Return-to-Work form) requires extra compliance measures (encryption, limited retention, etc.). Build those into the solution.

6. Test on Multiple Devices: If your audience includes mobile users (very likely for frontline employees or on-the-go managers), test the app on a smartphone and tablet. Canvas apps can be designed to be responsive, but it might need tweaking (e.g., using relative sizing, testing touch targets). The goal is an app that's easy to use on the devices your employees prefer. If something is clunky on mobile, adjust the layout or controls. A positive user experience will drive adoption.

7. Deploy and Train: Move the app into production (which might be as simple as saving it and sharing with users, or exporting as a solution for IT-managed deployment). Publish it for your intended audience – you can share an app with all employees or specific security groups. Provide a bit of communication: maybe an announcement email or a short guide. For example, "New HR Self-Service App now available – click here from your Teams toolbar!" Highlight how it benefits them ("update your info anytime without forms or waiting"). If needed, hold a brief training session or include the app intro in new hire orientation. Fortunately, most Power Apps are intuitive if designed well, so heavy training shouldn't be needed.

8. Monitor and Iterate: Use the Power Platform admin center or app analytics to see usage patterns. Are employees actually using the Training nomination app? Which features or screens are used most? Solicit feedback via a survey or within the app (some apps include a "Feedback" button). Over time, update the app with improvements or new features. For instance, after launching an HR Knowledge Base app, you might find employees keep asking a question that isn't in the FAQ – that's a cue to update the content or add functionality. Keep versioning and enhancing the app as HR needs to evolve (just ensure changes are tested and communicated).

Fictional Scenario – Power Apps in Action: *NOCKO Healthcare* operates several hospitals and clinics. Their HR team was overwhelmed with managing staff credential renewals – nurses and doctors must keep licenses and certifications up-to-date. Previously, HR tracked this in Excel and emailed individuals when they were due to renew, which often resulted in frantic last-minute compliance issues. NOCKO built a Credential Tracker Power App. Each clinician has a profile in the app (sourced from Dataverse), listing their required certifications and expiration dates. The app sends automated reminders via Power Automate when a cert is nearing expiration. Clinicians can log into the app from their phone, see what's expiring, and upload proof of renewal (photo of their new license) directly. The app then updates the central record and notifies HR. This solution saved HR an estimated 20 hours a month in tracking and chasing documents. More importantly, compliance improved – expirations that slipped through the cracks dropped to near zero. Clinicians liked the convenience: one nurse said it was "way easier than hunting for the right form and email." This story illustrates how a targeted Power App (in this case, a model-driven app with a Canvas front-end for ease of use) can solve an industry-specific HR challenge, whether in healthcare, manufacturing, finance, etc. The low-code approach meant IT and HR built it together in a few weeks, rather than buying an expensive niche system.

Exercise (Build a Simple HR App): In a workshop or on your own, try creating a basic HR app using Power Apps. For example, build a "Submit a Suggestion" app for employees:

- Create a new Canvas app (phone layout). Add a form where an employee can enter their name, department, and their suggestions to improve the workplace.

- Connect the form to a data source like a SharePoint list or Excel file to collect submissions.

- Add a screen that thanks the employee and perhaps displays recently submitted suggestions (to foster transparency).

- Test the app by submitting a few suggestions yourself. Then share the app with a colleague and have them submit one.

- Discuss or note how this app could streamline what might currently be an email-based process, and how you would extend it (e.g., adding a manager review step or categorizing suggestions).

- This exercise will familiarize you with Power Apps basics: creating screens, using a form control, and connecting to data. It demonstrates the speed at which you can turn an HR form into a user-friendly app.

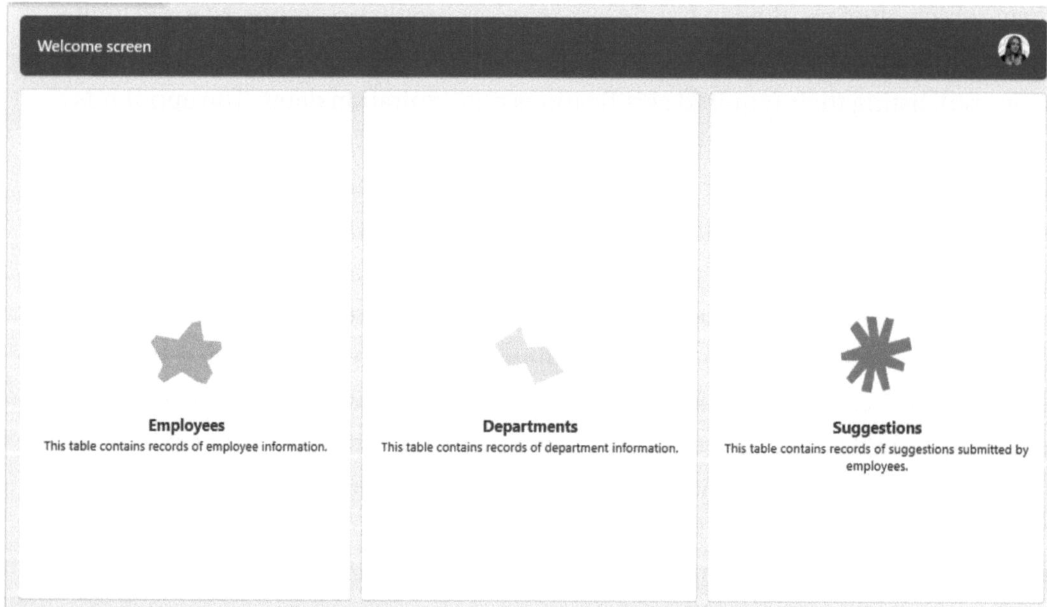

Figure 5-13. Submit a suggestion welcome screen in canvas app

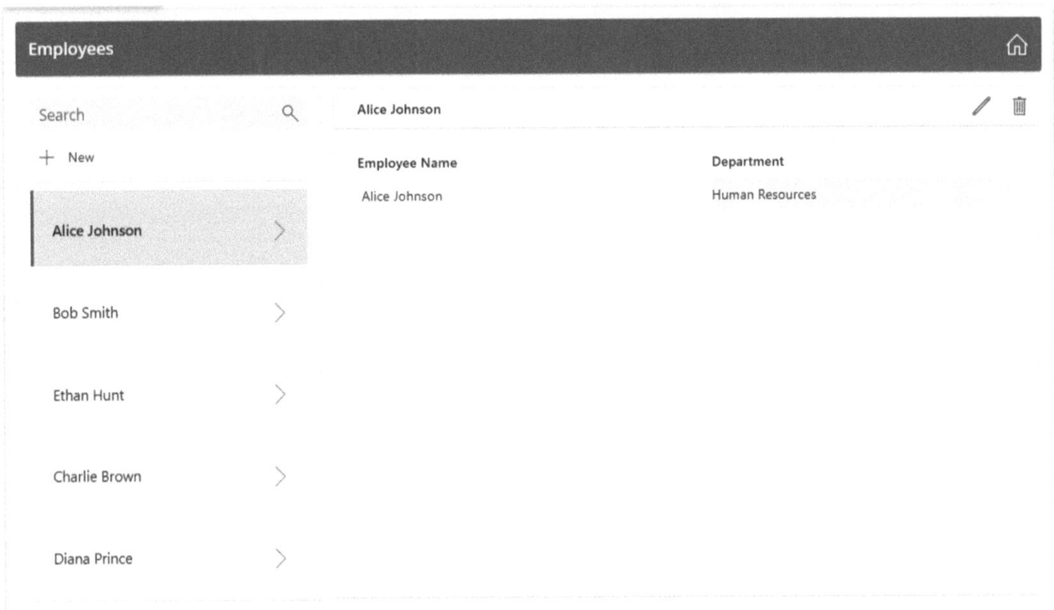

Figure 5-14. *Employee screen in suggestion canvas app*

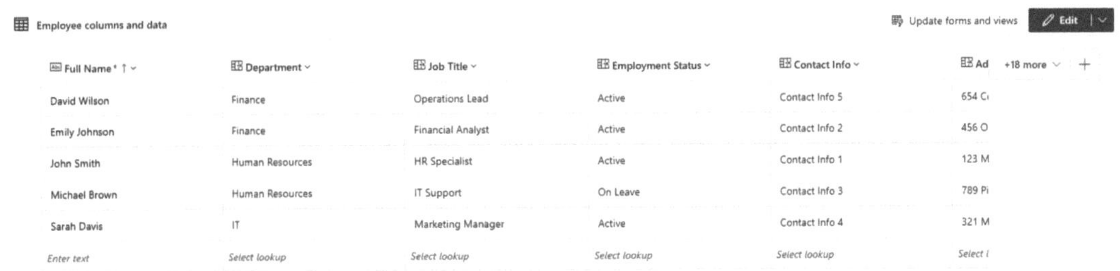

Figure 5-15. *Employee table structure and sample data*

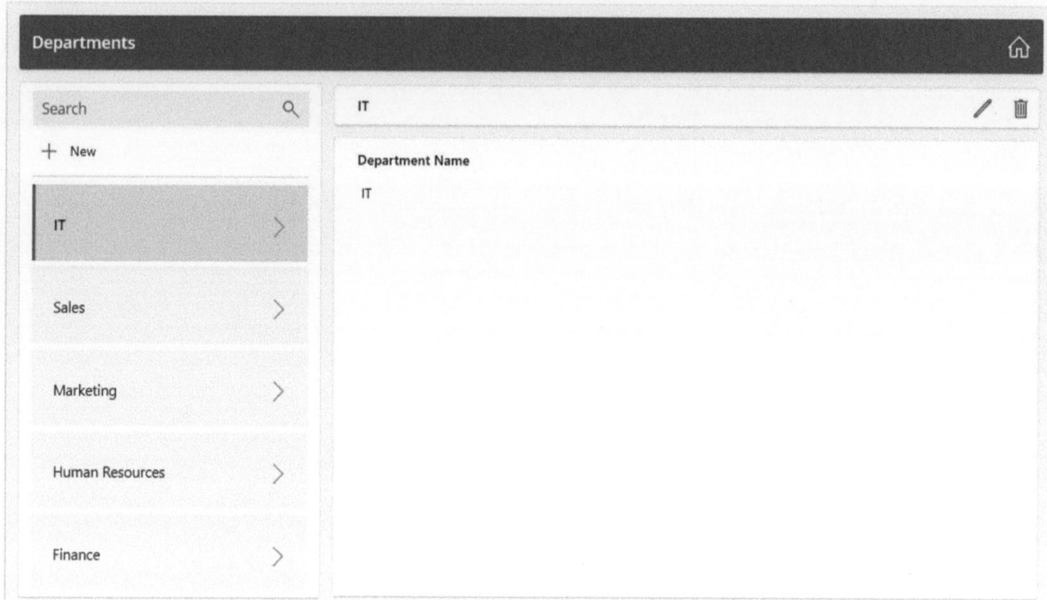

Figure 5-16. *Department screen in suggestion canvas app*

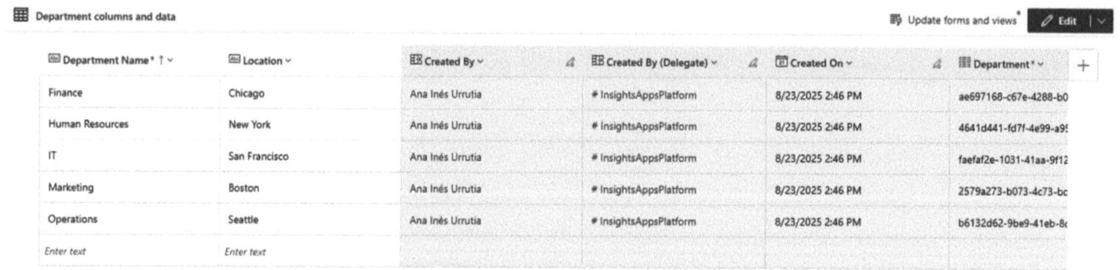

Department Name ▲	Location	Created By	Created By (Delegate)	Created On	Department
Finance	Chicago	Ana Inés Urrutia	# InsightsAppsPlatform	8/23/2025 2:46 PM	ae697168-c67e-4288-b0
Human Resources	New York	Ana Inés Urrutia	# InsightsAppsPlatform	8/23/2025 2:46 PM	4641d441-fd7f-4e99-a95
IT	San Francisco	Ana Inés Urrutia	# InsightsAppsPlatform	8/23/2025 2:46 PM	faefaf2e-1031-41aa-9f12
Marketing	Boston	Ana Inés Urrutia	# InsightsAppsPlatform	8/23/2025 2:46 PM	2579a273-b073-4c73-bc
Operations	Seattle	Ana Inés Urrutia	# InsightsAppsPlatform	8/23/2025 2:46 PM	b6132d62-9be9-41eb-8
Enter text	Enter text				

Figure 5-17. *Department table structure and sample data*

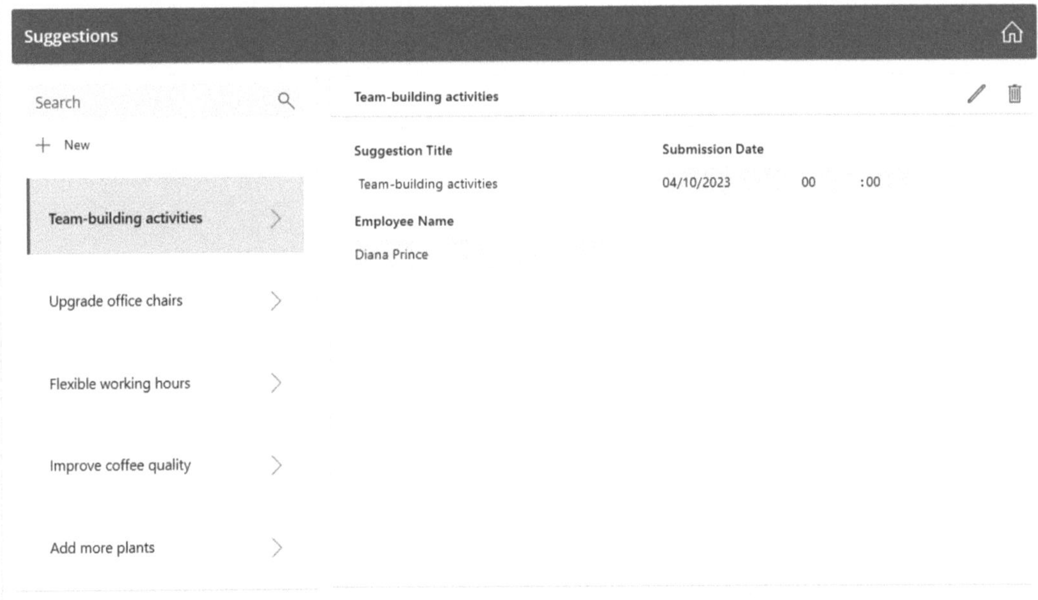

Figure 5-18. *Suggestions screen in suggestion canvas app*

Suggestions columns and data

Suggestion Title * ↑ ∨	Employee Name * ∨	Status ∨	Submission ... ∨	+18 more ∨
Add Reports	Eve	Approved	6/5/2024	
Bug Fix	Carol	Rejected	6/3/2024	
Improve UI	Alice	Pending	6/1/2024	
New Feature	Bob	Approved	6/2/2024	
Optimize DB	Dave	Pending	6/4/2024	
Enter text	*Enter text*	*Select option*	*Enter or pick date*	

Figure 5-19. *Suggestions table structure and sample data*

Power Pages: Engaging Employee and Candidate Portals

Power Pages (the newest member of the Power Platform) is a low-code platform for building secure websites and portals. In an HR context, Power Pages is incredibly useful for creating employee self-service portals, internal HR hubs, or external sites for candidates and alumni. It extends the idea of Power Apps into full-fledged web portals accessible via a browser to users inside or outside your organization. While Power Apps are often used for internal apps (and require sign-in via Microsoft Entra ID by default), Power Pages can be configured for external access, different authentication options (work accounts, personal emails, or anonymous for public info), and richer web content (text, videos, forms, etc.). Essentially, if HR needs a website for anything – be it an internal knowledge base or a public-facing job applicant site – Power Pages provides a faster path than coding from scratch.

Common HR use cases for Power Pages include:

- Employee Self-Service Portal: A one-stop HR portal for employees. This can include a knowledge base of HR FAQs and policies, a place to submit requests (like "Ask HR a question" or ticket logging), and links to other internal HR apps or resources. For example, an organization might create an HR portal where employees can *check their leave balance, download their latest pay slip, update personal information,* and read HR announcements – all in one website. This portal would be securely login-only (using work credentials via Entra ID) and can pull data from systems like D365 HR or SharePoint. The benefit is a consistent user experience: instead of emailing HR or navigating multiple systems, employees start at the portal. According to one overview, such Power Pages employee portals allow staff to access HR information, request time off, and update personal info easily, which streamlines HR processes and boosts employee satisfaction.

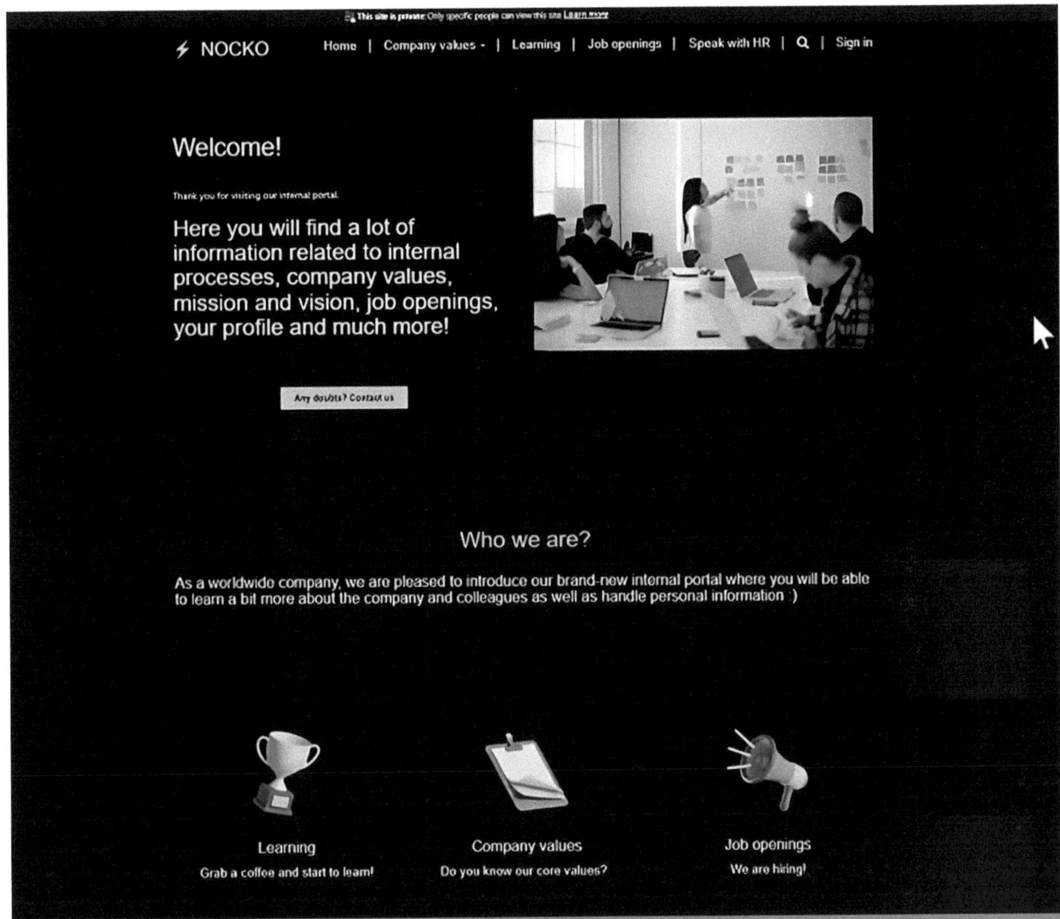

Figure 5-20. Employee self-service Power Portal

- Candidate or Onboarding Portal: External-facing site for job candidates or new hires. Imagine a "Candidate Portal" where applicants who have an offer can log in to complete pre-boarding tasks: fill out forms, read welcome materials, maybe start background checks. Power Pages can host this securely – new hires might authenticate with a personal email or a one-time code since they aren't in the company directory yet. This is more engaging than emailing PDFs back and forth. Similarly, a New Hire Onboarding portal could be public-facing where, after signing their contract, a new joiner can log in, see a welcome message from the CEO, find their orientation schedule, and complete HR paperwork. It creates a great first impression and reduces administrative overhead on Day 1.

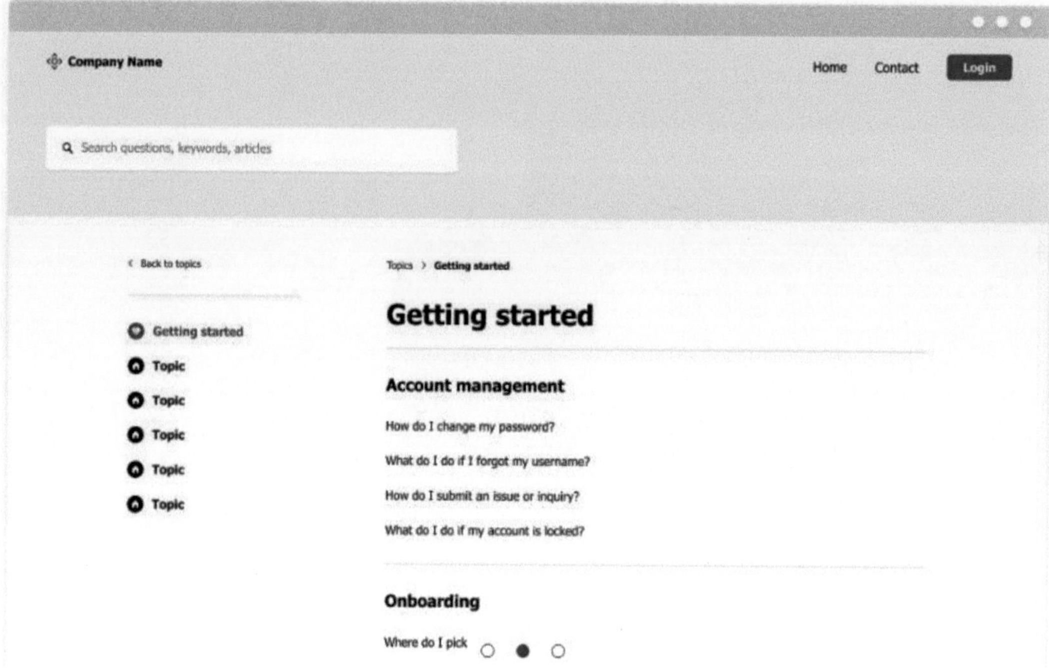

Figure 5-21. *Onboarding Power Portal*

- HR Community or Events Site: You might use Power Pages for things like a company career fair or wellness event sign-up site that both employees and maybe external partners can access. For instance, an internal job fair registration page where employees register for sessions – Power Pages can handle event registration forms and even payments, if needed (integrating with payment gateways). Or a Benefits Open Enrollment portal that walks employees (and perhaps spouses) through plan options with rich content and captures their selections (though this may integrate with other systems, Power Pages can provide the friendly front-end).

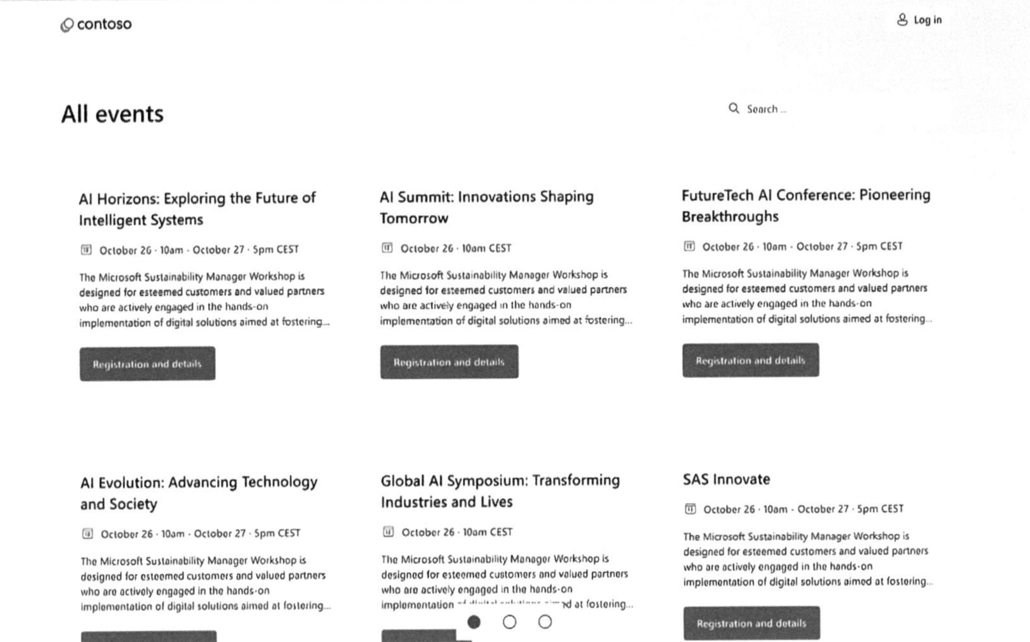

Figure 5-22. *Event Power Portal*

- Partner/Contractor Portal: Many organizations have extended workforce (contractors, vendors) who need access to certain HR-related information (like compliance training or time tracking). A Power Pages portal can be set up for these non-employees to log their hours, download policy docs, or complete mandatory trainings, without giving them full internal access. The portal can expose just what's needed from Dataverse or other systems in a controlled way.

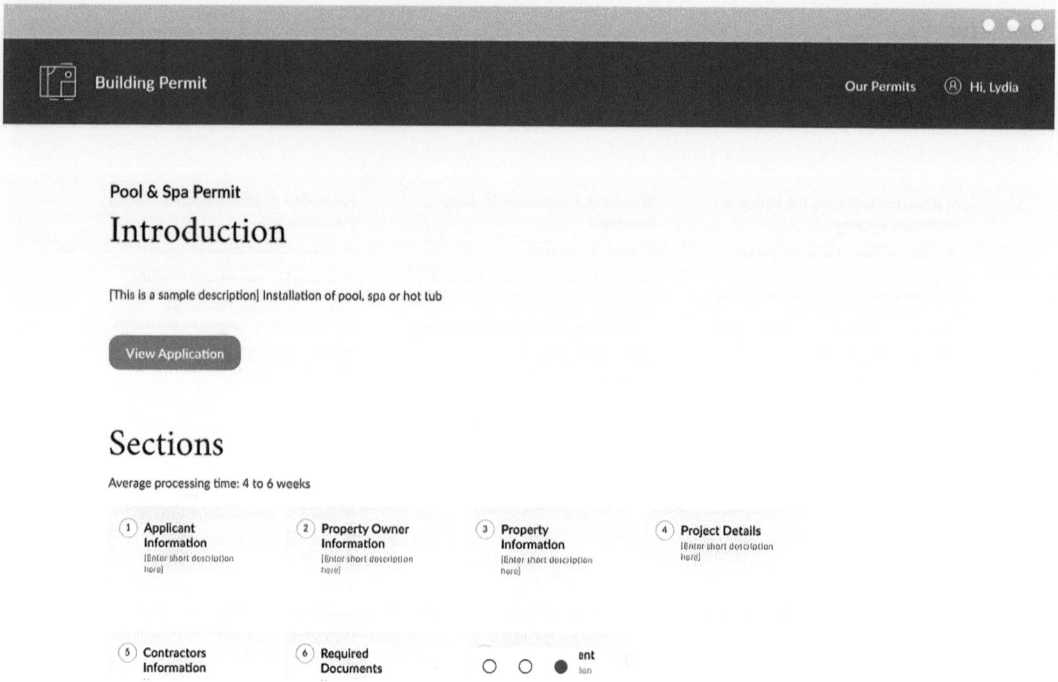

Figure 5-23. *Contractor Power Portal*

From a technical perspective, Power Pages is built on the same foundation as model-driven Power Apps (Dataverse). You design web pages, web forms, and use Dataverse tables for storing data collected from the portal (e.g., an "HR Questions" table for submitted inquiries). Under the hood, it's the evolution of what used to be called Power Apps Portals. It's designed to be more user-friendly with a new design studio for styling and layout, so HR or communications teams can have a role in designing the portal appearance (colors, images, text content) without coding. IT still plays a key role in setting up authentication, security roles, and integrating data.

Implementation Steps: Building an HR portal with Power Pages involves a mix of web design and app configuration. Here's how a team might go about it:

1. Define the Portal's Purpose and Audience: Clearly articulate what your portal will do and for whom. Is it internal (employees only) or external (candidates, former employees, public)? If internal, you'll likely use Microsoft Entra ID for login; if external, will users self-register or will HR invite them? For example, suppose HR wants an "HR Help Desk" portal where any employee can log in to submit HR questions and browse FAQs. The purpose is to reduce

repetitive questions coming to HR email and improve knowledge sharing. Audience: all employees. Knowing this, you'll design for authenticated internal users and focus on Q&A content and a support ticket form.

2. Plan the Structure and Content: Outline the site map – the pages and what goes on them. For an HR portal, you might have pages like "Knowledge Base" (with categorized FAQs), "My Requests" (showing the user's open HR cases or questions), "Forms & Docs" (downloads for common HR forms), and maybe "Contact HR." Engage HR content experts to gather the material (FAQs, documents, links) and decide how it should be organized. Also plan what interactive elements are needed: for example, a page for submitting a question (which likely ties to a Dataverse table of inquiries). Designing this on paper or a whiteboard first will save time.

3. Set Up Dataverse and Security: Work with IT to ensure you have a Power Platform environment with Dataverse ready. Define the data schema for any interactive elements. For instance, if building a "submit HR question" form, create a Dataverse table "HR Questions" with columns like Title, Details, Category, Employee, Status, Response, etc. If employees will log in with their work accounts, you can use their identity to link to their questions. Determine who in HR will manage the incoming data – those users might use a model-driven app or Power BI to view and answer the questions, so set up appropriate security roles (e.g., an HR Support role that can read/write the questions table). For external users (like a candidate portal), you'd configure contact records in Dataverse and set up authentication providers (like email, Microsoft Entra External ID, etc.) – a bit more complex, but manageable with IT's help.

4. Design the Portal in Power Pages Studio: Microsoft's Power Pages
    design studio lets you create pages visually. Start with a template,
    if one fits (there are starter layouts for things like scheduling, FAQ
    etc.), or start blank. Add text, images, and sections to match the
    structure planned. For dynamic content like lists of FAQs or forms
    for submission, you'll use Power Pages components: for example,
    add a *List* component connected to the FAQ Dataverse table to
    display questions and answers (you can allow searching, filtering),
    or add a *Form* component tied to the "HR Questions" table to
    let users submit new questions. Style the portal to align with
    company branding – add the company logo, use corporate colors,
    and ensure the design is clean and accessible (large enough fonts,
    etc.). This step is where a comms or design person can collaborate
    to make it look polished, while the HR/IT folks ensure the data
    bindings are correct.

5. Configure Authentication and Security on Pages: Decide which
    pages require login and who can see what. In our HR Help Desk
    example, the FAQ page could be public to any employee (since
    they log in anyway) and perhaps even indexed for search. The "My
    Requests" page should be restricted so users only see their own
    submissions – implement row-level filtering (Power Pages does
    this via *Web Roles* and table permissions; for example, assign all
    employees a web role that grants create/read on HR Questions
    where the contact equals their own login). Also, ensure HR staff
    have a secure way to view/respond to submissions – which could
    be via a separate secure page or by using a Power App internally.
    Power Pages allows creating an admin back-end, but often it's
    simpler that HR staff just use the model-driven app or Dynamics
    interface directly on the data. Test the login process: have a few
    employees log into a test site to confirm they can access and see
    only what they should.

6. Launch in Stages: Consider a soft launch or pilot. Perhaps open the portal to HR team members or a small department first to gather feedback. Check usage logs and ask pilot users: Could they find what they needed? Was the site intuitive? Did submissions go through okay? This feedback might lead to adjustments – maybe adding a missing FAQ, clarifying some instructions, or tweaking page layout for clarity. Once satisfied, roll out to the full audience. Communicate through company channels: for example, "Check out the new HR Portal – your 24/7 resource for HR questions and services!" Highlight top tasks they can do there (to entice usage).

7. Maintenance and Content Management: A portal is not a one-and-done – it requires content updates and oversight. Establish an owner (maybe someone in HR or HRIT) to keep the information fresh. If a policy changes, update the FAQ or document on the portal. Use metrics: Power Pages can integrate with analytics (like Azure Application Insights or even embed a Power BI web analytics dashboard) to see page views, search terms, etc. If employees frequently search the portal for "travel reimbursement policy" and get no results, that's a sign to add that content. Regularly review the incoming questions or usage patterns to continuously improve the portal's usefulness. Also, ensure security patches and platform updates are applied (Microsoft manages the infrastructure, but you should follow their recommendations for any changes needed).

Fictional Scenario – Power Pages in Action: *NOCKO Traders*, a global retail company, had a challenge with disseminating HR policy updates and answering employee FAQs across its 5,000 frontline workers. Many employees didn't have easy access to the corporate intranet while on the store floor, and HR was inundated with repetitive queries ("What's the holiday overtime policy?" "How do I update my bank info?"). NOCKO built an HR Central portal using Power Pages. Employees anywhere – even on their personal devices – can log in with their Microsoft account to access HR Central. The portal features a searchable knowledge base of 100+ Q&As, an announcement section for new policies, and an "Ask HR" form. Since launch, HR reports a 40% drop in basic HR inquiry emails, because employees find answers themselves on the portal. One interesting metric: the average time to resolve HR queries dropped from three days (waiting for email responses) to under one day, because questions are now routed and tracked through the portal's form, and HR can prioritize and respond faster (they set up an internal workflow to alert the HR team lead when a new question comes in, ensuring none get lost). Employees have reacted positively – especially those in different time zones or night shifts who can't call HR during normal hours. NOCKO's IT appreciated that Power Pages came with enterprise security, so they could allow personal smartphone access to the portal without exposing sensitive data publicly. This story underscores how a well-designed HR portal can boost efficiency and employee satisfaction by *making HR services more accessible.*

Exercise (Portal Planning Brainstorm): In a group or individually, sketch out a plan for an HR portal that would benefit your organization. Define:

- Purpose: For example, "Alumni Portal for retired employees to access benefits info" or "Campus Recruiting Portal for university grads to learn about our company and apply."

- Target Users: Who will use it and how will they log in? (Employees with company accounts, external users with email sign-up, etc.)

- Key Pages/Features: List 3–5 main pages and what each contains. For instance, "Home page with welcome text and navigation," "Jobs page where external users can see open positions and apply (perhaps linking to an external ATS)," "Contact page with a form to reach HR."

- Data/Integration Needs: Will you need to store data from the portal (like form submissions)? Will it pull data from an HR system (like showing a user their vacation balance from D365 HR)? Note any external systems to integrate.

- Security Considerations: Any confidential info? If so, how would you protect it?

After planning, discuss how you would implement this with Power Pages and what the impact might be. This exercise helps you think through the design of an HR portal step by step, even if you haven't actually built it yet. It's a crucial skill to align HR needs with Power Pages capabilities before diving into development.

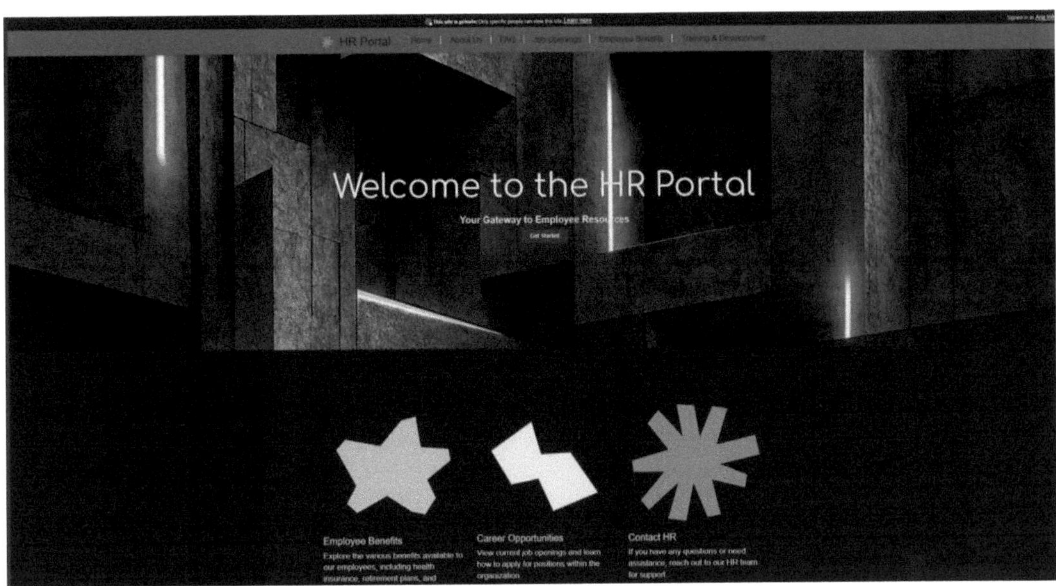

Figure 5-24. *Power Portal main screen*

Power BI: HR Analytics That Matter

Power BI brings data to life through interactive dashboards and reports, helping HR move from intuition-driven decisions to data-driven ones. With Power BI, HR leaders and analysts can consolidate data from various sources (HRIS, payroll, engagement surveys, etc.) and visualize key metrics in real time. Instead of static spreadsheets that are hard to parse, Power BI provides dynamic charts, graphs, and KPIs that answer pressing HR questions at a glance – and allows users to slice and drill down for deeper insight.

Every HR department has metrics it cares about. Some common HR dashboards and their typical insights include:

- Diversity and Inclusion Metrics: Monitor workforce diversity across various dimensions (gender, age, ethnicity, etc.) and by levels or roles. For instance, a dashboard could display the gender split by department or the trend of women in leadership over the last five years. If your organization has diversity targets, Power BI can show progress toward those (e.g., "We aimed for 50% female hires, we're currently at 45%"). These insights help HR ensure compliance with D&I goals and highlight areas for improvement.

159

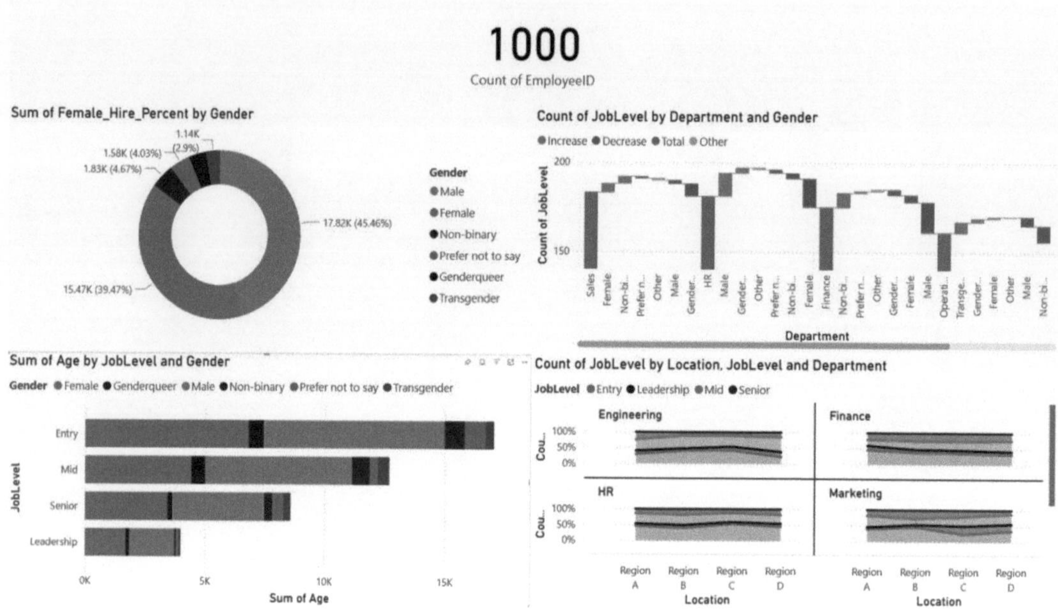

Figure 5-25. *Diversity and Inclusion metrics in Power BI*

- Headcount and Talent Movement: A report showing current
  headcount and how it changes with hires, promotions, transfers,
  and exits. Perhaps a visual "HR balance sheet" where each month
  you see how many joined, how many left, net change, and current
  total. Another visual might map internal mobility – how many people
  moved roles internally (which can be a health indicator of talent
  development). For larger firms, a *Sunburst* or Sankey diagram could
  even show flows of talent between departments (who is hiring from
  where internally).

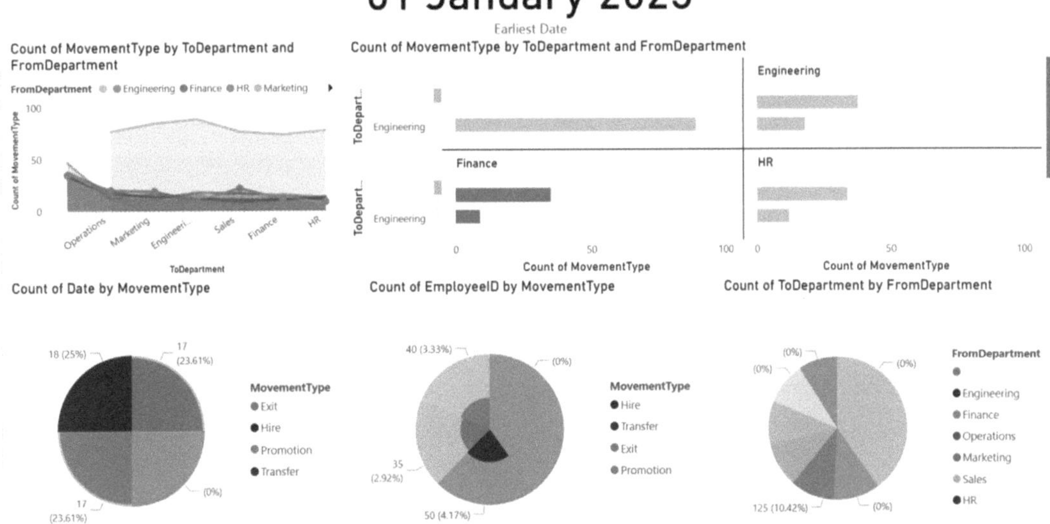

Figure 5-26. *Headcount and Talent Movement report in Power BI*

- Recruiting Effectiveness (Time-to-Hire): Measure how efficient the hiring process is. For example, average days to fill a position, broken down by department or by hiring stage (how long in screening vs. interviewing vs. offer). Bottleneck analysis: maybe the report reveals it takes an average of 20 days from requisition to first interview (too slow) or that offers are being rejected 30% of the time in a certain region. Visuals like funnel charts or segmented bar charts can identify at which stage candidates drop off. Having this data helps HR and recruiting leads target interventions (like streamlining interview processes or adjusting offers).

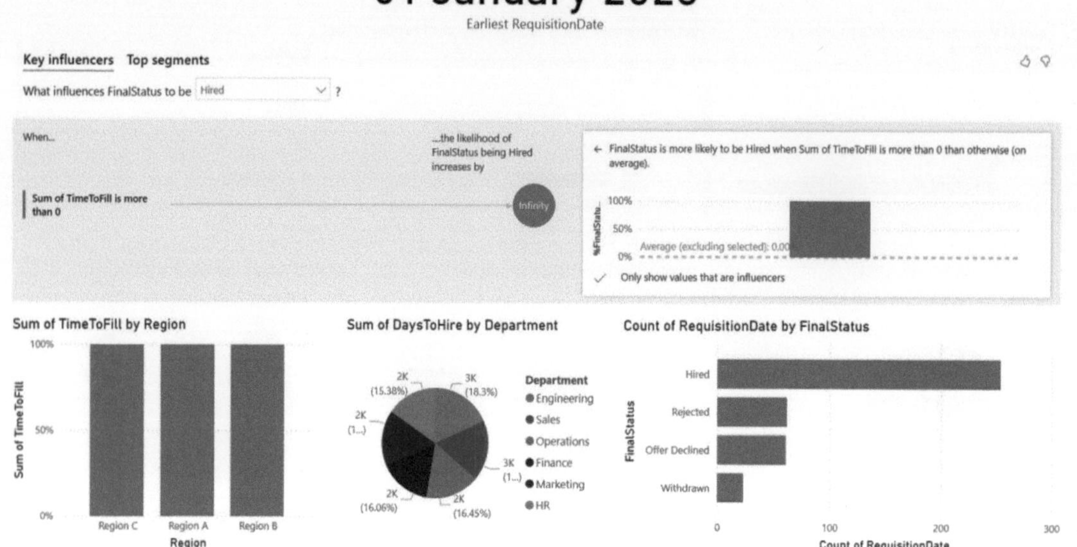

Figure 5-27. *Recruiting effectiveness report in Power BI*

- Training and Development Metrics: How many training hours
  per employee? Completion rates of mandatory courses? Is there a
  correlation between training and performance or promotion rates?
  A Power BI dashboard could combine LMS data with HR data to
  show, for example, that teams with higher average training hours
  have better retention. Or track certification completion by location,
  highlighting compliance in mandatory training.

These are just a few examples. The key is that Power BI answers questions. Before
building any report, it's crucial to ask: *"What decision will this inform or what behavior
will it change?"* For instance, an attrition dashboard is useful if it prompts managers to
act on retention strategies in hotspots.

Now, implementing Power BI for HR analytics:

Implementation Steps:

1. Data Identification and Collection: Determine what data you
   need for your chosen metrics, and where that data resides. HR
   data is often fragmented – some in the core HRIS (like employee
   profiles, salaries, positions), some in payroll systems, some in
   Excel sheets (like ad-hoc survey results), etc. List the data sources

(Dynamics 365 HR or other HRIS, ATS for recruiting, LMS for training, engagement survey tool, etc.). Work with IT or data analyst to establish connections. Power BI can directly connect to cloud systems via connectors (e.g., a Dynamics 365 connector, Oracle, SAP, etc.) or to files and databases. For example, connect to the HRIS for headcount and attrition data, to LinkedIn or an ATS for recruiting stats, and maybe to an Excel maintained by HR for mentorship program tracking. Ensure you have proper permissions to access and use this data – involving IT governance and data security teams as needed (especially if combining data across systems).

2. Data Modeling and Preparation: Often the hardest part. Bring the data into Power BI Desktop and model it – this means cleaning it (e.g., uniform date formats, consistent department names across systems) and relating tables (like linking an *employee table* with a *training records table* by Employee ID). You might create calculated columns or measures – for example, a measure for Turnover % = (# of exits in period)/(average headcount in period). Leverage Power Query to do transformations (like computing tenure in days from hire date, bucketing ages into ranges, etc.). A well-designed data model will make it easy to create visuals. If this sounds technical, note that Power BI has become more user-friendly, and Power Query's interface is mostly point-and-click for common tasks. Still, many HR teams partner with an analyst or take some training to get this right. It's worth it: a clean data model ensures your reports are accurate and update seamlessly.

3. Build Visualizations and Dashboards: Now the fun part – creating visuals that convey the insights. Start simple: maybe a line graph for attrition over time, a bar chart for attrition by department, and a card showing the current overall turnover %. Use slicers (filters) so users can slice data (e.g., filter everything by location or by employee tenure range). Make sure to follow data visualization best practices: choose appropriate chart types, label axes clearly, use colors consistently (perhaps the company's theme colors for style). The goal is an at-a-glance readability. Also consider adding

interactive elements: for example, clicking on a department in one chart could highlight that department's data across all visuals. HR leaders love when they can click on "Sales" and see every metric update for Sales. Keep each page of a report focused – one page might be "Workforce Diversity," another "Recruiting Funnel," etc., rather than overcrowding one page.

4. Implement Row-Level Security (RLS), if Needed: HR data is sensitive. Often, not everyone should see all data. You might restrict certain dashboards to HR leadership only. Or within a dashboard, use RLS so that, for instance, an HR Business Partner in Region A can only view data for Region A's employees. Power BI allows setting up roles and rules (like a filter: Region = "East" for the East HRBP role). This step is crucial for confidentiality (e.g., you don't want a manager accidentally seeing another department's salary or attrition figures, if that's not intended). Test RLS thoroughly by viewing as different roles. If dashboards are to be shared widely, aggregate the data enough to protect privacy (e.g., no personally identifiable info, just trends).

5. Publish and Share: Publish the report to the Power BI Service (cloud). From there, you can share it with specific users or groups (e.g., all HR managers). You might also embed the reports in Teams channels or SharePoint pages for convenience – for example, the HR team could have a Teams channel with an "Analytics" tab showing the live Power BI dashboard. Ensure those who get access know how to use it – maybe host a walkthrough meeting or short video to explain how to interact (slicers, drill-through, etc.). Often, giving a few example questions they can answer with the dashboard helps get people engaged (e.g., "This dashboard can tell you which department had the highest attrition last quarter – here's how to find that.").

6. Drive Action from Insights: Data is only useful if acted upon. As an HR leader, plan regular reviews of the dashboards. For instance, include key HR metrics in monthly leadership meetings via Power BI. Encourage managers to explore the data themselves by granting them access (with appropriate security). Some

organizations set up alerts (Power BI can email if a metric goes beyond a threshold – for example, turnover >10% in a month triggers an email to HR VP). Integrating analytics into decision-making processes solidifies its value. If the data shows a problem (like a spike in resignations in a team), have a process for HRBPs to follow up and address it.

7. Advanced Analytics and AI: Once foundational dashboards are in place, HR can leverage more advanced Power BI features and even AI. For example, Power BI's Quick Insights or AI visuals can detect anomalies (say, an unusual increase in sick leaves in a period) or provide key influencer analysis (what factors most influence engagement survey scores, etc.). Additionally, with the advent of Copilot in Power BI, even non-analysts can ask questions in natural language. An HR generalist could type "Show me attrition by manager for last year" and Power BI will generate a chart on the fly. This is powerful for ad-hoc questions without needing to create a whole new visual manually. It's like having a conversation with your HR data.

Fictional Scenario – Power BI in Action: *NOCKO Software* had a fast-growing workforce and a retention issue in their R&D department. The HR team deployed a Power BI dashboard for Attrition and Retention. Immediately, trends jumped out: the R&D attrition rate was 18% vs. company average of 10%. By drilling down, they saw most departures were employees with 2–3 years of tenure, and exit interviews (data brought in via text analysis in Power BI) frequently mentioned lack of career progression. These insights were presented to the CTO and engineering leaders. As a result, NOCKO introduced a formal mentorship and career path program in R&D. Over the next two quarters, attrition in that department fell to 12%, which was a significant improvement. The HR dashboard also revealed a positive correlation between employees taking at least five days of vacation and lower attrition – an unexpected insight that led the company to encourage managers to ensure their teams unplug (an example of analytics influencing culture). On the flip side, Power BI helped prove ROI of an initiative: NOCKO's HR had piloted a flexible work policy in one region, and the dashboard showed that region's engagement scores and retention improved compared to others – data they used to justify expanding the policy company-wide. This story illustrates how having the right HR data readily accessible can validate hunches or uncover issues that would otherwise remain hidden in spreadsheets. Many HR tech trends emphasize analytics – indeed, 46% of HR leaders say AI has boosted their analytics capabilities, and tools like Power BI are at the heart of that transformation.

Exercise (HR Data Dashboards): If you have access to sample HR data (or use a public dataset), try building a simple HR dashboard in Power BI:

- Use an example dataset like a CSV of employee attrition (there are sample datasets online with anonymous attrition info). Load it onto Power BI Desktop.

- Create a few visuals: perhaps a bar chart of attrition counts by department, a pie chart of attrition by reason (if data available), and a card showing overall % attrition.

- Add a slicer for gender or job role to see if attrition differs by those factors.

- Practice using the Q&A feature in Power BI: ask a question in the Q&A box like "average age of employees who left" (if age is in data) to see if Power BI can answer it.

- Discuss what the data is telling you. Can you identify a "story" (e.g., one department has much higher turnover)? What action might HR take in response?

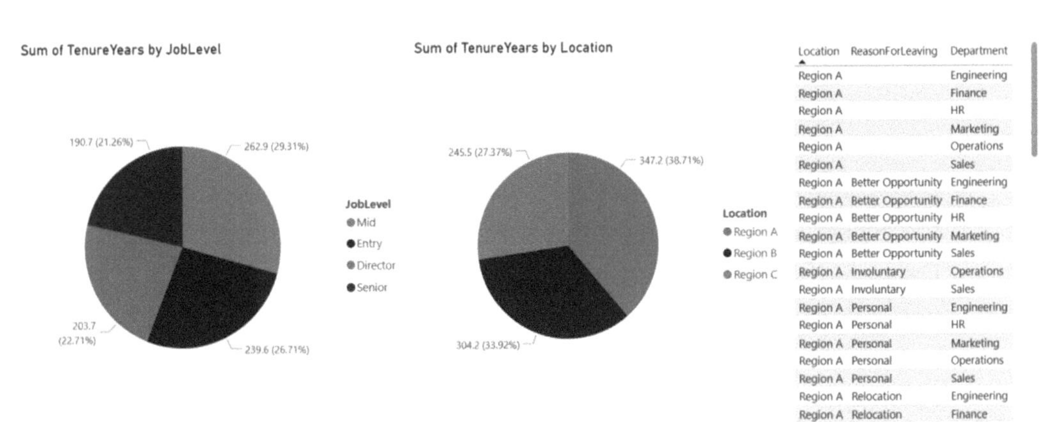

Figure 5-28. *Recruiting effectiveness report in Power BI*

This hands-on exercise helps demystify HR analytics. You'll see that with the right data, Power BI lets you explore and gain insights quickly, even if you're not a data scientist. It underlines the importance of both data quality and thoughtful visualization to support HR decision-making.

Copilot Studio: Conversational HR Agents (Former Power Virtual Agents)

Copilot Studio (formerly known as Power Virtual Agents, PVA) enables HR teams to create intelligent chatbots and AI assistants – effectively, a digital "HR front desk" that can engage with employees in natural language. These HR bots can be deployed in multiple channels: as a chat app in Microsoft Teams, on the company's intranet or HR portal (built with Power Pages, for example), or even on a public-facing website for candidates. They provide 24/7 self-service, handling common queries or tasks so that HR staff don't have to answer the same questions over and over.

What kinds of things can an HR chatbot do? Here are some example HR bot scenarios and their typical capabilities:

- Onboarding Assistant: A bot that welcomes new hires and answers their questions during the onboarding process. For instance, a new employee can ask, "When is my orientation session?" or "How do I set up direct deposit?" and the bot will respond with the relevant info (pulling from a knowledge base or the HRIS). It might also *guide* the newcomer through onboarding steps, like "Step 1: Complete your profile. Step 2: Upload your ID documents..." Integration examples: the bot could fetch the new hire's start date or manager's name from Dataverse (which might store employee data), or provide links to policy documents stored in SharePoint. This kind of bot ensures new hires feel supported and reduces the volume of basic questions to the HR team.

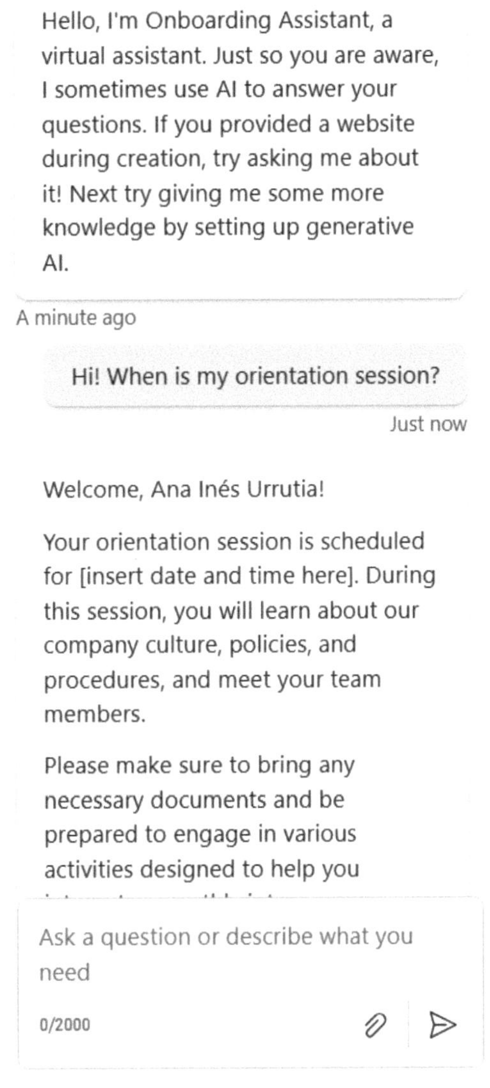

Figure 5-29. *Onboarding Assistant Copilot Studio*

- Time-Off FAQ Bot: Many HR teams field daily questions about vacation balance, leave policies, holidays, etc. A bot in Teams could answer questions like "How many vacation days do I have left?" by securely looking up the user's leave balance from the HR system.

It can also handle policy questions ("What is our parental leave policy?") by retrieving answers from an FAQ database or SharePoint. Integration: connecting to Dynamics 365 HR's Leave & Absence module for balances, or to the user's Outlook calendar to possibly suggest dates. This offloads a huge chunk of repetitive Q&A from HR staff – employees get instant answers any time.

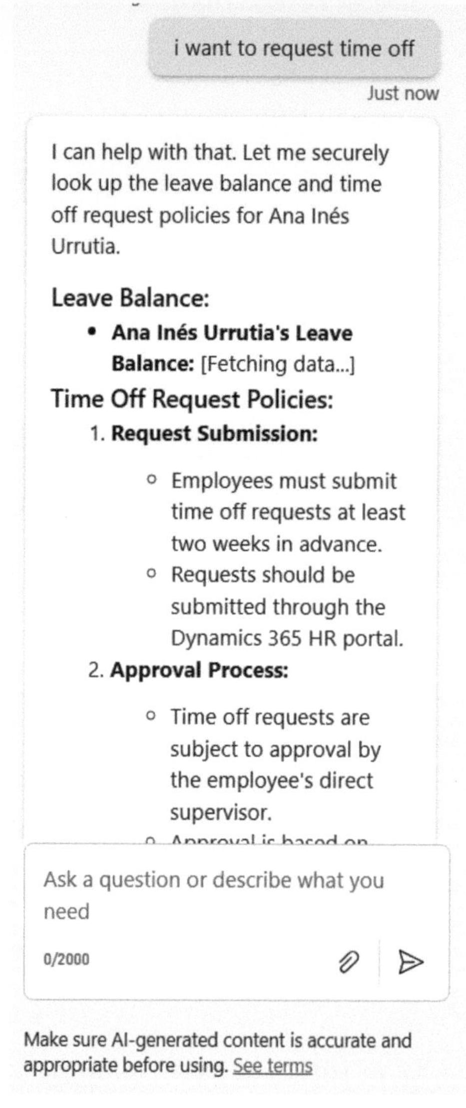

Figure 5-30. *Time-Off FAQ agent*

- Exit Interview Bot: When employees leave, gathering honest feedback is valuable. An Exit bot can conversationally ask a departing employee a series of questions about their experience, why they're leaving, what could be improved, etc. Because it's a bot, some employees might feel more comfortable sharing than in a live interview. The bot records their responses (both structured choices and open text) and stores them, say, in a Dataverse table or SharePoint list. It could also trigger sentiment analysis (with AI Builder) on the comments to categorize them (e.g., common theme: "lack of growth"). HR can then review these insights collectively. Integration: use Power Automate within the bot to, for example, send a summary of the exit feedback to the HRBP or log a ticket if the employee requests a follow-up.

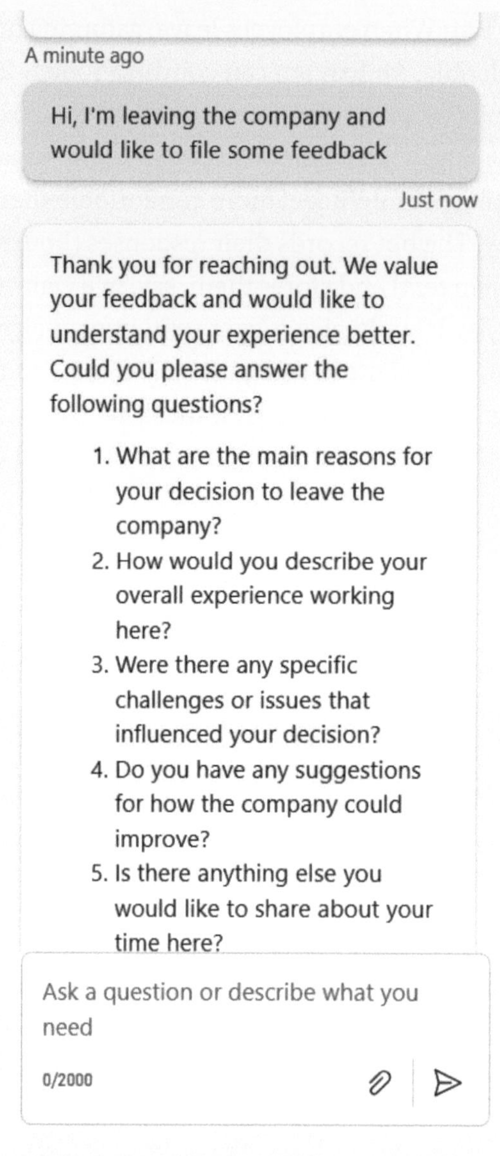

Figure 5-31. *Exit interview agent*

- Recruiting Status Bot: For hiring managers or even candidates, a bot could be used to check the status of open positions or applications. A hiring manager might ask, "How many candidates have applied to the Software Engineer position?" and the bot can retrieve data from the Applicant Tracking System or Dynamics 365 HR recruiting data. A candidate (external scenario) might ask, "Has a decision been made on my application?" with appropriate security (likely this would require an authenticated portal + bot scenario). This reduces the need for recruiters to manually update each manager or candidate.

- HR Policies and Compliance Bot: A bot that quizzes or guides employees on certain HR procedures. For example, a "Travel Policy Assistant" where an employee says, "I'm traveling to London, what's the meal reimbursement limit?" and the bot gives the answer. Or a "COVID Protocol Bot" where employees can ask about latest guidelines. These bots essentially serve as interactive policy manuals.

The power of Copilot Studio is that you don't need to be a coder to build these chatbots. Using a no-code graphical interface, HR professionals can define conversation topics, trigger phrases, and bot responses. You can incorporate decision trees (if user says X, go down that path) and integrate with other systems via Power Automate actions called "Bot Framework Skills" or using pre-built connectors.

And now with AI and Copilot capabilities built into Agents, creating and enhancing bots is even easier. For example, the new Copilot in bot-building allows you to simply *describe* what the bot should do, and it will generate topics and suggestions. You might tell the Copilot: *"Our employees often ask about expense reimbursement. Build a topic where if someone asks about expense policy or reimbursement procedure, the bot explains the process and can send them a PDF of our expense policy."* The AI would then create a draft topic with trigger phrases like "expense reimbursement," an answer pulling from existing content or a placeholder, and an action that shares a link to the policy PDF. You can then refine the wording or connections. This natural language approach can reduce bot development time dramatically, and it's great for HR folks who know the content well but aren't comfortable with bot frameworks.

Implementation Steps:

1. Identify Top Use Cases for a Bot: Don't try to make one bot do everything initially. Pick 1–2 high-volume or high-impact use cases. A good way to find these is to ask: "What questions or requests does HR get *all the time*?" or "Where do employees experience delays in getting info from HR?" Often, FAQs around leaves, benefits, and policies are low-hanging fruit. Alternatively, a

bot for new hires (since they have lots of predictable questions) is a popular starting point. Define the scope: for example, *"We want a bot that answers the top 20 HR FAQs and can handle checking leave balances."* Give your bot a friendly persona/name aligned with your company culture (like "HR Helper" or "AskHR Bot").

2. Prepare Content and Backend: Gather the knowledge the bot will need. This might be an FAQ document, policy manuals, or a Q&A list. Power Virtual Agents has an option to ingest an FAQ page or document to create a knowledge base – a great starting point. Also, set up any integrations needed. For a leave balance inquiry, you'll need a connection to your HR data. This could be done by creating a Power Automate flow that the bot calls: for example, a flow that takes an employee ID and returns their leave balance from the HR system. Get those pieces ready (the IT support here is to create any needed connectors or flows, and ensure data access is secure).

3. Use Copilot Studio to Build the Bot: In Copilot Studio (the updated interface for PVA), you'll create a new bot. The interface will let you define Topics. Each Topic is a dialog path, usually triggered by certain phrases. For example, a "Vacation Balance" topic triggered by phrases like "how many days off do I have," etc. Copilot can assist by suggesting topics if you feed it your FAQs or just by you typing "create a topic for vacation balance inquiry" – it may then prompt you to connect to a data source to fetch the answer. Design the conversation in a natural, friendly tone: welcome the user's question, present the info, maybe ask if they need anything else. Use bot variables to personalize (the bot can greet the user by name if integrated with Teams, e.g., "Hi Sam, happy to help with your question about time off."). For more complex processes, use the Power Automate integration: for example, if the user wants to *book time off*, the bot could trigger a flow to actually submit a leave request on their behalf – making the bot not just informational but transactional.

4. Test the Bot Thoroughly: Use the built-in test chat window to try various phrasings that employees might use. Ensure the bot understands them (the AI will match them to the right topic if phrases overlap, but you might need to add alternate phrasing). Check that the bot's answers are correct and up-to-date. Nothing will kill trust in the bot faster than it giving wrong info ("It told me I have 5 days left when I really had 10" – that'd be problematic). So test edge cases: what if the system it needs is down? (You might program the bot to respond, "Sorry, I can't retrieve that right now, please try again later"). Also, intentionally ask some unrelated or tricky questions to see how the bot handles it. Good bots have a default fallback: if it doesn't understand, it says so and perhaps offers options or a way to contact a human ("I'm sorry, I'm not able to answer that. Do you want me to connect you with an HR team member?").

5. Deploy to Your Channels: Decide where employees will interact with this bot. A very popular option is Microsoft Teams – you can publish the bot as a Teams app (like "AskHR Chatbot") and make it available to all users or specific groups. Employees can then converse with it just as they would message a colleague. Another channel is your intranet or Power Pages portal: you can embed the bot as a chat widget on an HR page ("Chat with HR Bot"). For external use (like a candidate site), you could embed it on a website. Copilot Studio allows multichannel publishing easily. When deploying, also plan some promotion – let people know this new resource exists. HR can send an announcement, "Got HR questions? Try asking our new HR bot in Teams!" Possibly provide examples of what to ask to encourage usage.

6. Monitor Bot Performance and Train: After deployment, use the analytics provided by Copilot Studio. You can see metrics like how many sessions occurred, what questions were asked, where the bot failed to provide an answer, etc. This is gold for improvement. For instance, if you see many users asking "Can I carry over my PTO to next year?" and the bot wasn't handling it initially, you can quickly create or tweak a topic to cover that.

Continual learning: update the bot's knowledge as policies change or as new questions come up. Treat it like onboarding a new HR team member – it needs ongoing training. Also monitor the user satisfaction if you include that (some bots ask at the end "Did I answer your question?"). If many say "no," investigate why – maybe the answers need more detail or clarity.

7. Hand-off and Escalation Plan: Design your bot experience to smoothly hand over to a human when needed. No matter how good the bot is, some queries will require human intervention (complex cases or simply a user who prefers a person). You can integrate the bot with Teams chat for HR or with your ticketing system. For example, if the user types "talk to a person" or if they are unsatisfied, the bot can offer: "I'm connecting you to an HR representative." This could create a ticket in the HR helpdesk system via Power Automate, or even directly tag an HR team channel for someone to step in. It's important employees don't feel *stuck* with a bot. Make it an augment, not a barrier.

Fictional Scenario – HR Bot in Action: *Litware,* a tech company of 1,200 employees, implemented an "HR Copilot" chatbot in Teams. Initially, it was set up to answer around 50 frequent questions (covering benefits, leave, office policies) and to handle a couple of tasks like checking vacation balances and helping employees find the status of their open HR tickets. Within the first month, the HR Copilot was used by 600 employees, with over 1,500 questions asked. HR noticed that one of the top queries was "How do I refer a candidate for a job?" which the bot hadn't been specifically programmed for. Seeing this in the logs, they quickly added a new topic guiding users to the employee referral portal and explaining the process. The next month, that topic handled dozens of inquiries that would've otherwise come to HR email. Litware's HR team estimates the bot resolved about 70% of Tier-1 HR queries without human intervention. That freed up the HR operations team to focus on more complex issues and proactive projects (they jokingly say the bot is like their new team member). One new hire gave feedback: "I love the HR chat – at my last company I had to wait two days for an email reply about setting up my 401k; here I got the answer from the bot in 10 seconds at 9 PM." This illustrates how a well-implemented conversational agent can significantly improve response times and employee experience. It's also a clear win for HR efficiency – less time on email, more on meaningful work.

Exercise (Design a Mini HR Chatbot): Even if you don't fully build a bot, you can go through the design thought process:

- Pick a simple HR topic (e.g., Paid Time Off policy).

- Write down 3–5 things an employee might ask about it in natural language ("How do I request PTO?" "How much PTO do we get per year?" "Does PTO carry over?").

- For each question, craft a concise answer as if you were the bot.

- Think of one action the bot could help with on this topic (e.g., "submit a PTO request" via integration – you won't build it now, just conceptualize it).

- Now, if you have access to Power Virtual Agents (even a trial), try creating a topic with those trigger phrases and have the bot respond with your answers. Test it in the demo chat to see if it works.

- If no access, simply role-play with a partner: one is the user asking questions, one is the "bot" answering with the scripted answers. This highlights if the answers are clear and if there are variations of questions you didn't anticipate.

This exercise teaches you how to structure a bot's knowledge and flow. It emphasizes understanding user intent and delivering information conversationally. You'll appreciate the nuance of how people ask questions and how a bot needs to be prepared to handle variations – which is exactly what Copilot Studio's AI helps with in real implementations.

Power Platform Across the Employee Life Cycle

One of the strengths of the Power Platform is how its components can interconnect to support every stage of the employee life cycle in a holistic way. Rather than seeing Power Automate, Power Apps, etc., as isolated tools, leading HR IT teams use them together to create seamless experiences. Let's map a few life cycle stages to Power Platform solutions to illustrate this end-to-end synergy:

Employee life cycle stage	Example solution	Power platform tools
Hiring (pre-boarding)	*Candidate Portal:* A site for new hires (after they've accepted offers) to complete forms, read welcome materials, and get a head start before Day 1. This might let them input personal data, sign policies, and learn about company culture.	Power Pages (external portal for candidates) + SharePoint or Dataverse (to store submitted forms) + Power Automate (to notify recruiters/HR of completion)
Onboarding (day 1–90)	*Onboarding Task Orchestration:* When a new hire is added to the HR system, automatically trigger and coordinate all onboarding tasks – IT account setup, equipment provisioning, scheduling orientation sessions, sending the new hire a welcome app, and reminding the manager to complete their onboarding checklist.	Power Automate (workflow automation across IT, Facilities, and HR systems) + Power Apps (a new hire onboarding checklist app for the employee and manager)
Development and training	*Learning Tracker:* An app and dashboard for employees to track their training and for HR to monitor development plans. Employees can see courses completed, get recommendations for next courses (perhaps using AI), and managers can view their team's progress. HR can analyze skills gaps.	Power Apps (for the user interface of the tracker) + Power BI (dashboard for HR to analyze learning data) + optionally AI Builder (to recommend courses based on role/skill)

(continued)

Employee life cycle stage	Example solution	Power platform tools
Engagement and well-being	*Pulse Survey Automation:* Automatically send out a short "pulse" survey to employees every quarter, then aggregate and analyze sentiment. Say 5 questions on a Forms or custom app, results are compiled and an AI model summarizes text feedback. HR can quickly gauge morale and engagement regularly.	Microsoft Forms (or a Power Apps survey form) + Power Automate (to distribute and collect results) + AI Builder or AI in Power BI (perform sentiment or keyword analysis on open-ended feedback) + Power BI (visualize the trends in engagement over time)
Offboarding	*Exit Process and Insights:* An exit chatbot (as described earlier) to conduct exit interviews and a structured offboarding checklist app. The bot gathers qualitative feedback; meanwhile, flows ensure all access removal and exit formalities happen. Finally, a report compiles exit data for analysis.	Copilot Studio (PVA bot to interview the leaving employee and answer questions about last paycheck, benefits, etc.) + Power Automate (to trigger IT tasks like disabling accounts, send farewell info) + Dataverse (store exit survey results) + Power BI (dashboard of exit reasons and trends)

In this way, from a candidate's first interaction with your company to the day an employee departs, the Power Platform can enhance the experience and efficiency. Automation ensures no step is forgotten (every new hire gets their equipment on time), apps give employees and managers easy access to what they need (no hunting through emails for forms), analytics provide insights at each juncture (spotting trends in hiring or exits early), and AI-driven tools add intelligence (predicting attrition, personalizing learning, etc.). For HR, it means a more proactive, well-managed life cycle; for employees, it often translates to a smoother journey with a digitally savvy employer.

Importantly, these solutions don't necessarily replace your core HR systems (like your HRIS or ATS); they *extend* them. The Power Platform acts as a flexible layer to adapt processes quickly. For example, if the business introduces a new mentorship program, instead of customizing the HRIS, HR can quickly spin up a Power App for mentorship enrollment and track outcomes in Power BI. This agility is crucial in modern

HR – as strategies change (think about the sudden shift to remote work in 2020, or new health checks during pandemic), being able to stand up new processes in days is a game-changer.

Governance and Sustainability

Adopting the Power Platform in HR brings tremendous capability, but it also requires strong governance to ensure solutions remain sustainable, secure, and compliant over the long term. Without guardrails, well-intentioned apps or flows could turn into maintenance burdens or even security risks. HR data is sensitive by nature, so governance is not optional – it's mandatory. Here are key governance practices and tips for HR applications of Power Platform:

- Environment Strategy: Set up dedicated Power Platform environments for different purposes (Development, Testing, Production for HR apps). For instance, you might have *HR-Dev* (where HR and IT experiment and build initial versions of apps/ flows), *HR-Test* (where you test with realistic data or do user acceptance testing), and *HR-Prod* (the live environment everyone uses). This separation means you can develop and break things in Dev without impacting users, and only promote to Prod when ready. Use managed Solutions to move apps/flows from Dev to Test to Prod in a controlled way – this packages all components and helps with version control. Having an HR-specific Production environment also allows you to apply HR-specific policies (discussed below) to just that environment.

- Data Loss Prevention (DLP) Policies: Power Platform DLP policies let admins control which connectors can be used together, to prevent data from leaking from secure systems to non-approved services. For HR, define a DLP policy that marks all HR and corporate systems as "Business" data (e.g., SharePoint, Dataverse, Office 365 Outlook, Azure SQL, maybe Workday or other HR system connectors) and marks personal or consumer services as "Non-Business" (e.g., Twitter, Gmail connectors). Then enforce that flows/apps in the HR environment cannot mix Business and Non-Business data.

For example, block any attempt to send HR data to social media or personal email connectors. This safeguards against someone accidentally (or maliciously) creating a flow that exports employee info to an unapproved location. Also consider Tenant-wide policies if HR data exists in other environments.

- Security Roles and Access Control: Ensure only the right people can create or edit HR solutions. Typically, you'd give the core HR IT team *Maker* permissions in the HR Dev environment and maybe some power users in HR as well after training. The Production environment should be locked down – most HR staff would only have *User* roles to use the apps, but not modify them. Manage permissions for data sources too: for example, if an app uses Dataverse tables with employee data, configure table permissions such that an HR user sees all data, but a manager only sees their team's data (if that app is manager-facing). This often involves aligning with your Microsoft Entra ID roles or D365 HR security roles. Regularly review who has access to what – especially if people change jobs. The principle of least privilege is your friend.

- Ownership and Life Cycle Management: Every app or flow should have clear owners – typically one business owner (HR side, accountable for ensuring the solution meets the process need) and one technical owner (IT or a technical HR analyst, responsible for maintaining the solution). Document these owners somewhere, even within the app (e.g., an "About" screen or description field). Also document what the solution does, what data it touches, and any known limitations. This helps if someone new has to take over support. Additionally, implement a process for change management: for example, if HR wants to update an app (add a new field to a form), they coordinate with IT to do it in Dev, test, then update Prod. Treat major Power Platform solutions like enterprise systems: test changes thoroughly and require approval before going live.

- Monitoring and Analytics: Use the Power Platform Admin Center and/or Center of Excellence (CoE) toolkit to monitor usage of HR apps and flows. Set up alerts for things like: when someone creates a new flow in the HR environment (so the platform admin can review if it's compliant), if a flow has failures, or if a certain connector is being used in the HR environment for the first time. Microsoft's CoE Starter Kit provides a dashboard that shows all apps, who's using them, etc. For HR, this oversight is important to prevent sprawl and to catch any issues early. For example, if an HR flow suddenly starts failing due to an API change, you might catch it in the admin logs even before users report a problem.

- Compliance and Audit: Check if any regulatory requirements apply to data handled by your Power Platform solutions (GDPR, HIPAA for health data in HR, etc.). Ensure you have retention policies for data (maybe you auto-delete Power Automate run history or certain app data after X time, if not needed). All user activities in Power Apps/Flows can be logged via Microsoft 365 Audit Log – make sure this is on, and you know how to retrieve logs if needed (e.g., to investigate who accessed or changed something in an HR app). Auditing is a big plus for these tools – you can demonstrate controls in place during audits by showing DLP policies, environment strategies, and logs of changes.

By instituting these governance measures, HR can confidently innovate with low-code tools while still protecting sensitive data and maintaining reliability. It's a balance of empowerment and control. The good news is Microsoft provides the tech capabilities to enforce most of these (unlike shadow IT where things might be totally uncontrolled). It's up to the HR IT leadership to design and enforce governance from day one. Perhaps create an "HR Power Platform Governance Charter" that outlines all the above for your organization – so everyone is on the same page about how HR apps are developed and managed.

A quick example: *NOVAX's HR team* built a great Recruitment app with Power Apps. Without governance, there was a risk that someone might build another redundant app or mishandle data. But NOVAX established that all HR apps must reside in the controlled HR-Prod environment, and only approved HR makers can publish. They also set a DLP policy preventing any flows in HR-Prod from using Dropbox or other non-approved storage. One day, a well-meaning HR employee tried to build a flow to save org charts to their personal Dropbox – the platform blocked it due to DLP, and the incident was logged. The HR IT team guided them to an approved solution using SharePoint instead. This story shows governance in action: it didn't stifle innovation (the employee had a creative idea) but channeled it safely.

AI and Copilot Enhancements for HR

As we've touched on throughout, the Power Platform is continually expanding its AI capabilities. Microsoft's vision of "AI as a copilot" is becoming reality in HR workflows. New Copilot features are embedding generative AI into the tools, helping HR teams build solutions faster and get insights more easily. Let's recap some of the ways Copilot and AI enhance the HR Power Platform experience:

- Copilot in Power Apps: This allows HR professionals (even those with no coding background) to auto-generate app screens and data models by describing their needs in natural language. For example, an HR specialist could type something like, "Create an app to track employee equipment requests, with a form for employees to request laptops or monitors and a view for IT to mark items as delivered." Copilot can interpret that and scaffold an app – creating a Dataverse table for Equipment Requests with fields (employee name, item, status, etc.), generating a basic form screen and a list screen. The HR specialist instantly gets a working prototype to refine, instead of starting from scratch. This dramatically shortens development time and lowers the expertise required to initiate an app. HR teams can thus prototype solutions on their own, then ask IT to polish or enhance security as needed. It makes app development a conversation rather than a laborious design task.

- Copilot in Power BI: This enables conversational data analysis. Instead of dragging fields and building charts manually, an HR analyst can simply ask questions in plain English and Copilot will create the visualization or report. For example, they might ask, "Which department has the highest six-month attrition rate among employees under 30?" and Copilot will query the data and produce a chart with the answer. It's like having a data analyst on call – the HR user focuses on *what* they want to know, not *how* to write a formula for it. This not only saves time but makes analytics more accessible to HR business partners or managers who may not be Power BI experts. They can interact with data through Q&A and get instant insights. The result: more people in HR can leverage data without intensive training, and can do so in real time during meetings or strategy sessions to inform decisions.

- Copilot in Copilot Studio: When building chatbots, Copilot assists in designing conversation logic using *plain language instructions.* For example, an HR bot creator could write, "If the user mentions a payroll issue, transfer them to the Finance bot or, if unavailable, create a ticket for the payroll team." The Copilot will interpret this request and set up the chatbot's flow accordingly – essentially writing the if/then branching logic for you. This is powerful because crafting a good chatbot conversation can be complex; Copilot helps ensure you don't miss important triggers or hand-offs. Additionally, Copilot can generate suggested topics from existing HR documents. You could feed in your employee handbook PDF, and it might propose topics like "Leave Policy Question" with content extracted. This jump-starts bot creation, leaving HR to fine-tune the answers. We've already discussed how Copilot can generate topics for FAQs – it's worth emphasizing how much faster bot building becomes. An HR team could stand up a new bot in days, not weeks, when leveraging AI suggestions.

- AI Builder Models and Natural Language Training: While not branded "Copilot," the integration of AI Builder with natural language deserves mention. HR folks can now train AI models (for predictions, classifications) by describing the outcome they want. For example, rather than manually selecting algorithms and features, an HR analyst could say, "Predict which employees are at risk of leaving based on their tenure, performance rating, and recent manager changes." The system understands that and helps configure a binary classification model. This means advanced analytics like attrition risk scoring, resume screening, sentiment analysis of comments, etc., become more reachable for HR departments that don't have data scientists. The AI does the heavy lifting under the hood.

- Business Process Automation with AI: Even in Power Automate, Copilot can suggest optimizations or next steps in a flow. Microsoft is introducing features where the flow can call GPT-based services for intelligent decisions – for example, analyzing text of an email and routing it based on content. For HR, an example might be automatically categorizing incoming HR helpdesk emails (benefits vs. payroll vs. employee relations) using AI, then triggering the right flow for each category.

In essence, these AI-driven enhancements mean HR solutions can be created and used with more ease and intelligence than ever. Natural language generation and understanding shrink the development cycle and make tools more intuitive. An HR generalist can literally "chat" with the system to build something or get an answer, rather than needing deep technical skills.

To illustrate, consider an HR intern who has never used Power BI – with Copilot, they can type, "Show me a chart of how many people joined each department this year" and get a result, then say "break it down by month" and see a trend. She's doing analysis from day one, without knowing DAX or data modeling. Or imagine a small-business HR manager who can now spin up a simple PTO tracking app by telling Copilot what they need, instead of spending days in Excel.

This democratization of development and analysis is a huge force multiplier for HR teams. It helps them be self-sufficient in solving problems and exploring data. And importantly, it injects AI into everyday HR processes: not as a futuristic concept but as embedded features that assist with the *boring stuff* (like writing formulas or routing messages) so HR pros can focus on human-centric work and strategy.

The Next Frontier: Project "Sophia" and AI Business Agents

Looking ahead, Microsoft is pioneering new AI-first experiences that could further revolutionize HR workflows. A prime example is Project "Sophia," which Microsoft refers to as an AI-powered *business research agent*. While still in preview, Project Sophia represents a next-generation approach to analyzing and interacting with business data in a very human way. It's like having a super-smart business analyst that you converse with in natural language across all your systems.

What is Project Sophia exactly? It's described as an AI-powered research canvas where you can ask any business question across domains and get guided, data-driven answers. It aims to help users solve complex, cross-functional business problems by allowing them to interact with data in new, conversational ways. Think of it as a mashup of Power BI, ChatGPT, and an analyst's brain – all in one interface. You pose a question, and Sophia can pull together data, generate charts, and even recommend next questions to ask. It's not limited to one dataset; it can reach across many (assuming they're connected and permissions allow) to find insights.

In an HR context, imagine what this could do. Today, you might use Power BI for known metrics, but suppose the CEO asks an unanticipated question like, *"Is there any correlation between our sales team's performance and their engagement survey scores or training hours?"* A complex, cross-domain query. With traditional tools, HR would have to collaborate with the data team to combine HR data, sales performance data, training records, etc., and run analysis – possibly weeks of work. In the vision of Project Sophia, you could ask this question in the canvas, and the AI agent would comb through connected data sources (sales results, engagement survey data, LMS, HRIS) to see if a relationship exists. It might generate a chart showing that teams with higher engagement scores indeed tend to meet sales targets more often, and suggest "It looks like engagement might impact performance. Perhaps explore attrition rates as well?" – guiding you to deeper insight.

Another scenario: during workforce planning, an HR leader could ask, *"What skills gaps do we have in our engineering department relative to industry trends?"* Sophia might integrate internal skills data (from LinkedIn or HR records) and external data (maybe job market data, which Microsoft's WorkLab or LinkedIn could feed) to answer. It could produce an output like: "Your engineering team is under-indexed in AI/ML skills compared to the industry average. 15% of engineers have AI skills vs. 27% industry-wide. Suggest investing in upskilling or hiring in that area."

Project Sophia essentially *contextualizes AI as a business advisor*. For HR, this could mean faster strategy formulation, more agile decision-making, and the ability to answer leadership's tough questions on the fly with data. It might also break down silos – for instance, linking HR metrics to business outcomes (showing how employee engagement influences customer satisfaction or how training impacts product quality).

We should note that Project Sophia is in preview and not widely available yet (as of this writing, limited to certain regions and scenarios). But it signals where things are heading: AI Business Agents that can span across Dynamics 365, Office 365, and other systems. Microsoft sometimes calls these *Business Copilots*. The idea is you won't need to pull reports from five systems and correlate – you'll ask the AI and it will do that heavy lifting, presenting you an answer with explanations.

For HR leaders and digital transformation directors, keeping an eye on Project Sophia is worthwhile. It represents the convergence of AI, big data, and user-friendly design. If it matures, HR might use it for tasks like:

- Quickly researching "What drives voluntary turnover in my company?" with answers gleaned from exit surveys, engagement data, and manager feedback notes.

- Simulating scenarios: "If we increase our engineering headcount by 10% next year, what does historical data suggest about recruiting lead time and cost?" – Sophia could analyze past hiring rates, capacity, and budget spend to project whether that's feasible or if constraints will arise.

- Answering board-level questions in real time: *"How has our employee demographic changed over the past 5 years and how might that impact our management training needs?"* – In a meeting, an HR exec could use Sophia to generate a quick report on the fly.

In summary, Project Sophia and similar AI business agents point to a future where interacting with data is as natural as having a conversation, and where AI doesn't just surface data but helps interpret and connect the dots across domains. For HR, which is inherently cross-functional (people affect every part of the business), this could be transformative. It aligns perfectly with the theme of HR becoming more strategic: if mundane tasks are automated and data analysis is turbocharged by AI, HR professionals can focus on higher-order work – culture, talent strategy, leadership development – armed with better insights.

As you implement Power Platform solutions today, it's encouraging to know that Microsoft's roadmap is adding more intelligence at every layer. Copilots within each tool are already boosting productivity, and soon AI agents like Sophia could amplify HR's ability to drive business outcomes. The message for HR and IT leaders is clear: embrace these AI capabilities as they emerge. They can augment your team (no AI won't replace HR, but HR who use AI may well outperform those who don't).

The conversation about next-gen HR workflows isn't complete without considering AI agents. While tools like Project Sophia are nascent, it's wise to experiment with previews if possible, build internal capability in data science, and think creatively about questions you'd want to ask such an AI. The companies that leverage these early will likely leap ahead in using data to inform every people decision.

Summary

Microsoft Power Platform gives HR and IT professionals an unparalleled toolbox to modernize and streamline HR processes. By harnessing these low-code tools together, organizations can

- Build custom apps and automated workflows that eliminate tedious steps and reduce wait times for routine HR processes. (No more emailing forms around for signatures or manually entering data in multiple places – the platform does it for you.)

- Automate key stages of the employee life cycle – from onboarding checklists to exit surveys – ensuring consistency and saving countless hours. With automation handling the busywork, HR teams can devote more attention to complex, human-centric tasks.

- Analyze workforce trends in real time, enabling truly data-driven decisions on hiring, retention, diversity, performance, and more. Dashboards update with the latest data, so HR and business leaders can spot issues or opportunities immediately, not months later.

- Embed AI and Copilot features into HR tools to make them smarter and more user-friendly. Think AI-driven chatbots answering employees 24/7, or analytics that anyone can query with a simple question. These innovations elevate HR services to be more personalized and proactive (and they're continually improving with Microsoft's investments in AI).

- Scale solutions safely through proper governance and partnership between HR and IT. The platform empowers HR to innovate, but guardrails – security roles, DLP policies, environment management – ensure that flexibility doesn't come at the expense of security or reliability. Clear ownership and documentation make sure each app or flow has someone looking after it throughout its life.

In short, with the Power Platform, HR can evolve from a service center into a driver of digital transformation and strategic value. Instead of being seen as paperwork-pushers, HR teams become solution builders and data-driven advisors. They can deliver faster and better experiences – imagine an employee completing onboarding in a day through a guided app, or a manager getting immediate answers from a chatbot at midnight – while the organization maintains full control over data and compliance.

The case studies and examples we've discussed show that this isn't theoretical: real HR teams are already saving time (often cutting process times by 50% or more), improving accuracy, and engaging employees in new ways thanks to Power Platform solutions. And they're doing it often without large IT projects, but in quick iterations that respond to the business needs.

For HR leaders, embracing these tools means being able to respond to change with agility – whether that's a sudden shift to remote work, a new regulatory requirement, or a CEO's request for analytics by end of day. For HR technology consultants and IT partners, it's an opportunity to deliver impactful solutions with faster ROI than traditional development.

Ultimately, the journey we've outlined – building workflows, reports, and automated dashboards to streamline HR processes – is about freeing HR to focus on what matters most: people. When administrative burdens are lifted and insights are readily available, HR can spend more time on talent development, culture building, and strategic initiatives that drive performance and employee well-being. The Power Platform, with its mix of automation, app experiences, analytics, and AI, is a catalyst to reach that state of an optimized, future-ready HR function. As you move forward, remember to start small, iterate, partner closely between HR and IT, and celebrate quick wins. The digital empowerment of HR is a journey – and with the Power Platform, you now have a powerful vehicle to travel that road.

PART III

Expanding the HR Toolkit

CHAPTER 6

Microsoft 365 for HR Collaboration

Introduction

Human Resources organizations are increasingly turning to Microsoft 365 as a unified platform to improve communication, collaboration, and efficiency. Microsoft's ecosystem – spanning Microsoft Teams, the Power Platform, Dynamics 365 Human Resources, and the Viva employee experience suite – offers an integrated toolkit that can modernize HR operations. By embracing this "One Microsoft for HR" approach, companies build a smart HR toolbox that addresses a wide range of needs. All these solutions share the Microsoft Cloud as a common foundation, meaning identity, security, and compliance (e.g., GDPR data protection) are managed in one place. This unified foundation is a relief for HR IT departments, since policies and access can be managed centrally rather than in siloed systems.

In this chapter, we explore how HR professionals, HRIS specialists, and consultants can use Microsoft 365 – especially Microsoft Teams – as a hub for HR communication and project coordination, enriched with Power Platform automation and Viva's employee experience capabilities. Real-world examples spanning desk workers to frontline employees (in industries such as manufacturing, healthcare, retail, and key HR functions like recruiting) will illustrate how a unified Microsoft approach helps HR teams and employees work smarter while maintaining enterprise security and compliance.

© Ana Inés Urrutia de Souza 2025
A. I. Urrutia de Souza, *The Microsoft AI Human Resources Handbook*,
https://doi.org/10.1007/979-8-8688-1781-6_6

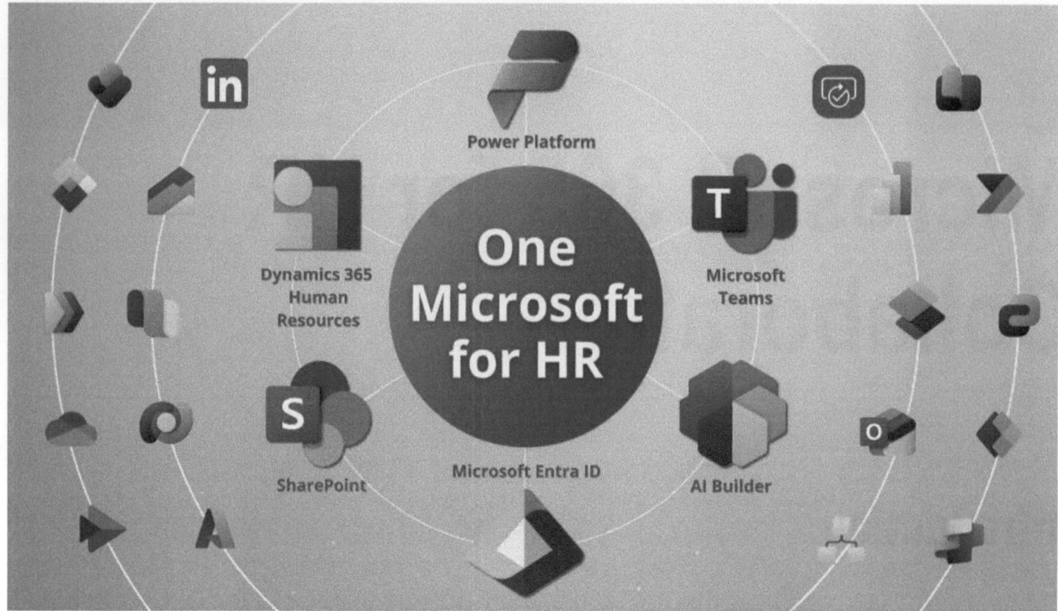

Figure 6-1. *One Microsoft for HR landscape and components*

Microsoft Teams As the HR Collaboration Hub

Microsoft Teams has become a central workspace where HR teams can communicate, collaborate, and coordinate projects in real time. As an all-in-one collaboration hub, Teams brings together chat, meetings, calls, file sharing, and a rich ecosystem of apps into one interface. HR departments typically create dedicated Teams and channels for their major functions and projects – for example, a Team for the Recruiting group with channels for open positions, another Team or channel for Onboarding new hires, and others for Talent Development, Employee Relations, etc. Within these digital spaces, HR staff (and other stakeholders like hiring managers or trainers) can easily hold discussions, share and co-edit documents, and organize virtual meetings or town halls – all without switching tools. This centralization of HR work improves organization and transparency.

HR Communication and Announcements

Teams also enables HR to reach employees quickly and interactively across the organization. Important HR announcements – policy updates, benefit enrollment deadlines, upcoming company events – can be posted in company-wide Team channels or shared via Viva Engage (the Yammer community app integrated into Teams). Unlike a traditional all-staff email, a Teams announcement allows two-way communication: employees can react with an emoji or ask questions in the thread, and HR can clarify in real time. HR leaders might also host live events or town halls through Teams (using the webinar or live event features), where leadership presents updates and employees engage via Q&A moderated by HR.

On a day-to-day basis, HR staff rely on Teams chat and calls for internal coordination and quick decision-making. For example, a recruiter can start a private Teams chat with a hiring manager to clarify interview feedback, rather than sending emails back and forth. An HR business partner might call a remote employee via Teams to discuss a sensitive issue – all with enterprise-grade security and compliance logging in the background. In all these cases, Teams provides a secure, logged channel for communications that may have once been scattered across unsecured texts or calls.

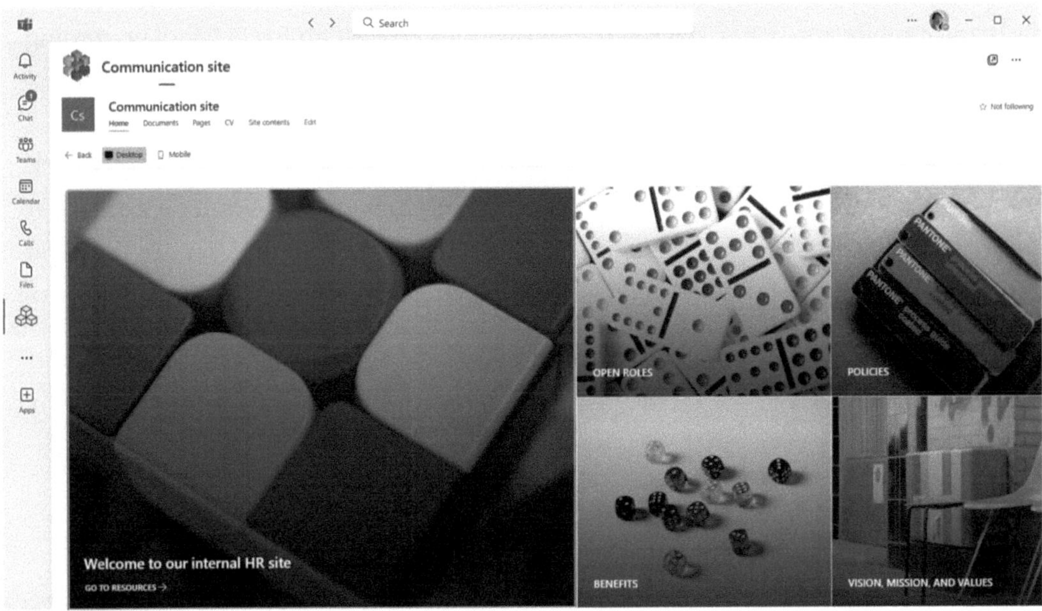

Figure 6-2. Microsoft Teams as the HR Collaboration Hub

Project Coordination and Task Management

Many HR initiatives are essentially projects (implementing a new HRIS module, organizing a company training program, running a recruiting campaign, etc.), and Teams provides built-in tools to help manage these. Teams integrates deeply with task management tools like Microsoft Planner and To Do, which helps HR project leads assign tasks, set deadlines, and track progress right alongside their conversations. A dedicated Planner board can be added as a tab in a Team's channel – for instance, a channel in the HR Team for "Leadership Retreat Planning" might have a Planner tab showing tasks and owners, so everyone has visibility into event preparation tasks. Team members receive notifications in Teams as tasks are assigned to them or marked complete. Additionally, Teams now includes a unified Tasks app (which consolidates Planner and personal To Do tasks) that shows each user all their tasks across projects. This means an HR professional can open Teams and see their task list in one place, helping them stay on top of their work.

Because Teams brings communication and task tracking together, HR projects run more efficiently. Consider a day in the life of an HR coordinator using Teams: in the morning they check their Teams Activity Feed for any @mentions or updates in HR channels. During their commute, they might join the daily stand-up meeting via the Teams mobile app. Later, back at their desk, they co-edit an Excel file of upcoming recruiting events with colleagues directly in a Teams file tab (leveraging SharePoint/ OneDrive integration in the background). In the afternoon, they review the Planner tab in the Recruiting channel to ensure all onboarding tasks for new hires are on track. By evening, a quick search in Teams brings up all the conversations and files related to tomorrow's HR leadership meeting, helping them prepare efficiently. This end-to-end scenario underscores how Teams can streamline HR work from start to finish by keeping everything in one place.

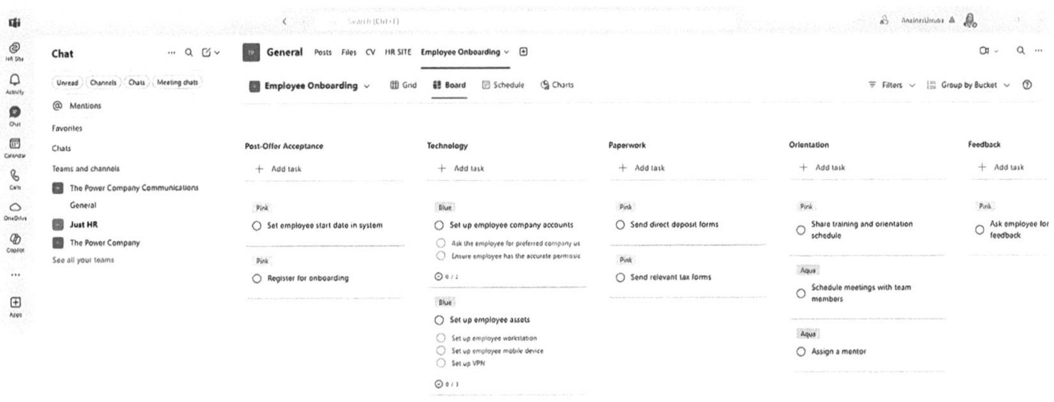

Figure 6-3. *HR Project Board in Teams (Planner)*

Empowering Desk and Frontline Employees via Teams

One of the strengths of Microsoft 365 (and Teams in particular) is its ability to serve different types of workers – from office-based HR staff to frontline employees – in a tailored way. Desk-based HR professionals (information workers) typically use Teams on their desktop or laptop throughout the day for persistent collaboration. They join Teams meetings, participate in chats and channel discussions, and work on documents stored in Teams/SharePoint. These users benefit from the full range of Teams features, such as advanced meeting capabilities (screen sharing, meeting recording with transcription) and deep integration with Office apps. For example, a corporate HR manager might host a virtual training session in Teams, share a PowerPoint during the call, then post follow-up PDF guides in the meeting chat for attendees.

By contrast, frontline employees – such as retail associates, factory floor workers, delivery personnel, or nurses – often use Teams primarily on mobile devices and need quick, on-the-go interactions. Microsoft has optimized Teams and related Microsoft 365 apps for these scenarios. Frontline staff can receive important communications and resources through Teams in a mobile-friendly way. For instance, workers can use Walkie Talkie in Teams for instant push-to-talk voice messages with colleagues. Scheduling and shift management is handled through the built-in Shifts app, which lets frontline employees view their schedules, swap shifts with manager approval, and request time off right from their phone. A retail store employee might get a Teams mobile notification when a new shift schedule is published or when their time-off request is approved – no need to check a bulletin board or call in. Frontline managers and supervisors use the Approvals app in Teams to review and authorize requests (like shift swaps or overtime) with just a few taps on their phone. Additionally, simple task checklists can be distributed via Teams: the Tasks app (integrating Planner) allows, say, a factory worker to tick off steps on a machine maintenance checklist and automatically report completion back to their supervisor.

Just as importantly, Teams connects frontline staff to the wider company culture and information, helping them feel included. Through tools like Viva Connections and Viva Engage embedded in Teams, a field employee can access company-wide announcements and resources that historically might have been missed if they weren't at a desk. For example, a nurse in a hospital could open the "HR Portal" via Teams (powered by Viva Connections) to read the latest HR news, submit a question to HR, or review an updated policy – all without needing to log into a separate system. Similarly, a sales associate can participate in a Yammer/Viva Engage discussion about a new product launch through the Teams app on their phone, sharing feedback or kudos that headquarters will see. Microsoft enables IT to tailor the Teams experience with appropriate licensing and policies for different roles (frontline vs. knowledge worker), so that each employee has access to the tools they need in a secure manner. The result is that both HR professionals and frontline employees are reachable and can collaborate through Teams in ways best suited to their work environment, increasing engagement and efficiency across the board.

Integrating Power Platform into HR Workflows

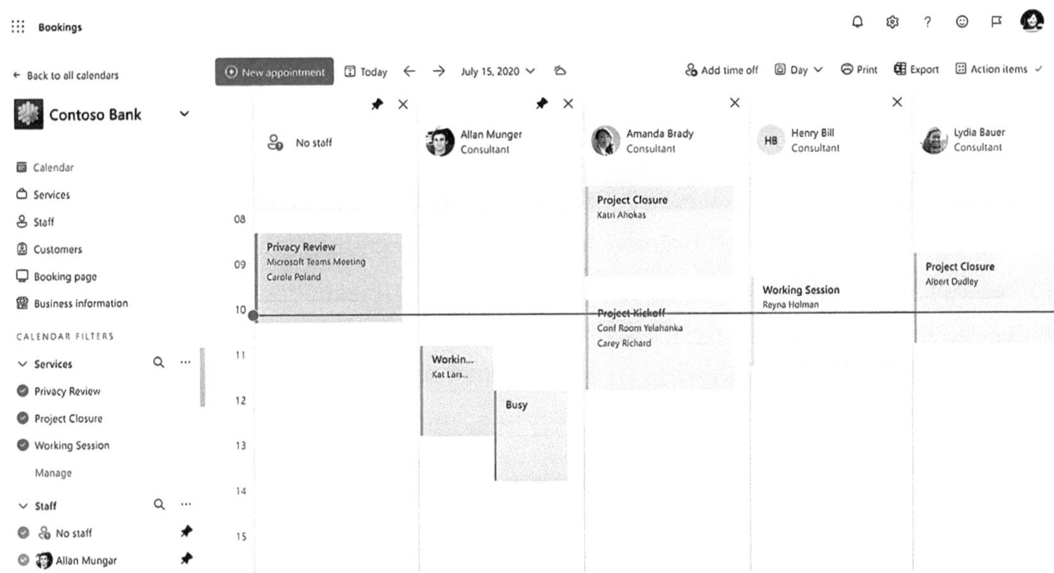

Figure 6-4. *Microsoft Shifts for frontline workers*

While Teams provides the communication layer, Microsoft's Power Platform extends Teams into a platform for automating HR processes and delivering custom HR applications right inside the flow of work. Many Power Platform components can be embedded within Teams, creating a one-stop shop in Teams for tasks that previously might have required separate systems or logins. Importantly, the Power Platform also connects natively with Dynamics 365 Human Resources and other data sources, enabling low-code integration across the HR tech stack. Key integrations include:

Power Automate (Workflow Automation)

Power Automate allows HR to automate repetitive tasks and integrate processes across Microsoft 365 and beyond. Inside Teams, Power Automate's capabilities surface through features like the Approvals app and via custom "flow" bots or notifications in channels. For example, suppose an employee submits a leave request through an HR app in Teams – a Power Automate flow can automatically route that request to the appropriate manager for approval and immediately notify the manager in Teams. The manager can approve or reject the request right within Teams, and the flow will then update the HR system (e.g., writing back to Dynamics 365 HR or SharePoint list) and send a confirmation to the employee – all in a matter of minutes, with the entire transaction tracked centrally. This kind of automation replaces what might have been a chain of emails or a paper form in the past.

HR departments also use Power Automate to send proactive reminders and alerts via Teams. For instance, a flow could post a message in an "HR Announcements" channel whenever a new company policy document is published, ensuring employees see it. Or a flow might ping employees with a 1:1 Teams chat message the day before a mandatory training course is due to be completed. Notifications about things like policy updates, approaching training deadlines, or timesheet cut-offs can be delivered directly through Teams, keeping employees informed and on-task. Moreover, Power Automate's library of connectors (including to third-party HR systems) means HR can bridge Microsoft 365 with other platforms, if needed – for example, automatically creating a ticket in an external payroll or service desk system when an employee submits a request in Teams.

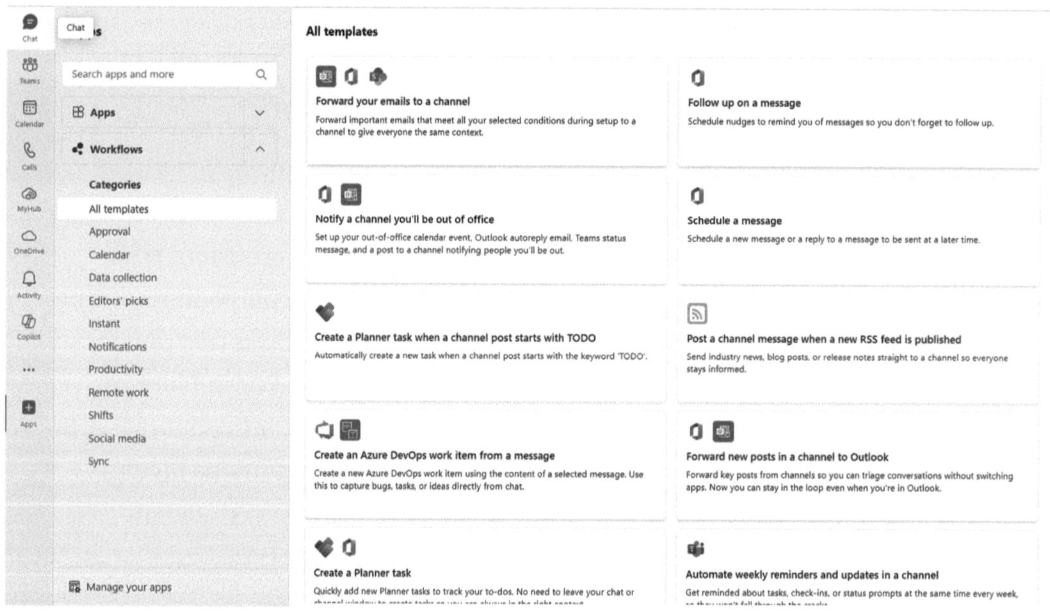

Figure 6-5. *Power Automate within Microsoft Teams for flow creation*

Power Apps (Custom HR Apps)

Power Apps empowers HR or IT teams to create custom applications and forms that run within Teams, tailored to specific HR needs. These can range from simple intake forms to more complex interactive apps. Using Dataverse for Teams (a built-in, lightweight data platform), an organization might build a "New Hire Onboarding" app that lives as a tab in the HR team's channel. This app could guide HR staff through each step of the onboarding checklist, update orientation session schedules, and capture new hire details – writing back to a central database (for example, updating records in Dynamics 365 HR or a SharePoint list).

Another example is an employee self-service app: rather than sending HR an email, an employee could open a Power Apps tab in Teams to update their personal contact information, request a certificate of employment, or view their remaining vacation balance. In fact, Microsoft itself provides a pre-built "Human Resources" Power App (template) integrated with Dynamics 365 HR, focused on leave and absence management. It enables employees to seamlessly request time off and view their leave balances/history, and allows managers to approve those requests – all in one interface within Teams (or via the Teams mobile app). By 2025, after Dynamics 365 HR's technical merge into the broader Finance & Operations infrastructure, this Teams-based HR app became the primary solution for leave management in the Microsoft ecosystem, illustrating Microsoft's commitment to embedding HR processes directly into the flow of work.

Organizations can extend this concept further by developing other Power Apps that tie into HR systems or data. For example, a company might build a Travel Approval app for HR that logs trip requests and approvals, or a Training Enrollment app that connects with Viva Learning to sign up for courses. These apps can surface in Teams' left navigation (pinned as personal apps) or as tabs in specific HR channels, meaning users don't have to leave Teams – or juggle multiple websites – to perform common HR tasks. The result is faster service delivery by HR and a more convenient, "in-context" experience for employees.

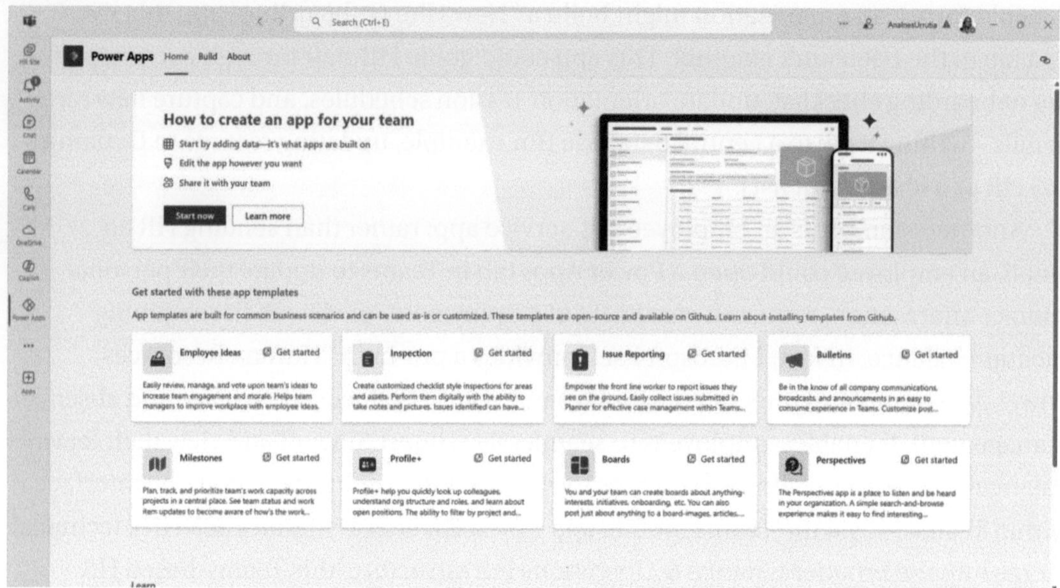

Figure 6-6. Power Apps Studio within Microsoft Teams for app creation

Power BI (Analytics and Insights)

Data-driven decision-making is crucial in HR for activities like headcount planning, diversity and inclusion efforts, or tracking the success of talent programs. Power BI dashboards can be embedded in Teams channels to put essential HR metrics at managers' and HR leaders' fingertips. For example, an HR leadership team might have a Teams tab containing a Power BI report that visualizes workforce demographics, turnover rates, or recruiting funnel statistics in real time. The data for this report can be pulled from Dynamics 365 HR, applicant tracking systems, or even Excel files – and updated on a schedule or continuously. Because it's in Teams, HR leaders can chat right alongside the data; they might tag team members in a conversation pane next to a chart to discuss why a particular metric changed and brainstorm responses, with the actual chart visible to all participants.

Microsoft's unified platform ensures that when sensitive HR data is shown in Power BI, it obeys the same security and permission rules as the source systems. Only authorized users (for instance, HR business partners or executives) will be able to view certain reports or slices of data. Row-level security can enforce that a manager sees only their own team's data, and so on. In practice, a regional HR manager could be in a meeting with operations and quickly pull up a Teams tab on their tablet that displays a

202

Power BI dashboard of overtime hours and absences in their factories, then discuss and annotate actions collaboratively – all without leaving Teams. Furthermore, Power BI can integrate data from tools like Viva Insights (the workplace analytics platform) to correlate HR outcomes (such as engagement or retention rates) with broader productivity or well-being metrics, giving a richer picture of what's driving those HR metrics.

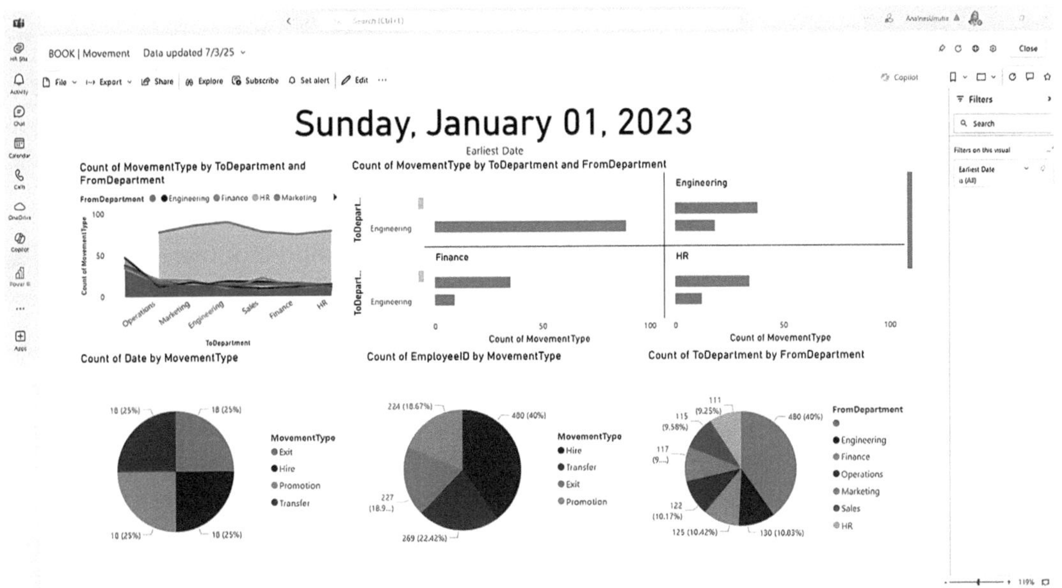

Figure 6-7. *Power BI within Microsoft Teams for data consumption*

AI agents and Copilot

One of the most exciting advances for HR is the use of AI-powered bots and assistants – often dubbed "Copilots" – to reduce manual effort and improve service quality. With Copilot Studio (now enhanced through Copilot capabilities in the new Copilot Studio), HR teams can create chatbots that live in Teams and answer common employee questions around the clock. For example, an "HR Help Bot" in Teams can answer queries about vacation policy, explain how to enroll in benefits, or outline the steps for onboarding a new team member. These bots are built without coding; HR subject matter experts can use a guided interface to add questions and answers or integrate the bot with live data (like querying remaining vacation days from the HR system). By 2025, such bots are supercharged with generative AI: using Microsoft's Azure OpenAI service, the bot can understand natural language inquiries more deeply and even generate helpful, nuanced answers based on HR knowledge bases or SharePoint policy libraries. A practical scenario might be an employee asking in the Teams chat: *"What's the process to apply for parental leave?"* – the HR bot (backed by Copilot AI) could respond with a concise summary of the parental leave policy and step-by-step instructions, and even provide a link to the leave request form or a button to open the appropriate Power App, all within seconds. This kind of AI-driven bot offloads a large volume of routine Q&A from HR staff, freeing them to focus on more complex requests.

Similarly, AI Copilots assist HR professionals directly in their daily work. Microsoft 365 Copilot – the AI assistant integrated across Office apps and Teams – can help draft content, analyze data, and answer questions in context. In a Teams chat or meeting, an HR specialist could invoke Copilot to help draft an announcement message for an upcoming policy change or holiday schedule, based on a few bullet points they provide. Copilot will generate a polished draft in moments, which the HR person can then review and tweak before posting to everyone. During a Teams meeting, Copilot can serve as a virtual assistant: it can listen to the discussion, summarize key points and action items, and even answer on-the-spot questions by referencing internal documents. For instance, if someone asks "What was our policy on volunteer leave again?" Copilot could quickly retrieve the policy document from SharePoint and highlight the relevant portion, right within the meeting notes. This is invaluable for HR meetings that might cover complex policies or legal guidelines – the AI ensures information is at the team's fingertips.

Microsoft has also introduced scenario-specific Copilot solutions for HR. For example, in recruiting, a "Recruitment Copilot" can help talent acquisition teams by analyzing job descriptions and large volumes of candidate résumés to surface the best matches. It could rank candidates based on skills and experience fit, significantly speeding up the sourcing process and helping reduce bias by focusing on objective criteria. The same Copilot might generate content for recruiters – it could draft a first version of a job posting based on a few inputs about the role, or even create an interview itinerary for a candidate's onsite visit, saving recruiters time. In performance management, an AI Copilot might help HR by summarizing employee engagement survey comments and suggesting possible action plans to address recurring issues.

Many of these capabilities are enabled via the combination of Copilot Studio (to design custom bots and assistants) and Microsoft 365 Copilot. By 2025, organizations can even craft their own AI assistants that leverage internal data securely. For instance, an HR team could build an "Onboarding Copilot" that automatically generates a personalized onboarding checklist for new hires based on their role and department.

The Copilot could pull in relevant training content (via Viva Learning), set up introductory meetings with key contacts on the new hire's Teams calendar, and present the new hire with an interactive guide – all triggered by an HR command or a new employee record being created. All told, embedding Power Platform workflows and Copilot AI into Teams means HR processes become more automated, intelligent, and employee-friendly. Routine transactions (like leave requests or expense approvals) turn into streamlined self-service workflows, and complex tasks (like analyzing attrition drivers or drafting policy documents) are augmented by AI-driven suggestions. HR professionals can thus focus on high-value strategic work, while trusting the Microsoft platform to handle data synchronization, notifications, and insightful analysis behind the scenes.

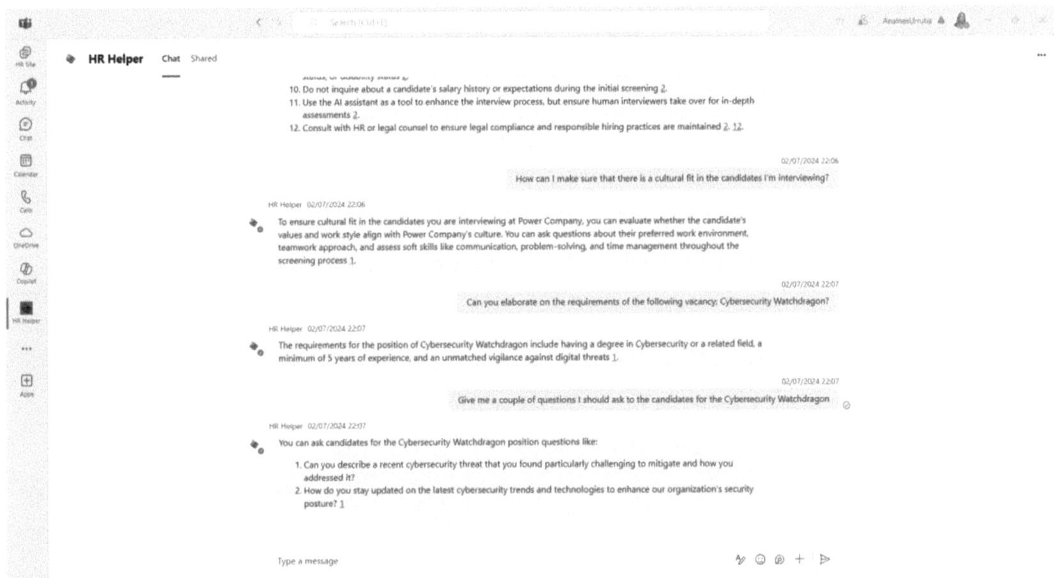

Figure 6-8. *Custom Copilot within Microsoft Teams for HR user interaction*

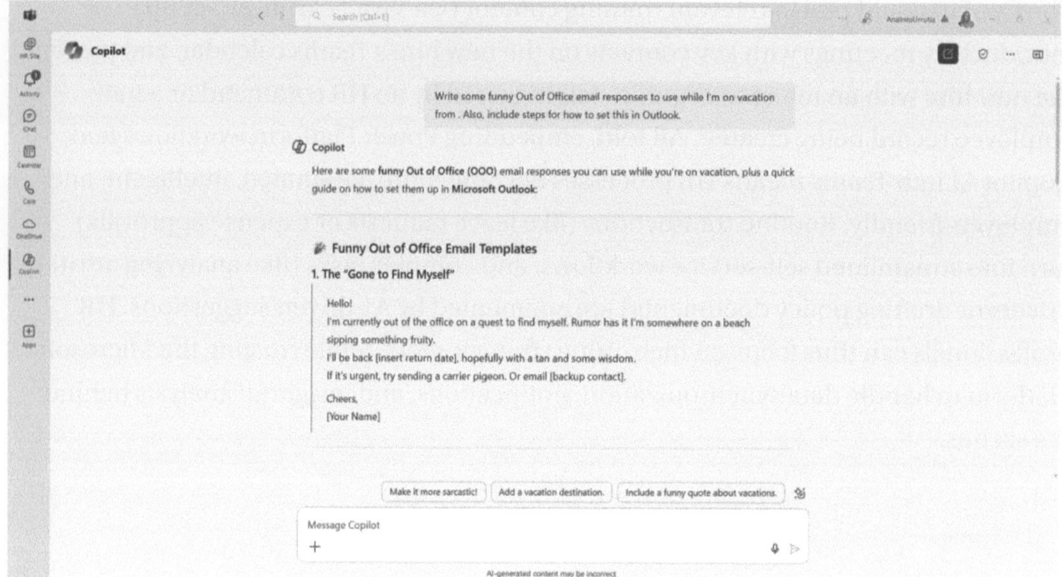

Figure 6-9. *Custom Copilot within Microsoft Teams for employee interaction*

Microsoft Viva: Enhancing Employee Experience and Learning

Microsoft Viva is an employee experience platform within Microsoft 365 (surfacing primarily through Teams) that focuses on improving engagement, learning, and well-being at work. Several Viva modules offer capabilities highly relevant to HR's mission of developing and supporting employees. In particular, Viva Learning, Viva Insights, and Viva Connections are key tools that HR can leverage to enrich the employee experience. All Viva components surface directly inside Teams, which means employees can access these resources in the flow of their normal workday.

Viva Learning – The Learning Hub in Teams

Viva Learning is a centralized learning hub in Teams that makes it easy to integrate training and professional development into everyday work. Instead of employees having to log into a separate Learning Management System (LMS) or track training in spreadsheets, Viva Learning brings training content right into Teams, where people are already communicating and collaborating. With Viva Learning, team members can discover, share, recommend, and complete learning content from both the organization's internal libraries and a multitude of external content providers – all without leaving Teams.

For example, an HR department can publish mandatory compliance training (say, a "Workplace Safety 101" course or a new GDPR policy module) through Viva Learning so that all employees are assigned to see it and complete it by a deadline. At the same time, employees have access to a broad catalog of courses from providers like LinkedIn Learning, Microsoft Learn, or other third parties if those are connected. From the Teams sidebar (or as a tab in a team's channel), a user can open Viva Learning to see a personalized dashboard of courses – including those their manager has assigned to them, as well as suggestions based on their role or interests. They might see a mix of content: for instance, a required "Cybersecurity Basics" training from HR, a recommended leadership course from LinkedIn Learning that aligns with their career plan, and some internal training documents or videos that colleagues have shared.

Viva Learning also makes learning more social and collaborative. Employees can easily share useful courses with colleagues via Teams chat or channel posts. For instance, an HR specialist might post in the HR team's channel, "@Team – check out this new Diversity & Inclusion training video," attaching the course directly into the conversation through Viva Learning. Important training can be pinned as a tab in a Teams channel as well – for example, a "Sales Onboarding" channel could have a Viva Learning tab that aggregates all required training content for new sales hires in one place. Managers and HR can track who has completed which courses through the reporting capabilities of Viva Learning. If certain courses are marked as required or recommended, the system shows completion statuses, which are visible to the recommending manager and HR. This helps ensure compliance training is finished on time and lets managers actively support their team's development.

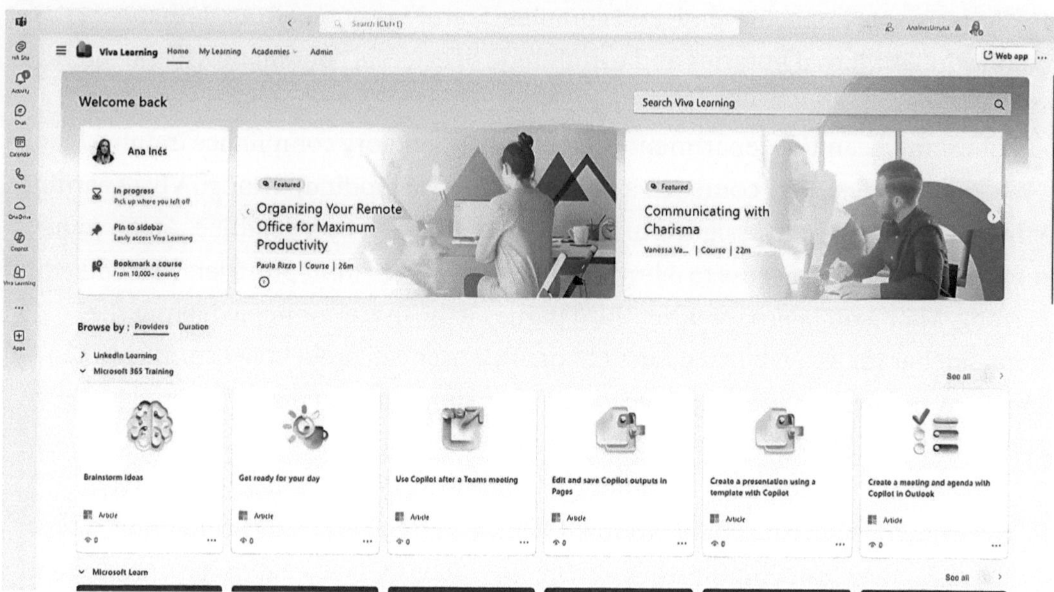

Figure 6-10. *Viva Learning within Microsoft Teams for learning and development*

As of 2025, these capabilities are mature and no longer in preview. Viva Learning supports integration with various external LMS platforms and content sources, meaning it can aggregate everything from formal e-learning courses to informal training PDFs hosted on SharePoint into the Teams experience. This is transformative for HR because it creates a one-stop learning portal that employees can access on any device. For example, a frontline retail employee can take a micro-learning course on their phone via Viva Learning during a quiet period at work (say, a short video on how to handle a new product return procedure), improving their skills without leaving the shop floor or scheduling dedicated training time. Meanwhile, HR and management gain insight into learning adoption and can identify areas that might need additional support or promotion (e.g., if a particular required course has low completion, they can send reminders or gather feedback). Overall, Viva Learning's seamless integration in Teams ensures that learning is not an afterthought but rather a natural part of the work day, promoting a culture of continuous learning across the organization.

Viva Insights – Well-Being and Productivity Data

Viva Insights provides data-driven, privacy-protected insights to individuals, managers, and leaders aimed at improving well-being and productivity. From an HR perspective, Viva Insights is a tool that can help monitor and enhance the employee experience at scale, using aggregate data about work patterns.

For individual employees, the Viva Insights app in Teams offers personal recommendations and nudges – for example, it might suggest scheduling regular focus time, taking breaks throughout the day, or setting up a virtual commute at the end of the day to reflect and decompress. These recommendations are derived from the user's own work patterns (such as long hours, after-hours emailing, or excessive meeting load) and are visible only to that employee, providing gentle guidance on work–life balance and productivity habits.

Managers get team-level insight cards (with aggregated, anonymized data) highlighting potential issues like an increase in after-hours work for their team, frequent meeting overload, or too little 1:1 time with direct reports. If Viva Insights surfaces that a manager's team has been consistently working late hours, it might prompt that manager to encourage taking time off or to review workload distribution. Similarly, if it shows meeting overload, the manager might consider streamlining standing meetings. These insights help managers proactively address burnout and foster healthier team norms.

HR business partners and leaders can leverage the advanced, organization-wide analytics (formerly known as Workplace Analytics) that Viva Insights provides. They can look at trends such as correlations between engagement survey results and collaboration patterns. For example, HR might discover that a department showing high burnout risk signals in Viva Insights (e.g., many employees working after hours or not taking vacation) also has higher turnover and lower engagement scores. This data can drive targeted interventions – HR could work with that department's leadership to implement a well-being program, adjust workloads, or provide additional resources.

Viva Insights can also complement HR's wellness initiatives. If HR rolls out a company-wide campaign on work-life balance, Viva Insights can support it by reminding employees to disconnect after hours and by providing HR with reports on whether after-hours work is decreasing over time. Well-being features like the virtual commute, breathing breaks, or integration with the Headspace meditation app can be promoted by HR as part of these initiatives. Importantly, all of this is done with privacy in mind – individual data is not visible to HR or management, and insights that HR sees are aggregated and de-identified. This ensures compliance with privacy regulations and builds employee trust, even as the organization gains valuable feedback on work habits and areas for improvement.

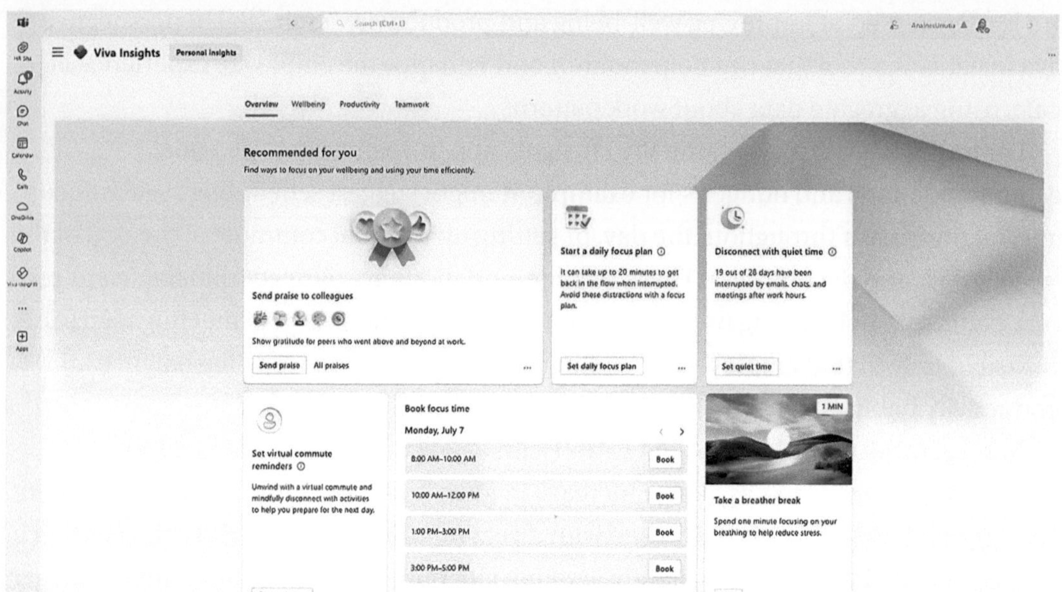

Figure 6-11. *Viva Insights within Microsoft Teams for well-being, productivity, and teamwork*

Viva Connections – The HR Portal in Teams

Viva Connections is essentially a gateway to the organization's intranet and employee resources, surfaced in Teams for easy access. It provides a customizable app (often branded with the company's name or logo) that delivers a curated feed of news, key resources, and interactive content to employees. HR can leverage Viva Connections as a modern employee portal, especially useful in companies with distributed or frontline-heavy workforces.

Through Viva Connections, HR can present a dashboard of HR and company resources right in Teams. For example, the home view might show: recent HR announcements or CEO messages, quick links to HR policies and FAQs, a personal status card (such as "You have 8 vacation days remaining" with a button to request time off), and even an embedded Yammer (Viva Engage) feed for company-wide discussions. Microsoft's platform allows integration of live data into this experience using Adaptive Cards. In practice, this means HR data from systems like Dynamics 365 HR can be pulled in so that each employee sees personalized info at a glance. An employee could open Teams, click on the company's Viva Connections icon, and immediately see a card saying "You have 8 vacation days remaining" alongside a "Request time off" action. If they click it, it might launch the time-off request form or app directly. Similarly, the Connections dashboard could show a "Payslip available" notice with a link to view the latest pay slip, or a "Training due" reminder if they have an outstanding course to complete. All of this happens within Teams, eliminating the need for employees to log into multiple different HR or intranet sites for basic information.

HR teams benefit as well: Viva Connections enables targeting content to specific audiences. For example, HR can configure certain cards or news posts to appear only for particular groups – such as showing a "License Renewal Reminder" card to healthcare staff whose professional certification is expiring soon (data which HR knows from D365 HR). Or manufacturing plant workers might see a safety tip of the week that desk workers don't see. This targeting ensures the content is relevant to the employee viewing it.

Viva Connections ties together various Microsoft 365 services – it uses SharePoint as the content backbone (for the intranet pages and news), Yammer/Viva Engage for community discussions, Stream for video messages, and Adaptive Cards to bring in data and actions from systems like Dynamics 365 or ServiceNow. The user experience is one integrated "dashboard" or feed in Teams that employees can access on any device.

Consider an example: at a manufacturing company, when a factory line worker starts their shift and opens Teams on a shared tablet, the Viva Connections dashboard might greet them with a *"Safety Tip of the Day,"* a link to a required training module (via Viva Learning) for a new machine they'll be using, and a prompt that says "Your home address on file is out of date – update now," which with one click opens a quick form (through a Power App or SharePoint page) to update their contact details. They can accomplish all of this within Teams during a pre-shift meeting. This kind of experience ensures important HR communications and tasks aren't lost in piles of paperwork or ignored because they're on a separate site – it meets employees where they already are.

Viva Connections is included with most Microsoft 365 enterprise plans, so deploying it doesn't incur additional cost – it's mainly about configuring the experience. This makes it a straightforward, cost-effective way for HR to reach all employees, from corporate offices to frontline sites, with a consistent portal. Implementing Connections furthers the vision of "One Microsoft" for HR: essentially, all HR information and services – whether it's pay, benefits, company news, or training – become accessible in one place with a consistent, user-friendly interface inside Teams.

In summary, Microsoft Viva augments the HR toolkit provided by Teams and Power Platform by focusing on the employee experience layer. Viva Learning ensures continuous development is woven into daily work; Viva Insights provides data and nudges to foster healthy work habits and organizational culture; and Viva Connections acts as the glue connecting employees with HR and company resources in Teams. Together, these tools help foster a more engaged, informed, and empowered workforce – which is ultimately at the heart of HR's objectives.

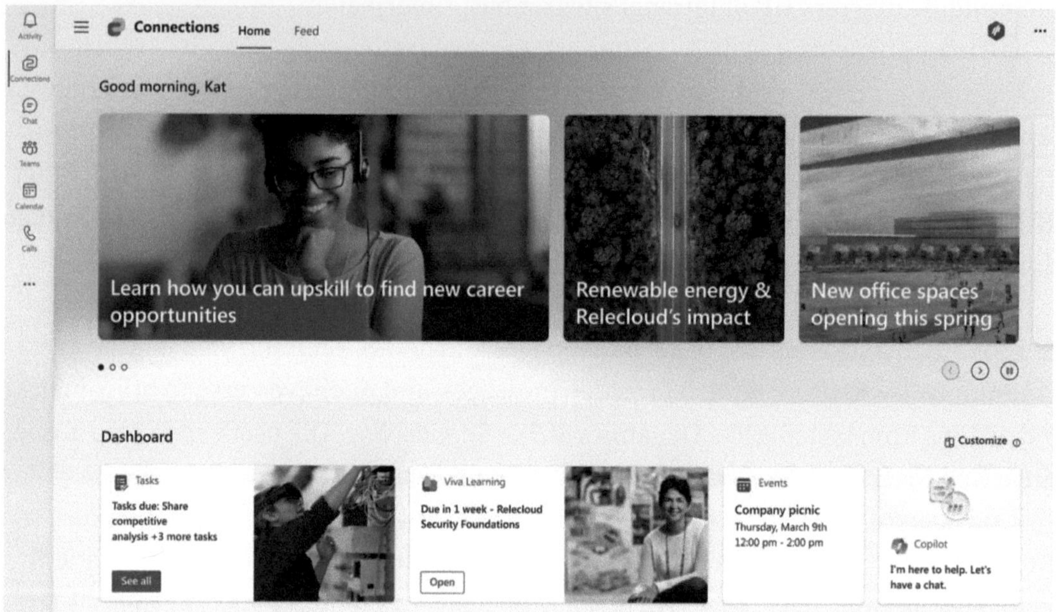

Figure 6-12. *Viva Connections within Microsoft Teams for company news and upcoming events or tasks*

Unified Vision: One Microsoft for HR

Bringing together Microsoft Teams, the Power Platform, Dynamics 365 HR, and Viva is not just about using multiple products – it's about a strategic unified architecture for HR IT. Microsoft's integrated approach allows HR organizations to break down technology silos and enjoy a connected ecosystem where data and processes flow seamlessly. Instead of a patchwork of disparate solutions (one system for core HR data, another for employee communications, another for analytics, and so on), organizations can leverage Microsoft's platform to build a robust HR technology stack in which each piece reinforces the other. As an HRIS specialist might say, "together we stand, divided we fall" – the more integrated and harmonized our tools, the stronger our HR service delivery becomes.

In practical terms, this "One Microsoft" vision manifests in several compelling ways:

1. Common Identity and Security: There is a unified identity and security model across Microsoft 365 and Dynamics. Every user – whether an HR staff member or an employee using self-service – is authenticated via the same Azure Active Directory (now called Microsoft Entra ID). With single sign-on, an employee can log in once and have access to Teams, their Outlook email, the HR self-service portal, Power BI reports, etc., according to their permissions. This improves user convenience (one username/ password, one login portal) and makes life easier for IT security: when someone leaves the company or changes roles, IT disables or adjusts their account in one directory, and that automatically governs access to all connected HR resources. The shared cloud platform also means compliance standards are uniformly applied. Company-wide retention policies, data encryption at rest and in transit, audit logs, and privacy controls are consistent across Teams, SharePoint, Power Platform, and Dynamics 365. For example, if a company needs to perform a GDPR data subject request (like exporting or deleting all of an individual's personal data), having HR communications in Teams and HR records in D365 under the same umbrella means one set of tools and processes can handle the request across both systems. This uniform approach to security and compliance significantly reduces risk and administrative overhead compared to managing multiple unrelated HR systems.

2. Simplified Data Integration: Data integration becomes much easier in a unified Microsoft environment. Dynamics 365 Human Resources – now built on the same infrastructure as other Dynamics 365 applications – can natively connect to the Power Platform and Microsoft 365 services. Microsoft provides built-in connectors and a common data model (via Dataverse) that drastically reduce the need for custom middleware or manual data exports. This ensures that data entered in one

place can be utilized in another without complex IT projects. A clear illustration is the synchronization between D365 HR and Microsoft Entra ID (Azure AD) for employee identities: as soon as HR creates a new employee record or updates an employee's phone number in D365 HR, that information can automatically flow to the central directory that Teams and Outlook use. The employee's contact card in Teams, therefore, stays up-to-date without any manual intervention. Likewise, organizational data like department membership or manager reporting lines (maintained in the HR system) can drive access control and group membership in Microsoft 365 – for example, automatically adding a new hire to the correct Teams channels or email distribution lists based on their department and manager. This saves both HR and IT significant time and minimizes errors. In the past, a change might have required updates in multiple systems (HR would update their system, IT would separately update Active Directory, etc.), but now the "enter data once and it syncs everywhere" principle applies. A unified platform also helps eliminate shadow IT in HR. Rather than HR feeling the need to buy a stand-alone tool for things like pulse surveys or case management, they can often use capabilities that exist within the Microsoft stack (e.g., Forms or Viva Pulse for surveys, or Lists or Power Apps for basic case tracking) that integrate out-of-the-box with their data. Fewer rogue tools means less data fragmentation and better compliance.

3. Unified User Experience: The user experience for both employees and HR staff is unified and familiar. Employees and managers primarily go to Microsoft Teams as their daily work hub, and from there they can access almost everything: they can chat with HR or colleagues, fill out an HR form or request (via a Teams app or bot), complete a required training module (via Viva Learning), and read the latest company news (via Viva Connections) – all through a consistent interface. For HR professionals, the tools they use regularly – Teams for meetings and chat, Office apps like Word/Excel, the Dynamics 365 HR administrative interface, Power BI for reports – all have a common look and feel and work

together fluidly. This reduces training needs (new features are adopted faster because they behave like other Microsoft tools) and increases adoption of the tools that HR rolls out to the workforce. Even the new AI capabilities like Microsoft 365 Copilot span across these experiences. For example, an HR manager could ask Copilot in Teams to gather data from a D365 HR attrition report and summarize it in a Word document for an upcoming meeting. Because Teams, Office, and D365 HR are integrated, Copilot can seamlessly fetch the data and generate a draft without the manager having to manually export or switch contexts. In essence, Microsoft often talks about a "Digital Fabric" woven across applications – HR stands to gain immensely from that fabric being tightly woven across all HR functions.

The bottom line is that a unified Microsoft approach to HR technology leads to a more connected, agile, and secure HR operation. It breaks down barriers between different aspects of HR work and between HR and the rest of the business.

Scenario Spotlights: Manufacturing, Healthcare, Retail, and Recruiting

- Manufacturing: In manufacturing companies, a large portion of the workforce is on the factory floor or in production facilities. Organizations have used Teams and Viva Connections to engage these frontline workers and provide streamlined access to HR services. For example, factory employees might share rugged tablets running Teams so they can receive safety bulletins or HR announcements digitally (replacing traditional bulletin boards). Through Teams, they can also access a knowledge base of equipment procedures or submit HR requests (like reporting an incident or requesting leave) without leaving the production floor. Companies often build simple Power Apps for these scenarios – for example, a machine maintenance checklist app that production workers fill out, which automatically logs training completion and maintenance data back to D365 HR to ensure compliance (only certified workers can operate certain machinery). When new manufacturing hires join, HR can onboard and train them via Teams as well: the onboarding process might include just-in-time training modules delivered through Viva Learning, and an Onboarding channel in Teams with resources and Q&A forums. All of this helps engage a workforce that typically doesn't sit at a desk, by delivering information and tools in a convenient, central way.

- Healthcare: In healthcare settings, the workforce includes clinicians and staff who must adhere to strict privacy and compliance rules (like HIPAA). Here, Teams is used for secure communication (with features like encrypted messaging and emergency alerts) among doctors, nurses, and administrators. For example, a hospital might use Teams for urgent care coordination or on-call scheduling, because it meets health data security requirements. Frontline healthcare workers coordinate shifts through the Teams Shifts app, and can access critical resources like clinical protocols or HR policies via a Viva Connections portal tailored to the hospital. An HR scenario in healthcare could involve using Power BI and Viva Insights data to monitor stress and workload levels: a hospital's HR might look at metrics indicating potential burnout in certain departments (e.g., consistently long hours or scarce breaks) and work with management to adjust staffing or provide support. Training is another focus – new procedures or compliance trainings (like patient privacy training) can be delivered through Viva Learning in Teams, ensuring that doctors and nurses can easily access the latest modules on their mobile devices. In some cases, this might be supplemented by mixed-reality training via Microsoft's Dynamics 365 Guides for hands-on practice, showing how seamlessly even advanced training tools can tie into the ecosystem. Overall, the Microsoft 365 toolset allows healthcare HR to support employees with flexible communication, accessible training, and data-driven wellness insights, all while maintaining the necessary privacy controls.

- Retail: Retail organizations often have geographically dispersed store teams and high employee turnover. Microsoft 365 provides a way to keep retail staff connected and informed. Retail associates typically use Teams on their smartphones provided by the employer. Through Teams, headquarters HR can send consistent communications to all stores – for instance, a policy change or a new promotion announcement can be posted in a company-wide Retail team, and store employees will see it on their phones and can ask questions. Quick pulse surveys can be sent via a Teams bot or Forms to get feedback from store employees after a new initiative. Day-one new hire onboarding paperwork can be completed through a Power Apps app in Teams (perhaps a simple checklist and forms app) so that even before a store employee's first day or during orientation, all required documents are filled digitally. Retail store managers use Teams for their management tasks too: for example, they approve shift swap requests or time-off requests via the Teams Approvals app, which automatically updates the shift schedule in Shifts – eliminating separate emails or paper forms. All of this happens with mobile-friendly interfaces that suit employees who may not have a PC at work. The outcome is that retail staff, who traditionally are hard to engage through email or corporate intranets, now have a direct line to HR and corporate resources through Teams. They feel more a part of the company, and HR can ensure critical updates (like safety procedures or benefits enrollment info) reach every employee consistently.

- Recruiting: The hiring process involves coordination between recruiters, hiring managers, and often external candidates – and Microsoft 365 offers tools to streamline this collaboration. Internally, HR recruiting teams create Teams channels or even separate Teams to manage recruitment for different departments or job openings. In these channels, recruiters and hiring managers can discuss candidates and share interview feedback in a transparent, organized way (instead of siloed email threads). Documents like job descriptions, resumes, and interview schedules are stored in the Teams files tab so everyone always has the latest version. Using Power Automate, some organizations integrate recruiting workflows: for example, when a hiring manager fills out an interview evaluation form (perhaps a Microsoft Form or a SharePoint list item), a flow can compile the feedback and notify the recruiter in Teams, speeding up the decision loop. Teams meetings are heavily used for interviews, especially in remote hiring – integrated with Outlook for scheduling and with features like lobby and recording for panel interviews. Additionally, AI has started to play a role: a Recruiting Copilot might sift through an applicant tracking system to find top candidates or even draft personalized candidate outreach messages for recruiters. While external candidates won't be in the company's Teams environment, they benefit from faster communication and scheduling thanks to the integration of Outlook and Teams on the HR side. Overall, by using Teams as the coordination hub (with Planner for tracking hiring stages, and maybe a Power BI dashboard to monitor recruiting KPIs like time-to-fill or diversity of pipeline), recruiting teams reduce friction and can fill roles faster. This scenario highlights how Microsoft 365 can support an HR function (talent acquisition) that is both collaborative and data-driven, even though part of the process extends outside the organization.

Conclusion

Microsoft 365's HR collaboration capabilities demonstrate how a unified technology platform can elevate the HR function from administrative to strategic. By using Microsoft Teams as the central cockpit – augmented by the Power Platform's automation and Dynamics 365 HR's robust data backbone – HR professionals can deliver services more efficiently and engage employees in more meaningful ways. Meanwhile, Microsoft Viva adds a crucial layer focused on employee experience, ensuring that learning, communication, and well-being are woven into daily work life rather than being afterthoughts. The overarching vision of "One Microsoft for HR" is about breaking down barriers: barriers between HR and employees (making HR services more accessible), between disparate systems (connecting data and processes), and between silos of data (unifying information for better insights).

The result is a more connected and agile HR organization that can support a diverse workforce of both desk workers and frontline workers, all while upholding global security and compliance standards. As we saw in examples from different industries, this integrated approach yields tangible outcomes – from faster onboarding and improved training compliance to higher employee engagement and data-informed decision-making in HR policy. HR teams become proactive partners to the business, leveraging the best of modern technology to focus on people rather than paperwork.

For HR leaders and enterprise consultants, the takeaway is that a holistic, integrated model is not only possible but already delivering value in many organizations. They can be confident that Microsoft's continually evolving cloud and AI capabilities (like the new Copilot services) will further empower HR in the journey ahead. The tools are now in place and proven; the task now is to thoughtfully weave them into the HR strategy. By doing so, organizations can create a modern, collaborative, and AI-enhanced HR environment that helps both people and the business thrive.

CHAPTER 7

Strategic Integration with LinkedIn

Microsoft's LinkedIn Acquisition and the Rise of Talent Solutions

Microsoft's relationship with LinkedIn began with a landmark acquisition in 2016, when Microsoft announced it would buy LinkedIn for $26.2 billion. This deal – Microsoft's largest ever at the time – was driven by CEO Satya Nadella's vision of combining Microsoft's productivity software with LinkedIn's vast professional network. The acquisition officially closed in December 2016, bringing LinkedIn's then 433 million members under Microsoft's umbrella. Nadella highlighted a shared mission: "to connect the world's professionals" and improve how people work. Analysts saw the move as a "massive growth play" for Microsoft, aiming to add new sales, marketing, and recruiting services to Microsoft's product suite and challenge competitors in the cloud software space. At that time, LinkedIn was already a powerhouse for hiring solutions – making most of its ~$3 billion annual revenue from recruiters and job seekers paying for networking and recruiting tools. Integrating this "social network for business" into Microsoft promised to unlock synergies in data analytics and AI, given both companies' rich stores of professional data.

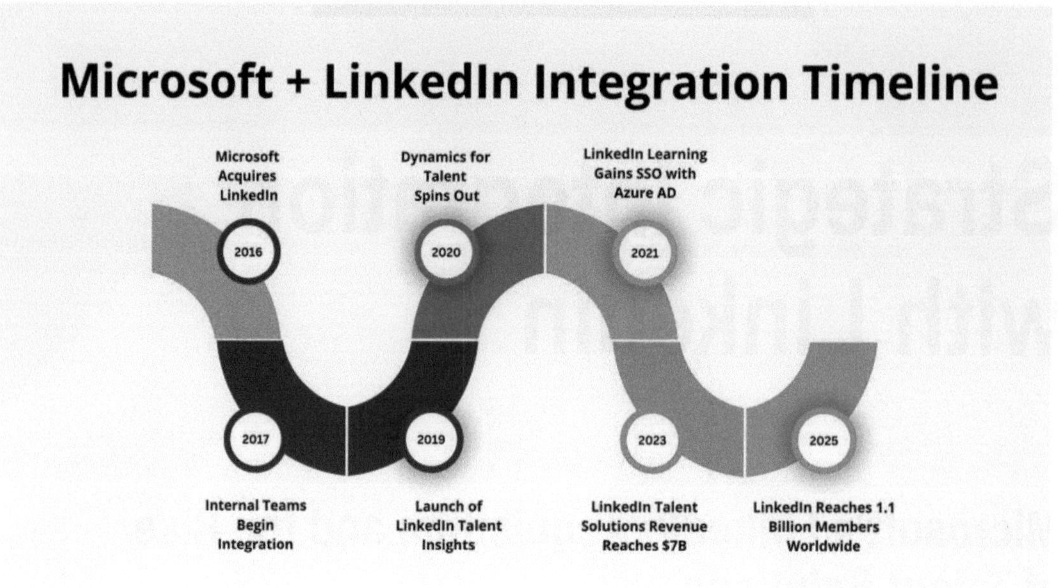

Figure 7-1. *Microsoft + LinkedIn Integration Timeline and development*

LinkedIn Talent Solutions: Overview and Purpose

Recruiter System Connect (RSC) uses secure APIs and enterprise connectors to synchronize data between LinkedIn Recruiter and ATS platforms like Dynamics 365 Human Resources. IT administrators can enable single sign-on (SSO) and provisioning via Microsoft Entra ID (formerly Azure AD) using SCIM protocols. LinkedIn Apply Connect uses OAuth 2.0 for secure authentication and candidate data transfer into ATS systems.

LinkedIn Talent Solutions (LTS) refers to LinkedIn's suite of products and services designed to help employers find, attract, and hire talent leveraging the world's largest professional network. In fact, LinkedIn now has over 1.1 billion members worldwide as of early 2025 – a massive talent pool that LTS taps into for recruiting. According to LinkedIn's own description, Talent Solutions provides "innovative recruiting tools to help you become more successful at talent acquisition" using LinkedIn's network. It is the company's biggest revenue driver, delivering about $7 billion of LinkedIn's total revenue in 2023. The goal of LTS is to enhance candidate sourcing and recruiting by connecting recruiters with the right professionals efficiently.

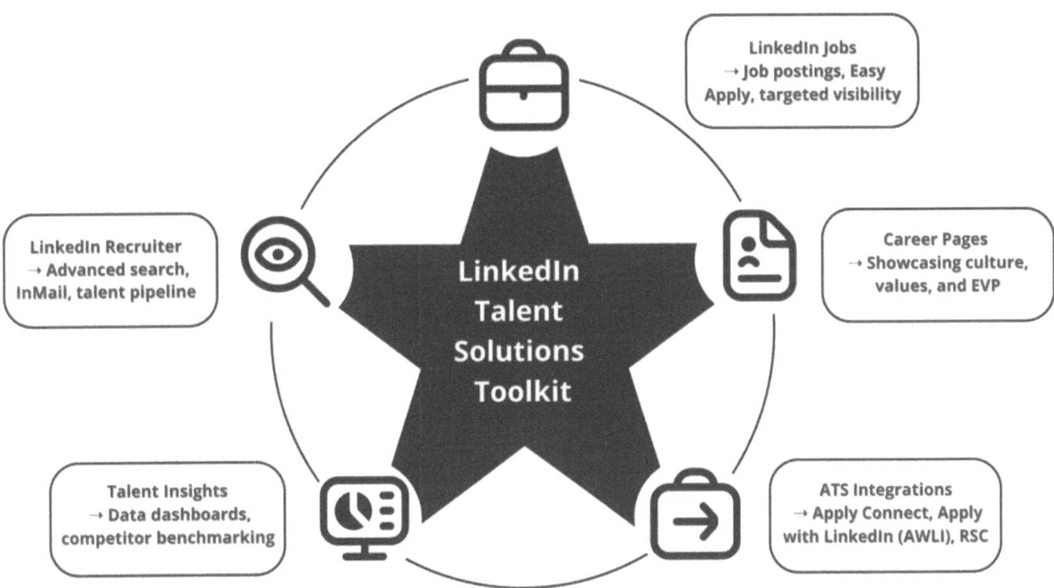

Figure 7-2. LinkedIn Talent Solution toolkit

What does LinkedIn Talent Solutions include? Primarily, it encompasses a range of hiring tools and platforms:

- LinkedIn Recruiter: A robust recruiting platform that lets hiring professionals search for and engage qualified candidates across LinkedIn. It offers advanced filters, InMail messaging, and candidate management features to streamline recruiting for multiple or hard-to-fill roles. LinkedIn describes Recruiter as a tool to "find, engage and hire qualified candidates" – essential for competitive hiring needs. There is also a scaled-down Recruiter Lite for low-volume hiring.

- LinkedIn Jobs: An online job posting service where companies can post job listings on LinkedIn and reach millions of active job seekers. Recruiters can target postings to specific audiences and manage incoming applicants. This platform makes it easy to attract and track candidates – "target your jobs to the right people" – and prioritize the best matches. Candidates often can apply with one click via their LinkedIn profile (using features like Easy Apply).

- Employer Branding & Insights: Solutions like LinkedIn Career Pages help organizations showcase their culture and values to attract talent. Meanwhile, LinkedIn Talent Insights provides analytics about talent pools, companies, and workforce trends, giving HR teams data-driven intelligence for strategic recruiting (for example, which cities have high concentrations of a certain skill, or how a company's employer brand is performing). These insights turn LinkedIn's data into talent intelligence to inform hiring decisions.

- Application & ATS Integration: Recruiter System Connect (RSC) uses secure APIs and enterprise connectors to synchronize data between LinkedIn Recruiter and ATS platforms like Dynamics 365 Human Resources. IT administrators can enable single sign-on (SSO) and provisioning via Microsoft Entra ID (formerly Azure AD) using SCIM protocols. LinkedIn Apply Connect uses OAuth 2.0 for secure authentication and candidate data transfer into ATS systems. Recognizing that many companies rely on Applicant Tracking Systems (ATS), LinkedIn offers additional integration tools via its Talent Solutions APIs. For instance, Apply with LinkedIn (AWLI) lets candidates autofill applications using their LinkedIn profile, while Apply Connect and Easy Apply allow job seekers to submit applications directly from LinkedIn, sending their data into the employer's ATS without manual entry. These features, along with RSC – which enables recruiters to see if a candidate already exists in their ATS and keep profiles in sync – enhance the candidate sourcing and recruiting experience by bridging LinkedIn's network with companies' internal systems.

In summary, LinkedIn Talent Solutions' goal is to be a one-stop, data-rich platform for talent acquisition. It essentially sells access to talent: recruiters pay for subscriptions (like LinkedIn Recruiter seats), for job advertisement slots, and for enhanced insights – all of which capitalize on LinkedIn's massive user base and data. As one source puts it, LTS is "designed to help recruiters attract, recruit, and hire professionals." This mission aligns closely with why Microsoft wanted LinkedIn in the first place – to connect professionals and empower recruiters with tools embedded in the platforms they use.

Impact of LinkedIn Talent Solutions

LinkedIn's prominence in recruitment is backed by notable data and industry research. The platform has become indispensable for recruiters in the digital age. Surveys indicate that around 72% of recruiters use LinkedIn when hiring new talent, and a majority report that candidates found via LinkedIn tend to be of higher quality than those from other sources. In fact, LinkedIn's extensive reach means that on average, seven people are hired every minute via LinkedIn, adding up to over 3 million hires through LinkedIn per year. Likewise, more than 9,000 LinkedIn members apply for jobs on the platform every minute – a testament to how embedded LinkedIn is in the job search and recruiting process.

Such scale and engagement have placed LinkedIn at the center of many companies' talent strategies. Gartner and other analysts often cite LinkedIn as a critical tool in talent acquisition. As early as the acquisition announcement, Microsoft noted that LinkedIn brought a network of hundreds of millions of professionals that could augment Microsoft's own enterprise offerings. Over the years since, LinkedIn's member base has skyrocketed (from 433 million in 2016 to 950 million+ by mid-2023), reinforcing its status as the world's largest professional network. Microsoft's FY2023 reports highlighted that LinkedIn's platform has become "mission critical" to over 950 million members for connecting, learning, selling, and getting hired.

From a business perspective, LinkedIn Talent Solutions has also been a strong performer. By mid-2023, LinkedIn's Talent Solutions segment surpassed $7 billion in revenue for the first time (over a 12-month period), reflecting growth in demand for its recruiting products. Industry observers like Forrester have pointed out that Microsoft's integration of LinkedIn is a major growth driver, one that few other tech mergers have achieved at such scale. The combination of LinkedIn's data with Microsoft's cloud and AI capabilities is often cited as a competitive advantage. For example, Microsoft expanded the total addressable market of its productivity and business process segment from $200 billion to $315 billion by incorporating LinkedIn's offerings, underlining how valuable LinkedIn's Talent Solutions and related services are in the broader Microsoft ecosystem.

Use Case: How Companies Leverage LinkedIn Talent Solutions

Organizations can centralize LinkedIn Talent Insights exports by integrating them with Power BI dashboards. While direct API querying is limited, data can be extracted using Power Automate or Azure Data Factory. This allows HR analytics teams to combine internal HRIS data from platforms like Dynamics 365 or SAP SuccessFactors with LinkedIn activity to visualize pipeline efficiency, source effectiveness, or candidate demographics.

To illustrate the power of LinkedIn Talent Solutions, consider a scenario based on real-world use cases (without naming specific companies). Imagine a mid-sized tech enterprise experiencing rapid growth and needing to hire dozens of specialized professionals (software engineers, product managers, etc.) across multiple regions. Traditionally, this company might rely on recruitment agencies or passive job postings, which can be slow and costly. Instead, the company adopts LinkedIn Talent Solutions to supercharge its hiring:

Sourcing Candidates: The recruiting team uses LinkedIn Recruiter to proactively search for candidates. With advanced filters (by skills, job titles, experience, location, etc.), they quickly identify a shortlist of potential hires from the over one billion LinkedIn profiles. The recruiters can see rich profile information – work history, skills, recommendations – and even whether someone is "open to opportunities." They reach out directly through InMail (LinkedIn's messaging) to engage these prospects. This direct, data-driven sourcing vastly widens the talent pool beyond who would apply on their own.

Job Advertising: Simultaneously, the company's HR posts its open jobs on LinkedIn Jobs. Thanks to LinkedIn's targeting algorithms, these job postings are shown to relevant candidates (for example, people with matching keywords in their profile or who have indicated interest in similar roles). Interested professionals can apply in a frictionless way – often with just a couple clicks using their LinkedIn profile via Easy Apply. Those applications flow straight into the company's applicant tracking system for review, or recruiters can manage them within LinkedIn's interface. This results in a higher volume of qualified applicants, as LinkedIn reduces barriers to apply (no lengthy forms for the candidate).

Efficiency and Quality: By using LTS, the company's recruiters become much more productive. Instead of juggling multiple platforms, they handle most recruiting tasks in one integrated environment. One real-life enterprise reported that adopting LinkedIn's Hiring Enterprise tools "immediately increased the productivity of our recruiters by 25%" – a significant efficiency gain. In our scenario, this means faster time-to-hire: roles that might have taken 3+ months to fill can now find good candidates in weeks. Moreover, because LinkedIn provides insights (like showing if a candidate knows someone at the company, or how they compare to others in the talent pool), recruiters can make better-informed hiring decisions. (Notably, 67% of recruiters say professionals hired via LinkedIn are of higher quality, reinforcing this point.)

Cost Savings: LinkedIn Talent Solutions can also cut recruitment costs. By leveraging LinkedIn's network directly, companies rely less on third-party agencies or recruiters who charge hefty fees. For instance, one organization in a public case study saved an estimated $500,000–$600,000 in one year by using LinkedIn to hire in-house, reducing spend on external recruitment agencies. Our hypothetical company similarly benefits by building an internal pipeline of candidates via LinkedIn, saving budget while gaining greater control over employer branding and candidate experience.

Talent Insights and Strategy: Through tools like Talent Insights, the company's HR can glean data to refine their strategy. They might discover, for example, that Data Scientists with AI skills are highly concentrated in City X or that their competitor is hiring aggressively in a certain domain. Such information (often available in LinkedIn Talent Solutions dashboards) helps in decision-making – whether it's opening a new office in a talent-rich location or adjusting salary offers to be more competitive. Essentially, LinkedIn's platform doesn't just provide candidates; it provides market intelligence for talent planning.

Overall, the use of LinkedIn Talent Solutions in this scenario leads to faster hiring of quality candidates and a more streamlined recruitment process. This fictionalized case mirrors many real-world outcomes – LinkedIn's customer testimonials include faster hiring cycles, improved recruiter productivity, and better hiring ROI. By tapping into LinkedIn's huge network and rich data, companies can fill roles that previously seemed tough to hire, all while elevating their employer brand among a global professional audience.

Dynamics 365 Human Resources Integration with LinkedIn

Dynamics 365 Human Resources stores job and applicant data in Microsoft Dataverse. This enables integration with LinkedIn Recruiter through APIs or Microsoft Power Platform tools such as Azure Logic Apps and Power Automate. Enterprises typically configure this through Azure Integration Services, with LinkedIn RSC authenticated by Microsoft Entra ID. Profile synchronization, application status updates, and interview scheduling can be automated using Power Platform flows.

One of the intriguing aspects of Microsoft owning LinkedIn is the potential for integration with Microsoft's own HR and business software. Microsoft Dynamics 365 Human Resources (formerly part of Dynamics 365 Talent) is an HR management platform that benefits from LinkedIn integration. Microsoft has indeed built links between Dynamics 365 HR and LinkedIn Talent Solutions, aiming to create a seamless hiring and HR workflow.

For example, Dynamics 365 for Talent (the earlier iteration of D365 HR) featured tight integration with LinkedIn Recruiter, allowing data to flow between the systems. This meant that a recruiter or HR manager using Dynamics 365 could view LinkedIn profile information – such as a candidate's work history, skills, and recommendations – directly within the Dynamics interface. Conversely, within LinkedIn Recruiter, they could see if a candidate already exists in their Dynamics 365 HR database or if any internal notes exist, etc. Essentially, the integration "draws together disparate information to build accurate candidate profiles and improve the ROI of the hiring process." Instead of treating LinkedIn and the HR system as separate silos, recruiters get a unified view. They might source a candidate on LinkedIn and one-click import them into Dynamics 365 as an applicant record, or automatically keep candidate statuses in sync between the two.

Concretely, Microsoft enabled this via Recruiter System Connect (RSC), an integration service that connects LinkedIn Recruiter with ATS/HR systems. Dynamics 365 for Talent: Attract (the recruiting module) was one of the ATS that supported RSC. Through such integration, when a recruiter logs a candidate in D365, they can see if that person matches a LinkedIn profile, and they can send them an InMail or view updated LinkedIn info without manual data entry. This "seamless communication and data exchange" between Dynamics 365 HR and LinkedIn helps streamline recruitment – saving time and reducing duplication. It also facilitates better insight: recruiters can leverage LinkedIn's extensive data within their HR system to make better hiring decisions.

Another aspect of integration is job postings. A Dynamics 365 HR user (recruiter) can publish a job opening in their HR system and have that job automatically post to LinkedIn Jobs through integration, ensuring broad reach. Conversely, applicants from LinkedIn can be funneled into D365 HR's recruiting app. Microsoft's documentation for the new Dynamics 365 HR Recruiting (preview) suggests that Microsoft is re-introducing a first-class recruiting module in D365 HR (after having deprecated the old Talent Attract app). While details are still in preview, it's likely this will come with even more LinkedIn connectivity given Microsoft's emphasis on leveraging LinkedIn's strengths in hiring.

From an HR practitioner's perspective, this integration is "cool" because it merges the power of LinkedIn's network with the enterprise data and processes of Dynamics. Recruiters no longer need to toggle between platforms to update candidate records or check for profile updates. They get a 360-degree view of the candidate in one place, and actions (like contacting a candidate or scheduling an interview) are streamlined. As one Dynamics 365 HR partner noted, a key benefit is the ability to "enhance the process of talent sourcing, recruiting and selection with LinkedIn Talent Solutions" directly within Dynamics. Also, features like scheduling interviews are improved – with Office 365 integration for calendars and LinkedIn integration for candidate info, Dynamics 365 HR can automate much of the admin work in hiring.

In summary, Dynamics 365 Human Resources integration with LinkedIn allows organizations to unify their talent acquisition process. It combines internal HR workflows (like job requisitions, candidate tracking, onboarding) with LinkedIn's external talent marketplace. This not only boosts efficiency but also improves candidate experience (candidates get quicker responses and more personalized communication) and gives HR teams richer analytics. It exemplifies the advantage of Microsoft owning LinkedIn – the enterprise software (Dynamics 365, Office 365) and the professional network (LinkedIn) can work hand-in-hand.

Evolving AI in Talent Acquisition

Copilot Studio is powered by Azure AI orchestration and supports custom scenarios using large language models (LLMs) such as those available through Azure OpenAI Service. In recruiting, organizations can extend these tools with custom plugins or data connectors that interpret candidate CVs, rank applicants, or summarize feedback from interviews. These AI capabilities are embedded securely in Microsoft Teams, Dynamics 365, or stand-alone applications using Microsoft authentication and role-based access.

Looking ahead, the partnership between Microsoft and LinkedIn is poised to drive further innovation in how companies attract and manage talent. A few future-facing trends and possibilities include:

Deeper Integration Across Microsoft's Ecosystem: We can expect LinkedIn to weave even more tightly into Microsoft's broad suite of enterprise tools. Beyond Dynamics 365 HR, think about integrations with Microsoft Teams or Viva (Microsoft's employee experience platform). In fact, Dynamics 365 HR already integrates with Viva Connections to deliver HR info in Teams. It's conceivable that LinkedIn could contribute content there too – for example, showing open roles or recommended internal candidates in Teams, or allowing employees to update LinkedIn-learning credentials through their MS profile. Microsoft has a history of integrating acquisitions gradually (as seen with LinkedIn Learning available through Azure Active Directory single sign-on, etc.), so further blending is likely.

AI-Powered Recruiting: Given Microsoft's heavy investment in AI (and the OpenAI partnership) and LinkedIn's rich dataset, the recruitment process is likely to become more AI-driven. We're already seeing early steps: LinkedIn has introduced AI features to optimize job postings and candidate matches. Microsoft's 2024 Work Trend Index (created with LinkedIn) noted that employees and recruiters are eager to embrace AI at work. In the near future, recruiters might have an AI Copilot (Microsoft's AI assistant concept) embedded in LinkedIn Recruiter or Dynamics 365 HR. This AI could automatically generate effective job descriptions, screen candidates by parsing their profiles, or even recommend top candidates for a role by analyzing LinkedIn data and a company's successful hires. The LinkedIn Talent Solutions roadmap for 2025 hints at "faster, AI-assisted sourcing" becoming standard. AI could also personalize how companies engage candidates – for instance, suggesting tailored content to send a candidate based on their background.

Unified Talent Ecosystem: Microsoft's long-term plan seems to be creating a holistic talent ecosystem – from hiring to onboarding to continuous learning and development – with LinkedIn at the core. Imagine a scenario where an employee's journey is fully connected: they are hired via LinkedIn Talent Solutions, onboarded through Dynamics 365 HR, upskilled via LinkedIn Learning, and even inside the organization they leverage LinkedIn's networking (via Viva) to find mentors or new internal roles. Some pieces of this are already in place (LinkedIn Learning is offered as part of many corporate learning programs, and Dynamics 365 can record learning progress, etc.). Future developments might close the loop, for example, using LinkedIn skill assessments to update an employee's profile and sync that with their HR record in Dynamics, so that internal recruiters can find internal candidates with the right skills.

Continued Growth and Influence: Lastly, LinkedIn's Talent Solutions will likely continue to grow in influence globally. With over a billion professionals on the platform, LinkedIn has a unique vantage point to observe labor market trends. We might see LinkedIn providing more macro-level insights (via its Economic Graph data) to help companies with workforce planning. Microsoft and LinkedIn already publish reports on talent trends, and as the integration deepens, these insights could feed directly into Microsoft's analytics tools (for example, LinkedIn data enriching Power BI dashboards for HR analytics). Gartner and McKinsey foresee a future where data-driven recruitment is standard – LinkedIn (with Microsoft's cloud AI) is well-positioned to lead that charge.

In conclusion, the Microsoft–LinkedIn partnership has evolved significantly since the 2016 acquisition. LinkedIn Talent Solutions today plays a crucial role in how organizations worldwide find and hire talent, offering unparalleled scale and tools for recruiters. Microsoft's stewardship (and integration of LinkedIn with products like Dynamics 365 Human Resources) has only strengthened these capabilities. By uniting productivity software, enterprise data, and the vast LinkedIn network, Microsoft is creating a powerful ecosystem for talent acquisition and management. And with ongoing innovations in AI and platform integration, the future of recruiting looks to be even more connected and intelligent, with LinkedIn Talent Solutions at the heart of that transformation.

Summary

Microsoft's acquisition of LinkedIn in 2016 laid the groundwork for a powerful synergy between productivity tools and professional networking. Today, LinkedIn Talent Solutions (LTS) is central to Microsoft's talent strategy, offering a suite of tools – LinkedIn Recruiter, LinkedIn Jobs, Career Pages, and Talent Insights – that help organizations source, attract, and hire top talent from LinkedIn's 1.1 billion-member network.

LTS enables seamless recruiting experiences through integrations with Applicant Tracking Systems (ATS), including Microsoft's own Dynamics 365 Human Resources. Features like Recruiter System Connect (RSC) and Apply Connect allow synchronized candidate profiles, automated status updates, and streamlined interview scheduling, improving hiring speed, quality, and cost efficiency. Organizations also leverage LinkedIn's insights in Power BI dashboards for strategic workforce planning.

The integration of LinkedIn with Dynamics 365 HR enables a unified talent workflow – from job posting and candidate sourcing to onboarding and profile syncing – all powered by Microsoft Entra ID authentication and the Dataverse platform.

Looking ahead, Microsoft is embedding AI capabilities across this ecosystem. Tools like Copilot Studio, Azure OpenAI, and Microsoft 365 Copilot are enabling AI-assisted candidate screening, job description generation, and interview feedback analysis. The vision is to create a unified talent ecosystem – from external recruiting on LinkedIn to internal mobility, upskilling through LinkedIn Learning, and HR analytics – integrated across Microsoft Teams, Dynamics 365, Viva, and Power Platform.

Ultimately, Microsoft and LinkedIn are shaping the future of connected, intelligent recruiting. By aligning enterprise software with the world's largest professional network and infusing AI at every stage, they are transforming how organizations find, engage, and develop talent globally.

PART IV

Optimizing Your HR Tech Stack

Data Security, Governance, and Compliance in the Microsoft HR Tech Stack

Role-Based Access Control with Microsoft Entra ID Across HR Systems

Implementing robust RBAC ensures that only the right people have access to sensitive HR data across Dynamics 365 Human Resources, Power Platform, SharePoint, and Teams. Microsoft Entra ID (formerly Microsoft Entra ID AD) serves as the unified identity and access management layer for all these services, enabling single sign-on and centralized control. This unified identity approach means that when an employee's role changes or they leave, updating their group membership or disabling their Entra ID account immediately updates access across all connected HR resources. Key best practices include:

- Use Entra ID Security Groups for Role Management: Define Microsoft Entra ID security groups aligning with HR roles (e.g., "HR-Core-Team," "HR-Managers," "HR-IT-Support"). Assign these groups the appropriate permissions in each application rather than assigning users individually. For example, in Dynamics 365 Human Resources you can create a Dataverse team bound to an Entra security group

© Ana Inés Urrutia de Souza 2025
A. I. Urrutia de Souza, *The Microsoft AI Human Resources Handbook*,
https://doi.org/10.1007/979-8-8688-1781-6_8

and assign the HR security roles to that team. This way, any user added to the Microsoft Entra ID group automatically inherits the correct role in D365 HR. Similarly, associate your Power Platform environments with an Entra security group so that only members are provisioned as users in that environment. This approach simplifies onboarding/offboarding and ensures consistency.

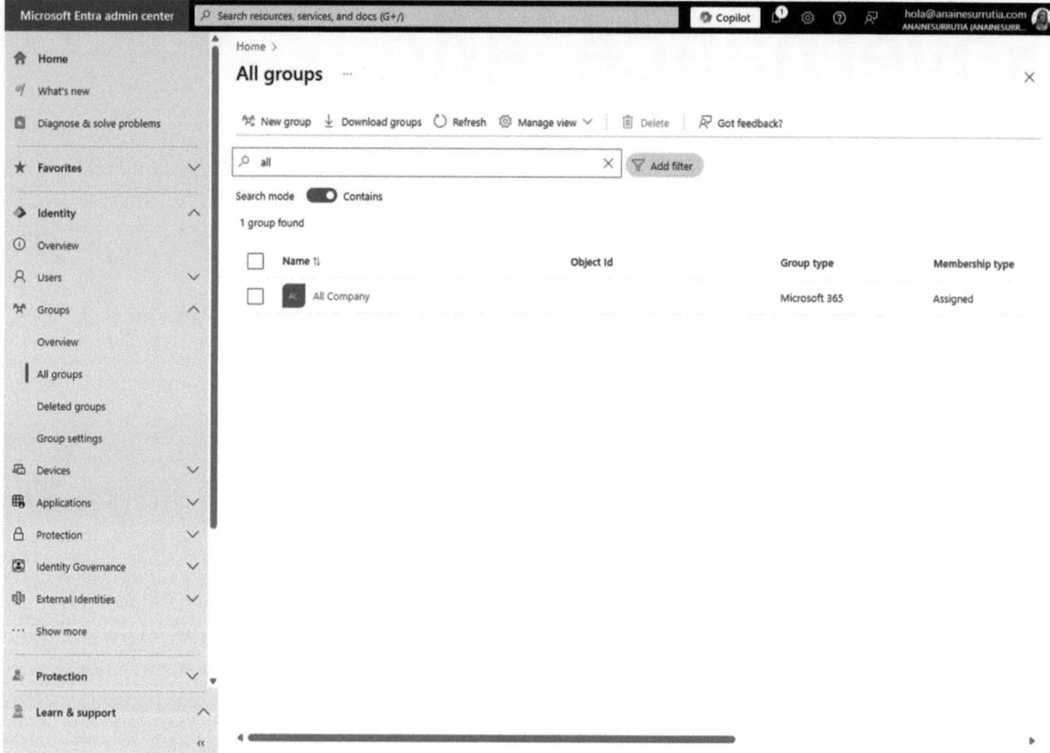

- Leverage Built-in Roles and Custom Roles: Microsoft 365 provides many built-in admin roles (e.g., "Dynamics 365 Administrator," "Power Platform Admin," "SharePoint Admin," "Teams Admin") that should be granted to IT staff on a need-to-have basis. Use least privilege principles – for example, an HR power user who builds Power Apps might only need the "Environment Maker" role in a specific environment, not full tenant admin rights. In SharePoint, grant HR site owners and members via Entra groups (or Microsoft 365 Groups) rather than individual users. In Teams, designate a limited number of Team Owners (possibly an HR group) who can manage membership of HR-related teams, and avoid adding broad distribution lists or "Everyone" to sensitive HR teams.

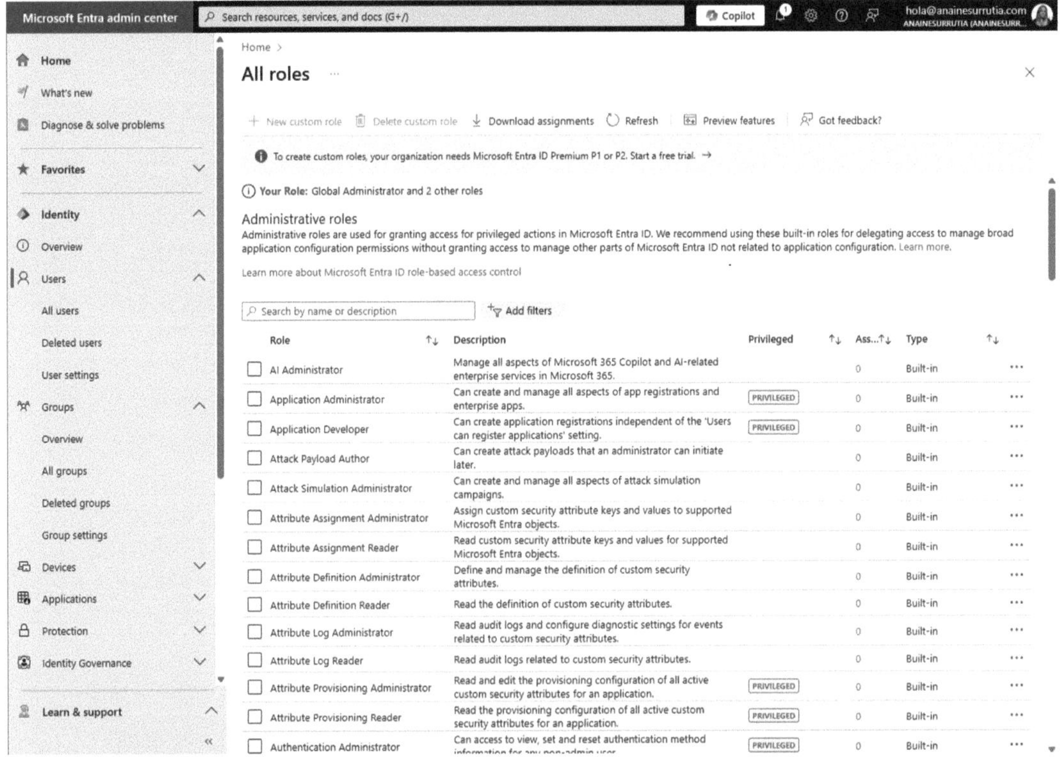

- Segregation of Duties: Divide admin responsibilities among roles to prevent overreliance on one account. For instance, the person managing Entra ID groups might be different from the person approving D365 role assignments. In critical cases, enable Microsoft Entra Privileged Identity Management (PIM) so that highly privileged roles (like Global Administrator or Compliance Administrator) are only active with just-in-time elevation. This reduces standing access to sensitive functions.

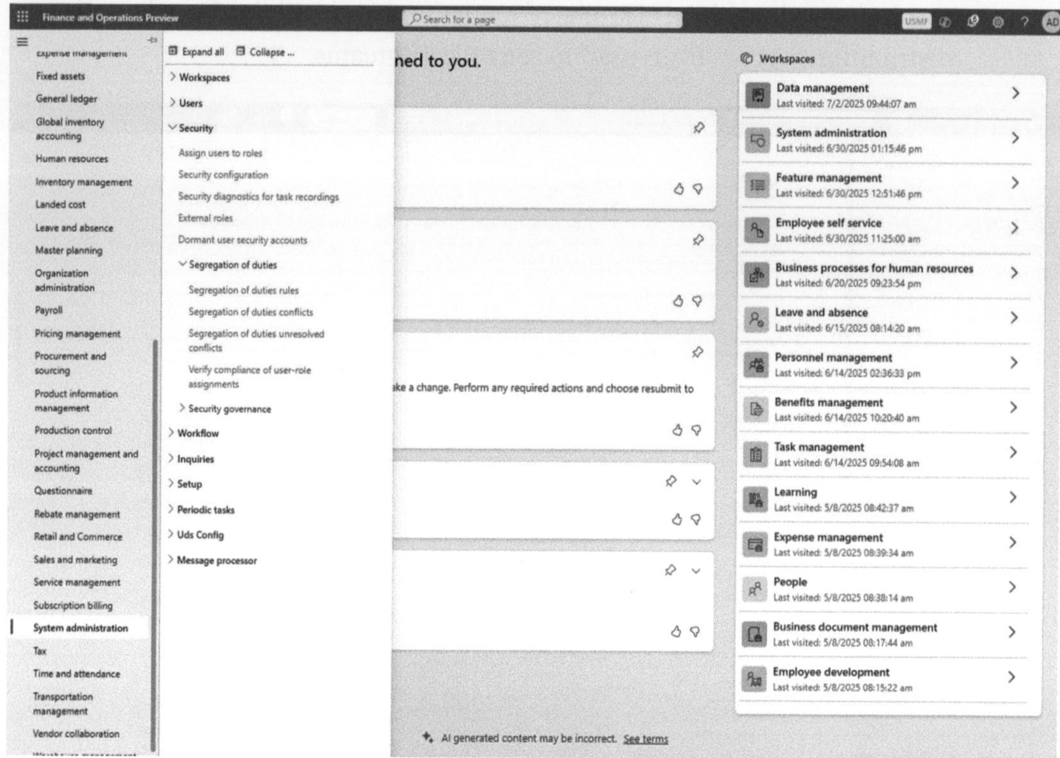

- Consistent Conditional Access Policies: Because all these HR systems
  authenticate through Entra ID, you can enforce uniform conditional
  access rules. Require multifactor authentication (MFA) for any HR
  application access, enforce location or device-based restrictions for
  HR data (e.g., only allow access to HR Power Apps from managed
  devices or specific networks), and consider using Microsoft Entra
  ID Identity Protection to flag risky sign-ins for HR accounts. These
  policies help ensure that even if credentials are compromised,
  unauthorized access to HR data is prevented.

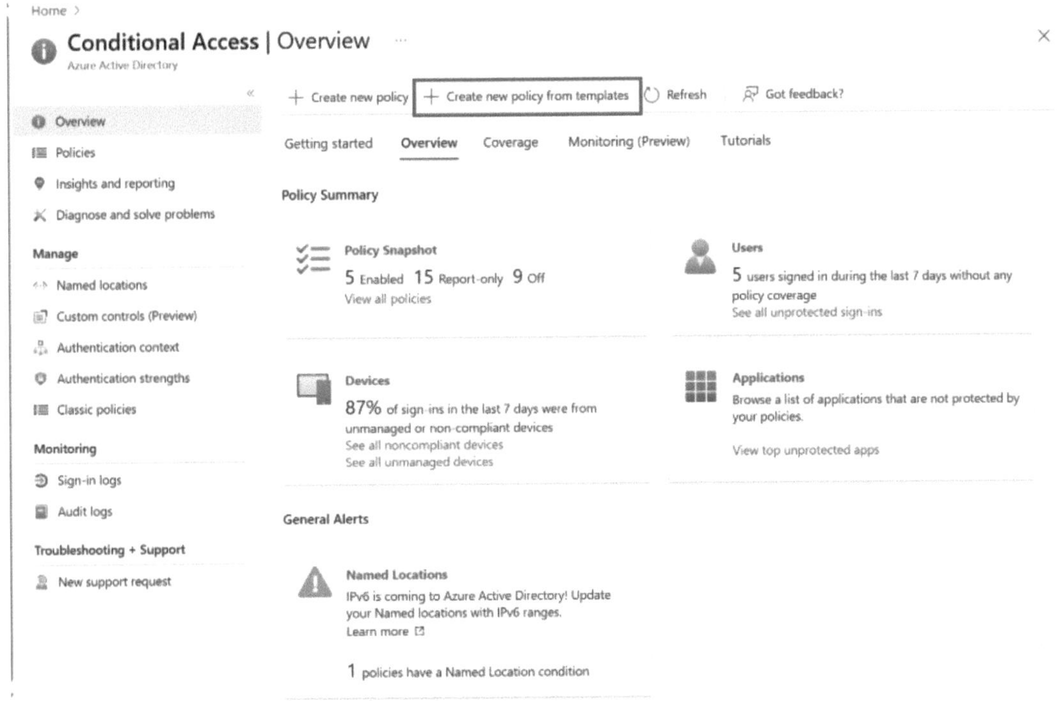

- Regular Access Reviews: Establish a process (perhaps quarterly) to review group membership and role assignments for HR systems. Microsoft Entra ID access reviews (part of Microsoft Entra ID Governance) can automate this by prompting group owners or managers to certify that each member still needs access. This helps catch permission creep over time. Likewise, use Dynamics 365's user role reports or Power Platform's Admin Center user list to audit who has access to what. Remove users who no longer need access or whose accounts are inactive.

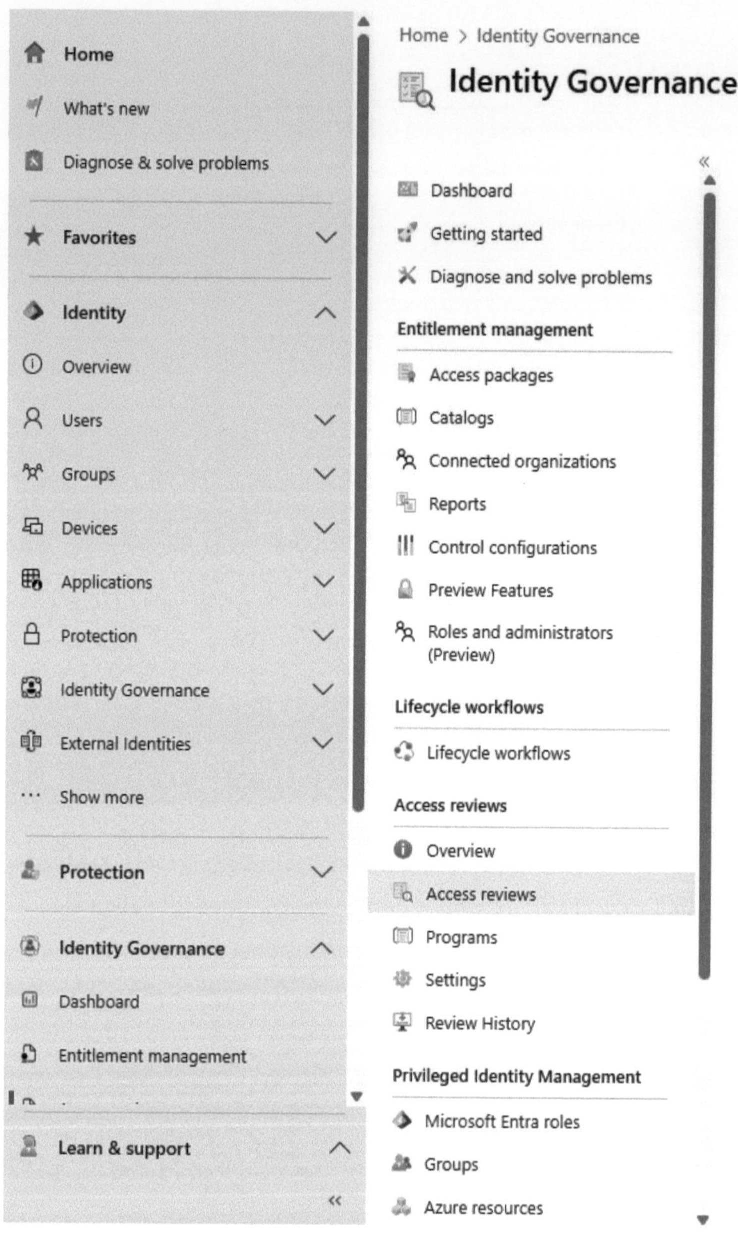

Be mindful that adding a user to an environment's security group in Power Platform doesn't automatically grant them rights to data – you still must assign a Dataverse security role for them to actually use apps or see records; if you later associate a security group with an environment that already has users, any user not in the group will be disabled in that environment. Plan group membership carefully and communicate changes to avoid surprises. Also, document your RBAC model – maintain a matrix of

Entra ID groups and which HR roles/systems they map to – so that HR, IT, and audit teams have a clear understanding of who can access which data.

Secure Power Platform Environment Architecture (Dev/Test/Prod)

When building HR solutions on the Power Platform (Power Apps, Power Automate, etc.), a secure environment strategy is essential. Segregate development, testing, and production into separate environments to protect live HR data and achieve compliance in change management:

- Dev/Test/Prod Segmentation: Use at least three environments – for example, HR-Dev, HR-Test, HR-Prod. Development environments (often set up as Sandbox type) allow makers to build and experiment without affecting real data. Test/UAT environments allow QA and user acceptance testing on realistic (but sanitized) data. Production holds the live HR apps and data with strict access. By isolating these stages, you ensure that incomplete or unapproved apps in Dev cannot accidentally leak data or impact users in Prod. Each environment should be linked to an Entra security group to restrict who can even enter it (for instance, only the HR IT developers in Dev, a broader group, including testers in UAT, and all employees, might have end user access in Prod).

- Solution-Aware Development & ALM: Always create Power Apps and Power Automate flows inside a managed solution rather than as individual, unmanaged components. Solution-aware flows and apps are much easier to move across environments and support robust ALM practices.

  For example, when a change is ready, you can export the solution from Dev and import it to Test or Prod, or use Power Platform pipelines to automate deployment with proper approvals. Within solutions, leverage connection references and environment variables to handle differences between environments (such as pointing a Dev flow to a Dev SharePoint site and a Prod flow to the Prod site). This

241

avoids hard-coding environment-specific info and makes promotion seamless. Also take advantage of solution features like version control – solution-aware flows support versioning and can store flow execution history in Dataverse for advanced tracking.

- Dataverse Security Roles and Data Policies: If your HR apps use Microsoft Dataverse (either as part of Dynamics 365 HR or a Power Apps database), enforce granular security within Dataverse. Define security roles that correspond to HR job functions – for example, an "HR Manager" role might have read/write access to employee records and compensation data, whereas an "HR Assistant" role has read-only access to certain tables, and "All Employees Self-Service" might only allow updating one's own profile. Assign these roles to users (or better, to Microsoft Entra ID group teams as described earlier). Leverage Dataverse's column security for particularly sensitive fields (e.g., Social Security Number, medical info) so that even if a user can see an employee record, they cannot see or update those protected fields without an additional role. Also consider using business units in Dataverse if your organization needs to segregate data (for instance, HR data for Europe vs. United States) – this can ensure a user in one BU cannot see data in another unless explicitly allowed.

- Managed Environments & DLP for Power Platform: Consider using Power Platform Managed Environments features if available, which provide enhanced governance for production environments (like weekly admin digest, limits on sharing, etc.). At a minimum, implement Data Loss Prevention (DLP) policies in the Power Platform Admin Center to control connector usage. In an HR context, you will likely mark internal services (Dataverse, Office 365, SharePoint, etc.) as "Business" connectors and block or isolate external services as "Non-Business." This ensures a flow in the HR environment cannot, say, accidentally send employee data to Twitter or Dropbox because those connectors would be disallowed in that environment. DLP policies are tenant-wide or environment-specific rules that prevent combining Business and Non-Business connectors in the same app/flow, thereby protecting HR data from flowing to unapproved services. For example, an HR Power Automate flow could be allowed to use SharePoint and Outlook (both business connectors), but if someone tries to add a Gmail connector, the policy would block it. These policies help maintain compliance with data handling rules and prevent makers from inadvertently introducing leaks.

When copying production HR data into lower environments for testing, mask or anonymize sensitive personal data whenever possible. Real employee data should not be freely accessible in a Dev environment that has weaker controls. Use tools or scripts to scramble names, emails, or identification numbers in test data. Also, set environment-level data integration accounts with minimum needed privileges – for instance, if using Power Automate to integrate D365 HR with Microsoft Entra ID AD, use a dedicated service account with a narrowly scoped role rather than a global admin's credentials. Finally, proactively monitor environment capacity (Dataverse storage, API calls, etc.) in Power Platform Admin Center. HR applications with lots of records or heavy usage might approach storage or service limits; configure alerts or check dashboards regularly to avoid disruptions.

Secure Power Platform Environment Architecture – at a Glance

When building HR solutions with Power Platform tools like Power Apps and Power Automate, security and structure are just as important as functionality. A well-planned environment architecture not only protects sensitive HR data but also supports scalability, compliance, and smooth app life cycle management. Below is a quick summary of the core components every HR tech team should have in place:

Dev/Test/Prod Segmentation

- Use **separate environments**: HR-Dev, HR-Test (UAT), HR-Prod

- Dev = Safe sandbox for makers

- Test = QA and UAT on sanitized data

- Prod = Live apps and data with strict access controls

- **Control access** via Microsoft Entra security groups

Solution-Aware Development and ALM

- Build **inside managed solutions** (not stand-alone apps/flows).

- Use **Power Platform Pipelines** or export/import for deployment.

- Use **environment variables** and **connection references** to avoid hardcoding.

- Benefit from **versioning** and **Dataverse flow history tracking.**

Dataverse Security and Data Policies

- Define **security roles** by HR function (e.g., HR Manager, Assistant).

- Use **column-level security** for sensitive fields (e.g., SSNs, medical data).

- Assign roles via **Entra groups** for scalable management.

- Use **Business Units** to segment data by region or entity.

Managed Environments and DLP

- Enable **Managed Environments** for governance and insights.

- Set up **DLP policies** to restrict risky connectors (e.g., block Gmail, Twitter).

- Separate connectors into **Business** vs. **Non-business.**

- Prevent accidental data leakage and ensure compliance.

Deploying a Power Platform Center of Excellence (CoE) for HR Solutions

Establishing a Center of Excellence helps govern and nurture your HR Power Platform usage at scale. Microsoft provides a CoE Starter Kit – a collection of components (apps, flows, dashboards) that you can deploy in your tenant to gain oversight of Power Apps,

Power Automate, and even Copilot Studio bots. For an HR IT team, the CoE acts as a "governance engine" ensuring compliance and best practices are followed by makers building HR apps. Key implementation steps and practices:

- CoE Environment and Initial Setup: It's recommended to create a dedicated CoE environment (Dataverse data store enabled) to install the kit solutions. This environment will store inventory and log data about all your apps/flows. Import the Core, Governance, and Nurture solutions from the CoE Starter Kit into this environment, following Microsoft's setup instructions. Part of setup involves establishing connections (e.g., the kit uses the Power Platform Admin connectors and Graph HTTP calls) and setting environment variables. Use the CoE Setup Wizard for governance components if available, which can streamline configuration. Make sure the account configuring the CoE has sufficient roles (Power Platform Admin or Dynamics 365 admin) and access to all environments, so it can scan and manage tenant-wide resources.

- Telemetry and Inventory Collection: A huge benefit of the CoE is the telemetry it gathers. The CoE kit includes "audit log sync" flows that pull usage data from the Microsoft 365 Audit Log (via Office 365 Management APIs) to track things like app launch counts, unique users per app, flow runs, etc. By default, the kit will inventory all Power Apps, Power Automate flows, etc., but usage fields (e.g., "Last Launched Date" or number of executions) will remain blank unless you set up these audit log flows. Action item: register a Microsoft Entra ID application and grant it ActivityFeed.Read for Office 365 Management API, then provide its Client ID/Secret to the CoE's environment variables. Once configured and turned on, the flows will regularly sync audit events so you can see, for example, that the "Employee Onboarding App" was launched 200 times this month by 150 users. This telemetry feeds into the CoE's Power BI dashboard.

- Power BI Dashboards and Reports: Microsoft provides a CoE Starter Kit Power BI dashboard that connects to the CoE Dataverse data. This dashboard gives you tenant-wide and environment-level insights into your HR apps and automations – number of apps, flows, chatbots, their owners, last launch dates, top connectors used, etc. Visualize the data to spot outliers: for example, a chart can show which environments or departments are creating the most apps, or map where app makers are located to ensure global HR solutions are properly supported. Below is an example of the CoE dashboard summarizing apps and usage:

Using this dashboard, HR IT can monitor adoption and identify potential risks – for example, an app with extremely high usage (maybe a mission-critical HR service app) should be reviewed for performance and compliance, whereas apps with no recent launches might be candidates for cleanup. The CoE also highlights if many apps are in the default environment (which might indicate shadow IT that should be governed) or if connectors are used in violation of policy (e.g., a Makers page can list all apps using certain connectors).

- Automated Life Cycle Governance: The CoE kit's Governance components include flows and apps that enforce standards automatically. For instance, compliance workflows can flag apps that are widely shared or business-critical and ensure they meet certain criteria. By configuring the Developer Compliance Center processes, you can require makers to provide metadata like business justification, support plan, data classification, etc., for their apps. The kit sets default thresholds – for example, if an app is shared with more than 20 users, or has over 30 launches in the past month, it's considered important and the maker will be asked for additional documentation. You can adjust these numbers (all stored in environment variables) based on your HR governance policies. When a threshold is exceeded, an automated flow kicks in to email the app owner asking them to fill out a compliance form. The maker receives a link to the Developer Compliance Center canvas app where they might answer questions like: "What business process does this app support? What data classification is the app's data? What's the impact if the app is down?" The maker's responses are saved in Dataverse and can be reviewed by admins.

- App Review and Cataloging Workflow: Once a maker submits the required info, the CoE provides an App Audit business process flow for administrators to review and approve the app. In a model-driven app interface (Power Platform Admin View), the admin can see all details of the app (description, connectors, last used, maker-submitted justification) in one place. They can then mark an app as Compliant or provide feedback to the maker if something needs change. A common decision point is whether the app should be moved to a managed Production environment or even added to a curated App Catalog for end users. The CoE toolkit supports marking an app as "Featured" (for a catalog) once it passes audit. For example, after an HR onboarding app is reviewed and approved, you might promote it to the official HR Apps catalog (perhaps a SharePoint site or Teams tab) so that employees know it's an IT-sanctioned solution. All of this workflow – from initial compliance request to final approval – is tracked, creating an audit trail of governance actions. It saves IT teams from manually chasing hundreds of app owners and instead implements a scalable, workflow-driven process.

- Center of Excellence as Ongoing Process: Beyond initial deployment, treat the CoE as a living program. Staff your CoE with roles like a Power Platform Admin (to monitor daily operations), a Business Liaison (from HR, to ensure apps align with HR's needs and policies), and perhaps a Champions community (power users in HR who advocate best practices). Use the CoE's Nurture components to train and support makers – for example, the kit can send automated welcome emails to new app makers with links to training content. Regularly update the CoE kit to get improvements (Microsoft releases updates periodically; plan for testing those in your CoE environment). Also, use the insights to refine governance – if you notice many orphaned apps (apps whose owners left the company), establish a process with HR to reassign or archive those. If certain departments (like Recruiting or Benefits) are creating many automations, maybe it's time to spin up a dedicated environment for them for better segregation. The CoE is not set-and-forget but rather a toolkit to continually improve your HR tech stack's hygiene.

Ensure that the service principal used by CoE flows has adequate permissions. For audit log ingestion, it needs permission to read audit data (ActivityFeed API) and your tenant's audit logging must be turned on (check in Microsoft Purview Compliance Portal). Also note, the CoE audit log sync incurs API calls – monitor for any throttling or consider scaling the frequency based on needs (e.g., maybe you don't need to sync every hour for moderate app usage). When makers get compliance emails, some may ignore or be confused – it's wise to socialize this program in advance ("Hey HR team, IT will be implementing an app compliance review – here's why it's important..."). You can customize the email templates in the flows to fit your tone and include contacts for questions. Lastly, exempt certain environments from CoE compliance flows if they are tightly IT-managed or system environments (e.g., your Prod HR environment where only IT builds might not need the same scrutiny as the Default environment where everyone can build). The CoE Admin View app allows setting an "Excuse from Compliance" flag on environments that should be skipped.

Leveraging Microsoft 365 Compliance Tools for HR Data Protection

HR data is highly sensitive – it includes personal information, salaries, performance notes, etc., and is subject to regulations (GDPR, etc.). The Microsoft 365 Compliance (Purview) suite provides several tools to ensure HR data is handled properly and to mitigate risks: audit logging, data loss prevention, and insider risk management are particularly relevant.

- Unified Audit Logging: Audit logs should be enabled and actively used for all HR systems. In Microsoft 365 (which covers SharePoint, Teams, Exchange, etc.), the unified audit log can track activities like file access, user deletions, permission changes, and more. Make sure auditing is turned on for the tenant (it usually is by default now, but double-check in the Compliance Center). For Dynamics 365 HR and Power Platform, enable auditing within those systems as well (Dataverse allows auditing at the entity and field level for changes to records; D365 HR, if on the Finance & Ops platform, has its own activity log). Use the Microsoft Purview Compliance Portal audit search to run queries when needed – for example, "who accessed the file containing executive compensation last week" or "export events from the HR site in SharePoint." Configure Alerts on sensitive activities: for example, get an alert if someone downloads over 100 HR files in an hour, or if a privileged account like an HR admin purges audit logs. Having audit trails is not just for security – it's often required for compliance (e.g., proving who accessed what data). Microsoft Purview's audit logs for M365 can retain data for 90 days by default (longer with advanced licensing). If your HR data needs longer retention for investigations, consider Advanced Audit which can retain certain high-value audit records for a year or more.

- Data Loss Prevention (DLP) Policies: In an HR context, you want to prevent sensitive information from leaking – whether through email, Teams chats, or via file sharing. Microsoft 365 DLP allows you to create policies that detect sensitive data patterns (like Social Security Numbers, health info, or other PII) and define actions if such data is found being shared inappropriately. For example, you might create a DLP policy that applies to Exchange and Teams: if a message contains a National ID or a keyword like "Performance Review" and is being sent to an external recipient, block it and notify the sender. Or a policy for SharePoint/OneDrive that if a file in the HR site or labeled "Confidential" is shared with anyone outside the organization, the sharing is automatically revoked or the file is encrypted. Leverage the built-in sensitive info types (Microsoft has many definitions like ABA routing numbers, passport numbers, etc.) or create custom types for things like "Employee ID" or internal project codes. For consistency, classify and label HR documents – for instance, use sensitivity labels in Purview to tag all files in your HR SharePoint site as "HR Confidential." These labels can be configured to enforce encryption or to simply serve as markers for DLP. When content is labeled or stored in specific HR locations, you can target DLP policies more narrowly (reducing false positives). In sum, DLP is your automated gatekeeper: it should be tuned to the kinds of data HR handles. Combine DLP with user education – if someone triggers a policy (e.g., tries to email a list of salaries), have the policy notify them with a friendly message about why it's not allowed, so they learn to use approved secure methods.

- Insider Risk Management: Not all data leaks are malicious; some are internal mistakes or even deliberate wrongdoing by insiders. Microsoft Purview Insider Risk Management is a solution that correlates signals to detect high-risk activities by users. In an HR scenario, you could configure insider risk policies to watch for indicators around HR data – for example, if an HR employee who has given notice of resignation starts downloading large volumes of files from the HR SharePoint or printing many documents, this could flag a risk. Similarly, unusual behavior like an employee accessing files they never do (e.g., someone in Sales trying to access salary info) could indicate snooping. Insider Risk Management allows you to incorporate HR signals (via the HR connector, you can input data like employment termination dates) so that the system can raise risk scores for users near their termination date. Your insider risk policies might target scenarios such as data theft by departing employees, inappropriate HR data access, or policy violations (like saving confidential data to personal cloud). When a risk alert triggers, a designated reviewer (often someone in HR, Legal, or a special investigations role) can investigate the case in the Purview portal. They can view the user's recent activities (files accessed, emails sent, Teams messages, etc. – privacy-trimmed as per policy) to determine if it looks truly risky. For example, an alert might show that "User X uploaded a file with sensitive info to a personal Dropbox account" – clearly a red flag. At that point, Insider Risk Management allows various actions: escalate to formal investigation, involve HR management, or even integrate with eDiscovery if legal action is needed. It's important to have HR involved in developing these policies because they understand the context of employee roles and can help set the right thresholds (and also to ensure you comply with employment laws and privacy when monitoring employees). Keep insider risk policies targeted – focus on areas of greatest concern (like confidential HR data and key insider groups). Also regularly review and tune them to reduce noise.

- Additional Compliance Measures: Aside from those three, other Purview tools could help HR. Retention policies – you might have rules to retain employee records for X years after they leave, or auto-delete certain data after Y years to comply with data minimization. Configure retention labels for content in SharePoint/Exchange related to HR (for instance, tag all content in an "Employee Investigations" library to auto-delete after seven years). Communication compliance – you might monitor for code of conduct violations in communications (e.g., harassment language in Teams or emails). If HR is responsible for ensuring workplace compliance, they could use this to get alerts on inappropriate behavior. Lastly, ensure Compliance Manager in Purview is tracking HR-related regulatory controls (like GDPR Articles that apply to employee data) – this tool can help you assess if you've implemented all required controls and even assign tasks (e.g., "Enable DLP for HR data" could be one control in Compliance Manager with status tracking).

When implementing DLP or insider risk policies, involve both IT and HR leadership. There may be legitimate HR workflows that trigger DLP (e.g., sending a spreadsheet of hires to a third-party benefits provider). In such cases, you might need to add exceptions (perhaps allow emails to that provider's domain even if they contain sensitive info, but still encrypt them). Test policies in Audit mode first – Purview allows you to see what would have happened without actually blocking content, which is invaluable for tuning. For audit logs, note that Dynamics 365 apps (including HR) might have separate audit settings – make sure those are on, and back up the logs if needed before they recycle. And remember, audit data and DLP alerts themselves can contain sensitive info – restrict access to the Compliance Center (via role-based access control like Compliance Admin or View-Only Auditor roles) so that only authorized personnel (e.g., HR privacy officer, security team) can view these details. You don't want just any IT admin poking through HR audit trails without cause. Finally, regularly review DLP incident reports and insider risk analytics – these will show you trends and help you continuously improve policies (e.g., if a particular type of sensitive data is often shared and blocked, maybe the HR team needs a secure collaboration solution for that purpose).

Managing AI-Driven HR Bots in Copilot Studio (Governance and Transparency)

As HR teams begin to leverage AI bots (such as custom Copilot agents for answering employee questions or assisting with onboarding), it's critical to manage these AI solutions with the same rigor as any HR application, if not more, given their ability to generate content and access data. Microsoft's Copilot Studio (part of the Power Platform) allows creation of custom AI-powered bots that can tap into your enterprise data. To implement these responsibly, focus on scoped data access, explainability of answers, and audit logging of bot activity:

Scoped and Secure Data Access: Copilot Studio agents should be designed to only access the data sources that are necessary for their function, and to respect user permissions on that data. In HR scenarios, this means if you build an onboarding Q&A bot, you might connect it only to a curated SharePoint knowledge base (policies, FAQs) or a specific Dataverse table of HR Q&A – not to every HR file or Teams chat. The principle "what the user can access, the bot can access" should apply: the agent will only have access to the data that the prompter (user asking it) has access to Microsoft's architecture by default enforces M365 credentials in Copilot experiences, but you must ensure any custom connectors or plugins you add to the bot also enforce proper auth. For example, if the Copilot uses a Graph API connection to read SharePoint, configure it to use the end user's identity (or a domain service account with limited privileges) rather than a super-user account. Use Microsoft Entra ID OpenAI service with your own data (if applicable) in a way that data is retrieved from an index that has only HR-approved documents. It's wise to have a review process for the knowledge sources your bot uses: HR and IT should jointly approve any content sources (to avoid inadvertently exposing a file that was not meant for broad consumption). Additionally, apply data classifications to AI-accessible content so that if, for instance, a document is tagged "Highly Confidential," the bot might either avoid using it or at least note that classification when answering.

Clear Explainability and Response Governance: An HR Copilot should provide transparent answers that users can trust and verify. Whenever possible, configure the bot to show the source of information it provides. For example, if an employee asks "What is our parental leave policy?" and the bot answers, the bot's response should ideally include a citation or reference (like "According to the 2025 Employee Handbook, page 5…" or a link to the policy document). This builds trust and helps the user confirm the answer's correctness. In Copilot Studio, one way to enable this is by structuring prompt responses to include sources when using the retrieval-augmented generation pattern – for example, include excerpts from the actual documents. Also, ensure the tone and boundaries of the bot are appropriate: for HR, bots should be factual and helpful but refrain from giving policy interpretations beyond what's written, and certainly avoid any sensitive judgments. Use prompt books or system messages to instill the bot with the right instructions (e.g., "If you are unsure or the question is outside the provided knowledge, do not fabricate an answer; instead direct the user to contact HR"). This prevents the AI from straying and improves explainability (since ideally, it will stick to known info). Maintain a change log of the bot's knowledge: if new content is added (say a new policy document), have a procedure to review and test how the bot responds to related questions, to ensure it's using the content correctly. In summary, treat the bot's "brain" as production code – changes to it (data or logic) should be controlled and understood.

Audit Logging and Oversight: Just as with any HR system, AI interactions need to be logged for compliance and possible investigation. Copilot Studio activities are automatically audited via Microsoft Purview. Every user prompt and the AI's response can generate audit log entries (if auditing is enabled) that record details like who the user was, which Copilot (agent) was used, and crucially, what files or resources the Copilot accessed to produce the answer. For example, if the Copilot pulled information from a file on SharePoint, the audit log entry will reference that file. Administrative actions in Copilot Studio – such as creating an agent, publishing it, updating its settings or connectors – are also logged

Action items: Ensure your compliance team knows that these logs exist and how to access them in the Purview Compliance Portal (under the Audit section, you can filter on Copilot-related activities). You might create custom alerts or scripts to monitor certain bot activities – for example, alert if an HR Copilot was asked a question that triggers a sensitive info disclosure (maybe detectable by certain keywords), or simply do periodic reviews of usage patterns (who is using the HR bot and for what). Microsoft also provides a specialized solution called Data Security Posture Management (DSPM) for AI – this allows security/compliance officers to review AI interactions in more detail, including reading the transcripts of conversations and verifying what data was accessed. Consider enabling DSPM for your tenant if you have Copilot agents handling sensitive HR topics. This way, if an issue arises (say, an employee claims "the HR bot gave me incorrect info about my benefits"), an authorized admin could retrieve the conversation transcript ID from the audit log and then fetch the full chat through DSPM to see what went wrong.

Policies for Responsible AI Use: Implement internal policies or guidelines for how AI bots are used in HR. For instance, decide which HR scenarios are appropriate for AI assistance and which are not. An onboarding FAQ bot or benefits Q&A bot is relatively low-risk (as long as answers are from vetted HR sources). But an AI-driven "HR Advisor" bot that tries to give personalized advice on employee relations issues would be much riskier and not advisable without human oversight. Clearly communicate to employees where an AI is being used ("This chat is with an HR virtual assistant.") and provide an easy path to reach a human if the bot cannot help or if the user is not satisfied. Monitor the feedback on the bot – Copilot Studio might not yet have built-in end user feedback loops, so create one (even if it's a simple form or email alias for bot issues). If the bot is deployed in Teams, you can use Teams App analytics to see usage and also encourage users to rate their experience. Incorporate AI systems into your incident response plan: for example, if the HR bot inadvertently exposed something it shouldn't (perhaps due to a misconfiguration), have a procedure to take it offline quickly and notify appropriate personnel. Also plan for model management – if you are using Microsoft Entra ID OpenAI under the hood, keep models up-to-date and evaluate them periodically for bias or inaccuracies on HR-specific queries.

Pitfalls and Tips: One challenge with AI bots is hallucination – the AI might sometimes produce an answer that sounds confident but is actually incorrect or not sourced from approved data. To mitigate this, continuously test your Copilot with realistic HR questions (possibly using a set of pre-production test cases whenever the knowledge source is updated). If hallucinations occur, adjust prompts or limit the scope further. Also consider using the "message limits" and moderation features: for example, limit the Copilot to only respond with a certain length to prevent it from spitting out an entire document, and use content filters to block any outputs that contain sensitive PII that shouldn't be in answers. In terms of security, treat your Copilot like a service identity – if it uses any plugins or connectors, keep those credentials safe (use Key Vault for secrets, as the Copilot Studio encourages) and revoke any that aren't needed. Audit logs will show if someone tries to tamper with the agent (like an admin updating the bot's authentication settings), so review those admin logs for any unauthorized changes. Finally, keep in mind user perception and privacy: HR topics can be personal, so ensure the bot's tone is empathetic and that it doesn't log or expose any more personal data than necessary. For instance, if someone asks the bot a question about leave balance, the transcript of that Q&A is technically HR data too – make sure access to those transcripts is limited and that you've communicated to employees that their interactions with the bot may be recorded for quality and compliance. Transparency builds trust in these AI solutions, which is essential for their success.

Monitoring and Alerting for HR Apps and Bots

Continuous monitoring is the final piece of a robust governance program. After implementing all the above controls, you need visibility into the health and usage of your HR applications (Power Apps, Automate flows, D365 modules) and AI bots, as well as a way to get alerted to issues or anomalies. Microsoft provides admin centers and analytics, and you can extend these with custom dashboards and alerting mechanisms:

Power Platform admin center Analytics: The Power Platform Admin Center (PPAC) offers out-of-the-box analytics for Power Apps and Power Automate. Go to the Analytics section in PPAC and review the App and Flow analytics for your HR environments. These dashboards show key metrics like the count of active users, session counts, error rates for flows, etc., over time. For example, you can observe if a particular HR app suddenly has a spike in errors or if a flow (such as one that syncs employee data nightly) has been failing. PPAC also provides insights into Capacity (storage, API calls) – set up the Capacity alerts to email admins when database storage or throughput consumption in an environment crosses a threshold (to avoid outages when limits are reached). In addition, monitor the Connection health – if connectors (e.g., to an external HR system or an email account) expire or fail, the Admin Center will show failed connection statistics. Establish a routine (weekly or monthly) to review these PPAC analytics for each HR-critical environment. This can catch issues like a flow that is approaching its performance limits or an app that hasn't been used in 90 days (which might be retired to reduce risk).

Custom Dashboards with Power BI: While admin center analytics are useful, combining data from multiple sources into a Power BI dashboard can give a holistic view. Building on the CoE data (which we covered earlier), you can use Power BI to create specialized views for HR application owners or executives. For instance, a dashboard might show: Number of HR service desk tickets related to the HR apps (from an ITSM system) vs. App usage trends - to see if a drop in usage corresponds to any reported issues. Or chart onboarding chatbot queries per week, categorized by topic, to identify if there are frequently asked questions that HR might want to address in communications or policy. If using Application Insights for bots or custom apps, you can ingest that telemetry (e.g., bot response times, error traces) into Power BI or Microsoft Entra ID Monitor workbooks. Another useful monitoring visualization is a system architecture map – using Power BI or Visio diagrams – that highlights data flows between HR systems (D365 HR to AD to SharePoint, etc.) with traffic light status (green OK, red problem) based on live data. This can quickly show if one part of the HR system integration is down (perhaps a flow failed that syncs data, so downstream systems are outdated). The key is to present the data in a way that both IT and HR stakeholders can grasp the state of the system at a glance.

Alerting and Notifications: Set up proactive alerts so that the relevant people are notified when something requires attention. Microsoft 365 offers some built-in alerting (e.g., via the Service Health Dashboard or Message Center when there is an outage or important change). But for your specific solutions, you might implement custom alerts. A few examples:

Use Power Automate to create an admin alert flow: the flow could run daily (or be triggered by a metrics change) to check conditions like "if any flow in environment X has failed in the last day more than 5 times" or "if the onboarding Power App has had zero users in the past week (possibly indicating an issue)," then send an email or Teams message to the support team. The Power Platform allows querying via the admin connectors or the CoE Dataverse tables to get these metrics programmatically.

If you have critical integrations (say between D365 HR and SAP or AD), consider using Microsoft Entra ID Monitor or Logic Apps with custom scripts to ping those and alert on failures or slow performance. Microsoft Entra ID Monitor's Log Analytics could aggregate logs from various sources (for instance, logs from D365 F&O if HR is on that platform, plus audit logs, plus system event logs) and you can set KQL-based alerts.

For AI Copilots, you might use Application Insights (if the Copilot or PVA bot is configured to log there) to set alerts on error rates. For example, if the bot encounters exceptions or if its output content filter triggers often (indicating users are asking disallowed things), have an alert go to the bot owner or HR IT. If you're leveraging DSPM for AI, any high-severity alerts from there (like attempts to access unauthorized data) should notify your security team.

Regular Reviews and Drills: Monitoring isn't just tools – it's also processes. Schedule regular operational review meetings for the HR tech stack. In these, review key metrics (uptime, usage, support tickets, upcoming changes). Use those sessions to fine-tune monitoring rules – for example, maybe an alert threshold is too sensitive and triggers too often, causing alert fatigue, so adjust it. Also rehearse incident response for HR systems: if an HR app goes down or a bot malfunctions during open enrollment, do you know who gets paged and how to communicate to users? Ensure contact lists are up-to-date and that both IT and HR stakeholders are aware of the protocols. You might integrate Power Platform alerts with a Teams channel or PagerDuty/ServiceNow, depending on your ITSM setup, so that critical issues generate immediate attention.

Power BI for Executive Reporting: Provide summarized compliance and usage reports to HR leadership periodically. For example, a quarterly "HR Systems Governance Report" generated via Power BI could show number of active apps, any security incidents (e.g., "3 DLP policy matches were resolved"), uptime stats, and upcoming compliance activities. This keeps leadership informed and demonstrates due diligence. It can also highlight the ROI of these systems (e.g., "The onboarding chatbot handled 500 questions this quarter, saving an estimated X hours of HR staff time"). Such reporting can justify continued investment in the platform and governance efforts.

Pitfalls and Tips: One common challenge is over-alerting – if you alert on every single flow failure, you may overwhelm your IT support. Classify your solutions by criticality and set different alert levels. For a low-risk HR survey app, maybe you just log failures for later review. But for the core "HR Employee Changes" integration flow, you alert on first failure because it could affect payroll or org data. Make sure alerts go to a group address or channel that is monitored even during off-hours if 24/7 uptime is required (some HR processes might not be 24/7, but things like systems that affect employee login or pay should be treated with high priority). Additionally, maintain documentation for each alert rule – what it means, who is responsible to act – so if someone on the team gets an alert at 2 AM, they know what to do. Leverage the CoE's capabilities too: the CoE kit has some built-in governance flows that can be repurposed as alerts (e.g., it flags orphaned objects, which you can treat as an alert to address security by removing or reassigning them). Finally, periodically review user feedback for both apps and bots – sometimes users will be the first to notice an issue (like a bot giving a wrong answer or an app page loading slowly). Provide easy channels for them to report issues (a "Report a problem" button that triggers a support ticket with context). In sum, combine automated monitoring with human feedback loops to get the full picture of your HR tech stack's health. With vigilant monitoring and responsive alerting in place, you can catch issues early, minimize downtime, and continuously improve the reliability and security of your HR solutions.

Summary

Chapter 8 outlines how Microsoft's HR tech stack – spanning Entra ID, Power Platform, Dynamics 365 HR, SharePoint, and Microsoft Purview – enables secure, compliant, and well-governed HR operations.

At the core is Role-Based Access Control (RBAC) through Microsoft Entra ID, ensuring only the right people can access sensitive HR data. Security groups, least privilege principles, conditional access, and access reviews help streamline onboarding, offboarding, and audit readiness.

Power Platform security is reinforced through environment segmentation (Dev/Test/Prod), Dataverse roles, and Data Loss Prevention (DLP) policies that prevent HR data from leaking to unapproved destinations. Managed Environments and masking of test data further strengthen protection.

Deploying a Center of Excellence (CoE) allows HR IT teams to monitor apps, enforce standards, and automate compliance checks. Dashboards and workflows help track usage, flag risks, and manage app life cycles efficiently.

Microsoft Purview adds layers of protection with audit logging, insider risk management, and retention/DLP policies tailored to HR data. These tools ensure visibility, legal defensibility, and proactive risk mitigation.

As HR teams adopt AI-driven bots via Copilot Studio, governance becomes essential. Bots must use approved data sources, show citation transparency, and log interactions. Admins can monitor usage and respond to misconfigurations using Microsoft's auditing and security tools.

Ongoing monitoring and alerting completes the picture, helping HR and IT detect anomalies, troubleshoot faster, and report on system health and compliance to leadership. Together, these controls build a secure, resilient, and trustworthy digital HR environment.

Templates, Playbooks, and Practical Frameworks for HR Tech Governance

This chapter is where thoughtful strategy meets day-to-day execution. The frameworks, guides, and templates provided here are not optional extras – they form the operational backbone for making HR technology initiatives secure, sustainable, and impactful. Whether an organization is implementing a new system through Agile sprints, a classic Waterfall rollout, or a hybrid approach, these tools are designed to be methodology-agnostic. They help translate high-level strategy into structured conversations, transform decisions into defined roles, and link roles to accountable outcomes.

Organizations are encouraged to leverage these tools in stakeholder workshops, during the scoping phases of transformation programs, or even as blueprints for retrospective health checks. Each tool is crafted with flexibility in mind: they can be printed, adapted, or annotated to suit specific needs. In practice, these resources have been applied in various forms by HR leaders, IT architects, and transformation consultants across both global enterprises and local teams. They are designed not for abstract theory but for practical facilitation – meant for use in boardrooms and project kickoff meetings, in Centers of Excellence (CoE) stand-ups and C-level reviews. In short, these tools are intended to be carried into the field and become an integral part of the work.

Governance Framework

One of the most persistent misconceptions in HR tech governance is that governance is a rigid structure suited only to large-scale, Waterfall-style implementations. In reality, a modern governance framework should be flexible and inclusive – able to adjust to the delivery rhythm of any organization. This section outlines a governance framework that works across all project methodologies by examining four interdependent "lenses" of governance: Strategic, Operational, Technical, and Life Cycle. Each lens offers a different perspective, yet all are connected in a continuous governance loop rather than a one-time sequence.

Strategic Lens – Aligning Vision and Value

The strategic lens ensures alignment between HR's business drivers and IT's architectural vision. It demands clarity on what success looks like, how value is measured, and which compliance boundaries cannot be crossed. Key questions under this lens include whether the system is being designed primarily for employee experience, efficiency, or compliance, and how those priorities influence the system's structure and features. It is crucial at this stage to define the strategic anchors of the project: identify the primary stakeholders or beneficiaries and determine how the new system's value will be demonstrated, measured, and sustained over time. For example, if the strategic goal is improved employee experience, the framework would establish metrics for user satisfaction and adoption rates, and ensure these metrics are tracked post-implementation.

Operational Lens – Defining Roles and Processes

The operational lens focuses on the human infrastructure behind the technology. It asks who owns each process and how various teams (such as HRIS, IT security, and legal) collaborate throughout the project. Here, role clarity becomes governance clarity. Informal practices and tribal knowledge are surfaced and recalibrated into formal policies or procedures. One practical exercise to apply this lens to is to walk through a simple HR process (for instance, an onboarding flow from a job offer to Day One system access) and log every stakeholder involved, each approval needed, and any security or compliance checkpoint at each step. This exercise often reveals gaps or overlaps in responsibilities. For instance, it may become apparent that both HR and IT believe the other is responsible for removing access for contractors at the end of their term. Identifying these ambiguities early allows the organization to update policies (e.g., an access revocation policy) and assign clear ownership for every operational step.

Technical Lens – Ensuring Secure and Scalable Architecture

The technical lens defines the system environments, access hierarchies, integration touchpoints, and platforms in use. The goal is to balance technical consistency with innovation. For example, if the organization provisions users and manages access through Microsoft Entra ID, the framework should ensure that this process is automated and auditable across all HR systems. At the same time, if the HR department is embracing low-code tools like Power Platform for innovation, guardrails should be established so that innovation can occur in "safe zones." Some companies formalize *safe innovation environments* (such as sandbox instances with anonymized or read-only data) for HR to experiment with new apps or AI features without risking production data. Under this lens, questions arise such as: *Are our environments (development, testing, production) properly segregated and governed? Who has administrative access to HR systems, and is it appropriate?* By addressing these, the technical lens ensures that the architecture supporting the HR technology is secure, compliant, and yet adaptable to new capabilities.

Life Cycle Lens – Adapting and Improving Over Time

The life cycle lens is often forgotten, but it is where governance truly becomes a living practice. This perspective asks how policies and processes will evolve alongside business changes and technological advancements. It mandates regular audits of decisions and encourages teams to capture lessons learned for continuous improvement. Rather than treating governance as a one-off project phase, the life cycle lens embeds it into the organization's ongoing rhythm. For example, many successful HRIT teams establish quarterly governance retrospectives (often run by the CoE or a governance board) where any new workflow, integration, or AI Copilot feature introduced that quarter is reviewed for compliance with policies, proper data lineage, and ethical considerations. The life cycle approach might include scheduled policy reviews (to update data retention rules when regulations change) and post-mortems after any incidents or exceptions. The key is to iterate rather than ossify policies and controls should be updated as the organization learns and grows.

These four lenses feed into each other continuously. Consider a scenario where HR is rolling out a new benefits management module in an HR system. The strategic lens ensures that this module aligns with the company's goal of improving employee satisfaction and that success will be measured by uptake and feedback. The operational lens designates an owner (perhaps the Benefits Administration team in HR) and defines how HR, IT, and Compliance will collaborate to support the module. The technical lens sets up the appropriate access controls in Entra ID and integration points (ensuring, for instance, that payroll data flows securely to the new module). Finally, the life cycle lens schedules a review after one quarter to evaluate how the module is performing, whether any policy adjustments are needed (e.g., adjustments to data access or retention), and to capture any insights for future rollouts. In this way, governance is not a linear checklist but a loop – a continuous operating cycle that adapts from planning through execution and into ongoing management.

Workshop Guide for Security and Governance Alignment

Introducing a structured governance framework often requires getting diverse stakeholders on the same page. This section provides a facilitated workshop guide to align security and governance responsibilities among HR, IT, and other partners. Consider a scenario: the HR Director, IT Security Lead, HRIS Business Analyst, and a Program Manager are all in a room to discuss an upcoming HR technology project. All participants agree that security and compliance are critical, but initially there is confusion over who is responsible for which aspect of governance. This workshop is designed to clarify boundaries and ownership in such situations, ensuring that nothing falls through the cracks when HR technology projects get underway.

Workshop Overview

The Security & Governance Alignment Workshop is a facilitated session (about three hours in total) that brings together business and technology stakeholders to clarify responsibilities and identify risks in HR tech governance. The primary goal is to map out "who does what" for key governance areas and to ensure consensus on how security and compliance will be managed throughout the project. By the end of the session, the team should have a shared mental model of governance and possibly a draft governance RACI matrix tailored to their project (identifying who is *Responsible, Accountable, Consulted,* and *Informed* for major tasks).

Key objectives of the workshop include establishing clear ownership for data security and privacy tasks, defining the collaboration points between HR, IT, and other departments (like Legal or Compliance), and initiating any documentation that may be missing (such as an access control policy or data handling procedure). It is not about blaming gaps, but about collectively discovering them and assigning accountability going forward.

Workshop Preparation

Proper preparation ensures that the workshop is efficient and evidence-based. Before running the session, the organizer or facilitator should gather relevant background information and artifacts. Ensure that

- Current Access Artifacts are available: All attendees should have access to up-to-date organizational charts (to understand team structures and reporting lines) and current permission sets or access control lists for HR systems. This ensures discussions start with a clear picture of who currently has access to what.

- Directory Role Data is gathered: Export the Microsoft Entra ID (Azure AD) group and role membership data for HR applications in advance. Having a tangible role matrix of existing access will help the group identify any discrepancies or over-provisioned accounts.

- Audit and Incident History is reviewed: Review recent audit findings, security reports, or system support tickets related to access issues or data breaches in HR systems. Real examples of past incidents (for instance, an HR app that had unauthorized access or a data retention lapse) will ground the conversation in concrete lessons and emphasize why certain governance measures are needed.

By equipping participants with these materials, the workshop can quickly move from hypothetical discussion to addressing actual conditions in the organization's HR tech environment.

Workshop Agenda and Facilitation

The workshop itself is structured into three distinct hours, each with a specific focus, to systematically cover the landscape of security and governance alignment:

- Hour 1: Role and Risk Mapping – The facilitator opens with a scenario to spark discussion. For example: *"A new contractor joins via the HR system (e.g., Dynamics 365 Human Resources). Who controls what that person can see? Who ensures their data is only kept as long as necessary? Where are the audit trails for their access?"* Participants collaboratively trace this contractor's journey through various systems, identifying each point of access (such as SharePoint folders, Power Apps, the HR database in Dataverse, Teams channels, etc.). For each access point, the group notes the current owner or gatekeeper (HR business partner, IT admin, third-party vendor, etc.) and highlights any gaps or overlaps in responsibility. This exercise makes visible any areas where, for instance, two departments assume the other is handling a security check or where no one is clearly accountable. The facilitator can use a whiteboard or a digital collaboration tool (like a Miro board) to map these points in real time. By the end of Hour 1, the team will have a visual map of the current state of role-based access and a list of noted risks or ambiguities requiring attention.

- Hour 2: Governance Maturity Check-In – In the second part, the group assesses the organization's current governance maturity (using the maturity model introduced later in Section 4 as a reference point). The facilitator might present a preliminary assessment of whether the organization is Reactive, Managed, Defined, etc., and ask the team to discuss where they believe they currently stand and why. The aim is not to reach a unanimous verdict but to encourage discussion. One participant might point out, for example, that while some policies exist (suggesting a "Managed" level), inconsistent enforcement might actually put them closer to "Reactive" in practice. Another might note progress in certain areas (like regular access reviews, indicative of a "Defined" level). This dialogue helps surface perceptions and evidence of governance effectiveness (or lack thereof). The facilitator captures different viewpoints on a flip chart. The immediate outcome of this segment is a clearer, shared understanding of strengths and weaknesses – for instance, consensus that incident response is ad-hoc (a weakness) but awareness of data privacy is growing (a strength). This sets the stage for targeted improvements.

- Hour 3: Initial RACI Draft and Action Planning – The final hour is action-oriented. Based on the gaps and misalignments identified earlier, the group works to draft a high-level RACI chart (Responsible, Accountable, Consulted, Informed) for key governance activities.

For example, an action might be "Conduct quarterly access reviews for HR systems" – HRIS might be designated Responsible, the IT Security Lead Accountable, with Legal and Internal Audit as Consulted, and so on. The facilitator encourages the team to assign *temporary owners* for any gap areas if a permanent owner is not yet clear – someone who will take the next steps to find the right owner or develop the needed process. Additionally, the group defines the next review point or follow-up meeting to revisit these assignments, ensuring this workshop's outcomes have continuity. It's emphasized that the goal is not to achieve perfection in one meeting but to commit to accountability and traceability. For instance, if it was discovered that no one was formally managing the life cycle of HR data retention, a follow-up action could be: "Draft a data retention policy for HR records and have it reviewed by Legal within 30 days." By the end of Hour 3, the team leaves with a draft governance map or action list specifically tailored to their organization's landscape, and with clarity on who will drive each action forward.

RACI Matrix

This sample chart illustrates how responsibilities can be distributed across key roles in an HR tech governance project

	Human Resources	IT Security	Legal	Project Manager
Define data access policy	Responsible	Accountable	Consulted	Informed
Review integration security	Consulted	Responsible	Consulted	Accountable
Maintain risk register	Informed	Responsible	Informed	Accountable
Approve AI/automation tools	Consulted	Consulted	Accountable	Responsible

RACI Matrix

This template illustrates how responsibilities can be distributed across key roles in an HR tech governance project.

	Human Resources	IT Security		
Task 1				
Task 2				
Task 3				
Task				

At the conclusion of this workshop, the various stakeholders should have a shared mental model of HR tech governance in their organization. Misunderstandings are reduced, and each participant knows their role in maintaining security and compliance. Equally important, the group has initiated documentation (such as updating an org chart with governance contacts or compiling a list of needed policies) and has agreed on tangible next steps. This alignment early in an HR technology initiative dramatically lowers the risk of security gaps later on. In practice, organizations that conduct such cross-functional workshops find that subsequent project phases run more smoothly: for example, when a new feature is about to be deployed, everyone knows who needs to sign off on the security review and who will handle training and communications.

Gap Analysis and Requirements Discovery Canvas

Complex projects often fail not due to technical hurdles but because critical gaps in understanding or process are discovered too late. To combat this, a Gap Analysis and Requirements Discovery Canvas is introduced as a tool to surface mismatches early – whether they be in expectations, in ownership, in compliance measures, or in data integrity. Rather than simply listing areas of concern in isolation, this canvas is meant to be used interactively, ideally in a facilitated session with cross-functional stakeholders (representatives from HR, IT, Security, Compliance, etc.). It provides a structured way to walk through the key categories of governance and uncover where the "current state" might not align with the "desired state" for the upcoming HR tech initiative.

The canvas is divided into five major categories, each posing critical questions to prompt discussion and discovery:

1. Data Access and Control – *What data is considered sensitive? Where does that data reside? Who has access to it today, and who should have access to it in the future state?* This category forces the team to identify sensitive data elements (for example, employee personal information, salary data, medical leave details, or performance reviews) and map out their locations (in an HRIS, in spreadsheets, in emails, etc.). Just as importantly, it challenges assumptions about access: perhaps currently a broad group of HR staff can see certain personal data, but the goal in the new system is to tighten that to a need-to-know basis. Discussing these points might reveal, for instance, that contractors or external partners have access to data they shouldn't, or that data is duplicated in multiple places without clear control. Such insights allow the project team to plan early for remediation – like cleaning up permissions, consolidating data sources, or establishing new access policies – before the new system or process is rolled out.

2. Identity and Provisioning – *How are user identities managed and provisioned? Is identity provisioning (e.g., via Entra ID) automated and consistent? How are non-employee roles (contractors, consultants, interns) handled in the system? Are there any shared or generic accounts still in use that could pose security risks?* In this part of the canvas, stakeholders examine the joiner–mover–leaver processes and the integration of HR systems with identity management. They might discover gaps such as accounts not being deactivated promptly when someone leaves, or that contractors are given full employee access due to system limitations. By writing these down, the team can formulate requirements like *"The new system must integrate with Entra ID to automatically provision and deprovision accounts based on HR status"* or plan cleanup activities (for example, eliminating shared accounts in favor of individual accounts with proper roles). The

discussion here ensures the project addresses identity life cycle issues as a core requirement, rather than as an afterthought.

3. Center of Excellence (CoE) and Innovation Channels – *Does the organization have a defined innovation space or CoE for HR tech, where new ideas (like Power Platform apps or pilot programs) can be safely tested? If such channels exist, is there visibility and governance over those innovations once they are launched?* This category explores how the organization encourages innovation while maintaining oversight. For example, perhaps HR has been using a "shadow IT" approach to build a quick solution in Power Apps for a survey or a workflow. The canvas discussion would uncover whether these innovation efforts go through any review or if they bypass security review entirely. A mature approach might involve a sanctioned CoE that provides a sandbox environment for experimentation and a process to review and promote successful experiments to production. If the discussion shows a gap (e.g., lots of little apps or bots being built with no central tracking or governance), the project requirements might include establishing an HR Technology CoE or at least guidelines for innovation (such as requiring new apps to register with IT or go through a data security assessment if they use sensitive data).

4. Copilot and AI Readiness – *Are AI-driven features (such as an HR Copilot or other machine learning tools) enabled by default in the current systems? Who is responsible for configuring their context and boundaries? Has there been any "red team" or risk assessment exercise to test the outputs of these AI features for bias, accuracy, or security issues?* This is a forward-looking category recognizing that many modern HR systems and platforms (like Microsoft's Dynamics 365 or Viva with Copilot capabilities) come with powerful AI components. Stakeholders need to gauge their readiness to govern AI: for instance, if HR data is being used to feed an AI that suggests answers to employee queries, do policies exist to limit sensitive data exposure? The canvas helps teams articulate concerns such as *"We lack a process to review AI suggestions for compliance"* or requirements like *"AI features*

should be enabled only in a controlled environment until we define an ethics and compliance checklist." If the organization has not yet thought about AI governance, this discussion could prompt the creation of new governance artifacts (perhaps an AI usage guideline or an AI ethics committee including HR, IT, and legal). It ensures that if the new project will leverage AI, the necessary guardrails and accountabilities are put in place from the outset.

5. Compliance and Audit Capability – *Can the current system(s) produce audit logs that show who accessed or changed sensitive information (for example, who accessed salary records last quarter)? Is there a standard data retention policy in place for HR data, and can the system enforce it or support it?* Under this category, the team assesses how well compliance requirements are supported. Perhaps regulatory obligations (like GDPR, which grants employees the right to request their data or have it deleted) are not clearly mapped to system capabilities. The discussion might surface that *"We can track user logins, but not every read of a confidential field,"* or *"We have a data retention policy of X years for candidate data, but the current recruiting system retains everything indefinitely."* Such gaps lead directly to requirements or actions: for instance, to configure auditing on critical fields, or to implement data retention workflows. It is often useful to have the actual text of relevant policies on hand during this discussion (e.g., the corporate data retention policy for HR records) to compare stated policy vs. practice. For each of these five categories on the canvas, it is recommended to provide ample space (literally, if using a physical whiteboard or a virtual canvas) to write down notes on the actual vs. target state. Encourage candor: participants should feel comfortable noting, for example, "Actual: All HR staff have access to all personnel files; Target: Limit access to HR Business Partners and managers only, with audit trails." The canvas will likely end up looking messy, filled with comments, arrows, and highlights – and that is good, because it means real issues are being uncovered and debated. The goal is not a neat document, but an honest portrayal of where misalignments exist.

Data Access and Control

Who sees what, where data
lives, and how it's protected.

Current state
Desired state
Key Actions
Risks

Identity and Provisioning

How accounts are created, updated, and deactivated,
especially for non-employees.

Current state
Desired state
Key Actions
Risks

Current state
Desired state
Key Actions
Risks

CoE and Innovation

How new tools and
experiments (like Power Apps)
are governed or supported.

Current state
Desired state
Key Actions
Risks

Copilot and AI Readiness

How AI features are reviewed,
controlled, and monitored for
risks.

Current state
Desired state
Key Actions
Risks

Compliance and Audit

How access is tracked, policies
enforced, and data privacy
obligations met.

Current state
Desired state
Key Actions
Risks

After working through the five areas, the project team should step back and review the canvas in its entirety. This holistic view helps in several ways: it identifies the *must-have requirements* for the upcoming project (areas where gaps could be project-killers if not addressed), it highlights *policy or process changes* needed in parallel with technical changes, and it reveals *dependencies* (for example, realizing that a successful rollout might hinge on updating an identity management process first). The canvas becomes a living artifact that can be revisited throughout the project to ensure those gaps are indeed being closed. It also serves as excellent input for risk registers and project plans.

By using this canvas early in the project life cycle, teams can discover lurking issues in a structured way and avoid costly surprises late in the game. It reinforces the proactive ethos of governance: find the gaps before they find you.

HR Tech Maturity Model

In order to chart a course for improvement, it helps to know where the organization currently stands in its HR tech governance journey. The HR Tech Maturity Model presented here is not meant to pass judgment but rather to provide orientation. Every organization can be placed somewhere along this maturity spectrum, and what matters most is not the exact label, but having a realistic understanding of current state and a vision for where to go next. This model outlines five levels of maturity in HR technology governance, from the most basic (Reactive) to the most advanced (Strategic):

- Level 1: Reactive – Governance is ad hoc or informal. Policies and processes are minimal or nonexistent. Security gaps and issues tend to be discovered only after they have caused incidents. For example, an organization at this level might only realize that an HR system lacked proper access controls *after* a data breach or an audit failure. Audit trails for HR systems are incomplete or not enabled, making it hard to investigate incidents. The focus at this stage is often firefighting rather than planning – addressing issues as they occur, with little bandwidth for preventive measures.

- Level 2: Managed – There are some policies and repeatable processes, but they may not be consistently enforced or fully comprehensive. Basic controls exist but might rely on manual effort. For instance, there could be a data loss prevention (DLP) rule set up for HR data, but it's applied manually or to only a subset of systems. Similarly, one part of HR might be tagging apps or data for sensitivity, but others are not, leading to uneven coverage. The organization is beginning to pay attention to governance, perhaps due to a recent scare or compliance requirement, but the approach is still siloed or reactive. Progress is being made, yet governance is not integrated into everyday workflows.

- Level 3: Defined – Governance processes are clearly documented and have dedicated owners. Roles and responsibilities in HR tech governance are understood across the organization. Regular reviews or audits occur to ensure policies are being followed. At this stage, for example, there might be a formal governance committee or a Centre of Excellence in place that reviews all new HR tech initiatives for compliance with standards. The use of platforms like Power Platform or new SaaS HR tools is under control – perhaps an inventory of apps is maintained, and there is an approval process before something new is launched. However, while things are under control, they may not yet be optimized or fully aligned with broader business strategy. There is a foundation, but integration between HR governance and enterprise governance (or between tools and strategy) might still be maturing.

- Level 4: Proactive – Governance is now embedded in the delivery and development cycles of HR technology. Instead of reacting to issues, the organization anticipates them. Risk assessments are a standard part of developing or onboarding any new application or feature – for instance, before a new AI-based recruiting tool is implemented, a privacy impact assessment and bias test are conducted as a matter of course. Centers of Excellence and governance committees not only exist, but they actively guide projects, and business stakeholders welcome their input (rather than seeing governance as a hurdle). Innovative practices are in place, such as "pre-mortems" (to predict what could go wrong) for major changes, and continuous monitoring of key controls. AI outputs and automation workflows are reviewed regularly to ensure they remain compliant and ethical. At this level, the organization can often prevent incidents and is agile in updating policies when the business or regulatory environment changes.

- Level 5: Strategic – At the highest maturity, governance is not just a protective measure, but a source of competitive advantage and agility. HR, IT, Legal, and Security teams work in seamless collaboration, treating governance as a shared responsibility that enables innovation rather than stifling it. The effectiveness of governance is tracked with Key Performance Indicators (KPIs) – for example, metrics such as "time to provide or revoke access," "percentage of projects passing governance review first time," or "audit issues found per quarter" are measured and continuously improved. The organization can confidently pursue advanced technologies (like AI and robotics in HR processes) because it has established trust and transparency mechanisms – AI decisions are explainable and audited, data usage is well-governed, and employees and regulators alike have confidence in the HR systems. At this stage, governance considerations are embedded in strategic planning: for instance, when the company plans to enter a new region or launch a new line of business, the HR tech governance implications (data residency, new compliance laws, etc.) are part of the conversation from the beginning. In short, governance is part of the organization's DNA, enabling it to innovate quickly while maintaining control and integrity.

Using this maturity model, a team can self-assess where they fall and use the levels as a roadmap for improvement. For example, an organization might realize they are at Level 2 (Managed) because they have some policies but lack consistency. Their goal might then be to reach Level 3 (Defined) within a year by formalizing the governance committee, documenting all processes, and enforcing existing policies more uniformly. Another organization already at Level 4 (Proactive) might aim for Level 5 (Strategic) by investing in cross-training between HR, IT, and legal teams and by introducing metrics to track governance performance.

The model is also useful for communicating with leadership: being able to articulate "We are currently at a Defined level of HR tech governance and aim to become Proactive in the next budget cycle" helps justify certain investments (for example, new tooling for monitoring or hiring a compliance analyst). It shifts the conversation from abstract compliance talk to a more concrete maturity goal that can be measured and tracked.

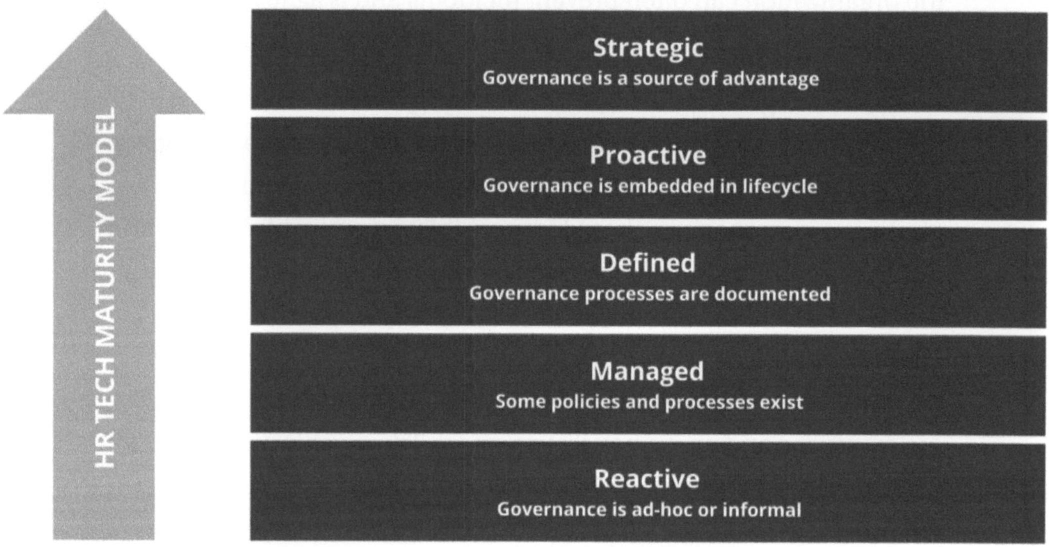

In summary, the HR Tech Maturity Model helps organizations understand their current governance posture and chart a clear path forward. It emphasizes that improvement is a journey: what matters is recognizing strengths, addressing weaknesses, and steadily moving governance from the background to an integrated, strategic function.

Project Kickoff Playbook

Embarking on a new HR technology project without proper alignment can lead to chaos, miscommunication, and false starts. The Project Kickoff Playbook is a guide to give any HR tech initiative a strong start from day one, ensuring clarity, alignment, and structure are in place at the outset. This playbook distills best practices for the initial phase of a project – when expectations are set, teams are formed, and the groundwork for governance is laid. By following a structured kickoff approach, organizations can drastically reduce confusion and set a tone of proactive governance and collaboration for the entire project.

Setting the Stage: The kickoff phase should begin by defining the project's scope and objectives in human terms. This means articulating the problem being solved and the value to be delivered in a way that all stakeholders can understand. Rather than immediately diving into technical specifications, the focus is on the *why* and *for whom* of the project. For example, clarify what pain points the project addresses: *"We are automating the employee onboarding process to eliminate manual data entry, which currently causes delays and errors."* Also specify whose daily work will improve: *"This will improve the experience for new hires and reduce workload for HR coordinators."* These are not rhetorical questions or feel-good statements – they shape everything else in the project. Getting consensus on the fundamental purpose and beneficiaries provides a north star for the team when making decisions later. It can be helpful to document these in a brief project charter or vision statement at the very start.

Once the vision is established, there are several preparatory steps to undertake to ensure the team is ready for execution:

- Secure Access to Key Systems: Make sure the core project team has access to all necessary systems and tools from the get-go. For an HR tech project, this often includes environments in systems like Dynamics 365 (for HR modules), SharePoint or other document repositories, and the Power Platform (if app development or automation is in scope). If there are data environments or testing sandboxes needed, request those early. For instance, if a developer will need a Power Apps environment to prototype forms, have that set up and accessible. Early access prevents delays and enables initial assessments of data and configurations.

- Confirm Core Team and Stakeholder Availability: Identify the core project team members across HR, IT, and any other relevant departments (such as a representative from the Privacy office or PMO) and ensure their availability for key meetings and work. This might involve coordinating calendars for the first few sprints or milestones. It also means clarifying roles: for example, confirming who the HR process owner is, who the IT systems lead is, and who will act as the project manager. Explicitly confirming these roles and their time commitment helps avoid the situation where a critical person is unknowingly double-booked on another project or out of office during a crucial period.

- Document and Circulate a Glossary of Terms: One often overlooked step is establishing a common language. HR technology projects are cross-functional, and terminology can cause confusion (an IT person's understanding of "production environment" might differ from an HR person's notion of "go-live," for example). By creating a glossary of key terms, acronyms, and definitions at the kickoff, the team can reduce miscommunication throughout the project. For instance, clarify what "Go-Live" entails in this project, or define what "Copilot" features mean in the context of your HR system. Circulate this glossary to all team members and stakeholders and encourage additions if new terms arise. With the groundwork laid, the project leader should convene a formal Kickoff Meeting with all stakeholders. A structured agenda for this meeting ensures that everyone gains a mutual understanding and that nothing important is left unaddressed. Below is a guide for a typical kickoff meeting agenda:

  - Introductions and Roles: Begin with introductions, especially if team members come from different departments or outside the organization. Each person should understand who is on the team and what their expected role or contribution is. For example, the meeting should clarify who will serve as the executive sponsor, who is the project manager, who represents HR operations, who covers IT architecture, etc. This sets a tone of accountability from the start.

- Problem Statement and Desired Outcomes: Reiterate the core problem the project is solving and the key outcomes desired. Even if this was discussed in pre-meetings, stating it in the kickoff ensures alignment. For instance, *"Our current onboarding process takes 3 weeks; our goal is to reduce that to 3 days while improving data accuracy and compliance."* All stakeholders should agree that these are the targets the project will be judged against.

- Implementation Methodology: Outline how the project will be executed. Will it follow an Agile approach with defined sprints and iterative releases, or a Waterfall approach with defined phase gates and sign-offs, or a hybrid model? Clarify the cadence of work: for example, *"We will use two-week sprints with review sessions every other Friday"* or *"Key milestones are design, configuration, testing, UAT, and deployment, each with stakeholder reviews."* Also mention any checkpoints or governance reviews that will be embedded (for example, a security review before go-live). This portion of the agenda gives everyone a mental model of how the project's work will progress over time.

- Overview of Governance Framework and Initial Owners: Introduce the governance framework (such as the one described in Section 1 of this chapter) that will be applied to this project. This means explaining that the project will consider strategic, operational, technical, and life cycle governance aspects throughout. Identify initial owners for governance activities – for example, designate who will be responsible for monitoring compliance tasks, who will maintain the risk register, and who ensures that decisions are documented. If a formal governance board or steering committee exists, note how this project will report to that body. Essentially, this part of the meeting instills the message: governance is part of the project's fabric from day one, and here are the people championing it.

- Q&A and Open Discussion of Risks: Allow time for questions from the team. New projects often surface uncertainties or known concerns. It's wise to openly discuss any known risks or challenges at the kickoff. For instance, someone might raise, *"Our last project had a delay because of integration issues with payroll – do we anticipate that here?"* Acknowledge these and note them. This isn't the time to solve everything but to make sure no major worry is hiding unspoken. It also shows that project leadership is aware of potential pitfalls and is not shying away from them.

After the kickoff meeting, certain follow-up actions help maintain momentum and solidify the planning:

- Distribute a Kickoff Summary: The project manager or facilitator should send out a summary of the kickoff discussion. This document typically includes the list of attendees, the key points covered (problem statement, methodology, roles, etc.), and any decisions made. Crucially, it should enumerate agreed-upon action items, with owners and due dates. For example: "Action: Set up weekly project status call – *Owner: John (PM), Due: Friday*.*" This summary becomes the reference point for everyone and is especially useful for those who could not attend the meeting.

- Finalize and Publish Roles and First Deliverables: If not fully done in the meeting, immediately work to confirm each team member's specific responsibilities and the first set of deliverables or milestones. For instance, identify who will draft the requirements document, who will configure the first prototype, who will prepare the data for migration, etc., along with target dates. Publishing this as a one-page RACI or responsibility chart can be very helpful for clarity. This goes hand-in-hand with governance: ensure there is an assigned governance owner (even if this is a temporary assignment until a formal person is named). The governance owner's role is to keep an eye on compliance and risk considerations as the project progresses and to liaise with any external governance bodies.

- Initiate an Access Audit (if applicable): Immediately after kickoff is an ideal time to review "who has access to what" in the context of this project. This might involve auditing the current HR systems to check that only the appropriate personnel have administrative or sensitive access. If the project involves new systems or environments, set up the process for approving access to them. For example, if a development environment is created for the project, decide who should have access and ensure accounts are created for them (and conversely, that when the project ends, these accounts will be reviewed or removed). This proactive audit serves two purposes: it gets everyone thinking about security from the start, and it can catch any legacy access issues that should be resolved now rather than discovered later. It's much easier to fix access issues in the early stages than to deal with a breach or permission error mid-project.

In short: These are the must-do actions that set your HR tech project up for success. From defining the "why" to locking down access and ownership, this list ensures you're not just starting fast – but starting right.

- Define project scope in human terms.

- Identify project beneficiaries.

- Secure access to Dynamics 365, SharePoint, Power Platform.

- Confirm core team roles (HR lead, IT lead, PM, Privacy).

- Circulate glossary of terms.

- Schedule kickoff meeting.

- Clarify implementation methodology (Agile/Waterfall/Hybrid).

- Assign initial governance owners.

- Draft kickoff summary and distribute.

- Finalize roles and first deliverables.

- Initiate access audit.

By following this kickoff playbook, the project gains a strong foundation. Every team member starts with a clear understanding of goals, roles, and processes, and governance is positioned as a help rather than a hindrance. A well-run kickoff cannot guarantee project success on its own, but it *significantly tilts the odds in favor of success*. It creates a shared sense of purpose and a culture of accountability that will carry through the sprints, milestones, and eventual go-live.

Self-Assessment for Governance Readiness

Sometimes the most illuminating insights come from asking direct, candid questions. The Self-Assessment for HR Tech Governance Readiness is a tool designed to prompt reflection on how well-prepared the organization is to govern its HR technology environment. This is not about obtaining a "passing score" or assigning a grade – there is no numerical score at the end. Instead, it's about sparking honest conversations and revealing blind spots. The assessment consists of a series of key statements or questions. For each item, stakeholders should consider whether it holds true in their organization, and if not, why not. The value lies as much in the discussion these points generate as in the answers themselves.

Consider the following ten self-assessment prompts as a starting point:

1. Inventory of HR Applications: *We maintain a living inventory of all HR-related applications and data flows.* – This checks whether the organization actually knows all the tools (from major systems to minor shadow IT spreadsheets) in use for HR and how data moves between them. If the immediate answer is "we're not sure" or the inventory is outdated, it indicates a governance gap because one cannot secure or govern what is not known. An actionable outcome might be to start (or update) such an inventory.

2. Defined Ownership: *Every system has a named business owner and a named technical owner.* – This ensures accountability. If a system or integration doesn't have clear owners on both the business side (e.g., an HR manager responsible for the content or usage of the system) and the technical side (e.g., an IT administrator or system architect), decisions and maintenance can fall through the cracks. Lack of ownership often correlates with systems that are neglected or fail to meet requirements because no one feels fully responsible.

3. Controlled Use of AI Tools: *AI tools (such as HR-focused Copilots or AI assistants) are enabled only in controlled environments.* – This question probes how cautiously (or freely) the organization adopts AI in HR. A "controlled environment" could mean a pilot program, with limited access and monitoring, rather than turning on an AI

280

feature for all employees without preparation. If AI tools are in widespread use, the follow-up is: have the boundaries and uses been thought through (e.g., preventing an AI from inadvertently exposing private data or making employment decisions without human oversight)? Answering "yes" suggests a deliberate approach; "no" might flag a need for an AI governance policy.

4. Power Platform Governance: *Our use of low-code or automation tools (e.g., Microsoft Power Platform) is documented and governed by clear guidelines.* – Many HR teams use tools like Power Apps, Power Automate, or similar platforms to create custom solutions or automate tasks. This statement checks if there's governance around that: Is there documentation of what apps and flows exist? Are there policies (like requiring business approval or IT security review for new automations)? If the organization cannot readily point to such documentation or guidelines, it suggests potential risk – for example, someone might build a workflow that unintentionally exposes sensitive data.

5. Sensitive Data Traceability: *We can trace who has accessed sensitive fields (such as compensation, health data, or performance notes) in our systems.* – Essentially, do audit logs or monitoring tools exist such that if someone questioned "Who looked at Employee X's salary details in the last six months?" the organization could provide an answer. If the answer is no, that implies that if a breach or inappropriate access occurred, the organization might never know. It highlights the need for better logging or tools to monitor access to critical data fields in HR systems.

6. Life cycle for Apps and Automations: *There is a policy for retiring or decommissioning unused HR applications and automation flows.* – Over time, organizations accumulate many tools and scripts. This point checks if there's a clean-up mechanism. Without a retirement policy, outdated systems might linger (posing security risks if not patched, or confusion as data might be duplicated). An example of a good practice here is having an

annual review of all apps/flows, identifying those that haven't been used in, say, 12 months, and evaluating whether they should be turned off after confirming they're not needed. A "no" here means the environment could be cluttered with legacy artifacts that no one owns but still have access to data.

7. Data Subject Access Requests (DSAR) Handling: *We are capable of fulfilling data subject access requests (DSARs) or similar privacy requests within required regulatory time frames.* – Regulations like GDPR give employees (as data subjects) rights to request their data or demand deletion, etc. This question asks if the organization has a process and capability for that, particularly since HR holds a lot of personal data. If fulfilling such a request would require a scrambling of emails and manual effort across multiple systems, it's a sign that data governance is not streamlined. Being able to confidently say "yes, we have a process for DSARs and have tested it" is a sign of maturity in privacy governance.

8. Inclusive Governance Discussions: *Our governance discussions and committees include representatives from HR, IT, Legal, and Security.* – Effective governance is cross-functional. If the answer is "no, it's mostly just HR and IT" (or even just IT), then the perspectives may be too narrow. Including Legal ensures compliance with laws, including Security ensures alignment with broader infosec practices, and HR ensures that the practical impact on people and process is considered. This point often uncovers whether governance is siloed.

9. Regular Governance Reviews: *We conduct regular (e.g., quarterly or annual) workshops or meetings to evaluate and update our HR tech governance practices.* – This measures whether governance is treated as an ongoing activity or a one-time setup. A "yes" would mean the organization has a cadence (like the quarterly CoE retrospectives mentioned earlier) where policies, issues, and improvements are discussed. If "no," governance improvements

might only happen after something goes wrong. It's the difference between continuous improvement vs. stagnation in the governance approach.

10. Onboarding Includes Governance Orientation: *New team members (whether in HR, IT support for HR systems, or related roles) receive an orientation on our HR tech governance policies as part of their onboarding.* – If new HR staff or IT administrators join and are not educated on things like data handling policies, security protocols, or relevant governance procedures, then compliance will be inconsistent. A "yes" indicates governance awareness is embedded in the culture; a "no" might reveal that governance knowledge is mostly tacit or limited to a few individuals, which is a risk if those individuals leave or if others inadvertently violate policies out of ignorance.

After presenting these statements, it is useful for the core team (or governance committee) to individually reflect and perhaps even write down whether they think each statement is true, partially true, or false for the organization. Then, gather the group to discuss the responses. It's not necessary (and often not productive) to force a single "consensus answer" for each – differences in perspective can be illuminating. For example, IT might believe there's a solid inventory of HR apps (because they have a list of servers), but HR might know of cloud services or spreadsheets not captured in IT's list. Such a discussion immediately identifies areas where better alignment or communication is needed.

The outcome of this self-assessment should be a set of discussion points and potentially an action list. The goal is to turn any "no" or hesitant "maybe" answers into future "yes" responses through concrete improvements. If, say, question 8 (on cross-functional involvement) got a "no," a resulting action could be to formally add a Legal representative to the governance meetings. If question 5 (on audit logs for sensitive data) is a "no," an action might be to evaluate tools or system settings that enable such logging.

It's worth noting that this assessment can also serve as a baseline to measure progress. The organization might revisit these same questions in a year and find that several "no" answers have turned into "yes" after deliberate effort – an encouraging sign of governance maturation.

Most importantly, treat this self-assessment as a conversation starter, not a final exam. The value is in the dialogue it opens; it raises awareness among stakeholders about what good governance entails and where the organization might be falling short. The exercise can be done as a simple workshop activity or even as an anonymous survey followed by a meeting to discuss results, depending on the culture. The emphasis is on collective insight rather than individual scores. Everyone should come away with a clearer picture of the governance landscape and a shared resolve to address the most pressing gaps.

From Structure to Practice

The templates, playbooks, and frameworks discussed in this chapter are meant to be picked up, adapted, and put into practice. Think of them as scaffolding rather than scripture. They provide structure and support, but each organization will tweak and evolve them to fit its unique culture, risks, and goals. True governance excellence emerges not from static documentation alone but from a repeated commitment to practice and improvement. It comes from the ongoing alignment of teams and the willingness to treat governance as a dynamic part of the organization's rhythm, rather than a one-time checklist.

In practical terms, this means printing out templates and scribbling notes in the margins, bringing playbooks into meetings and adjusting steps based on what the team learns, and using frameworks as common reference points during debates and decisions. Over time, as these tools become ingrained, governance will start to feel less like an external requirement and more like a natural habit. When an organization reaches the point that governance considerations are second nature – where every project kickoff instinctively includes a security review, every innovation is accompanied by a conversation about compliance, and every team member feels responsible for safeguarding data – governance stops being a hurdle and becomes an enabler of success.

Make these frameworks your own. Refine the templates, fill in the canvases with real data, and let the maturity model and self-assessments guide your progress. In doing so, governance will evolve from a formal structure into lived practice, one that empowers HR technology to truly support and drive the business with confidence and integrity. When governance is woven into daily work, it ceases to be just a policy or a document – it becomes a habit, and ultimately, part of the organization's competitive advantage.

Summary

Chapter 9 provides practical tools and frameworks for making HR technology governance structured, actionable, and adaptive. It emphasizes that governance is not a rigid set of rules but a living, flexible practice that should align strategy with execution across HR, IT, and compliance teams.

A four-part governance framework – Strategic, Operational, Technical, and Life Cycle lenses – guides organizations in aligning goals, clarifying roles, ensuring secure architecture, and continuously improving processes. These lenses help make governance an ongoing loop, not a one-time task.

To operationalize governance, the chapter offers:

- A Security and Governance Alignment Workshop to map responsibilities, surface risks, and create a RACI chart.

- A Gap Analysis Canvas for uncovering blind spots in access, identity management, AI readiness, and compliance.

- An HR Tech Maturity Model outlining five stages from Reactive to Strategic, providing a roadmap for improving governance maturity.

- A Project Kickoff Playbook to establish clarity, roles, access, and alignment from day one of any HR tech initiative.

- A Governance Readiness Self-Assessment to prompt honest discussion and prioritize improvements.

Ultimately, these resources help teams move from abstract principles to tangible actions, fostering a culture where governance becomes a habit, embedded in how HR technology is planned, delivered, and maintained. Governance excellence emerges through practice – by continuously adapting, collaborating, and aligning governance with business goals.

CHAPTER 10

AI for the Future of HR

Human Resources is undergoing a transformation driven by artificial intelligence. No longer confined to back-office administration, HR is becoming a strategic data-powered function – and AI is at the heart of this shift. As we look to the future, AI is reshaping how companies attract talent, engage employees, and manage performance. In this chapter, we explore emerging trends in AI applied to HR processes (from talent acquisition to employee engagement and performance management), and consider how to implement these technologies strategically. We will examine both cutting-edge Microsoft solutions and notable approaches beyond the Microsoft ecosystem. Critically, we will emphasize governance, compliance, and auditability – including how the new Model Context Protocol (MCP) is redefining the way HR AI agents handle data and user interactions to ensure security and transparency.

The New AI Frontier in HR

AI has quickly moved from pilot projects to core components of HR operations. Recent surveys show that nearly half of organizations already use AI in some HR capacity, and by 2025 an estimated 80% of organizations will integrate AI into HR functions. What began with simple chatbots answering routine questions has evolved into sophisticated AI systems that can screen thousands of candidates in minutes, predict employee turnover with striking accuracy, and even draft personalized coaching plans. HR leaders are now under pressure to leverage AI for efficiency and strategic insights, while also navigating the complexities and risks it brings.

AI in Talent Acquisition: Reinventing Recruiting

For many companies, talent acquisition has been the entry point for HR AI adoption. Hiring at scale is labor-intensive and fraught with inefficiencies that AI is well suited to address. Intelligent screening tools can parse resumes far faster than any human,

© Ana Inés Urrutia de Souza 2025
A. I. Urrutia de Souza, *The Microsoft AI Human Resources Handbook,*
https://doi.org/10.1007/979-8-8688-1781-6_10

using natural language processing to evaluate experience, skills, and even subtle cues in a candidate's profile. This drastically cuts down time-to-hire – studies report AI can shorten hiring cycles by up to 50% on average, while also reducing costs per hire by automating initial filtering and outreach. For example, AI-driven Applicant Tracking Systems now routinely filter out 30–40% of job applications before a human recruiter even reviews them, flagging the most promising candidates from massive pools.

Beyond resume screening, AI chatbots and assistants have become virtual recruiters. They engage candidates in human-like conversations: answering questions about the company, scheduling interviews, and even conducting initial assessments. Candidates might interact with a chatbot that asks pre-screening questions and uses the answers to rank their fit. These bots operate 24/7, ensuring no candidate's query goes unanswered and freeing up recruiters from repetitive Q&A tasks. AI is also writing recruitment content – generative AI models can draft tailored job descriptions and persuasive outreach messages in seconds. Microsoft's Copilot Studio, for instance, includes a *Job Craft Agent* that helps HR teams generate clear, role-aligned job descriptions and even suggest interview questions from minimal input. Such tools not only save time but also help standardize language to avoid subtle biases and ensure consistency in how roles are described.

Use Case – Smarter Hiring at Contoso: Consider a global software firm (let's call it Contoso) hiring hundreds of engineers a year. Traditionally, recruiters at Contoso spent countless hours skimming resumes and manually coordinating interviews. By adopting an AI-driven talent acquisition platform, Contoso transformed its recruiting process. An AI resume parser now evaluates incoming applications against job requirements within seconds, scoring candidates on skill match and even flagging "hidden gems" – candidates who might be overlooked due to nontraditional backgrounds. Meanwhile, a conversational AI assistant handles routine candidate inquiries (e.g., "What is your remote work policy?") and automates interview scheduling by syncing with hiring managers' calendars. Within the first year, Contoso saw time-to-fill for key roles drop from 45 days to under 30. Recruiters credited the AI for handling the drudge work and surfacing stronger shortlists, allowing them to spend more time actively courting top candidates. However, the rollout was not without challenges: the team discovered the AI's training data led it to favor candidates from certain schools, an unintended bias in its recommendations. Catching this, Contoso's HR analysts retrained the model on more diverse data and instituted bias checks. This illustrates both the breakthrough – a dramatically more efficient hiring funnel – and the risk – that unchecked AI can reinforce biases, requiring vigilant human oversight.

Looking outside the Microsoft ecosystem, a number of specialized HR tech firms are pushing AI in recruiting even further. Companies like Eightfold AI and Phenom use machine learning to build rich candidate profiles by aggregating data from resumes, social media, past applications, and more; they then match candidates to jobs (and vice versa) with predictive algorithms. AI video interview platforms have also emerged – for example, tools that analyze recorded candidate interviews for word choice, facial expressions, or tone. These promise insights into competencies and personality traits, though they raise serious ethical questions about bias and privacy. Indeed, 58% of companies say they now use AI for video interview analysis, yet regulators have warned that some of these practices may be invasive or unfair. We will revisit the governance of such tools later, but the trend is clear: talent acquisition is becoming an AI-driven domain. Recruiters in forward-thinking organizations are partnering with AI "co-recruiters," using the technology to widen the candidate funnel, eliminate grunt work, and make data-informed hiring decisions.

AI in Employee Engagement: The Intelligent Workplace Coach

Once employees are through the door, AI is increasingly used to keep them informed, supported, and engaged. Modern workers, especially digital-native generations, expect workplace services that are as responsive and personalized as the apps on their smartphones. This is where AI shines in the employee experience.

Virtual HR Assistants are now common in large organizations, often accessible through chat in Microsoft Teams or other collaboration tools. These AI assistants give employees a single, immediate point of contact for HR needs. An employee can ask a question in plain language – "How do I update my health insurance beneficiaries?" – and the AI will retrieve the relevant policy or form. Or an employee might tell the assistant, "I need to take tomorrow off," and behind the scenes the AI will log the leave request in the HR system automatically. Such a scenario is not science fiction: a consulting firm in the Middle East built an HR chatbot that could do exactly this, integrated with backend HR systems via APIs. If an employee said *"I want to take tomorrow off as annual leave,"* the AI assistant would instantly make the booking in the leave management system on the employee's behalf. This kind of seamless service not only saves employees and HR staff time, it also meets the modern expectation for instant, self-service transactions.

AI is also elevating employee wellness and development. Consider Microsoft Viva, an employee experience platform that incorporates AI to promote engagement and well-being. Viva Insights, for example, uses AI-driven analytics on Office 365 data to provide both employees and managers with feedback on work patterns – like how much time is spent in meetings or after-hours emails – and offers nudges to prevent burnout. A related AI Wellness Check agent (available through Copilot Studio) goes further: it can proactively recommend well-being activities during the workday. As Microsoft describes, this *Wellness Check* agent pulls data from trusted health sources (like the CDC or NIH) and suggests personalized exercises – perhaps a breathing exercise at midday, a reminder to take a screen break, or a journaling prompt – all delivered via Teams in a friendly, conversational manner. The goal is to treat employee wellness not as a periodic HR initiative but as a continuous, proactive conversation supported by AI.

Sentiment analysis is another AI application transforming engagement. Through surveys, feedback platforms, and even analysis of anonymized communication patterns, AI can gauge the mood of the workforce in real time. Traditional engagement surveys might be done annually; AI-powered platforms like Viva Glint (or its competitor Workday Peakon) now enable always-on listening. They use intelligent algorithms to parse open-text feedback and spot themes in what people are saying. This provides HR and leaders with up-to-the-minute insights on morale and potential issues. In fact, AI can detect subtle warning signs: for example, analyzing thousands of comments or help-desk tickets to identify a rise in negative sentiment from a particular department, which might indicate a leadership problem or overwork. One statistic often cited is that predictive models can anticipate employee turnover with up to 87% accuracy by analyzing such data patterns. While the exact figure may vary, it's true that machine learning models have become adept at identifying combinations of factors (like declining engagement, fewer internal networking interactions, increased absenteeism) that correlate with someone becoming a "flight risk." This allows HR to intervene early – perhaps a manager's check-in or a tailored retention plan – before a valued employee decides to leave.

Use Case – The Mood of the Organization: Imagine a large retail company, RetailCo, with tens of thousands of frontline employees spread across stores. RetailCo uses an AI-driven engagement tool to keep a finger on the pulse of this distributed workforce. Employees have an app that occasionally asks, in a chat interface, questions like "How was your day?" or "Do you feel supported by your manager this week?" Many employees respond candidly, thinking they're simply chatting with an HR bot. On the backend, the

AI aggregates these responses and analyzes text sentiment. Over the holiday season, the AI detects a sudden dip in positive sentiment among warehouse employees in one region and flags "potential burnout or dissatisfaction" to HR. Digging in, HR discovers those warehouses had mandatory overtime due to a surge in orders, and employees felt strained. Armed with this insight (which surfaced weeks earlier than a traditional survey could have), RetailCo's HR leaders quickly roll out a bonus pay program and hire temporary staff to ease the burden. They also task the AI with monitoring whether sentiment improves. Over the next two weeks, the AI reports a modest uptick in morale. In this scenario, AI became an always-listening coach – not replacing human managers, but providing early detection and data-driven recommendations so that leadership could respond in a human way.

It's worth noting that employees are generally receptive to AI's involvement in engagement when it clearly benefits them. A recent industry poll found 65% of employees feel more engaged when AI is used in HR processes (for example, to personalize learning or quickly resolve issues), and 50% of employees even trust AI to provide unbiased feedback on their performance and development. The trust in "unbiased feedback" likely stems from the perception that an AI analyzing objective data might be less prone to favoritism than a human manager. However, trust is fragile – if AI is used for surveillance or seen as making unfair judgments, that trust will erode. Therefore, companies have to be very transparent about how AI is used in monitoring engagement and make clear that the goal is to support employees, not to spy on them.

On the technology front, in addition to Microsoft Viva's suite, numerous external tools leverage AI for engagement. Chatbots like Leena AI and Moveworks integrate with HR systems to provide employees instant answers and route their requests (functioning as AI help desks). Platforms like Qualtrics and CultureMonkey use AI to automate analysis of engagement surveys and suggest action plans to HR. And a new category of AI coaching apps has emerged – these are personal coaching agents that employees can interact with confidentially. For example, an employee might tell the AI coach they're nervous about a presentation, and it could provide tips or even generate a quick practice script. Some companies are offering these AI coaches as a perk to help employees navigate day-to-day challenges or career growth conversations, in addition to traditional mentorship programs.

Overall, AI in employee engagement is about creating a more responsive and personalized workplace – one where each employee can get tailored support and development at scale, and where leaders have data-driven insight into the human heartbeat of the organization.

AI in Performance Management: Toward Data-Driven Fairness and Growth

Performance management, long a domain of annual reviews and subjective assessments, is being reinvented with AI. Organizations are shifting to continuous performance management models, and AI is playing assistant coach, scorekeeper, and occasionally referee in this new model.

One significant trend is using AI to analyze performance data for patterns and potential. Modern enterprises collect myriad data points on employee performance: sales numbers, project deliverables, peer feedback, customer satisfaction scores, and beyond. Making sense of this deluge is a task suited for AI. Machine learning systems can crunch multidimensional performance data to identify who the rising stars are, which employees might be struggling and why, and even suggest the next steps for development. For instance, an AI might analyze a software developer's output (code quality, tickets resolved, mentorship activities) and compare it with peers or historical data to predict the developer's promotion readiness or risk of attrition. These insights help managers avoid blind spots and base decisions on evidence rather than gut feeling.

AI is also being used to support managers in delivering feedback and coaching. Writing constructive, unbiased performance feedback is hard – so some companies now provide managers with AI-generated draft feedback. A manager can input some bullet points about an employee's performance, and a generative model (like GPT-4 tuned for corporate tone) will produce a well-structured paragraph highlighting achievements and growth areas. This is similar to features now built into Microsoft's Dynamics 365 Copilot for HR case management: it can generate email responses or summaries for HR staff handling employee cases. In performance reviews, an AI might generate a summary of an employee's year based on goals and outcomes logged in systems. The manager can then edit and personalize it. This saves time and also helps less experienced managers provide quality feedback. However, companies must ensure that managers do not abdicate their judgment entirely – the AI can assist, but the emotional intelligence in delivering feedback remains a human art.

Perhaps the most promising area is AI-driven personalized development. Instead of the old one-size-fits-all training, AI can help create tailored growth plans. After evaluating an employee's skills, performance, and career aspirations (often gathered via surveys or talent profiles), an AI can recommend specific courses, stretch assignments, or mentors that align with that individual's needs. For example, if an employee's performance data shows strong technical skills but weaker leadership scores, the system might suggest a leadership training program or assign them as a mentor to junior staff to build that muscle. This is often done via internal "talent marketplace" platforms – many large organizations (including those using Workday or LinkedIn's Learning Hub) employ AI to match employees to internal gigs or roles that will develop particular skills. The result is a more dynamic performance and development environment, where AI helps employees chart personalized career paths (indeed, surveys indicate 70% of employees expect AI to help create personalized career development plans by 2025).

Use Case – Fair and Efficient Promotions: One instructive example comes from IBM's HR department, which faced a daunting performance management challenge: processing promotions for tens of thousands of employees every quarter. The task involved HR partners pulling data from multiple systems into giant spreadsheets to decide who met the criteria for promotion – a process that took up to ten weeks each cycle. IBM's solution was to introduce an AI-powered digital HR agent nicknamed *HiRo* to handle the data drudgery. HiRo automatically gathers and compiles all the relevant performance and skills data for employees eligible for promotion, eliminating the need for HR staff to manually assemble that information. In a pilot, this automation saved IBM 12,000 hours in one quarter and cut the promotion processing time in half. Importantly, IBM designed HiRo with governance in mind: the system makes *no autonomous decisions* about who gets promoted – it simply presents the data in a digestible format for human managers and HR business partners to make the calls. By doing so, IBM ensured that the final decisions remained with people (maintaining accountability), while HiRo handled the tedious work. They also conducted a thorough ethics assessment of HiRo, aligning it with principles like explainability (making it clear that HiRo does not decide promotions, people do), fairness (applying uniform criteria and displaying the same data for every candidate to avoid favoritism), and privacy (ensuring personal data is secure and only used in approved ways). The result was a performance management process that was both more efficient and fairer – managers could focus their energy on discussing *why* someone deserves a promotion rather than spending hours on *collecting* the evidence, and employees could trust that the evaluations were grounded in complete data, not just whoever advocated loudest.

This example highlights a broader theme: AI can make performance management more objective by grounding decisions in data. But it can also exacerbate problems if done poorly. A poorly designed performance algorithm might inadvertently penalize those who take parental leave or who don't log long hours online, if those factors aren't carefully accounted for. And if employees feel a "black box" is deciding their fate, it can undermine trust even more than old opaque human processes did. Transparency and human oversight are crucial. Many organizations are therefore adopting a principle that AI provides *input* into performance decisions, but never the final *output* without human review.

We also see AI enabling continuous feedback loops. Rather than waiting for annual reviews, companies are using tools where employees can get real-time feedback from peers or even from the work itself. Some sales teams, for example, use AI to analyze client meetings (through transcripts or recordings) and give representatives immediate coaching tips on their sales technique. In software development, AI code review tools not only catch bugs but can identify patterns in a programmer's work – for instance, noting if they frequently struggle with a certain type of task – and then recommend specific training modules. These are subtle shifts, but over time, they change performance management from a periodic evaluation to a continuous, supportive process where AI is an ever-present guide.

Implementing AI in HR: Strategy and Practical Considerations

The promise of AI in HR is great – but realizing it requires careful strategy and practical execution. HR leaders and IT teams must collaborate closely to integrate AI into HR workflows in a way that delivers value and is accepted by users. This section explores how to approach AI implementation in HR, from selecting the right projects and technologies to managing change in the organization.

Start with Strategic Pain Points

A key to success is to identify the HR processes that will benefit most from AI. Rather than adopting AI for AI's sake, leading companies start by pinpointing their biggest pain points or opportunities. For example, if a company is struggling with high turnover among new hires, an AI solution that predicts flight risk or improves onboarding might be high-impact. If the recruiting team is drowning in applicant volume, an AI resume screener or chatbot could yield quick wins. By aligning AI projects to pressing HR challenges, you ensure there is a clear value proposition. This also helps get buy-in from stakeholders – it's easier to rally support for an AI tool when you can say, "This could reduce our 42-day average time-to-fill for positions," or "This might improve our abysmal onboarding completion rates."

It's often wise to start with pilot projects in a sub-area of HR before scaling up. For instance, pilot an AI-driven AskHR chatbot for a single business unit or location, gather feedback, and refine it before enterprise-wide rollout. Microsoft itself followed this approach internally: their HR team developed an internal "AskHR" app on Dynamics 365 with embedded AI capabilities to handle employee inquiries. They rolled out features stepwise and observed how both employees and HR staff engaged with them. By piloting, you can measure results (e.g., reduction in response times, user satisfaction scores) and also catch unexpected issues early. A small success can then be showcased to build momentum for broader AI adoption in HR.

Integrating with Existing HR Systems

One practical consideration is how AI solutions will integrate into current HR technology stacks. Enterprise HR is often an ecosystem of platforms: HRIS (like SAP SuccessFactors, Oracle HCM, or Workday), applicant tracking systems, learning management, case management tools, etc. Introducing AI usually means either augmenting these systems with new capabilities or connecting external AI services to them. A classic example is using an AI service to analyze data from your HRIS and then writing back insights or flags into that system.

This is where technologies like Microsoft's Power Platform and AI Builder come into play for Microsoft-centric organizations. Power Platform's low-code tools (Power Automate, Power Apps) combined with AI Builder allow creating custom workflows that inject AI into routine processes. For example, one could build a Power Automate flow that listens for a new employee survey submission, then uses an AI Builder sentiment analysis model to rate the sentiment, and finally logs a case in an HR dashboard if the sentiment is very negative (so a human can follow up). Microsoft reports using AI Builder internally for tasks like analyzing user sentiment in HR support cases and auto-triaging them to the right queue. This kind of integration can often be done *without* replacing your core systems – instead, AI works alongside them, accessing data via APIs or connectors.

Notably, Microsoft has been weaving AI capabilities into its flagship HR-related systems. Dynamics 365 Human Resources (part of the broader D365 suite) can embed Copilot services that draft responses or summarize employee cases. Microsoft Viva, integrated with Teams, connects to Office 365 data and uses AI to produce insights or training suggestions in the flow of work. And as discussed, Microsoft Copilot Studio now provides a unified way to build AI *agents* that connect with various data sources. Copilot Studio's approach is particularly interesting: it allows HR or IT professionals (even those not deeply technical) to configure AI *agents* with natural language prompts and connect them to data via pre-built connectors. Microsoft offers ready-made agent templates for common HR scenarios – for example, a *Leave Management agent* to handle time-off requests, or an *Awards and Recognition agent* to help run employee award nominations. An organization can deploy these agents and customize them to their environment, integrating with their HRIS for pulling policy info or with their payroll system for updating records. The low-code design means you don't need a team of AI scientists to embed these into your processes; your existing HR IT analysts or power users might do it with some training.

For non-Microsoft environments, similar integration strategies exist. Major HR tech vendors have opened to AI partnerships: Workday, for example, enables integration of third-party AI models via its Extend platform and acquired an employee feedback AI company (Peakon) to bolster its offerings. Oracle's HR Cloud touts its built-in machine learning for things like "Best Candidate" scoring and offers an API framework for adding custom AI services. And then there are stand-alone AI HR products (e.g., a tool like Beamery for talent analytics) that must be integrated via APIs to the core HRIS. Interoperability is key – HR leaders should ensure whichever AI solutions they consider can securely plug into their existing systems and data without massive custom development.

This brings us to data. AI in HR is only as good as the data it can use. Practical data considerations include: Do we have quality data to train or feed the AI (e.g., well-tagged performance data or a corpus of past job descriptions)? Is our data siloed, and how will we connect it? Enter the Model Context Protocol (MCP), an emerging open standard that directly tackles this integration challenge.

The Model Context Protocol (MCP): Connecting AI to HR Data

One of the hardest parts of implementing AI in enterprise workflows is connecting AI systems (which are often cloud-based and evolving) to the myriad enterprise data sources securely and efficiently. Historically, hooking an AI assistant or model up to internal databases, SaaS tools, or knowledge bases required custom integration work for each source – essentially building one-off "pipes" for each data feed. This is burdensome and hard to maintain, especially when systems update or new data sources need to be added. It also raises consistency issues: how do you ensure all these custom integrations enforce the same security and logging standards?

Model Context Protocol (MCP) has emerged as a solution to this problem. Developed initially by Anthropic and now gaining wider industry support, MCP is essentially a universal adapter for connecting AI to enterprise systems. Think of it as *USB-C for data*: instead of every integration using a different plug, MCP provides a standard interface. Technically, it defines a simple client-server architecture: an *AI agent or assistant* acts as the client that needs information, and the *enterprise system* (be it an HR database, an ATS, or a payroll system) runs an MCP *server* that exposes certain data or functions in a standardized way. When the AI needs something – say an answer to "How much PTO does Alice have left?" – it sends a request via MCP; the HRIS's MCP server receives the query, fetches the relevant data (Alice's PTO balance), and returns it in a structured format the AI understands. All of this happens with strong security controls and auditing baked in by the MCP protocol.

In the HR context, MCP can be transformative. Imagine an AI HR assistant that via MCP can seamlessly talk to *all* your HR systems: the recruiting system, the core employee database, the learning platform, etc. Instead of building and maintaining separate integrations for each system (and updating the AI's API calls whenever systems change), you rely on MCP connectors. If you switch, for example, from one HRIS to another, as long as the new system has an MCP server exposing similar capabilities, your AI assistant doesn't need a rewrite – it's like unplugging one hard drive and plugging in another to a USB port. This drastically reduces integration time and cost for AI projects. Microsoft recognized this potential and has integrated MCP into Copilot Studio, meaning any custom Copilot agent can use MCP to connect to external tools and data with minimal fuss. By 2025, MCP was generally available in Copilot Studio, allowing HR teams using Microsoft's platform to quickly hook their agents into systems like Workday or ServiceNow via MCP connectors (in fact, Microsoft provided pre-built connectors for common enterprise apps).

But beyond technical ease, MCP redefines how AI agents manage data with governance in mind. MCP provides a centralized layer through which all AI data access is channeled. This has huge implications for compliance and auditability: every time the AI agent accesses a piece of HR data or triggers an action, it goes through the MCP server which logs the interaction in a standard, reviewable format. For HR – where data is sensitive and regulations like GDPR or employment laws are strict – this unified audit trail is invaluable. Security teams can review logs to see, for instance, that the AI pulled salary data for an analysis on June 1 at 2:00 PM and that it only retrieved aggregated, non-personalized figures because the MCP server was configured to mask personal identifiers. Without MCP, such oversight is much harder when multiple integration methods are in play. Additionally, MCP lets administrators centrally enforce access controls: the MCP server will only expose what the AI is allowed to see or do, ensuring the AI can't accidentally or intentionally perform unauthorized actions. For example, you might allow an HR AI agent to *read* certain data (like training records or anonymized engagement scores) but not to *write* any changes, except perhaps logging a service ticket. MCP essentially sandboxes the AI's capabilities to a well-defined set of tools and data, which is a cornerstone of safe deployment.

Another advantage is consistency. HR organizations often update or even swap out AI models over time – today's cutting-edge large language model might be replaced by a better one next year. MCP helps here as well: because it standardizes how the AI model talks to systems, you can change the model without redoing all integrations or worrying that the new model will behave inconsistently with regard to data access. Governance policies remain consistent even if the underlying AI model changes changes, because those policies are enforced at the MCP layer (outside the model). This means companies can experiment and upgrade their AI models with less risk, as long as they keep the MCP connections stable.

To illustrate, let's say a company's HR AI agent was initially powered by Model X. All queries for employee data went through MCP to the HRIS. Now the company wants to switch to Model Y, which is more powerful. Thanks to MCP, Model Y can be plugged in and immediately gain the same controlled access to HRIS data – it "learns" the available MCP endpoints (like getEmployeeRecord, updateLeaveBalance) rather than some bespoke API from Model X's era. And it will still be constrained to those endpoints, so any rogue behavior (however unlikely) by Model Y can't go beyond what Model X was allowed to do.

In practice, what MCP means for HR IT is that data integration for AI becomes more plug-and-play. Early adopters in other domains (like software development and customer support) have reported dramatically faster deployment of AI solutions thanks to MCP. In HR, we can expect similar gains – connecting an AI coaching tool to a learning management system, for example, could be as simple as installing an MCP connector and granting the appropriate permissions. The end result is faster innovation cycles: HR teams can pilot an AI idea (say, an internal career advisor chatbot) in days by snapping together an AI service and relevant data sources, rather than the weeks or months of integration work that used to be required.

It's still early days for MCP in HR, but the vision is compelling. A future HR IT architecture might include an MCP "hub" where all HR systems (recruiting, HRIS, benefits, etc.) publish a set of capabilities. AI agents – whether Microsoft Copilot-based, IBM's Watson, or open-source LLMs – could then be authorized to use certain capabilities. This not only speeds up deployment, it enforces a deliberate process of defining which AI can do what. That very process is a form of governance: it forces HR and IT to decide, for instance, that the recruiting AI can read candidate data and write interview feedback (because you want it to auto-score interviews), but it cannot directly send offer letters without human sign-off. Those rules get baked into the MCP configuration instead of hidden in some code.

In summary, MCP offers a pathway to integrate AI with HR data securely, flexibly, and with full auditability. As HR AI usage grows, adopting such standards will likely become a best practice for any enterprise-scale deployment. We now turn to the broader topic of governance and compliance, of which MCP is an important part, but not the whole story.

Governance, Compliance, and Auditability: Managing the Risks of HR AI

For all its potential, AI in HR also carries significant risks. HR deals with people's livelihoods, rights, and sensitive personal information – a misstep can lead to allegations of unfair practices or breaches of privacy. Thus, governance, compliance, and ethics in HR AI are paramount. This section discusses how organizations can harness AI's benefits while ensuring accountability, fairness, and legal compliance. We will also see how the technical measures like MCP and broader governance frameworks work together to create an AI that is not just smart but trustworthy.

Navigating the Ethical and Legal Minefield

AI systems, especially those powered by machine learning, can behave in unintended ways. In recruitment, we saw how an AI might *learn* to prefer candidates of a certain profile if trained on biased historical data. In performance management, an algorithm might inadvertently penalize someone for taking maternity leave if not carefully designed. These are not hypothetical – real companies have faced backlash over AI-driven HR tools that were found biased. In 2018, for example, Amazon had to scrap an experimental hiring algorithm that started downgrading resumes containing the word "women's" (as in "women's chess club captain"), reflecting the male-dominated data it was trained on. Such stories underscore that AI can inadvertently perpetuate or even amplify bias if we are not vigilant.

Regulators have taken notice, and the regulatory environment for HR AI is tightening. The European Union's upcoming AI Act explicitly classifies AI systems used in employment (hiring, promotion, firing decisions, etc.) as "high-risk" applications. This means organizations deploying AI for these purposes in the EU (or affecting EU citizens) will face strict obligations: conducting risk assessments, documenting how the AI works, ensuring human oversight, and more. The AI Act is expected to become law by 2024 and fully enforceable by 2026. Companies have a short window to get compliant, and those that cannot meet the transparency and safety requirements may have to pull certain AI tools off the market or cease their use in HR. Similarly, in the United States, the Equal Employment Opportunity Commission (EEOC) has signaled that unexamined AI hiring tools could violate anti-discrimination laws, and local laws (like New York City's bias audit law for hiring algorithms) are already in effect. The direction is clear: using AI in HR will soon come with formal regulatory responsibilities akin to handling personal data under privacy laws.

So what does good HR AI governance look like? Firstly, organizations should establish an AI governance body or steering committee. This group – comprising HR leaders, data scientists, legal counsel, and ethicists if available – would set policies for AI use, evaluate new AI tools, and monitor outcomes. Part of their job is to stay abreast of global regulations (since AI is borderless) and ensure the company's practices meet the highest applicable standards. They would also develop or endorse ethical guidelines for AI in line with company values. For instance, they might adopt principles similar to IBM's, which include transparency (employees should know when AI is being used and how), fairness (AI decisions must be free of prohibited biases), and privacy (personal data used by AI must be protected and minimal).

Another best practice is conducting algorithmic impact assessments for any AI that has material effect on people. This is analogous to privacy impact assessments companies do for GDPR. Before deploying an AI model in, say, screening candidates, the company should analyze: what data goes in? Could those data encode bias? How does the model make its predictions (is it a black box or interpretable)? What are the potential harms (e.g., could it systematically reject minority candidates)? And importantly, what processes exist for humans to review or override the AI's decisions? Such assessments help identify risks early. Some jurisdictions will likely make them mandatory for high-risk AI – the EU AI Act in draft form essentially requires documentation of these aspects. But even absent a mandate, it's a prudent step. If the assessment finds, for example, that an AI tool lacks transparency, the company might decide to avoid it or to pressure the vendor for a more explainable version.

Transparency is a theme that cannot be overstated. Whether due to regulation or employee expectations, companies will need to be transparent about their use of AI in HR. This includes informing employees or candidates when AI is involved in decision-making that affects them. Many companies have started updating their privacy notices or handbooks to mention AI – for instance, telling job applicants that an automated system may be used to evaluate their application, but also reassuring them of the human oversight and fairness checks in place. Transparency also extends internally: HR and IT should maintain documentation of how each AI tool works, what data it uses, and how it was vetted. In case of an audit or an incident (like a claim that the AI was discriminatory), this documentation is crucial evidence of due diligence.

Critically, maintaining a "human in the loop" is emerging as both a best practice and likely a legal requirement in many cases. What this means is ensuring that for consequential decisions (hiring, promotion, termination, etc.), AI outputs are reviewed and validated by a human, rather than being fully automated black-box decisions. The Mercer report on the EU AI Act advises avoiding fully automated black-box HR tools altogether. Instead, if AI scores candidates or flags employees for promotion, that should feed into a human-driven process, not replace it. Having a human final say provides a safety net for judgment and empathy that AI lacks, and also assigns clear accountability (it is still the manager or HR making the decision, not blaming "the algorithm"). The IBM promotion case with HiRo illustrated this: the AI presented data, but "any decision that involves a pay raise or a nomination is made by the manager [and] HR Business Partner," not by HiRo. That approach kept the process ethical and compliant while still using AI to its fullest extent for efficiency.

Technical and Process Controls

On the technical side, protocols like MCP that we discussed are a powerful tool in the governance toolkit. By routing AI's access to data and actions through a controlled interface, MCP inherently supports key governance pillars: security, auditing, and fine-grained permission control. Every HR AI project should have logging and auditability from day one – if an AI model is interacting with personal data, you need records of what was accessed, when, by which system, and for what purpose. MCP provides that out of the box. But even if one isn't using MCP, architects should implement similar logging around AI interactions. For example, if you integrate an AI via an API, ensure those API calls are logged. Some companies generate a unique identifier for each AI "decision" so it can be traced later. Others store the raw outputs of AI (like scoring recommendations) for a period, so that if someone challenges a decision, it can be reviewed.

Security is another facet: HR data is often highly sensitive (think health info, salaries, performance notes). If AI models are cloud-based (like many generative AI services), one must ensure that sending data to them doesn't violate any data residency or privacy rules. Many vendors now offer enterprise plans where AI processing can happen in a private environment or at least with contractual assurances of data handling. Alternatively, companies can use open-source models deployed internally for extra control. Regardless, any AI usage should go through the same security review as other IT systems: checking encryption, access controls, vendor risk, etc.

Then there is bias monitoring. Don't "set and forget" an AI system. Just as we monitor business KPIs, we need to monitor AI outcomes for signs of bias or error. This might mean periodically sampling AI decisions and doing a manual review: for example, take 100 rejected job applicants that the AI screened out and see if a diverse group is represented or if there's an odd skew. Some organizations have deployed fairness dashboards – tools that continuously track metrics like selection rates by gender or ethnicity for AI-driven decisions. If an anomaly is detected (say the AI is selecting men at twice the rate of women for a certain role), the system raises an alert for investigation. This kind of proactive approach is increasingly feasible with analytics tools and is highly recommended to ensure the AI remains within ethical bounds.

Finally, companies must plan for the auditability of their AI. Auditability means that if someone asks "why did the AI do X?", you have the means to answer. This is tough with black-box deep learning models, but there are ways to approximate an explanation. Some AI systems provide saliency maps or feature importance scores indicating which factors weighed most on a decision. Others allow a form of "counterfactual" probing – for example, how would the recommendation change if we altered this input? If the stakes are high, consider simpler models that are intrinsically interpretable, even if they are a bit less accurate, especially if required for compliance. The audit trail from MCP again is valuable – it doesn't explain the model's inner workings, but it records the chain of events (what data was accessed, what the AI asked for). Combined with logs from the AI system (some keep conversation histories), an auditor could piece together context for a particular decision.

From a compliance perspective, having these controls in place is not just defensive; it can be a competitive advantage. Regulators and clients are more likely to trust and approve AI uses if you can demonstrate robust governance. In highly regulated industries (finance, government, etc.), the ability to show detailed audit logs and explainability for your HR AI might even be a prerequisite to use it at all. It's telling that many of the biggest players are investing heavily in AI governance – Microsoft, for example, has an internal AI ethics committee and has baked responsible AI checks into its product development. They have toolkits for fairness assessment and require teams to document AI systems' intended uses and limits. Enterprises adopting AI in HR would do well to mirror these practices at their scale.

Use Case – A Tale of Two Chatbots: Consider two companies that each deploy an HR chatbot to answer employees' benefits questions. Company A chooses a popular AI service and gives it access to their HR policy wiki. They launch it quickly without much oversight. Initially, it's a success – employees love the instant answers. But one day, a glitch causes the bot to expose an employee's personal data (in answering a question, it pulled up the wrong info). The incident reveals that the bot had no proper access controls; it was over-permissioned on data. Worse, because there were no detailed logs, it's hard to trace how many times it may have served up data incorrectly. Trust in the tool plummets, and Company A has to shut it down and report a breach. Meanwhile, Company B took a slower, more deliberate approach. Their chatbot was integrated via an MCP-like gateway: it could only fetch data from a specific FAQ database and had rules to mask any personal identifiers. Company B's IT had set up monitoring and kept transcripts of the bot's answers (which employees were aware of via a disclaimer). When a new overtime policy rolled out, a few employees asked the bot about it and got slightly misleading answers (because the AI hadn't been updated yet). Thanks to logs, HR noticed the pattern of questions and the answers given. They quickly corrected the source info and used the transcripts to *teach* the AI the correct responses. The bot's accuracy actually improved over time, and employees grew to trust it more, seeing that it was consistently updated and accurate. In the end, Company B's careful governance not only averted disaster but made their AI more effective in the long run.

Balancing Opportunity and Complexity

The future of HR is undeniably intertwined with AI. The opportunity is immense: we're talking about HR teams free from drudgery, able to focus on strategic people initiatives, employees empowered by on-demand support and personalized growth paths, and organizations gaining predictive insights to make better talent decisions. This is the vision of *augmented HR*, where AI is a co-pilot to HR professionals and to employees themselves – not replacing the human element, but enhancing it. As one HR analytics leader put it, "AI isn't about replacing people but empowering them to do more valuable work… freeing up time for meaningful human interaction." In HR, those meaningful interactions – a manager coaching an employee, a recruiter passionately convincing a candidate, an HR business partner devising a plan to improve team morale – are irreplaceable. AI's role is to clear the path and provide the insights to make those interactions count even more.

Yet, realizing this opportunity comes with complexity. HR leaders must grapple with integrating new technologies into old processes, overcoming skepticism and fear among staff, and ensuring that the AI they introduce is fair and compliant. There will be missteps along the way. Not every AI project will yield the expected ROI; some might even backfire if not managed well. The key is to approach AI adoption in HR as a journey of continuous learning and iteration. Start small, build trust with early wins, involve stakeholders (including employees – get their feedback on tools that affect them), and scale up with confidence. The complexity can be managed by cross-functional teamwork: HR bringing domain knowledge, IT and data teams bringing tech expertise, legal ensuring compliance, and perhaps most importantly, executives setting the tone that AI in HR is a priority for the business's future.

In the coming years, we can expect AI to become as embedded in HR systems as Internet connectivity is today. Think about how unremarkable it is now that an HRIS has basic analytics or self-service – soon, having AI-driven recommendations and chat interfaces will be just as standard. Those HR organizations that have laid the governance groundwork will flourish in this AI-rich environment, because they'll be able to deploy new capabilities quickly and responsibly. They will have earned the trust of their employees that AI is there to help, not judge. They will also be able to attract forward-thinking talent; younger workers entering the field will gravitate toward employers that use modern tools to enhance their career and work life.

On the flip side, HR teams that avoid or delay AI adoption risk falling behind. If routine tasks stay manual, HR staff will remain bogged down and less able to contribute strategically. If decisions continue to be made on instinct alone, organizations might miss out on patterns that AI could reveal – patterns that could be the difference in retaining a top performer or catching a budding culture issue. However, it is equally true that rushing in without proper oversight is a risk; a scandal involving AI (for example, a biased hiring AI that hurts the company's reputation) could set a firm back years. Thus, the balance: be proactive and bold in embracing AI, but do so with eyes open to the responsibilities.

To conclude, AI is not a magic wand for HR – it is a powerful tool that *augments* the capabilities of HR professionals and the experience of employees. The organizations that succeed with AI in HR will be those that combine narrative depth with practical utility: they will craft a vision for how AI can elevate the human potential in their workforce (the narrative), and they will roll up their sleeves to integrate, govern, and fine-tune these technologies in the trenches (the practical work). As we have seen, the technologies are advancing rapidly – from generative AI assistants that can converse naturally, to predictive models that can foresee issues, to integration protocols like MCP that tie it all together. HR leaders, IT experts, and consultants must collaborate more closely than ever to harness these advances for the good of organizations and their people.

"AI for the Future of HR" ultimately means HR that is more efficient, informed, and empathetic. The efficiency comes from automation of the mundane; the informed part comes from data-driven insights and predictions; and the empathy – somewhat paradoxically – is enabled by giving humans more time and information to focus on the human side. With strong governance and a clear purpose, AI will help HR professionals fulfill the perennial mandate of their function: to align human potential with organizational goals, in a way that people thrive. It's an exciting future – one where HR can truly become the driver of organizational success, powered by AI and guided by human wisdom.

Summary: AI for the Future of HR

AI is reshaping HR from an administrative function into a strategic, data-driven partner. From recruiting and engagement to performance and development, AI is enhancing efficiency, personalization, and insight – while introducing new governance challenges.

Recruitment and Talent Acquisition

AI tools now screen resumes, generate job descriptions, and engage candidates via chatbots. These solutions reduce time-to-hire and recruiter workload, but require bias checks and oversight to avoid reinforcing systemic inequities.

Employee Engagement and Support

Virtual HR assistants in platforms like Teams handle routine requests, while tools like Microsoft Viva use AI to monitor well-being and flag burnout risks. Sentiment analysis offers real-time insights, enabling faster, targeted interventions.

Performance and Development

AI supports continuous performance management by summarizing feedback, suggesting development paths, and analyzing promotion readiness. The goal is not to automate decisions but to inform them with better data and consistency.

Implementing AI Strategically

Success depends on starting with clear pain points, piloting in targeted areas, and integrating AI into existing systems. Microsoft's Power Platform and Copilot Studio offer low-code options for embedding AI into HR workflows.

Model Context Protocol (MCP)

MCP is a new integration standard that enables secure, auditable AI access to HR systems. By acting as a centralized gateway, it simplifies connections while enforcing consistent access control and governance across tools and models.

Governance and Compliance

With rising regulation (e.g., EU AI Act), HR AI must be transparent, fair, and accountable. Best practices include maintaining audit trails, involving human reviewers, conducting impact assessments, and setting strict data access policies.

A well-governed AI project can enhance trust and productivity. Poorly managed tools risk breaches, bias, and loss of credibility.

AI will not replace HR – it will augment it. When implemented responsibly, AI helps HR teams focus on what matters most: people.

PART V

Conclusion

CHAPTER 11

The Future of Work Is Now

For years, the phrase "future of work" evoked distant speculation – robots replacing jobs, virtual offices, AI-driven everything. But in today's HR and workplace reality, the future of work is no longer on the horizon. It's here. Organizations are now facing the convergence of radical flexibility, distributed teams, intelligent systems, and human-centered design. Technology isn't just changing how we work – it's changing why we work, and how we thrive while working.

This chapter closes the book by examining the transformative journey that HR is undergoing, how Microsoft's ecosystem enables that shift, and what leaders must do now to build organizations that are resilient, responsive, and human.

The Great Redefinition: From Process to Purpose

In the past, HR technology was often equated with efficiency: faster payroll, better scheduling, fewer manual errors. But in the age of AI and hybrid work, HR's mission is expanding beyond transactions. It's about building meaningful experiences, fostering adaptability, and shaping culture at scale.

The Microsoft HR tech stack is increasingly designed around this ethos. Viva, Power Platform, Dynamics 365 Human Resources, and Copilot tools are all focused on helping employees feel supported, connected, and empowered. This is no small shift. It requires HR to stop thinking like an administrator and start thinking like a designer – of systems, workflows, and above all, experiences.

Consider the redesign of performance management. Rather than once-a-year appraisals, organizations are enabling continuous development through learning nudges in Viva, real-time feedback loops using Power Apps, and AI-generated growth plans via Copilot Studio. These tools make development visible, accessible, and individualized.

Or take onboarding. Where legacy systems created isolated tasks (forms, training modules), new HR environments create journeys. A Power Platform onboarding app embedded into Teams might welcome a new hire, guide them through setup, connect them to buddies, and introduce cultural norms – all orchestrated through flows and dashboards.

The transformation isn't just digital – it's philosophical. HR is becoming less about managing headcount and more about curating ecosystems. Employees don't just want jobs– they want to understand how their work fits into something bigger. Microsoft's solutions help operationalize that purpose, turning intangible goals like "belonging" or "clarity" into trackable outcomes.

Companies that embrace this redefinition are building cultures that are resilient, because they are inclusive by design. This means being able to onboard from anywhere, support multiple languages, personalize training to role and learning style, and surface opportunities based on skills – not titles. With tools like LinkedIn Skills Graph integrated into Viva, even the traditional resume is being challenged in favor of skills-based journeys.

The Tech Stack As a Culture Stack

Tools reflect culture – and they shape it, too. If HR tools are clunky, siloed, and unintuitive, they reinforce a culture of fragmentation. But when tools are integrated, conversational, and proactive, they reinforce connection and trust.

With Microsoft Entra ID, identity becomes fluid and secure. With Power Platform, creativity is democratized. With Viva, wellness and alignment move from side conversations into the heart of work. With Copilot, information becomes accessible – filtered through guardrails and enhanced through AI-driven summaries.

Together, these aren't just tools. They form a "culture stack."

- Security becomes psychological safety. When employees know their data is protected, and that access is role-based and accountable, they feel safe to engage.

- Automation becomes time reallocated to meaning. When routine tasks are delegated to AI and flows, people can focus on work that matters.

- Insights become dialogue. With tools like Viva Insights, organizations don't just report on burnout – they act on it.

The implications go further: culture stacks can be portable, especially in distributed or hybrid teams. An HR system that's designed for transparency and inclusion helps anchor company values – even across borders, time zones, and working styles. Think of a global employee who logs into Teams each day and sees a personalized feed of wellness resources, learning prompts, manager messages, and community chats – all surfaced based on role, behavior, and timing. That's not just technology. That's trust made tangible.

Adaptive HR: Leading in a Nonlinear World

The future of work is nonlinear. Talent doesn't follow a straight ladder, work doesn't follow a 9-to-5 rhythm, and careers don't follow fixed job descriptions. In this new world, HR must become an adaptive function – capable of sensing shifts, responding with agility, and designing for resilience.

Microsoft's ecosystem is uniquely suited to support this adaptiveness:

- Copilot Studio enables rapid development of AI agents that meet emerging employee needs – whether it's a policy assistant or a learning path recommender.

- Dataverse provides a unified data layer that supports personalization and trend analysis.

- Power BI and Viva Glint offer visibility into engagement, sentiment, and productivity – so decisions are driven by patterns, not assumptions.

This approach turns HR teams into experience designers and digital product owners. Rather than operating in the background, they prototype and ship: onboarding journeys, mentorship networks, feedback bots, internal mobility hubs. They act on data and iterate based on employee feedback. They think like product teams – shipping versions, testing uptake, and measuring impact.

The best HR organizations now operate on three time horizons:

- Today: Delivering support, benefits, and policy with reliability

- Next: Surfacing trends and experiments (e.g., new reward mechanisms, talent marketplaces)

- Beyond: Shaping culture through foresight (e.g., preparing for AI-literate workforces, upskilling at scale)

Five Takeaways for HR Leaders

1. Governance Is Strategic, Not Bureaucratic. Whether implementing AI, provisioning access, or building apps, governance ensures trust. Use RACI charts, audit trails, and MCP-driven integrations to embed accountability and empower ethical deployment.

2. Experience Is the New Productivity. Employees thrive when their tools support flow, not friction. Consider the employee journey as a design challenge – and use Microsoft's low-code tools to solve it across roles, regions, and devices.

3. AI Requires Guardrails. Copilot can do amazing things, but it must be deployed with ethical design, explainability, and human oversight. Think "co-pilot," not "auto-pilot." Establish AI use guidelines, transparency standards, and escalation paths.

4. Innovation Belongs to Everyone. With Power Platform and Copilot Studio, innovation is no longer the domain of engineers. HR teams can build bots, apps, and insights on their own – with IT support and strategic enablement.

5. HR's Mandate Is Expanding. You're no longer just hiring, paying, or retaining talent. You're shaping the digital habitat of your organization. Every automation, every interface, every AI prompt is a cultural artifact – treat it with intentionality.

From Function to Movement

The HR function has always been about people. But in the era of AI, remote work, and radical change, that mandate is evolving. HR is no longer just supporting the business – it's designing the future of the business. And technology is not a constraint on that mission – it's the toolkit that makes it possible.

We must also acknowledge the shift from digital transformation to digital normalcy. There is no going back. Employees now expect personalization, transparency, and agency in how they experience work. HR systems must not just meet these expectations – they must evolve ahead of them. Microsoft's tools are designed not as silver bullets but as scaffolding: what you build with them reflects your culture.

As you leave this book, remember: the future of work isn't something we prepare for – it's something we shape. The tools are in your hands. The question is: What will you build? And who will you build it with?

Because the future of work is not a solitary destination – it's a co-created journey.

Glossary: Microsoft HR Tech Stack

AI (Artificial Intelligence): Technology that mimics human thinking. In HR, it helps analyze data, automate tasks, and provide personalized recommendations – for example, suggesting training for employees or screening job applicants.

AI Builder: A tool within Microsoft's Power Platform that lets non-technical users build AI features (like predicting employee attrition or analyzing survey responses) with easy drag-and-drop steps.

AI Copilot: A built-in assistant in Microsoft tools (like Word, Excel, or Teams) that can help write, summarize, analyze, and suggest content using AI. Think of it as a helpful "co-pilot" that boosts productivity.

Applicant Tracking System (ATS): A software system used by HR to post jobs, collect resumes, and track applicants during the hiring process.

Business Process Automation: The use of software (like Power Automate) to reduce or eliminate repetitive manual HR tasks (like sending reminders or approvals).

Canvas App: A type of Power App where the layout and user experience are designed from scratch (like painting on a blank canvas). Often used for custom mobile-friendly apps.

Copilot Studio: A tool to create chatbots – automated helpers that can answer employee questions 24/7. It doesn't require programming knowledge and is often used in HR for onboarding bots, time-off inquiries, and more.

Culture Stack: A phrase used in this book to describe how integrated tools (like Teams, Viva, and Power Platform) reflect and shape a company's values, behavior, and experience.

Custom App (Power App): A small, purpose-built application (like a form or dashboard) created by HR or IT to solve specific needs such as collecting feedback or tracking training.

Data Loss Prevention (DLP): Security settings that stop sensitive data (like salaries or personal info) from being shared outside the organization by mistake.

Dataverse: Microsoft's secure data storage service used to hold employee and HR information that apps and automation tools can access.

© Ana Inés Urrutia de Souza 2025
A. I. Urrutia de Souza, *The Microsoft AI Human Resources Handbook*,
https://doi.org/10.1007/979-8-8688-1781-6

Dynamics 365 Human Resources (D365 HR): Microsoft's main HR system used to manage employee records, leave, compensation, and performance. It integrates with other Microsoft apps like Teams and Outlook.

Employee Experience (EX): The total set of interactions employees have with their workplace – from onboarding to learning to how supported and valued they feel.

Employee Self-Service (ESS): Tools that let employees manage HR tasks (like requesting time off or updating their contact info) without needing to email or call HR.

Entra ID (formerly Azure AD): Microsoft's system for managing user access and login security. It ensures the right people have access to the right tools – and only those tools.

Governance: Rules and systems that ensure technology is used responsibly and securely. In HR, this includes who can see employee data, how apps are approved, and how AI is monitored.

HR Portal: A website or app that acts as a central point for employees to access HR resources like policies, pay stubs, or support tickets.

HRIS (Human Resources Information System): A digital system for managing employee data, job history, benefits, and more.

Insights (Viva Insights): A Microsoft Viva feature that provides summaries of work patterns, well-being indicators, and productivity metrics to help improve work–life balance.

Integration: The connection between two tools that allows them to share data – for example, syncing job applicants from LinkedIn into Dynamics 365 HR.

Journey Mapping: A way to design and visualize the steps employees go through – from hiring to exiting – to improve experience at each stage.

LinkedIn Talent Solutions: LinkedIn's suite of hiring tools used to find, attract, and hire talent. Includes job posting, recruiter search, and candidate analytics.

Low-Code: A way to build apps or workflows with minimal programming, using visual tools (like drag and drop). Microsoft's Power Platform is low-code.

Model Context Protocol (MCP): A secure and standardized way for AI systems to request data from HR systems. It ensures that every AI request is safe, logged, and controlled.

Model-Driven App: A type of Power App that is based on a structured data model. Often used for internal HR systems like tracking job requisitions or approvals.

Onboarding App: A digital tool that guides new hires through forms, policies, team intros, and tasks during their first days at a company.

Performance Management: The process of tracking and supporting employee growth, goals, and feedback. Microsoft tools like Power Apps and Viva help automate and personalize this.

Power Apps: Microsoft's tool for building small HR apps to replace spreadsheets, paper forms, or manual processes. Often used for things like leave requests, checklists, or nomination forms.

Power Automate: A Microsoft tool used to build workflows – automated processes that save time and reduce errors (like sending reminders or approvals).

Power BI: A reporting and dashboard tool that helps HR visualize data – like attrition trends, training completion rates, or hiring funnel efficiency.

Power Pages: A tool to build secure websites or portals – for example, a candidate portal, an employee help desk, or a public-facing HR FAQ.

Power Platform: Microsoft's suite of low-code tools that lets users create apps, automate workflows, build dashboards, and create chatbots without needing full coding expertise. It's widely used in HR to streamline work.

RACI Matrix: A planning tool used in projects to clarify who is Responsible, Accountable, Consulted, and Informed for specific tasks or decisions.

Role-Based Access Control (RBAC): A method for managing who can see or change what in HR systems. Access is based on a person's job role.

Security Roles: Permission levels in Microsoft tools that define what a user can access or do. For example, a manager can see their team's data, but not other departments.

Self-Service Portal: A site or app where employees can take action on their own – like downloading a policy or submitting a form.

Teams (Microsoft Teams): Microsoft's collaboration platform, combining chat, video calls, file sharing, and HR tools in one place. Often used as the main HR communication hub.

User Adoption: The process of helping employees learn, accept, and use new HR tools.

Viva Connections: A Microsoft Viva module that acts as a customizable intranet hub inside Teams. Think of it as a homepage for HR and company updates.

Viva Engage: A social communication tool (similar to Yammer) inside Teams that lets employees share ideas, celebrate wins, or ask questions.

Viva Glint: A Viva tool that collects and analyzes employee feedback to measure engagement and sentiment.

Viva Insights: A Microsoft Viva module that helps individuals, managers, and HR teams understand productivity and wellness trends.

Viva Learning: A centralized learning platform that brings required and suggested courses (from LinkedIn Learning, internal content, etc.) into Teams.

External Resources for HR Tech and Microsoft Ecosystem

Microsoft Learn: Official documentation, tutorials, and modules for Dynamics 365, Power Platform, Microsoft 365, and Viva. Ideal for HR and IT professionals who want to deepen their technical knowledge or validate implementation decisions. *https://learn.microsoft.com*

LinkedIn Talent Solutions Blog: Articles and case studies on modern recruiting strategies, employer branding, and integration best practices using LinkedIn tools. *https://business.linkedin.com/talent-solutions/blog*

Microsoft WorkLab: Research-backed insights from Microsoft on productivity, hybrid work, AI in the workplace, and employee engagement trends. *https://www.microsoft.com/en-us/worklab*

Gartner HR Research: Reports and insights on global HR trends, digital HR strategy, employee experience, and vendor comparison tools. *https://www.gartner.com/en/human-resources*

Society for Human Resource Management (SHRM): The world's largest HR association, offering legal updates, implementation guides, and AI ethics frameworks in HR contexts. *https://www.shrm.org*

European Commission: AI Act Resources: Information and draft legislation regarding the European Union's AI Act, which affects high-risk applications such as AI in HR systems. *https://artificialintelligenceact.eu/*

Microsoft Security and Compliance Center: Central portal for managing compliance, data loss prevention (DLP), audit logs, and security settings across Microsoft cloud services. *https://compliance.microsoft.com*

Anthropic: Model Context Protocol (MCP): Technical specification and overview of MCP, a secure integration standard for AI agents, co-developed with Microsoft for safe enterprise use. *https://www.anthropic.com/index/model-context-protocol*

Microsoft AI Principles and Responsible AI Resources: Guidance and tools developed by Microsoft for implementing responsible, ethical, and transparent AI systems across industries. *https://www.microsoft.com/en-us/ai/responsible-ai*

© Ana Inés Urrutia de Souza 2025
A. I. Urrutia de Souza, *The Microsoft AI Human Resources Handbook,*
https://doi.org/10.1007/979-8-8688-1781-6

Power Platform Adoption Hub (Microsoft): Resources for adopting Power Platform at scale: governance templates, CoE Starter Kit, security models, and ROI examples. *https://adoption.microsoft.com/en-us/powerplatform/*

Apress HR Tech Book Catalog: For readers looking to expand into related titles on HR analytics, digital transformation, and AI integration across enterprise systems. *https://www.apress.com/gp/business-it/hr-tech*

Index

E, F

G